Arguing About Britain and Europe in Parliamentary Discourse

Marlene Herrschaft-Iden

Arguing About Britain and Europe in Parliamentary Discourse

Imagined Communities in Liberal Democrat Leaders' Debate Contributions (1997–2010)

PETER LANG

**Bibliographic Information published by the
Deutsche Nationalbibliothek**
The Deutsche Nationalbibliothek lists this publication in the Deutsche
Nationalbibliografie; detailed bibliographic data is available online at
http://dnb.d-nb.de.

Library of Congress Cataloging-in-Publication Data
A CIP catalog record for this book has been applied for at the
Library of Congress.

Die Autorin wurde von der sdw mit einem
Promotionsstipendium gefördert.

Cover illustration: Houses of Parliament. © Marlene Herrschaft-Iden

Printed by CPI books GmbH, Leck

ISBN 978-3-631-78559-1 (Print)
E-ISBN 978-3-631-79451-7 (E-PDF)
E-ISBN 978-3-631-79452-4 (EPUB)
E-ISBN 978-3-631-79453-1 (MOBI)
DOI 10.3726/b15838

© Peter Lang GmbH
Internationaler Verlag der Wissenschaften
Berlin 2019
All rights reserved.

Peter Lang – Berlin · Bern · Bruxelles · New York · Oxford · Warszawa · Wien

This publication has been peer reviewed.

www.peterlang.com

Für Arnold

Acknowledgements

I would like to thank the Anglistik/Amerikanistik team at the University of Passau, especially my supervisors Prof. Dr. Jürgen Kamm and Prof. Dr. Bernd Lenz, for supporting this research project. Thank you also to Prof. Dr. Bernhard Stahl and Prof. Dr. Birgit Neumann for making valuable suggestions.

Stiftung der deutschen Wirtschaft helped to fund this project with a PhD grant and offered many thought-provoking seminars as well as the chance to meet fantastic people.

I would also like to thank the Parliamentary Archives in London and their unfailingly friendly and helpful staff.

Thank you to my colleagues and fellow doctoral candidates at the University of Passau who acted as advisors, role models, timekeepers, proofreaders… and who became friends in the process.

Maria and Christian – I will never forget your unparalleled generosity. I am so glad to know you and call you my friends.

I am grateful to my family, especially Bine, Jürgen, and Bernhard, who each gave what they could to support me on this journey.

To Noah, whose expected arrival helped me to get my priorities straight and to cross the finish line – and who lights up every single day since his birth.

And most of all, to my husband Daniel – without your love, patience, and unwavering support, none of this would have been possible.

Contents

List of Abbreviations

B	BSE	Bovine Spongiform Encephalopathy
C	CDA	Critical Discourse Analysis
	CAP	Common Agricultural Policy
	CFSP	Common Foreign and Security Policy
	CON	Conservative and Unionist Party
E	EC	European Communities
	EEC	European Economic Community
	ECSC	European Coal and Steel Community
	EFTA	European Free Trade Association
	Euratom	European Atomic Energy Community
	EMU	Economic and Monetary Union
	EU	European Union
H	HoC	House of Commons
	HMG	Her Majesty's Government
	HMO	Her Majesty's Opposition
L	Labour	Labour Party
	Lib Dem	Liberal Democrat
	Lib Dems	Liberal Democrats
M	MEP	Member of the European Parliament
	MP	Member of Parliament
N	NATO	North Atlantic Treaty Organisation
P	PM	Prime Minister
	PMQs	Prime Minister's Questions
Q	QMV	Qualified majority voting
S	SEA	Single European Act
U	UK	The United Kingdom of Great Britain and Northern Ireland
	UKIP	United Kingdom Independence Party
W	WEU	Western European Union

1. Introduction

The result of the Brexit referendum on 23 June 2016 in the UK put a spotlight on the difficulties in British-European relations. But even long before this, to misquote Jane Austen, it was "a truth universally acknowledged" that European policy was and still is one of the most controversial issues in British politics:

> There are thus two key dimensions to the Westminster-and-Europe syndrome. First, it is deeply controversial – controversial between the United Kingdom and its partner Member States; controversial between Government and Opposition; controversial within the major political parties as well as between them. (Giddings 2005b: "Westminster" 217)

Indeed, ever since the inception of the European institutions, questions like 'to join or not to join' (be it the common market or the common currency) and to 'opt out or not to opt out' (or indeed whether to opt back in) have divided opinions. Disagreement over European issues has split governing and opposition parties alike, caused parliamentary rebellions as well as nationwide pro- and anti-campaigns, toppled ministers and whole governments and has arguably even given rise to wholly new parties whose raison d'être is linked to British-European relations, like the United Kingdom Independence Party (UKIP). The absence of a general consensus on European policy in the UK thus represents the backdrop against which discursive struggles between Eurosceptics and pro-Europeans have been played out for a long time.

Hugo Young summarises the dominance of Eurosceptic discourse in the UK at the beginning of the Labour government period in 1997:

> By far the greatest portion of the belonging had been spent under the hand of ministries, culminating in Major's, that never – not too strong a word – found a single thing to exalt about membership of 'Europe'. Destiny had dragged Britain there, but the British discourse seldom moved beyond the narrow modes of complaint, lecture and demand. (1999: 472)

In line with this assessment, Daddow postulates that "the British were kept in a permanent state of discursive war with the continent, in which a hegemonic Eurosceptical [sic] discourse acted as both frame and limit on the way the British people called Europe to mind" (Daddow 2011b: *New Labour* 65). As a result, as former diplomat Stephen Wall reports, the other EU members worried already in 1997 that "British Eurosceptic opinion might drive Britain to leave the EU altogether" (Wall 2008: 165). This shows how thin the ice has been for a long time and how important the British discourse on Europe can be judged in this context.

How British political parties have positioned themselves in this political mine-field has indeed been the subject of many studies. Yet while Blair and his proclamation of a new pro-European agenda in a bid to overcome this powerful discursive formation that framed the EU as negative attracted large media and academic coverage, the Liberal Democrats (Lib Dems) have been starkly neglected. Third-largest party from 1997 to 2010, they are consistently described as pro-European, yet their contribution to the discourse on Europe and EU policy has not been comprehensively studied yet. Given that as a third party, they had only slim chances of having to prove the viability of their policy proposals in government, they can be expected to have challenged the existing Eurosceptic discourse even more confidently than New Labour. This study will argue that the Lib Dem position on European policy during the 13 years of Labour governments from 1997 to 2010 constitutes an important part of the puzzle that is the difficult relationship between Britain and Europe, and that it, therefore, merits scholarly attention.

1.1 Research Interest and Questions

As mentioned above, the Lib Dems are invariably described as "Europhile" or "pro-European" both in academic works and journalistic publications; Russell and Cutts even see them as the "most Europhile of all British parties" (2009: 75). Very often, however, this claim is only substantiated by recounting the Lib Dem MPs' voting behaviour. The way they talk about Europe has been completely ne-glected so far. Jones and Norton claim that

> [t]he UK's relationship with the European Union (EU) has been marked by a mixture of antipathy and disinterest. […] It suggests that British attitudes to Europe reflect a deep-rooted distrust of all things European, which have not been challenged by British political leaders regardless of party affiliation. (2010: 615)

I will seek to rebut this verdict in the following, addressing the ensuing questions: how often did Lib Dem party leaders refer to Europe in parliamentary debates, i.e. how important did they rate this issue? Did the Lib Dems as an alleg-edly pro-European party really leave the Eurosceptic discourse unchallenged? This dissertation will delve deep into parliamentary discourse on European policy and uncover the self-image of the UK in relation with the EU or "Europe" offered by the Lib Dems in order to close this research gap.

British foreign policy is almost invariably said to be of a pragmatic nature, focused on the 'national interest' in any given situation (Black 2006: 3) and thus not influenced by a certain ideology. Ultimately, however, Heindrichs claims that Euroscepticism cannot be explained by economic interests alone and suggests that other factors have to be taken into account:

Das britische Verhalten in der Europapolitik liegt vielmehr auch in unverwechselbaren, identitätsstiftenden Normen begründet, die politisch, historisch und kulturell bedingt sind und die integrationsskeptische Rolle Großbritanniens in der Europäischen Union bedingen. (Heindrichs 2005: 19)

He thus argues that there must be other, less tangible reasons for the distinct British role in European integration, anchored in norms that form an important part or indeed the basis of British identity. Based on this understanding, I postulate the hypothesis that behind the dispute and political debate surrounding European integration lies the fear of many Britons that they might lose their identity (or that it may at least be eroded) through a progressing Europeanisation. The ambivalent relations between the United Kingdom and 'Europe' could then be traced back to a self-understanding which is constituted against (a continental) 'Europe' as its 'Other'. This specific identity concept would then, of course, stand in the way of a hard-headed 'rational' debate based on factual arguments since discussing Europe and the relation with it simultaneously calls British identity itself into question. The rejection of further engagement in and with 'Europe' would then become a crucial part of how British politicians define 'Britishness' and thus an essential question of survival. The Lib Dems can be expected to counter these fears by a discourse that frames the UK as part of Europe, and the European Union as a non-threatening entity.

Following this line of argumentation, such a self-understanding must certainly manifest itself in political discourse on Europe and influence both the choice of words, i.e. the selection on the paradigmatic axis, and the structure of arguments advanced. The most important actors exercising influence in this discourse are the political leaders (Jones and Norton 2010: 615; Geddes 2004: 1). Their speeches and contributions to the debate on European policy thus seem the most promising place to start and shall, therefore, be investigated to chart the development in context and to see if the hypotheses set out above can be confirmed by empirical evidence. In a nutshell, this study aims at shedding light on which cultural, identity-shaping norms can be discovered in Lib Dem contributions to parliamentary debates.

The following research questions will, therefore, be addressed:

• How important is the topic of 'European policy' in the New Labour years? How often is it addressed in parliamentary discourse?
• How are Britain and Europe portrayed in Lib Dem party leader's speeches during the Blair and Brown governments?
• Which discursive strategies are employed and how do the party leaders use certain words and metaphors to characterise both Europe and Britain? How

does their "discourse reality" concerning the British-European relations look like?

- How do they seek to rebut Eurosceptic positions and political offers in the UK?
- When it comes to specific European policies, which course of action do the Lib Dem party leaders, as members of the opposition, propose and which arguments and rhetorical devices do they use to justify their recommendations?

The time frame of 1997 to 2010 is deemed to be especially relevant because several important developments on the European level have taken place in the same period: the debate on Economic and Monetary Union and the introduction of the common currency, the euro; the signing of European reform treaties including the (failed) European Constitution project and its 'comeback' as the Treaty of Lisbon as well as the 'Eastern' enlargement of the European Union. These events were subject to controversial discussion on member-state level, and in this light, the debate can be expected to yield interesting results as to how a British self-understanding is negotiated in this specific context. Additionally, considering that European policy became a central element of the Conservative Party (CON)'s opposition strategy after the election loss in 1997 (Meier-Walser 2001: 26), this can be expected to impact on the Lib Dem discourse as well.

Summing up, the central research interest is to retrace how the party's position on European policy was expressed and justified, ultimately seeking to achieve a more detailed and differentiated understanding of the underlying identity concepts and inner logic of the Lib Dem party leaders' contributions when debating European policy in the British Parliament. The ultimate aim of this thesis is to discover possible reasons inherent in pro-European discourse explaining why the attempt to argue in favour of the EU was not successful. Hopefully, this will add to the understanding of the UK position, which the UK's European partners have been lacking more and more (Watt 2014), a fact that is also evident in the way in which the still ongoing Brexit negotiations have been conducted.

1.2 State of Research

Unsurprisingly, given its controversial nature, the relationship of the United Kingdom with "Europe", a term often used synonymously with the institutions of the EU in British debate, has attracted much academic interest and coverage. An impressive number of historic accounts of UK-Europe relations exists since WWII, e.g. Jansen et al. (1995), Geddes (2004), Robbins (2005), Charmley (2005), Casey (2009), and Rose (2011). Grob-Fitzgibbon (2016) retraces

British-European relations and summarises his assessment neatly in the title of his book, *Continental Drift*.

More recently, both the prospect and result of the in/out referendum in the UK have called forth many shorter treatises, seeking to forecast and explain these developments, e.g. Glencross (2016) who focuses on the political events leading right up to the referendum, and Clarke et al. (2017). However, none of them focus on pro-European voices in more depth. Yet in order to understand why the UK will now leave the EU, the discursive attempts to keep it in surely merit a closer look, too.

Most authors seem to agree with George that the United Kingdom is the "awkward partner" among the EU member states (1998): see e.g. James and Oppermann (2009: 285), Kingdom (2003: 118). The British are consistently described as "reluctant" (Jones and Norton 2010: 636) or even "bad" Europeans (Budge 2007: 162). The relations are characterised as an "uneasy partnership" (Watts 2000) or a "very rocky marriage" (Black 2006: 67). In a British standard text book for students of politics, the relations with Europe are even simply captioned as a "crisis issue" (Budge 2007: 166). This assessment seems to be widespread, whereas pro-European positions on the political level and third parties are completely absent from the bigger picture.

The influence of European integration on the British political system has been detailed in standard works on British government and politics, explaining the European institutions and highlighting polity changes, e.g., in Dunleavy et al. (2006), Budge et al. (2007), Kavanagh et al. (2006), and Kingdom (2003). The 'European issue' is, however, usually restricted to a separate chapter among others covering foreign and defence policy or domestic policies of the UK governments.

Focusing more on political actors rather than events and structure, the European policies pursued by individual British Prime Ministers have been addressed by, e.g., Pine (2007), Wanninger (2007), and H. Young (1999). H. Young's *This Blessed Plot* takes an actor-centred approach at Britain's relationship with Europe and shows how often British politicians, regardless of party affiliation, have changed their mind (he calls this "vacillation" the "chronic disease" (1999: 471) having befallen British politicians) and claims that a coherent strategy or vision of Britain in Europe has been lacking from the beginning. He argues that Europe has also remained an issue because of party politics (elections as well as government-opposition conflicts).

Deighton comments that "[t]he EU is one of the great but unloved issues of our time" and that "[m]ischief from opposition parties can bring easy electoral gains. Some sectors of the press have fuelled this problem" (cited in Seldon 2001: 307). This indicates that the opposition discourse has a role to play, but she ignores pro-European voices. Euroscepticism is thus foregrounded in the academic literature, e.g. in Forster's *Euroscepticism in Contemporary British Politics: Opposition to Europe in the Conservative and Labour Parties Since 1945* (2002), while not much attention has been dedicated to the pro-European discourse in the UK.

When it comes to the New Labour years, which are the subject of this study, Blair's proclaimed policy change concerning Europe triggered scholarly interest in the discipline of political science, leading to a good coverage where political content analyses of New Labour's policies and comparisons between words and deeds are concerned, e.g. Wanninger (2007) as well as James and Oppermann (2009) and Daddow (2011b).

Yet the political discourse during these years has been largely neglected: there is only little published work on political speeches by British politicians in this period. Earlier research confirms its relevance, though: In *The Language of Empire,* MacDonald provides an overview of important myths and metaphors of popular imperialism (1994: 15), thus showing how important rhetoric devices can be in shaping a whole discourse. Rhetoric in British political discourse was also studied by Grond (2004), and in Norman Fairclough's *New Labour, New Language?* (Fairclough 2000), speeches during the first Blair government are analysed more closely. Wanninger (2007) also focuses on Blair's speeches with the aim of contrasting promised policies with the actual outcomes. Indeed, most other political accounts of British parties' policies on Europe evaluate policy outcomes, but neglect the language aspect.

A notable exception is Daddow (2011b): he published the only comprehensive and systematic discourse analysis of speeches by Blair and Brown, focusing on New Labour's use of historical references in their discourse on Europe. Musolff (2000) traced the use of metaphors in British and German public debate on European integration in media reports and commentaries. A further promising approach was followed by Teubert (2001), who used discourse analysis to identify 25 key words of British Eurosceptic discourse in 2000. Similarly, Mautner (2000) addressed *Der britische Europa-Diskurs* in her study, analysing British daily newspaper articles about European policy. She proposed an integrated approach drawing on both qualitative methods for textual analysis as well as corpus linguistics in order to be able to handle large data sets and not just a small number of (exemplary) texts. She based her work on Critical Discourse Analysis (CDA), a research tradition established in the late 1970s (Mautner 2000: 35). This study will adapt parts of this framework for research.

Furthermore, identity-related aspects are rarely mentioned, and questions concerning possible identity conflicts in British political positions on Europe have not yet received satisfying answers in the existing literature. While Menno

Spiering takes a long view and explores possible roots of the difficult relationship between Britain and Europe in his *Cultural History of British Euroscepticism* (2015) and Linda Colley's (2005) account of how the British nation was forged in the past has become a classic, they do not focus on present-day politics. Promising approaches in this direction can be found in Risse (2001), Ichijo and Spohn (2005), as well as Guisan (2012), but only Risse addresses the British context specifically. He focuses on the government level, however, thus leaving out the opposition as well as leaving most of the New Labour years uncovered. Leith and Soule confirm a research gap here: "Only limited work has been undertaken to consider how political parties operating within [...] the wider UK have employed a sense of national identity" (2012: 41).

In general, research interest in this subject seems to have peaked around the millennium and to have abated ever since. Especially the election victory of the Labour Party under Blair and the hope of a new chapter in British-European relations seem to have generated a high number of academic studies – but the number has declined during New Labour's years in power. This is in stark contrast to the high relevance of the British debate on Europe going on today and its development from 1997 onwards until 2010, amid a fully-fledged global economic crisis which impacted heavily on the European Union and its member states.

Especially opposition discourse about Europe from 1997 to 2010 has been starkly neglected so far; the limited attention focused mostly on election campaign periods (see e.g. Meier-Walser 2001). There is no systematic analysis focusing on the rhetoric on Europe in opposition speeches from 1997 to 2010. The extensive study by Diez (1999) on British discourses on Europe is highly elucidating but does not feature the Liberal Democrats and does not cover the New Labour years. The existing approaches shall be integrated in the present dissertation and the identified research gap thus closed.

Overall, the allegedly "most Europhile of all British parties" (Russell and Cutts 2009: 75) has not been the subject of any dedicated qualitative study of their actual spelt-out position on Europe, and no systematic corpus of political speeches on Europe by the Liberal Democrats in the British Parliament has been analysed. This dissertation project seeks to address this gap and thus to contribute to the highly topical debate on the relations between the UK and Europe.

1.3 Outline

This book is structured as follows: Chapter 2 sets out the theoretical framework underlying the analysis of the selected primary sources. Chapter 3 provides the necessary context, briefly introducing the development of British relations with Europe and European institutions after the Second World War (starting with Winston Churchill's famous 'Zurich Speech') is briefly outlined, providing a timeline containing the milestones in European integration and British involvement in it up to 2010 and beyond. The process of data selection, data gathering, and subsequent analysis will be made transparent in the following chapters. Chapter 4 outlines the British political system with a special focus on parliament as well as (opposition) parties and their functions. Additionally, this chapter addresses the importance of political speech in British political culture and explains which speeches have been selected for analysis. Subsequently, the methodology adopted for the analysis of the primary sources is discussed in Chapter 5, and the connections to the theoretical considerations are highlighted.

The following chapters present the results of the completed analysis and discuss them. Chapter 6 outlines the quantitative results, while chapter 7 contains the qualitative ones. Chapters 7.1 to 7.5 correspond to the five big content clusters which emerged from the data analysis: firstly, Economic and Monetary Union (the euro as the common currency), secondly, the European dimension of British foreign and security policy, followed by a third chapter dealing with the EU treaties debated during the researched period. Fourthly, the Common Agricultural Policy (CAP) is discussed, and lastly, the enlargement of the EU. These findings are briefly set in their (political) context at the beginning of each chapter. The final chapter summarises and evaluates the analysis results. Additionally, it relates the findings to the political developments after 2010 and lists further and remaining research questions ensuing from the results of this study.

2. Theoretical Framework and Definitions

In order to achieve a high level of reliability, qualitative work must make the research process transparent and lay open the theoretical stance from which the interpretation takes place (Silverman 2014: 282). The basis of the theoretical framework underlying this study is discourse theory as developed by Michel Foucault. These foundations are complemented with the considerations on the nature of political discourse by Chilton and Fairclough.

While, as Chilton notes, the "analysis of political discourse is scarcely new", with the "classical tradition of rhetoric [as] a means of codifying the way public orators used language for persuasive and other purposes" (Chilton 2004: ix), he argues that there is a "deep link between the political and the linguistic" (Chilton 2004: xi). He claims that "[e]mbedded in the tradition of western political thought there is in fact a view that language and politics are intimately linked at a fundamental level" (2004: 4). This link been can be traced back to Aristotle's *Politeia*, where he terms man a "political animal" endowed "with the power of speech" which makes mankind unique (qtd. in Chilton 2004: 5).

The functions and properties ascribed to language have changed over time; in this context, the linguistic turn occurring in the 1960s has to be mentioned here. It describes the theoretical reframing of language, which had hitherto been considered a transparent and neutral medium, i.e. merely serving to transport meaning. It was recognised that language must be considered a standalone research object (Stiersdorfer 2005: 132). Besides the study of political rhetoric, there are also strands of research focusing on the performative aspect of language (see e.g. Austin: *Doing Things with Words*). Chilton separates two main functions of language, saying that people use it to "interact with one another and exchange mental pictures of the world" (Chilton 2004: xi).

The "'social construction of reality' is a formula by Berger and Luckmann [meaning that] [l]anguage and reality are connected, discursive practices can constitute a reality" (Nünning and Nünning 1996: 16). This is corroborated by Hunt when she draws the conclusion from her empirical research that "[w]ords did not just reflect social and political reality; they were instruments for transforming reality" (Hunt 1989: 17). In her studies, she found that "political language could be used rhetorically to build a sense of community and at the same time to establish new fields of social, political, and cultural struggle" (Hunt 1989: 17). It is, therefore, important to look at the language used in its specific context, especially at important and critical junctures or when the politicians in questions are trying to establish a new perception of a given context, such as the continuing British involvement with the European Union. Hunt also makes explicit the connection to Foucault's idea of power and its inextricable links to language: "linguistic practice, rather than simply reflecting social reality, could actively be an instrument of power" (Hunt 1989: 17).

2.1 Discourse Theory

In the attempt to detect larger argumentative patterns and clusters of images concerning the relationship between Britain and Europe in political speeches, however, further theoretical input is necessary. Going beyond speech act theory, which concentrates on the micro-level of single speech acts, the aim of this analysis is to focus on discourse as a larger entity embedded in a specific context. It is thus discourse theory that needs to be included as well. Michel Foucault's theoretical focus on discourse and power provides a suitable framework for a study of political speeches and is both topical and increasingly popular in Cultural Studies.[1]

There are many views on what the term 'discourse' entails. For this study, the following working definition is adopted: Chilton states that "[d]iscourse consists of coherent chains of propositions which establish a 'discourse world', or 'discourse ontology' – in effect, the 'reality' that is entertained by the speaker" (2004: 54). Discourse can thus be defined as "the coherent body of categories, concepts, and principles by means of which individuals apprehend and concep-tualize reality" (Cabrera 2004: 22). It is, therefore, interesting to deconstruct dis-course and analyse the "chains of propositions" (Chilton 2004: 54) uttered by relevant speakers to understand which perceptions of 'reality' underlie them.

Although he is one of the most cited authors in cultural sciences, Foucault's ideas and theoretical assumptions have changed more than once during his lifetime, making it hard to pin down one particular 'theory' he has developed (Stiegler 2015: 11). The focus on discourse is something that lasted, though. Storey summarises Foucault's view of discourse as "organized and organizing bodies of knowledge, with rules that govern particular practices (ways of speaking, thinking and acting)" (Storey 2015: 133). According to Foucault, discourses fulfil three functions: "they enable, they constrain, and they consti-tute" (qtd. in Storey 2015: 133). A discourse is thus a particular way of making

---

1   See e.g. the recent introduction of a new journal dedicated to studies on power and discourse, *Coils of the Serpent. Journal for the Study of Contemporary Power*, which explicitly refers to Michel Foucault's seminal work in this area.

sense of phenomena, which excludes other possible interpretations at the same time. It also constructs the phenomenon in so far as it appears in the way it was described according to the rules of the discourse. This means a discourse does not describe a reality that exists outside of it, nothing that is part of 'nature', but "a product of 'culture' " (Storey 2015: 134). Discourse can thus be conceptualised as a social practice because it also "produce[s] subject positions" that are occupied by individuals (Storey 2015: 134) – a pro-European Lib Dem leader, for example.

In their all-encompassing quality, discourses thus shape identity: "all the things we are, are enabled, constrained and constituted in discourses" (Storey 2015: 134). According to Foucault, "[i]t is in discourse that power and knowledge are joined together" (Foucault 2009: 318). The political stage is one discursive domain in which such discourses and the power struggle over the accepted knowledge, the accepted 'reality', are played out. However, Foucault rejects the notion that power always suppresses, clarifying that it can also be productive: "[i]n fact, power produces; it produces reality; it produces domains of objects and rituals of truth" (1979: 194).

Detailing the last point, Foucault explains that whole "regimes of truth" govern discourses, i.e. they determine what is believed and what is rejected. Foucault insists that "[e]ach society has its own regime of truth, its 'general politics' of truth – that is, the types of discourse it accepts and makes function as true" (Foucault 2002a: "Truth and Power" 131). He is interested in "how men govern (themselves and others) by the production of truth" (Foucault 2002b: "Question" 230).

While Foucault's thinking does not deny that anything exists non-discursively, he postulates that the way it is 'constituted', i.e. how it is interpreted, whether it is accepted or rejected, is entirely dependent on the discourse around it. This means we cannot talk 'about' something but we 'constitute' it in a certain way while we are talking (Storey 2015: 134), summarising Foucault's ideas expressed in the first volume of *The History of Sexuality* from 1981.

A further relevant keyword that needs to be defined is "discursive formation". Storey summarises that these "consist of the hierarchical criss-crossing of particular discourses" (Storey 2015: 134). According to Daddow (2011b: *New Labour* 2), the anti-European discourse had the upper hand when New Labour took office. While he comes to the conclusion that Labour tried to change this and failed, it is interesting to see how the Lib Dems go about the attempt to establish a counter-discourse. The idea of resisting a powerful discourse with its established regime of truth is also built into Foucault's thinking, who claims discourses are not fixed but can change:

> We must make allowances for the complex and unstable process whereby discourse can be both an instrument and an effect of power, but also an [sic] hindrance, a stumbling block, a point of resistance and a starting point for an opposing strategy. Discourse transmits and produces power; it reinforces it, but also undermines it and exposes it, renders it fragile and makes it possible to thwart it. (Foucault 2009: 318)

How subjects in the dominating discourse on Europe seek to accomplish just that, to destabilise and expose it, will be analysed in the following.

Fairclough and Fairclough (2012) argue that political discourse is distinct (Fairclough and Fairclough 2012: 15) from other discourses and that it is "primarily a form of argumentation" which involves "more specifically *practical* argumentation, argumentation for or against particular ways of acting, argumentation that can ground decision" (1). Political actors thus weigh the pros and cons for specific actions and consider alternatives, a process they term, with reference to Aristoteles' *Nicomachean Ethics*, "deliberation" (Fairclough and Fairclough 2012: 1). They suggest that "politics is most fundamentally about making choices how to act in response to circumstances and goals, it is about choosing *policies*" (Fairclough and Fairclough 2012: 1) and such choices are the result of deliberation. The process of deliberation includes "practical reasoning about what should be done" (Fairclough and Fairclough 2012: 11) based on the speaker's goals and values, and at least one counter-argument must be considered (Fairclough and Fairclough 2012: 11). The expected result of such a process is then a

> reasonable decision (including a political decision) [which] will emerge from sufficient critical examination of reasons, from considering and balancing reasons in favour but also, essentially, from considering reasons *against* a proposed course of action, i.e. from at least a minimal process of deliberation. [...] [T]he goal of practical reasoning is arriving at a reasonable judgment that can ground reasonable decision-making and reasonable action (Fairclough and Fairclough 2012: 11).

Fairclough and Fairclough discern an objective (or systemic, i.e. the circumstances/environment or the political system in which something takes place) and a subjective aspect (i.e. the people who act in this environment). They argue that the subjective aspect is especially important when analysing political discourse, since a political discourse features "groups of people with different interests and objectives, who are competing to make their own particular choices, policies and strategies prevail" (Fairclough and Fairclough 2012: 3). Taking the example of the global financial and economic crisis, they define the subjective aspect further as

> those aspects which have to do with the agency of political and other actors in making decisions and developing strategies and policies in response to the crisis [which] can

most fruitfully be seen in terms of the Aristotelian account of political action as based upon the liberation that leads to a decision. This entails recognizing that deliberation (and practical argumentation) is an essential part of the responses of actors to the crisis. From this perspective, in which argument is the main analytical category, the 'narratives', 'mental conceptions' and 'imaginaries' discussed in these accounts are elements of practical arguments: narratives of the crisis are incorporated within what we will call 'circumstantial premises' of practical arguments (premises which represent the context of action): 'imaginaries' for possible and desirable state of affairs are incorporated in our account within the 'goal premises'. Practical argumentation can be seen as 'means-ends' argumentation where the claim or conclusion ('we should do *A*') is a judgement about what means should be pursued to attain the end (goal). (Fairclough and Fairclough 2012: 3–4)

They complement their definition by adding that "practical arguments are often problem-solution arguments" (Fairclough and Fairclough 2012: 11).

They cite other approaches, such as

Jessop (2002: 6–7, 92–94) [who] emphasizes '*strategies*' and the '*narratives*' and '*imaginaries*' associated with them. Crises create the space for competing strategic interventions to significantly redirect the course of events as well as for attempts to 'muddle through', and which strategies prevail partly depends upon 'discursive struggles' between different 'narratives' of the nature, causes and significance of the crisis and how it might be resolved, including economic and political 'imaginaries' for possible future states of affairs and systems. (qtd. in Fairclough and Fairclough 2012: 3)

However, in their view "[t]he study of narratives, explanations or imaginaries is pointless unless we see them as embedded within practical arguments, as feeding into and influencing processes of decision-making, briefly, as premises in arguments for action" (Fairclough and Fairclough 2012: 3).

Fairclough and Fairclough continue their reasoning by suggesting that "different accounts of the crisis involve different descriptions, narratives and explanations of the context of action, which are present in the (circumstantial) premises of arguments. Along with the goals of arguers (in the goal premise) – and these may involve various 'imaginaries' or visions – and a means-goal premise, they provide reasons in favour of particular courses of action (the conclusion of the argument). How the context of action is represented (or narrated, explained) affects which course of action is proposed, which explains the intense competition and conflict over winning acceptance or imposing one account (one narrative, one explanation) of the crisis rather than others" (2012: 7).

They propose a four-fold structure of premises for practical arguments: first, "a circumstantial premise, which represents the existing state of affairs and the problems it poses; a goal premise, which describes (and 'imagines') the future state of affairs agents want to bring about or think ought to be brought about; a value premise, expressing the values and concerns which underlie the agents' goals (but also affect how they represent the context of action); and a means-end premise, which represents the proposed line of action as the (hypothetical) means that will presumably take agents from the current state of affairs to the future state of affairs that is their goal" (Fairclough and Fairclough 2012: 11). It follows that analysis of an argument is then "a matter of identifying within an argument its premises and its conclusion and the relations between them" (Fairclough and Fairclough 2012: 11).

Fairclough and Fairclough also consider emotions as well as motivation and their role in argumentation. They make clear that in their view, an appeal to emotions (pathos) can strengthen an argument and is not necessarily manipulative in a negative way; the "premises for practical arguments include what we shall call 'concerns' as well as beliefs, and concerns subsume emotions and emotional dispositions. Without a motivational and emotional investment, no belief could ever lead us to act at all, because nothing would really matter to us" (Fairclough and Fairclough 2012: 15).

The role of values is clarified as well: a separate category of premises expresses "the goals and values of action" (Fairclough and Fairclough 2012: 15). The goals, i.e. the envisaged future state of affairs, are dependent on the values held by the agent. They also acknowledge the interdependence of values and 'concerns' with the perception of circumstances (objective or system environment). This means that there is a subjective component to the "objective" aspect, too:

> The context of action, as a problem, is of course objective, not of our own making, but it can be described or represented in various ways. These alternative ways of representing it can even support radically different claims for action. Facts, in other words, have evaluative content, and can therefore support various normative conclusions. (Fairclough and Fairclough 2012: 15)

Summing up the approach by Fairclough and Fairclough, it can be stated that they combine concepts of Critical Discourse Analysis with argumentation theory and arrive at the conclusion that arguments should take precedence in political discourse analysis, rather than representations (2012: 17). I will argue, however, that the focus depends on the research question(s) asked. For this study, the incorporation of both the analysis of argumentation as well as the analysis of representation is deemed useful to answer the research questions.

2.2 Imagined Communities

In the second edition of his seminal work, *Imagined Communities* (1991), Anderson claims that "the United Kingdom of Great Britain and Northern

Ireland [has] the rare distinction of refusing nationality in its naming", which "suggests that it is as much the legatee of the pre-national dynastic states of the nineteenth century as the precursor of a twenty-first century internationalist order" (Anderson 1991: 2). To emphasise his argument, he asks "what nationality its name denotes: Great Brito-Irish?" (Anderson 1991: 2).

Based on the observation that in the 1990s, many 'new' countries applied for membership of the United Nations, he argues that even

> many 'old nations', once thought fully consolidated, find themselves challenged by 'sub'-nationalisms which, naturally, dream of shedding this sub-ness one day. The reality is quite plain: the 'end of the era of nationalism', so long prophesied, is not remotely in sight. Indeed, nation-ness is the most universally legitimate value in the political life of our time. (Anderson 1991: 3)

Anderson foresaw the disintegration of the Soviet Union and Yugoslavia, but his observations are also very topical for the contemporary political situation; looking at the developments in Europe, where Catalonia has been trying for some years now to establish a sovereign state and break away from Spain and where the independence referendum in Scotland in 2014 could have led to a break-up of the United Kingdom and a second 'indy-ref' is still being debated after the Brexit referendum result.

Possible objections raised against Anderson's theoretical approach include the fact that he developed it with a focus on South-East Asia and the Americas and made no pretensions to a global applicability. Nevertheless, it seems that with the concept of Britishness in crisis and the rise of nationalism and nationalist parties in the UK and many other European countries, his notions can be fruitfully adapted to the present study. Anderson suggests that "nationality, or, as one might prefer to put it in view of that word's multiple significations, nation-ness, as well as nationalism, are cultural artefacts" (Anderson 1991: 4). His explanation of the development of these "cultural artefacts" and "why [...] they command such profound emotional legitimacy" is of particular interest; the hypotheses governing the present study are derived from his reasonings in this context.

Anderson offers the following definition of a nation, which serves well as a foundation for this study:

> it is an imagined political community – and imagined as both inherently limited and sovereign. It is imagined because the members of even the smallest nation will never know most of their fellow-members, meet them, or even hear of them, yet in the minds of each lives the image of their communion. [...] In fact, all communities larger than primordial villages of face-to-face contact (and perhaps even these) are imagined. Communities are to be distinguished, not by their falseness/genuineness, but by the style in which they are imagined. (Anderson 1991: 6)

He adds that Gellner (1964: 169) makes a similar point when he claims that nationalism invents nations. Anderson explains further:

> The nation is limited because even the largest of them, encompassing perhaps a billion living human beings, has finite, if elastic, boundaries, beyond which lie other nations. No nation imagines itself coterminous with mankind. [...] It is imagined as sovereign because the concept was born in an age in which Enlightenment and Revolution were destroying the legitimacy of the divinely-ordained, hierarchical dynastic realm. Coming to maturity at a stage in human history when even the most devout adherents of any universal religion were inescapably confronted with the living pluralism of such religions, and the allomorphism between each faith's ontological claims and territorial stretch, nations dream of being free, and, if under God, directly so. The gage and emblem of this freedom is the sovereign state. [...] Finally, it is imagined as a community, because, regardless of the actual inequality and exploitation that may prevail in each, the nation is always conceived as a deep, horizontal comradeship. Ultimately it is this fraternity that makes is possible, over the past two centuries, for so many million people, not so much to kill, as willingly die for such limited imaginings. These deaths bring us abruptly face to face with the central problem posed by nationalism: what makes the shrunken imaginings of recent history (scarcely more than two centuries) generate such colossal sacrifices? (Anderson 1991: 7)

As becomes clear in the concept of a nation as an 'imagined community' proposed by Anderson, the limited nature of a nation necessitates the existence of other nations. This concept of an 'other' can be directly related to identity and identity formation as proposed, e.g., by Paul du Gay and Stuart Hall: when an identity is in crisis, it can no longer rely on the tacit acknowledgement of the members of a certain group (in this case those who consider themselves members of a nation) but has to be reaffirmed in order to secure its continued acceptance among the imagined community. To achieve this, the people interested in keeping up a certain national identity have to rely on discourse enabling the perpetuation of the latter. Alternatively, some actors might attempt to establish a new or changed identity; convincing voters that the UK has a European identity might be such a new identity concept designed to update a formerly isolationist and solely national conceptualisation of the British nation. Speeches represent a prime means for politicians to spread their ideas of what characterises their nation. This study thus rests on the hypothesis that British identity was in crisis when New Labour came to power and that would, therefore, be explicitly mentioned in political discourse. Secondly, this study proposes that Europe as an entity beyond the limits of the British nation may serve either as an 'other' against which the boundaries and limits of the nation and its identity are defined, or indeed that political actors seeking to overcome this gap will try to frame the UK as part of Europe, thus extending Anderson's "horizontal comradeship" to other countries and thus pushing the limits of the imagined community to include not just the nation but members of a larger organisation.

Although he concedes that "Anderson's account is useful in linking forms national identity with modes of communication", Barker summarises the criticism levelled at Anderson's theory in this context:

> Anderson tends to overstate the unity of the nation and the strength of nationalist feeling. In doing so, he covers over differences of class, gender, ethnicity, and so forth. Indeed, the proliferation and diversification of contexts and sites of interaction, constituted in and through discourse, prevent the easy identification of subjects with a given, fixed identity. Consequently, in the context of the accelerated globalization of the late modernity [...], we have begun to talk about hybrid cultural identities rather than a homogeneous national or ethnic cultural identity. Further, the instability of meaning in language, différance, leads us to think of culture, identities and identifications as always a place of borders and hybridity rather than fixed stable entities (see Bhabha 1994). (Barker 2012: 259–260)

Leith and Soule (2012), however, argue that in political party discourse, 'us vs. them' differentiations are quite common, e.g. one's own party vs. political opponents, left vs. right (in terms of political ideology) or the "classic nationalistic sense of 'us' and 'them'" (46). They further state that

> [f]or any nation to exist and be considered separate there must be a sense of belonging to the nation. This means that out-groups will be created – individuals or other groups who do not belong to the nation – and parties will seek to portray their political opponents as not operating in the national interest. (Leith and Soule 2012: 46)

While this statement refers to the Scottish context, it seems to describe accurately the situation of European policy debates on the UK level in Westminster.

Ungari (2009) asserts that "[s]crutiny and imagination play a key role in constructing and perceiving places. Over the years Australia and Europe have scrutinized and imagined each other, and constructed and reconstructed their reciprocal perception" (353). I will argue that, although the sea separating Britain from mainland Europe is not as wide as the oceans between Britain and Australia, a similar process of scrutinising and imagining the Other can be identified in the latter relationship. Summo-O'Connell concurs that the "discourse around the mutual alterity of subject and Other" (2009: 4) is a worthwhile research objective.

2.3 Othering and Identity

Nünning and Nünning make an important connection between discourse and identity when they explain that "a people's collective identity, just like personal identity, is neither natural nor stable, but discursively constructed" (Nünning and Nünning 1996: 20). This makes the investigation of political discourse plausible when the aim is to discover concepts of British identity in relation to Europe. Similarly, Leith and Soule describe national identity "a discourse at both mass and elite levels" (2012: xiii). Adding to this, "[i]dentity, deduced from Hollinger and Kristeva, is thus not an ontological but a functional term; it is the arena where the political and the personal overlap, and it is most significantly a battlefield of power" (Däwes 2003: 218–219). This emphasises the importance of power when attempting to establish a certain identity as an accepted 'truth' and confirms the centrality of the discursive process in national identity formation. The heterotypification of the UK as an "awkward partner" (see above) has been sufficiently established so far; the autotypification of the UK by a British party claiming to be pro-European, however, represents a research gap as it is still waiting to be filled.

As Said remarks, "no identity can ever exist by itself and without an array of opposites, negatives, oppositions" (1993: 60). According to this conception of identity, a hierarchy is established over the course of the formation process that claims the self is usually superior to the 'other'. With regard to British collective identity, this principle seems to have been dominant in the identity formation process ever since: in their study on fictions of empire, Nünning and Nünning state that "by establishing oppositions between 'us' and 'them', between self and other, fictions of empire served as an important means of maintaining an advantageous British self-image and of constructing Britain's national identity" (1996: 20). Bringing this line of argumentation back to Said, the link to power becomes apparent once more when he explains that Orientalism can be understood as synonymous with "discourses of power" (Said 1978: 205). The question that arises in this context is whether this mechanism can also be observed in the more contemporary political discourse on Europe, i.e. whether the Lib Dems use their relative power as part of the British political elite to try and establish an identity that includes a European element or whether a discourse of 'othering' Europe and the EU as inferior can be observed in the Lib Dem leaders' speeches.

2.4 Euroscepticism

It is very difficult to find definitions of being "Europhile" or "pro-European"; is it the absence of critical views? The general support for EU membership of one's country? Does it mean accepting ever-closer union as the *finalité* of the Union? Does it preclude calling for a referendum to legitimise political decisions concerning EU policy? The phenomenon of Euroscepticism, on the other hand, is similarly complex; here, however, more effort to define the term have been undertaken so far. When it comes to party-based Euroscepticism, the best-known definition has been offered by Szczerbiak and Taggart, who differentiate "between principled (Hard) opposition to European integration and contingent (Soft) opposition, with attitudes towards a country's membership of the EU being viewed as the ultimate litmus test" (Szczerbiak and Taggart 2008: 240). They claim that 'Soft Euroscepticism' "involves contingent or qualified opposition to European integration, which expresses itself in terms of opposition to the specific policies or in terms of the defence of national interest" (Szczerbiak and Taggart 2008: 241), whereas 'Hard Euroscepticism' means "fundamental opposition to the idea of political and economic integration, a principled objection to the current form of integration in the European Union on the grounds that it offends deeply held values" (Szczerbiak and Taggart 2008: 240).

In summary, they define

> party-based Hard Euroscepticism as being where there is a principled opposition to the EU and European integration and therefore can be seen in parties who think that their countries should withdraw from membership, or whose policies towards the EU are tantamount to being opposed to the whole project of European integration as it is currently conceived. (240)

While this definition seems quite clear-cut, the second form of Euroscepticism is subtler and, therefore, harder to identify but probably more widespread:

> Party-based Soft Euroscepticism, on the other hand, [is] where there is NOT a principled objection to European integration or EU membership but where concerns on one (or a number) of policy areas leads to the expression of qualified opposition to the EU, or where there is a sense that 'national interest' is currently at odds with the EU trajectory. (240–241)

For the purposes of this study, these definitions of party-based Euroscepticism are used *ex negativo* to determine whether the discourse contributions by Lib Dem leaders form a genuine counter-discourse to the dominant Eurosceptic attitudes in the UK or if they also contain Eurosceptic elements.

3. Historical Background: Britain and Europe

The British today are confronting different cultural and economic realities than in the past when they had a more clearly defined world role and a greater sense of national identity (Oakland 2011: 17). Arguably, the relations between the United Kingdom and the (rest of the) European continent have been ambivalent for a long time, marked by hesitation and reserve. This is a widespread judgement in the academic literature covering the UK-EU relations, well summed up by Oakland: "[i]n recent centuries, Britain has rarely seen itself as an integral part of mainland Europe. It has sheltered behind the sea barrier of the English Channel and its outlook has been westwards and worldwide" (2011: 7). This reservation manifests itself in the famous quote by Winston Churchill from the 1930 essay "The United States of Europe":

> We see nothing but good and hope in a richer, freer, more contented European commonality. But we have our own dream and our own task. We are with Europe, but not of it. We are linked but not compromised. We are interested and associated but not absorbed. [...] We belong to no single continent, but to all. (Qtd. in G. Schmidt 1989: 1)

3.1 After 1945

Following countless wars and ententes, many historians and political scientists see a watershed after the Second World War (see e.g. Daddow 2011a: *Britain and Europe*, H. Young 1999) which left the UK in serious economic difficulties and without most of the remaining Empire (e.g. Oakland 2011: 7). Evaluating the subsequent loss of status and influence, Thackeray concludes that at the end of the war, "Britain's days as an independent great power in Europe were over" (Thackeray 2002: 170, see also Birch 1998: 228). This resulted in what Oakland calls "debates, re-evaluation and pressures" on "traditional notions of Britain's place in the world" (2011: 7). G. Johnson goes one step further and makes out a deep identity crisis (2005: 1). Morisse-Schillbach concurs when she writes that some believe that the identity crisis is not yet overcome (2006: 90). The historical context, therefore, renders the period after the Second World War especially interesting when it comes to the UK's external relations, its self-image and image of others when dealing with countries and also organisations like the European Communities and later the European Union: Political leaders must explain why they think Britain should act in a certain way because there are no fixed determinants anymore.

However, the change in perceptions of the continent was slow; Churchill revisited the idea of a UK that is geographically close but remains aloof from the rest of Europe in the famous "United States of Europe" speech, held in September 1946 at the University of Zurich. While it was seen on the continent as a promise of closer ties in the future, it became soon clear that the then British Prime minister (alongside many of his fellow countrywomen and countrymen) did not see the UK as an average European country, but rather as a country with a special role to play on the stage of world politics (G. Schmidt 1989: 1). Indeed, the UK was to be a "friend and sponsor" of a European community led by Germany and France, alongside "mighty America", the Commonwealth of Nations and the Soviet Union (Churchill 1946: "USE"). This concept of the 'three circles' placed the UK at the intersection of Europe, the Commonwealth and the 'special relationship' with the USA, thereby seeking to uphold its status as world power. Kastendiek and Stinshoff see this approach as part of the post-war consensus in the UK (2006: 99).

This position did not significantly change in the 1950s, and when the Treaty of Rome was signed between the six founding members of the EC, the UK, having declined the invitation to join the meeting, stood by and watched: "Britain did not join then, but instead helped to create the European Free Trade Association (EFTA) in 1959" because they did not wish "to be restricted by close European relationships" (Oakland 2011: 131). Oakland explains this with a historically grown distrust among the British: "An old suspicion of Europe also caused many British people to shrink from membership of a European organization, which they thought might result in the loss of their identity and independence" (2011: 131).

European integration, meanwhile, had developed considerably during this time. This dynamic nature makes it difficult to define the precise nature of the European Union. It has been described as "an evolving set of treaties and institutions (Díez Medrano 2003: 2). Its beginnings lie in the founding of the European Community for Coal and Steel in 1951 by Belgium, Germany, France, Italy, Luxemburg, and the Netherlands. The Treaty of Rome (1957/1958) then created the "European Economic Community" (EEC), also called the 'Common Market' (European Commission: "History 1945–1959"), as well as the "European Atomic Energy Community" (Euratom).

By the 1960s, the UK began to realise that the days where 'splendid isolation' from the continent constituted a viable alternative were indeed over. Official involvement of the UK with the European Communities began in 1961, when Conservative British Prime Minister Harold Macmillan made the first formal application to join the EC which was ultimately vetoed by French president de

Gaulle in 1963. Sicking and Müller state that the UK only applied for membership of the EEC when its role as independent world power had become visibly
eroded and the community had developed into a successful reality (1999: 7).
The Merger Treaty of 1965/1967 combined the EEC and Euratom, leading to
the denominator "European Communities" (EC). The Labour Prime Minister
Harold Wilson decided to apply a second time for membership in May 1967,
but de Gaulle vetoed this one as well. The British efforts to join were upheld,
however, and Wilson's successor Edward Heath could successfully complete
membership negotiations in 1970 (Pine 2007: 1). On 1 January 1973, the United
Kingdom entered formally into the European Economic Community (EEC),
the ECSC, and EURATOM, together with Ireland and Denmark. In 1975, only
two years after the UK had joined the then EEC, the (generally perceived to be
unfavourable) terms of British membership were renegotiated and then put to
a public vote in a referendum by Prime Minister Harold Wilson, which confirmed the UK's belonging to the 'single market'. Highlighting the relevance of
political discourse for these developments, Sicking and Müller claim that it was
mainly the economic advantages of membership in the trade community that
were highlighted in British political debates at the time of joining under Heath
in 1973 and the ensuing referendum under Wilson in 1975 (Sicking and Müller
1999: 7).

Once a member of the EC, Sicking and Müller claim that the 1980s were
characterised by the conflicts between Thatcher's government and Brussels over
questions of the EC budget and the planned progress towards a European Union
(1999: 7). Also commenting on Thatcher's European policy, J. Young states: "The
11 years of her premiership saw some surprising developments. Sceptical about
European integration, she contributed much to one of its greatest advances, the
Single European Act" (1999: 209). The SEA was indeed ratified in 1985 and codified the goals to create a single market as well as agreeing European Political
Cooperation, which would later develop into the Common Foreign and Security
Policy.

On 3 October 1990, Germany was reunited. Furthermore, the 'European
Summit' in Rome established the European exchange rate mechanism. Both
developments went ahead notwithstanding the resistance by Margaret Thatcher,
who decried the latter as 'Europe through the backdoor' (qtd. in J. Schmidt
2011: 357). The treaty of Maastricht of 1992 was even described as "national
suicide" by Thatcher (qtd. in J. Schmidt 2011: 371). Among other important
developments such as the decision to introduce a single European currency, this
was the treaty with which the institutional compact was renamed "European
Union" (EU). Under Thatcher's successor Major, the UK government obtained

an opt-out both from the single currency and the Social Chapter (J. Schmidt 2011: 371). With these exceptions agreed, the UK government under Major signed the Maastricht treaty after long negotiations in February 1992 (J. Schmidt 2011: 373). In the autumn of 1992, on 'Black Wednesday' (26 September 1992), the government had to take the pound Sterling out of the European exchange rate mechanism and the pound heavily lost value as a result (Kastendiek and Stinshoff 2006: 110). Meier-Walser attributes Labour's election victory in 1997 partly to this event (Meier-Walser 2001: 12). It also had inner-party consequences: anti-European CON MPs made it difficult for Major to pass the laws that would ratify the Maastricht Treaty. After losing the first parliamentary vote in 1993, ratification was delayed until August that year, when it passed with a slim majority (J. Schmidt 2011: 381).

Sicking and Müller refer to the relationship between the UK and the EU as problematic in the 1990s and claim it grew even more so since the Maastricht treaty paved the way to a European economic and monetary union (Sicking and Müller 1999: 7). Similarly, Giddings recounts that ever since the inception of the European institutions, "the UK has struggled to develop its relationship with its European partners" (Giddings 2005b: "Westminster" 215). He explains this continued unease with the ever-changing nature of the European Union and the increase in its competences and power: "A primarily trading and economic bloc developed its social and political aspirations, generating significant political tensions in the UK" (2005b: "Westminster" 215). He concludes that ever since the UK joined the EC, " 'Europe' has been a topic of high political controversy, within and between the governing parties" (Giddings 2005b: "Westminster" 215).

3.2 New Labour, New Dawn? British Political Parties and European Policy 1997–2010

The general election in May 1997 can be described as a watershed moment for the UK's relationship with the EU. The CON, who had dominated British politics and whose former leader Margaret Thatcher left a decidedly Eurosceptic legacy that her successor John Major did not change notably, suffered their heaviest defeat since 1906, winning only 165 seats. The Labour Party with its then leader Tony Blair won the General Election with a surprisingly high margin, gaining 418 seats in the House of Commons. The Lib Dems in third place won 46 seats with 16.8 % of the vote. Shortly after having been elected, Labour signed up to the Social Chapter, which Major had refused to do (J. Schmidt 2011: 402). Blair's pro-European rhetoric and his promise to lead the UK to the 'heart of Europe' gave rise to a sense of new beginnings: the UK's European partners perceived – at least in the first Labour years – a distinct change in Blair's attitude towards Europe, which contributed to the decision to award him the International Karlspreis in 1999 (Sicking and Müller 1999: 8). Sicking and Müller recount that Blair spoke of a "Europe of citizens" as his vision, specifically addressing social and cultural concerns (1999: 11). Ludwig concludes that this demonstrative policy change, the strategic turn towards Europe by Labour and the positioning of the CON as an anti-European alternative, shows that there was no 'permissive consensus' concerning European integration in the UK in the years after 1997. Ludwig claims that in comparison with other EU member states, the UK was quite singular in this regard (2011: 31).

As salient issues and priorities in British EU policy during Labour's first of three consecutive terms of office, Ludwig names the "adaptation of the European economic and social policies, the reform of European institutions and treaties, the EU's enlargement and its Common Foreign and Security Policy" (2011: *Abstract*). In the general elections 2001, Labour retained their huge majority in the HoC by winning 412 seats, and the Lib Dems could again improve their results by gaining 52 seats. The CON, on the other hand, gained only one more seat than in 1997, totalling 166.

In his account of British European policy, Wall confirms that the years from 1992 to 2004 were of crucial importance in the UK-EU relationship since the Treaties of Maastricht, Amsterdam, and Nice as well as the Constitution fall into this period. His evaluation of the implications for British politics is quite sobering: "All of those institutional changes posed serious substantive and political problems for the British governments which had to wrestle with them" (Wall 2008: vii–viii). Giddings concurs when he names "the single currency, immigration and asylum; and defence arrangements" together with the European Constitution as "particularly sensitive" policy areas (2005b: "Westminster" 216).

The following general elections on 5 May 2005 saw a decrease in the number of seats won for Labour to 355, and the CON won 198 seats, winning only one additional seat. However, the Lib Dems could win 62 seats, the best result for a third party since 1923, and saw the biggest increase in popular vote share to 22 %. Russell and Cutts argue that this increase was due to a vote swing from both big parties, thus increasing the third party's voter base: "Voters who might term themselves one-nation Conservatives were targeted by the Liberal Democrat campaign rhetoric that suggested that the Conservative Party had surrendered to the Eurosceptic right" (2009: 78). From these election results, the conclusion can be drawn that despite not being in government, the Lib Dems succeeded in making their positions heard and found approval for them.

In terms of European policy during this third term of the Labour government, the European summit in June 2005 failed to produce an agreement because Schröder and Chirac demanded a stop for the British budget rebate, a demand Blair only wanted to accept if the CAP was reformed profoundly in return (J. Schmidt 2011: 446). Further important developments were the Lisbon Treaty, which was negotiated to replace the failed EU constitution.

Oakland summarises Labour's European policies from 1997 up to 2010 as follows:

> The previous Labour government wanted a strong Europe in which Britain could play a central role; supported the enlargement of the EU; backed the Lisbon Treaty; was in principle in favour of Britain entering the European common currency (euro); and proposed a common defence and foreign policy for the EU. But it was against the concept of a federal 'superstate', favoured the Council of Ministers as the key decision-making body and was against enhancing the powers of the European Parliament. (2011: 135)

The policy goals of New Labour were thus clearly pro-European; however, a certain reserve towards the movement of decision-making powers to EU institutions was apparent. Comparing the proclaimed policy goals with the actual policy outcomes during New Labour's three consecutive terms of office, Oakland concludes:

> However, it did not take Britain into the first wave of the euro in 1999. Its policy was to wait until Britain's economy was in line with those of other members, see how the currency developed and then put the issue to a referendum. Polls in recent years have consistently suggested that a majority of Britons are against joining the euro. A MORI poll in February 2005 found that 57 per cent of respondents were against the euro and 55 per cent would not change their minds if the government strongly urged support. Feelings in Britain about the Lisbon Treaty (a revamped and rejected constitutional treaty) have also been volatile, with many people feeling that Britain should have had a referendum on the issue. (2011: 135)

Against the background of these political developments, Oakland thus summarised in 2011 that "British membership of the EU continue[d] to be difficult" (2011: 134). Among the UK's grievances, he lists "its contribution to the EU budget [...], the agricultural and fisheries policies; and [...] movements towards greater political and economic integration" (Oakland 2011: 135). Labour thus sent mixed messages in European policy during their time in office. Even after 13 years of Labour governments, Oakland claims that

> the relationship between Britain and Europe continues to be problematic and new associations have been forced by events and circumstances rather than wholeheartedly sought. A scepticism about Europe and the historical impulses to national independence and isolationism still appear to condition many British people in their dealings

with and attitudes to the outside world, despite their reliance on global trade and international relationships. (2011: 8–9)

The political stance of the biggest opposition party, the CON, leaned more and more towards "Eurosceptic" criticism of the EU, whereas the Lib Dems are typically counted as Europhile, i.e. supporters of all steps towards a more integrated EU. Given that "British support for the EU peaked in the 1980s but has since been eroded, and Britain is now the least enthusiastic of the EU countries" (Oakland 2011: 136), the political discourse on this policy area with its different positions certainly merits a closer look. Especially the "Europhile" side represented by the Lib Dems is interesting to look at.

Summarising the overall Lib Dem performances in the Blair years, Russell and Cutts claim that "Tony Blair was good for the Liberal Democrats. Throughout his leadership of the Labour Party the fortunes of the Liberal Democrats, Britain's third party, were boosted" (2009: 65). They account for this with the unpopularity of the CON during this time and also disenchantment with New Labour towards the end of their time in government, leading to impressive election results: "[i]n parliament, the Liberal Democrats tripled their numbers across Blair's three election victories and in Scotland and Wales they were able to share power in the new devolved institutions" (Russell and Cutts 2009: 65). Commenting on Charles Kennedy as leader of the Lib Dems during many of these successes, Russell and Cutts conclude: "His avuncular public image enabled the party to have a distinct voice in British politics" (2009: 71). Building on this influence and importance, the Lib Dems became more confident subsequently: "Under Kennedy the Liberal Democrats amended the tone of election campaigning from 'constructive opposition' to 'effective opposition'" (Russell and Cutts 2009: 66).

Highlighting their consistency when it comes to parliamentary votes on European policy, A. Jones found that "[m]ost British political parties have changed their position on the issue of Europe. Only the Liberal Democrats (and the SDLP in Northern Ireland) have been consistent supporters of membership" (2016: 178). When it comes to the Lib Dem position on Europe under Clegg's leadership, however, Russell and Cutts draw attention to one incident where

> [i]ncredibly, the most Europhile of all British parties managed to engineer a parliamentary split on the issue of Europe – as Clegg's instruction to abstain on the need for a referendum on the European Union constitution led to rebellion from a fifth of the parliamentary party, two resignations from the Liberal Democrat shadow cabinet and ridicule in the popular Tory press. (2009: 75)

This indicates that the debate on the EU Constitution and a possible referendum on it is one of the 'hot' topics which have caused a high amount of controversy even among the Lib Dem MPs and, therefore, merit a closer look if one wants to understand the dynamics of today's political turmoil when it comes to the British relationship to the EU.

3.3 2010 and Beyond – Brexit Ahead

On 6 May 2010, the General Election produced the following result: The CON won 306 seats (36.1 %), whereas Labour only won 258. The Lib Dems were still the third biggest parliamentary party with 57 gained seats; these results meant a hung parliament. After frenzied negotiations, a coalition government between CON and Lib Dems with David Cameron as Prime Minister and Nick Clegg as Deputy Prime Minister was formed (J. Schmidt 2011: 459). One of the most divisive issues was, as could be expected given the opposing approaches adopted by the two parties in the preceding years, the European policy to be pursued by the coalition. This was further illustrated by the two different campaigns for the following general election in 2015: The CON promised a referendum on staying in the European Union and won an overall parliamentary majority whereas the Lib Dems suffered painful losses and were effectively swiped off the electoral map, with the Scottish National Party (SNP) subsequently taking over the position as third-largest parliamentary party in Westminster.

The Brexit referendum in June 2016 with its unprecedented result has ever since been the event that dominates British politics and is the subject of much scholarly analysis. This book argues, however, that in order to fully understand the dynamics leading up to the current complicated situation, the years preceding the coalition government are much more interesting – and much more in the dark as yet.

4. Text Selection: Parliamentary Discourse

In the following, the scope and limits of this study's material basis will be set out. Teubert states that "[t]he general discourse in Britain consists of all the spoken and written texts that have been communicated within the British discourse community" (2001: 45). Because the general discourse in Britain is thus far too large to be analysed or even captured in its entirety at any point, "[a]ll discourse analysis can ever hope for is to look at sub-discourses, small selections of texts, defined by parameters such as time span, authorship, audience, region, domain or medium" (Teubert 2001: 45). Teubert allocates these selection tasks to the researchers interested in such a sub-discourse when he points out that "[i]t is the discourse analysts who determine the parameters of the special discourse they want to study" (2001: 45). This task is consequently approached in the following, and the decisions made are justified by providing background information on the British political system and the role of parliament in it, as well as the actors creating and shaping the British sub-discourse dealing with European policy.

When it comes to political discourse in the UK, Teubert claims that "[t]he discourse community includes British politicians, business people, academics, journalists and the public at large" (Teubert 2001: 45). Regarding the parameter authorship, this study proposes to focus on British politicians as important contributors to the (considered essentially political) debate on British relations with Europe. Leith and Soule criticise that many academic studies focusing on national identity are limited to elite conceptions of these concepts; however, they recognise the importance of political elites in this field (2012: 12–13). Several experts in British politics and European policy agree that the most important actors and influencers in this discourse are the political leaders (Jones and Norton 2010: 615; Geddes 2004: 1).

The next step is to determine which politicians forming this elite are relevant. In the following, it will be outlined in more detail that the British Parliament has a central function in the British polity. It will equally be argued that speeches held there possess significant relevance for the national discourse on Europe, which makes them a worthwhile object of research. Party leaders' speeches in Parliament are especially interesting because of the latter's' predominant position in the parliamentary system.

Although European policy traditionally lies with the Foreign Secretary, reflecting both the fact that it was seen as a foreign policy domain as well as the composition of the General Council in Brussels responsible for negotiating treaties (Wall 2008: 190), the importance of heads of government, who meet in the European Council and decide on the strategic direction of the EU, has grown in recent years (Wall 2008: 195). As has been shown in the introduction, this development is reflected in the numbers of academic studies focusing on government leaders and their take on European policy, while the opposition parties have been neglected in this regard. To redress this imbalance, it makes sense, therefore, to focus on the opposite numbers of the Prime Ministers over a given period, namely the opposition party leaders (rather than shadow ministers). Hence, the present study favours an examination of British party leaders' contribution to political discourse on Europe, thus aiming at determining the "elite" aspect of the overall discourse. This is not perceived as limiting, though; rather, it allows for robust results obtained through a rigorous in-depth analysis of empirical data based on a large and systematically established corpus containing all speeches made in the particular environment of parliament by the chosen members of the political elite.

4.1 The Importance of Parliament in the British Political System

Kamm and Lenz advocate seeing the present as a result of the past and claim that without knowledge of the historical developments, the current constitutional and legal system cannot be satisfactorily understood (Kamm and Lenz 2004: 10). It is thus important to bear in mind that the current political system in the UK evolved from different traditions introduced by the numerous settlers on the islands: Romans, Angles, Saxons, and Angles left traces as well as the Vikings and then the Normans. The monarchy with its feudalistic system installed by the latter contributed eventually to an empowerment of the nobility when they faced weak kings, and in 1215 King John Lackland had to cede some rights to the barons (lords), set down in Magna Carta (Kamm and Lenz 2004: 16). This historical event, whose 600th anniversary was celebrated in 2015, arguably laid the foundations for the developments and establishment of the present-day political system with parliament at its heart. The most radical change to this centralised system in recent years has indubitably occurred with the devolution process: the Scottish parliament in Edinburgh and the regional assemblies of Wales and Northern Ireland have acquired rights and competences of their own. The relations with the EU, however, are decided upon at state level. Therefore, it is the British parliament at Westminster which is the main focus of this study.

Today, the British political system is a constitutional monarchy. In what is called the Westminster system of parliamentary government (Kastendiek and Stinshoff 2006: 103), the sovereign is not the people, but the monarch in Parliament (the monarch is indeed also literally called the sovereign). The monarch's role, however, is today all in all only symbolical and the actual power lies with the political party wielding a majority in the House of Commons, and, therefore, almost always constituting the government. It is thus not the monarch but parliament (or more precisely the political party commanding a simple parliamentary majority in the House of Commons, which is necessary to win a division) who can, therefore, theoretically pass and abolish any law it chooses. This principle is a pivotal feature of "parliamentary sovereignty". Johnson claims that the "sovereignty doctrine [...] is still widely held to underpin the claims made by the lower house of Parliament" (N. Johnson 2005: 21). Giddings says that this doctrine has indeed "acquired a mythical status" (Giddings 2005a: "Purpose" 259) and that "in the debates about Britain and the European Union and about the role of the courts, the myth of parliamentary sovereignty plays a central but deeply confusing role" (Giddings 2005a: "Purpose" 259), while some experts in constitutional law argue that this principle was in fact undermined with the Single European Act signed by Margaret Thatcher.

Even though the executive has a powerful position in the Westminster system (Kastendiek and Stinshoff 2006: 106) and "parliamentary sovereignty is effectively hijacked by the executive" (Kingdom 2014: 459), parliament nevertheless stays "the constitutional seat of sovereignty in Britain" (Kingdom 2014: 459). Parliament thus occupies an outstanding role. However, Stuart admits that the "idea of parliament in decline is one of the most resilient themes in British political science" (2009: 189). Nevertheless, he says that "[t]he Blair decade ended with parliamentarians better resourced than ever before, and if not wholly representative of the wider public, then a great deal more so than they had been previously" (Stuart 2009: 189). Equally addressing the "claim that Parliament is in decline today" (Ryle 2005: 4), which he attributes largely to a hostile media representation (7), Ryle argues that "Parliament – particularly the House of Commons – plays a more active, independent, and influential role in Britain today than at any time for many years" (Ryle 2005: 4). Summarising this discussion, Kingdom claims that "[w]hatever its faults, Parliament remains the nation's central democratic forum. Even though debate rarely leads to direct policy change, it can have a longer-term influence by shaping public opinion" (Kingdom 2003: 408). Indeed, Giddings feels sure that on complex issues such as the euro and the European Constitution where a referendum was planned and the parties split, Parliament could provide the best forum for debate: "If fully exploited the Parliamentary forum, notwithstanding the pressures on the Westminster timetable, can provide fuller and richer exploration of these issues than any discussion on Newsnight,

Today, or Panorama, or a multitude of features in newspapers, however distinguished" (Giddings 2005a: "Purpose" 225).

Picking up on the role of the media for politics in the UK, Negrine, and Seymour-Ure argue that they prefer to report on debates in the Chamber (the House of Commons) because they tend to be

> general, populist, argumentative, talking largely in non-technical language, responding fairly quickly to topical issues, reflecting and helping to set the political agenda. The extreme case is Prime Minister's Questions, when to a significant extent the Members talk past the opposition benches to the outside world. (2005: 239)

Ryle summarises the power of opposition in Parliament in relation to the media as follows: "Governments can no longer ignore parliamentary opinion. MPs must be heeded or the media will put the Government in the dock for being 'out of touch' with the public" (2005: 9). Even in today's age of (online) mass media, sound bites, and TV debates, parliament remains the location where all important policy issues are discussed in detail and where long-term political strategies are controversially debated. It can be concluded, therefore, that despite attempts of the executive to dominate parliament and a changing media environment, it remains the central institution where opposition discourse is heard and can influence both public opinion and government actions.

It has to be noted, though, that Parliament is no monolithic institution, but possesses a multi-layered structure. Firstly, it is a bicameral parliament, with two different chambers: the House of Lords and the House of Commons (Giddings 2005a: "Purpose" 258). The latter is democratically elected, which results today in what Giddings calls the "primacy of the House of Commons as the elected chamber" (Giddings 2005a: "Purpose" 262) in the legislative process. All laws and important government decisions are presented and discussed there (UK Parliament: "Parliament's Role"). This is one of the main functions of parliament today, together with the role of being "a scrutineer of government and administration" (Giddings 2005a: "Purpose" 259). Kingdom states that "the House of Commons is also the chamber of the prime minister, the leading ministers and opposition front bench [...] the site where political Titans confront each other on a daily basis" (2003: 367–368). The House of Commons is made up by individual MPs representing one constituency each. The House of Lords, on the other hand, is composed of a varying number of hereditary and life-time peers. It has the right to propose, debate, and suggest amendments to laws, too. However, even though partially reformed in 1999, the make-up of the upper chamber does not reflect the election results and many members do not belong to a political party at all. The functions of Parliament are also carried out in committees. There were two parliamentary committees in the House of Commons working in the subject area of British-European relations, namely the European Scrutiny Committee (ESC) and the European Standing Committee. However, the 'minutes of proceedings' of the committee sittings do not contain the recorded discussions, but only the agendas of each session and division results. Some documents are classified as 'closed' under the 30-year-rule; they contain Explanatory Memoranda and the correspondence with Ministers or other civil service employees. The minutes of the debates in the European Scrutiny Committee are not released (only informal notes are produced) and can, therefore, not be accessed for research, not even under the Freedom of Information Act (FOI).[2]

Giddings points out that next to the binary structure of HoC and House of Lords, there are "two other dualities, which divide both chambers and are built into the very fabric of the place, physically and culturally – the first between government and opposition, and the second between front-bench and back-bench" (Giddings 2005a: "Purpose" 258). These features will be explained in more detail in the next section.

4.2 Parties and Parliament

Baedermann (2007: 5) argues that electoral systems and laws vary markedly from (European) country to country. Anchored in the respective political systems, they influence and are influenced by it. One of the most direct and visible effects of electoral laws on the political system is the make-up of the political party system: electoral laws determine which people are elected to the legislative body in a country, and the parties are usually the reservoir from which the candidates are recruited (Baedermann 2007: 5).

In the British political system, political parties are the central element; indeed, parliament "is largely energized by political parties" (Kingdom 2014: 459). The UK's Westminster system is characterised by its two-party system: the majority vote electoral system (first-past-the-post) means that in every constituency, the candidate who wins the (simple) majority of ballots cast wins the parliamentary seat for this constituency (Worcester 2011: ix). This usually results in clear majorities; since the 1920s, it has furthered the dominance of two big parties in Parliament, namely the Conservative and Unionist Party, usually referred to as the Conservatives (also called 'Tories'), and the Labour Party (Cole and Deighan 2012: 44). The party with the absolute majority in parliament (50 % plus 1 of

---

2   I am grateful to the ESC clerk in 2015, Sarah Davies, for providing this information.

the total of seats) can form the government. This electoral system is designed to produce stable majorities in parliament (Kastendiek and Stinshoff 2006: 103). In the twenty-first century, however, this system has produced and is likely to produce further so-called 'hung parliaments', i.e. a situation where none of the two big parties wins an absolute majority. The CON-Lib Dem coalition government from 2010 to 2015 and the general election results in 2017 showed that. It means that smaller parties (like the Liberal Democrats) have recently gained more importance and can act as kingmakers when the two big parties fail to win a majority.

Traditionally, though, the role of third parties in British politics is a difficult one: "A third party in Britain is likely to face a battle to establish credibility" (Russell and Cutts 2009: 76) because their chances to participate in government are slim in a two-party system. The Lib Dems were the third-largest party in the British political system from 1992 until 2015. They came into being as a political party in 1988 as a result of the official merger of the Liberal Party and the Social Democratic Party but never came close to importance in general election results, mainly due to the electoral regime favouring the two biggest parties. Nevertheless, in 2010, the Lib Dems became part of a coalition government, and their leader at the time, Nick Clegg, became 'deputy Prime Minister'. This suggests that they had previously worked hard at achieving enough credibility – and the tools at their disposal were words. The conclusion by Russell and Cutts seems appropriate: "This suggests that the political impact of the third party may be measured in something other than sheer parliamentary size" (2009: 76).

The parties also serve an important selective function for political programmes and politicians themselves: to become an influential actor on the political stage, one will usually join a party, stand for election and win a constituency to become an MP, and then rise through the ranks of the party to become a 'front-bencher' and have more opportunity to contribute to debates (Baedermann 2007: 5). It is thus the party 'elite' and especially the party leaders who are relevant in this regard: "Privy Councillors (cabinet and ex-cabinet members and leading members of the opposition parties) enjoy certain privileges: 'right honourable' rather than 'honourable', they receive precedence in debate" (Kingdom 2003: 368). The leaders of the Lib Dems as members of the Loyal Opposition have been appointed as such Privy Councillors for life. The party leaders of the two major opposition parties thus enjoy privileges that show their importance and set them apart from other members of the opposition. The deputy speaker of the House of Commons also made this clear on 24 March 2010:

Order. The House should also hear the response of the leader of the Liberal Democrat party. Can I say to the House, as many hon. Members seem unaware, that there is a clear convention that the responses to the Budget by the Leader of the Opposition and the leader of the Liberal Democrats are not interrupted? [Official Report, 24 March 2010, Vol. 508, col. 269]

The internal management of parliamentary parties is in the hands of the "whips". Giddings explains that the "prevailing mindset is that *any* refusal to follow the party line is rebellion – and with its concomitant 'discipline', prejudices a successful career" (Giddings 2005a: "Purpose" 266). This raises the question why so many MPs rebel when it comes to matters European – they must feel very strongly about it if they risk their career by doing so, or they feel confident that the party leadership will accommodate their views, since the "whips can terrorise the few, but must bend to the many" (Giddings 2005a: "Purpose" 266). Thus, whips are required "to give warning when the leadership's take on a question cannot be sold" (Giddings 2005a: "Purpose" 266). It can, therefore, be assumed that should the official party line go against most of the parliamentary parties' members, substantial rebellions will occur, and the policy will be adapted accordingly.

4.3 Parliamentary Speeches

In the particular context of the British political system and British political culture, political speeches retain a highly relevant position (2001: 172). Parliament is used by British politicians as a debate chamber and national public forum (Tönnies and Viol 2001: 172). Given that public speech has a high significance and long tradition in the Anglosphere, still visible today, e.g., in the countless university debating societies which still play their part in preparing the political elite, British politicians try and influence public opinion by the means of speeches. Political decision-making equally relies on them (Tönnies and Viol 2001: 171–172). Especially speeches made in Parliament allow valuable insights into political developments and the different positions taken by political actors (Tönnies and Viol 2001: 171–172). Ryle concurs when he defines the main role of Parliament as follows: "Parliament does not govern but is the forum for public debate and criticism of the policies and acts of government" (2005: 5). This definition with its emphasis on the "central function of Parliament as a critical forum" (8) highlights the crucial importance of speeches made in Parliament, and particularly those made by the opposition whose chief function is to critically evaluate government. Particularly well-known and relevant where scrutiny is concerned are Prime Minister's Questions (PMQs). Debates in the House of Commons are thus the most prominent platform for political speeches. This makes the selection of speeches held in the House of Commons plausible because they contain carefully worded statements directed to a public the speaker seeks to convince, and are, as such, an especially promising corpus to be analysed.

In terms of the audience addressed, parliamentary speeches can be considered multi-faceted. The following quote shows that parliamentary debate is also aimed at the (voting) public, which is sometimes even explicitly mentioned:

> Mr. Speaker: Order. If hon. and right hon. Members do not stop shouting, I may have to ring some sort of helpline myself –or, worse still, suspend the sitting. This sort of noise and ranting makes an extremely bad impression on the British public. I appeal to the House to have some regard for the way in which we are viewed by the electorate. [Official Report, 2010, Vol. 506, col. 294]

The politicians speaking as well as the speaker are clearly very aware that they address not only their physically present political friends and opponents but also journalists, as well as their prospective voters.

Content-wise, Tönnies and Viol conclude that the question of the UK's role in the world is still an issue being controversially debated in political speeches (2001: 175). In general, they conclude that political speeches are part of material culture and windows into the discourse reality of a specific moment in the past:

> Reden lassen, wenn auch meist in durch den Redner manipulierten Form, die Geschichte zu Wort kommen. Sie reflektieren gesellschaftliche Stimmungen und Problemlagen, geben dem späteren Leser einen Einblick in die Selbstwahrnehmung, den Vorstellungshorizont und die Zukunftserwartungen einer historischen Periode und vermitteln nicht zuletzt Einsicht in den zeitgenössischen Diskurs, also die besondere Beschaffenheit der Sprache, derer sich Redner und Adressaten bedienen, um politische Ideen vorstellbar und kommunizierbar zu machen. (Tönnies and Viol 2001: 173)

Having established the British Parliament as the central institution in the political system of the UK and having explained its basic structures and functions, this sums up and confirms the adequacy of analysing political speeches to answer the research questions of this study.

4.4 Summary: Relevant Actors and Selected Speeches

Summing up, the political discourse on Europe in the time frame of 1997–2010, i.e. during the New Labour governments, has been chosen to be the main focus of this study. The research is limited to the period from the General Election in May 1997 until the General Election in May 2010. These dates mark the beginning and end of 13 years of Labour governments under Tony Blair (1997–2007) and Gordon Brown (2007–2010), with Tony Blair stepping down on 27 June 2007 and Gordon Brown, the former Chancellor of the Exchequer, taking over. This allows for a longitudinal research design where results show developments over time. This particular period is especially relevant in the context of this project because several important developments on the European level took place in the same period of time: the debate on Economic and Monetary Union and the introduction of the common currency, the euro; the signing of European reform treaties and the (failed) European Constitution project as well as the 'Eastern' enlargement of the European Union. These events were subject to controversial discussion on member-state level and in this light, the debate can be expected to yield interesting results as to how a British self-understanding is negotiated in this specific context.

During this time, the Lib Dems were the third-largest party in parliament. As relevant and yet largely ignored actors when it comes to the supposedly Europhile discourse in the United Kingdom during this time, the Lib Dems are central to this study. The fact that they negotiated a coalition agreement with the CON after the general election 2010 and thus governed as coalition partners from 2010 to 2015 brings their positions during the times of opposition to the forefront of political interest as well. Moreover, despite being described repeatedly and consistently as "pro-European", this claim is insufficiently grounded in data or quotes from party members themselves. It is, therefore, particularly interesting to see how their (opposition) policy proposals in the field of British-European relations are justified, and whether they indeed see and describe themselves as pro-European or whether this label is ascribed to them from outside, by journalists, analysts, and academics.

In the context of the British political system where parliament plays an eminent role and speeches held there by prominent party members are of particular relevance, the corpus analysed in this study focuses accordingly on speeches made in the House of Commons. The corpus under scrutiny thus includes all oral speeches and statements by the party leaders of the Lib Dems made in parliament during the chosen period. As shown above, they had a privileged position and had the right to comment on the prime minister's statements as well as to be heard uninterruptedly (i.e. they were not obliged to 'give way'). This study does not deny that there were and are conflicting views on policy positions in every political party, the multitude of which cannot be captured when only the leaders' speeches are selected. However, they represent the dominant and official party line. The function of political parties as selective mechanism for policies having been asserted above, dissenting views will not be included in the corpus. Moreover, the Lib Dem MPs were united in their position on Europe except for one case of rebellion (Lynch 2011: 220).

Tab. 1: Lib Dem Party Leaders and Their Terms of Office

Lib Dem Party Leader	Term of Office
Paddy Ashdown	until 9.8.1999
Charles Kennedy	9.8.1999–7.1.2006
Sir Menzies Campbell	7.1.2006–2.3.2006 (interim leadership)
	2.3.2006–15.10.2007
Vince Cable (interim leader)	15.10.2007–18.12.2007
Nick Clegg	18.12.2007–11.5.2010 and beyond

In the period under review, the Lib Dem parliamentary party was led by Paddy Ashdown, until 9 August 1999. After that, Charles Kennedy was elected as new leader and remained in this position until 7 January 2006. His deputy Sir Menzies Campbell took over as interim leader then and was endorsed as official leader two months later, on 2 March 2006. He resigned on 15 October 2007. Vincent Cable then acted as interim leader until Nick Clegg won the leadership contest on 18 December 2007 and stayed on until 2015. The following table provides an overview of these dates.

5. Data Analysis Methodology

After having defined a specific part of the British political discourse on Europe as the subject of analysis, the next step is to decide how to analyse such a discourse. Frenken et al. suggest considering the following criteria when analysing political speeches: speaker, type of speech, date, place, issue, length and audience, as well as the occasion (2008: 20–21). These criteria will be included in the analysis, where debates are first sorted according to the issue(s) they address, and then analysed chronologically per speaker. Although all speeches are made in the House of Commons, the types of speech vary, from the weekly PMQs sessions to debates occasioned by contextual events, either recurring (such as the 'Debate on the Address', which comes first in every new parliamentary session, and bi-annual EU Council meetings) or occasioned by one-off events. The audience of parliamentary speeches is discussed in general in the previous chapter, while the length of debate interventions is not considered.

The analysis of a large corpus of textual data can be approached from a multitude of angles (Tönnies and Viol 2001: 172–173), using quantitative as well as qualitative methods. In the light of the research questions and the empirical material to be analysed, namely recorded speeches, a qualitative approach seems the best choice. Indeed, Mayring postulates that all content analyses consist of at least one qualitative step, namely deciding what exactly will be analysed and what will not – thus employing a qualitative judgement (2010: 20–21). There are numerous ways to approach a qualitative analysis of data: hermeneutics, critical (dialectical) approaches, narrative approaches, descriptive as well as explorative (theory-building, like grounded theory) ones (Mayring 2010: 9–10). Mayring argues, however, that an integration of qualitative and quantitative methods can produce better results than insisting on the alleged opposition of the two method types (2010: 51). He specifically advocates the use of quantitative steps in a qualitative analysis where they usefully complement the steps already taken, especially the number of items in one category which may indicate its significance (Mayring 2010: 51). Where such a combination is employed, he calls for an extensive justification and interpretation of results (Mayring 2010: 51). Kuckartz agrees that most research implicitly relies on a mixed-methods approach and that contemporary research explicitly uses them in a bid to overcome the opposition between quantitative and qualitative methods (2012: 18–19). When it comes to generalising the found phenomena, Mayring says that quantitative steps may be appropriate (Mayring 2010: 51).

In order to obtain comprehensive, rich, and sound results, it is thus deemed appropriate for this research project to combine several methods, i.e. using a mixed-methods approach. With such a method triangulation, the results can additionally be considered more valid and reliable. Based on these considerations, the chosen analytical methodology for this research project is set out in the following.

5.1 Preparation of the Corpora

In a first step, all speeches made by Lib Dem party leaders between May 1997 and May 2010 were looked up in *Hansard*, the official parliamentary records in the UK where all speeches made in Parliament are recorded and archived. They could be retrieved online and were stored. The importance of *Hansard* as a record of contributions to parliamentary debates is often demonstrated when MPs cite what they or their opponents have said on previous occasions. When something is 'on the record', it can be read, re-read, and proven to have been said, thus giving rise to reactions and contributing to making up the MPs' minds when it comes to taking a decision. By using the archived protocols of parliamentary speeches, i.e. data that has been processed (transcribed) from an oral genre to a written form of text, a number of communication details are invariably lost (such as intonation, speed, volume, gestures, facial expressions, etc.). However, the focus of this study will be on arguments and metaphors, which survive the transcription process in their entirety.

There were two main forms of archived information encountered during the study of these primary sources: the historic *Hansard* and the present-day *Hansard*. For debates in the period of 1803 until March 2005, the historic *Hansard* keeps the records. It was thus accessed to examine the speeches made by the leaders. The procedure was as follows: first, the entries held in the historic *Hansard* were sorted by name to obtain a list with all the speeches by the party leaders in question. Then, these lists were narrowed down to only include their terms of office as party leaders. The entries were sorted chronologically.

The same procedure was applied to the records in the current *Hansard*, which holds all records from April 2005 until the present in reverse chronological order. The online records for the parliamentary session 2005/2006 differ from the publications after 2006 in that they can be sorted by name of the person speaking, but contain a keyword listing, i.e. a tag, instead of giving the dates on which the tagged subjects were debated. I inserted these dates after having checked the entries for mentions of Europe gone unnoticed.

In conclusion, there were thus three different forms of archived speeches during the selected research period, which I have modified to make them comparable concerning the information they give, by adding the date or the subject of the debate where it was missing. The total of speeches resulting from the process laid out above, containing all speeches made in the House of Commons by all selected politicians from 2 May 1997 until 11 May 2010, forms the first corpus (corpus one). This forms the basis for the next analytical step, namely a content analysis of all speeches in corpus one.

5.2 Content Analysis

Leith and Soule argue that "[w]hile parties generally, as they must, give attention to a broad range of ideas and policies [...], they also differ markedly in relation to what they believe significant" (2012: 46). It is, therefore, highly interesting to explore, in a first analytical step, which topics were addressed at all, and thus deemed important, by the party leaders. This will yield first results concerning the respective party priorities and the place that Europe occupied amongst them. Leith and Soule advocate a "quantitative content analysis" in order to achieve this (2012: 167).

Mayring summarises the properties of content analysis in the social sciences as follows: it is concerned with the systematic analysis of fixed (i.e. written or recorded) communication, defined as a transfer of symbols (2010: 13–14). The analytical steps are carried out according to certain rules, which allow for the analysis to be reproduced and tested. Additionally, it is theory-led in that it seeks to answer a research question against a specific theoretic background via interpretation of the results (Mayring 2010: 14). This method is, therefore, considered especially suitable as a first step in an analytical process aiming at understanding British discourse.

A simple way to analyse content is by counting the occurrences of certain elements in the data set and to compare them with the frequencies in which others occur – a frequency analysis (Mayring 2010: 13). The necessary steps are (in this order): formulating a research question, defining the corpus, establishing categories, defining analytical units (i.e. minimum/maximum text bits that fall under a category), coding, calculating, and comparing frequencies, and visualising and interpreting the results (Mayring 2010: 15). A first step on the way to shedding light on the research questions set out at the beginning of this study is thus a quantitative assessment of how often European policy or British-European relations play a role in parliamentary contributions by party leaders at all, and how this number compares with the overall number of their contributions. This relation should give an indication as to how salient the topic was in each parliamentary session, in the three parliaments 1997–2010 and in the research period overall.

In order to calculate this ratio, all contributions to parliamentary debates made by Lib Dem party leaders were coded manually according to the rules for a qualitative content analysis. The procedure was as follows: the debates with interventions by the chosen actors were accessed via the links provided in the *Hansard* online archives and coded manually to indicate which subjects were brought up in the specific debates. Where European policy was explicitly mentioned or implicitly referred to, the speeches or relevant parts of it were copied into a MaxQDA file and saved for further analysis; they subsequently formed corpus two. When speeches did not touch on anything connected with European policy, the entries were subsequently excluded from further analysis. To summarise the process laid out above, the relevant speeches (i.e. talking about Europe in some way) were chosen to form the smaller, second corpus (corpus two) representing the Lib Dem parliamentary opposition discourse on Europe as defined for this study. This forms the basis for all subsequent analysis steps, namely a qualitative assessment of the speeches mentioning Europe.

In order to be able to calculate shares of a total, a unit of analysis must be chosen. In this study, the number of debates separately titled in *Hansard* in which the party leaders spoke is defined as the total to calculate the ration between corpus one and two. The units of analysis in this case are thus the different debates in which the speakers made one or more contributions. If, for instance, Charles Kennedy mentioned the CAP) three times in one debate, the debate in question would count as one occurrence and one unit of analysis. Leith and Soule confirm that "[t]he relative importance given to specific policy areas can then be considered by measuring the individual codes against the total" (2012: 42). The results of the calculations are given per parliamentary session and overall for the 13 years of Labour governments that are researched. When it comes to the content analysis of speeches in corpus two, this means that the total can be more than 100 % when more than one subject was mentioned in a debate.

I have used the software "MaxQDA" to code corpus two, i.e. the complete data set consisting of all contributions containing references to Europe. After having coded 10 % of the speeches manually, automatic coding was employed. Automatic coding means that the software checks the whole text for instances of the search terms (e.g. "enlargement") and assigns the code I have selected (in this case the code category is synonymous, i.e. "enlargement") to the sentence containing the search term. The automatic coding instances were then checked manually for accuracy and coding boundaries (size of the coded text segments), and were modified where necessary. The coded segments were then subject to the further analysis steps, which will be set out in the following.

Adapting the approach by A.D. Smith (2003), Leith and Soule argue that "[e]lites regularly employ the relationship between nationalism and history in their attempts to create, maintain and legitimise the nation and a sense of nationhood" (2012: 41). History is an important element in that "[e]mploying the past of golden ages and mythical heroes to more recent, and perhaps mundane, political events regularly takes place" (Leith and Soule 2012: 41). Coakley similarly argues that the "capacity of elites to shape political outcomes by influencing the way in which the past is perceived is a well-known characteristic of public life" (2004: 531). Leith and Soule claim that "[n]ational political elites employ nationalist symbols and myths to support their political programme" (2012: 41). In their work on Scottish party manifestos, they found that there were "few expressions or direct policy statements expressing a distinct sense of either Scottishness or Britishness" (2012: 60). They note that the content analysis using codes has its strengths, but also weaknesses: it does not allow to capture implicit meaning and "limits interpretation" (2012: 61). To remedy this, Leith and Soule suggest to "comment on the rhetoric and tone of specific language", acknowledging the "need for greater rhetorical investigation" (2012: 61) because political statements may carry more meaning than just the obvious policy area they refer to. They put the case for "a study of the nuances and discourse [...] [which] may provide further insight into the nature of national identity, as envisaged and employed by [...] political parties" (2012: 61).

5.3 Political Discourse Analysis

After having clarified the theoretical properties of discourse in Chapter 2, the next step is to decide how to analyse such a discourse. Foucault did not leave a manual as to how to operationalise his ideas and set about a 'discourse analysis' (Stiegler 2015: 13–14). Several different methods[3] have, therefore, been developed: amongst them are historical discourse analysis, conversation analysis, and CDA (see e.g. Keller 2013). For this study, the latter approach is favoured. The second qualitative analysis step thus draws on "political discourse analysis", an approach specifically adapted to the analysis of political texts. As laid out in

---

3 The label "discourse analysis" (DA) often used for them all is deceptive, since it looks like a method but serves as an umbrella term for various approaches to the analysis of discourses.

Chapter 2.1, it was developed by Fairclough and Fairclough (2012) and is based on CDA. Critical discourse analysis emphasises the inclusion of context und interdisciplinarity:

> Furthermore, one important characteristic arises from the assumption that all discourses are historical and can therefore only be understood with reference to their context. Therefore, these approaches refer to such extralinguistic factors as culture, society and ideology in intricate ways, depending on their concepts of context and their research methodologies and ways of data collection. Hence, the notion of context is crucial for CDA, since this explicitly includes social-psychological, political and ideological components and thereby postulates interdisciplinarity. (Wodak and Meyer 2012: 20–21)

In line with the definition of political discourse as deliberation, Fairclough and Fairclough argue that, in addition, political actors weigh the pros and cons for specific actions and consider alternatives in political discourse. Therefore, they argue that the

> analysis of texts should focus upon the generic features of whole texts rather than isolated features of the text [...]. In particular, analysis should focus on how discourses, as ways of representing, provide agents with reasons for action. Analysis of non-argumentative genres (narrative, explanation) should also be viewed in relation to the arguments in which they are usually embedded. (Fairclough and Fairclough 2012: 1)

They claim that with this approach, "more familiar focuses (e.g. on representation, identities, narratives, metaphors)" can be analysed and interpreted "in ways which account much better for their political significance and effectiveness" (Fairclough and Fairclough 2012: 2). "Agents' choices, decisions and strategies are political in nature, they are contested by groups of people with different interests and objectives, who are competing to make their own particular choices, policies and strategies prevail" (Fairclough and Fairclough 2012: 3). This approach is, therefore, considered ideally suited to the analysis of opposition speeches, which by nature present alternative policies and seek to convince the audience. Additionally, it allows for the incorporation of earlier results pertaining to, e.g., metaphors and word choices.

According to Fairclough and Fairclough, the analysis of an argument is "a matter of identifying within an argument its premises and its conclusion and the relations between them" (Fairclough and Fairclough 2012: 11). The proposed analytical steps are, therefore, the following: first, to extract the descriptions of certain contextual facts. In a second step, the presented goals will be classified. In a last step, the analysis of the values possibly underlying these goals follows, and the alternative ways of how to reach them as presented by the respective speakers will be summarised.

This proceeding is deemed a useful approach for this study because often in the speeches under scrutiny, mentions of specific European policy areas or actions and events related to it are connected to others; as prerequisites, as reasons for, or as goals of developments under discussion. With political discourse analysis, the premises of arguments and how they relate to each other will be uncovered. In a nutshell, the following four analytical steps will be carried out:

- Extracting the descriptions of certain contextual facts (evaluation of status quo)
- Collecting the presented goals
- Naming the values possibly underlying these goals
- Identifying the alternative ways proposed to reach the proclaimed goals

5.4 Metaphors and Word Choice

A rhetorical text analysis will then delve deeper into the selected parliamentary speeches as a genre with particular characteristics. Confirming the usefulness of this approach, Tönnies and Viol claim that political speeches are

> natürlich auch als Texte zu analysieren, die mit einer festgelegten Absicht vor einem bestimmten Publikum vorgetragen werden und klar auf die Erfüllung dieses Zwecks zugeschnitten sind. Im Vordergrund steht hierbei die Frage nach dem Wie der rednerischen Vermittlung. Wie z.B. sehen die Textstrategien aus, die der Redner benutzt, um die Zuhörer für seinen Redegegenstand zu interessieren, ihre möglicherweise vorhandene Ablehnung zu überwinden und sie schließlich von seinen Meinungen, Vorhaben oder Vorschlägen zu überzeugen? (Tönnies and Viol 2001: 179)

In order to reach this goal of convincing the audience, Tönnies and Viol list a number of rhetorical devices the speakers (authors) may use, such as

- metaphors (also emphasised by Leith and Soule (2012: 62–64))
- appealing to emotions
- word choice
- figures of speech (it may be especially useful to include metonymies in the analysis since they are closely related to metaphors)
- only selective use of information
- logical structure
- the mentioning and then rebutting of the opponent's positions
- use of statistics (presented as rational or seemingly neutral and incorruptible information)

(Tönnies and Viol 2001: 181–182)

The following analysis shall look for such stylistic devices and explain their function. Deictic choices such as the use of the pronoun "we" with its function of stressing a collective quality, creating a community, rousing patriotic feelings, and including the listeners will also be included.

Viebrock claims that political speeches are a communication process and that the addressee is important. A speech will usually anticipate who will listen and thus 'create' the audience (Viebrock 1974: X). Perelman further states that for a speech to be effective and reach the goal of persuading individuals, there has to be a good fit between this constructed audience and the actual listeners, who may be very different from each other: "To win over the different elements in his audience, the orator will have to use a multiplicity of arguments. A great orator is who possesses the art of taking into consideration, in his argumentation, the composite nature of his audience" (1974: 21–22). Viebrock concludes that especially parliamentary speeches have to respect this and that the audience may include one's own party, as well as the press and public opinion, and even foreign governments (Viebrock 1974: X).

In addition to that, Viebrock lists a number of necessary elements for argumentation: first, speaker and audience must want to get into contact (e.g. when both have an interest in the topic addressed). Secondly, they have to speak the same language (Viebrock 1974: IX). Communication and cooperation are also needed, says Perelman (1979: 15–16). According to Luhmann, communication is not a mere "Vorgang der 'Übertragung' von Sinn, bzw. Information; sie ist gemeinsame Aktualisierung von Sinn, die mindestens einen der Teilnehmer informiert" (Luhmann 1971: 42). This means that a common basis concerning topic, language, and ideology is necessary for a rhetorical process where the speaker influences his audience (Viebrock 1974: X).

5.5 Summary

In a nutshell, the analysis of the corpus will be carried out using a combination of quantitative and qualitative methods. To begin with, a corpus containing the transcripts of all speeches made in the House of Commons by all selected politicians from 2 May 1997 until 11 May 2010 (corpus one) was compiled. This corpus forms the basis for the next step, the subsequent analysis of the collected primary sources. Conducting a content analysis allowed for the formation of a second, smaller corpus (corpus two). It contains those speeches found to be related to the subject matter 'Europe (an policy)'. The speeches in this second corpus were furthermore analysed with regard to the argumentation structure (political discourse analysis) as well as the metaphors they employ and word choices they make. Drawing on the context, the results will then be interpreted within the context of the theoretical framework.

6. Quantitative Results

In the following, the results of the analysis will be presented. To begin with, an overview of the quantitative results in relation to the parliamentary calendar will be outlined: the research period is divided into parliamentary sessions, covering approximately 12 months unless there is an election. Tab. 2 provides an overview of the dates forming the basis for the analysis.

Tab. 2: Parliamentary Sessions 1997–2010

	Parliamentary Session	State Opening	Prorogation	Number of Sitting Days
	General Election on 1 May 1997			
52nd Parliament	1997/98	14 May 1997	19 Nov 1998	241
	1998/99	24 Nov 1998	11 Nov 1999	149
	1999/2000	24 Nov 1999	30 Nov 2000	171
	2000/01	6 Dec 2000	3 May 2001	83
	General Election on 7 June 2001			
53rd Parliament	2001/02	20 June 2001	7 Nov 2002	202
	2002/03	13 Nov 2002	20 Nov 2003	162
	2003/04	26 Nov 2003	18 Nov 2004	157
	2004/05	23 Nov 2004	7 April 2005	65
	General Election on 5 May 2005			
54th Parliament	2005/06	17 May 2005	8 Nov 2006	208
	2006/07	15 Nov 2006	30 Oct 2007	146
	2007/08	6 Nov 2007	26 Nov 2008	165
	2008/09	3 Dec 2008	12 Nov 2009	136
	2009/10	18 Nov 2009	8 April 2010	69
	General Election on 6 May 2010			

As explained in Chapter 5.2, corpus one contains all speeches made by Lib Dem leaders in the research period, whereas the smaller corpus two includes only those speeches relating to Europe. I have used complete debates, i.e. those with a separate title in *Hansard*, as units of analysis. This means that whenever a party leader mentioned even one aspect related to Europe or European policy, the whole debate in which this contribution was made was counted as "Europe-related" and thus part of corpus two.

Overall, the Lib Dem party leaders contributed to 546 separate parliamentary debates. These form corpus one. During the content analysis, 115 of them, a share of 21.1 %, were coded as related to Europe and thus assigned to corpus two. The general salience of European policies can, therefore, be described as high in the context of Lib Dem party leaders' speeches, with roughly every fifth contribution by a Lib Dem party leader in parliament addressing at least one aspect of it. This confirms the relevance of the Lib Dem discourse on Europe and serves as a basis for the following analysis. When it comes to the Lib Dems during the New Labour years, the claim that Europe has been treated as a marginal topic by British politicians can thus be refuted.

These results are visualised in the following graph (Fig. 1), showing the percentage of EU-related speeches of Lib Dem leaders in relation to their overall contributions per parliamentary session. The figures are not given separately for every leader but calculated using the total per session even when the leader changed during a session in order to foreground the party line, not individual speakers' priorities.

The graph shows that the parliamentary sessions of 1997/1998 and 1998/1999 had the highest share in Europe-related speeches, which coincides with the preparation for the introduction of the euro in the first eurozone countries, giving rise to the question if the UK should join or not. The hypothesis that this political context had an influence on the quantitative share will have to be confirmed or falsified by the salience of this topic in the Lib Dem parliamentary discourse. Equally, the other percentages will be compared to the salience of topics in the course of this study.

It is remarkable that the lowest share of speeches addressing Europe-related policies can be found in the three sessions including the election campaigns for a general election, namely in the parliamentary sessions 2000/2001, 2004/2005, and 2009/2010. This makes the conclusion plausible that the issue of Europe was not considered a vote-winner by the party leadership and downplayed in the months preceding the elections as a consequence. A further factor could help explain the low salience in the session 2004/2005, taking into account the low share in 2003/2004 as well: the Eastern enlargement of the EU, which came into effect in January 2004, was endorsed by both the governing Labour Party as well as the Official Opposition, the CON. This would make it less necessary to focus on European policy because no counter-discourse needed to be established. Again, this hypothetical explanation has to be confirmed by the topic analysis.

Fig. 2 shows the relations between overall contributions (corpus one) and those relating to Europe (corpus two) during the three Parliaments (1997–2001, 2001–2005, 2005–2010). With a share of 21.3 %, Europe is most often debated in

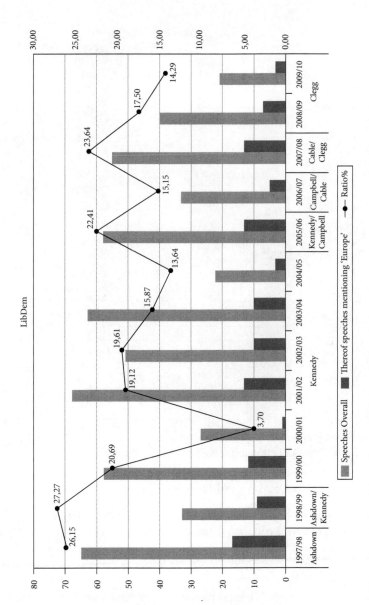

Fig. 1: Percentage of Contributions Relating to Europe

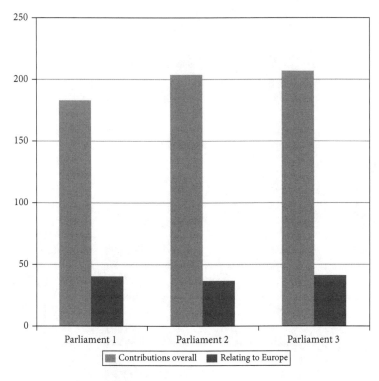

Fig. 2: Relation between Lib Dem Leaders' Overall Contributions and Europe-Related Ones in the Three Parliaments

the first Parliament under Labour. The second Parliament has the lowest share of the three, with 17.6 %. The third Parliament is in the middle between the two, with a share of 19.8 % of contributions mentioning Europe.

6.1 The Lib Dem Leaders Addressing Europe

In a further step, the ratios between the two corpora have been calculated for each party leader individually, and the results over the whole research period are visualised in the next graph, Fig. 3. It shows the relation of total contributions against those related to Europe for every party leader of the Lib Dems during the research period.

It can be seen that of all the party leaders that were considered, Ashdown addressed Europe most often percentage-wise: he had the highest share of

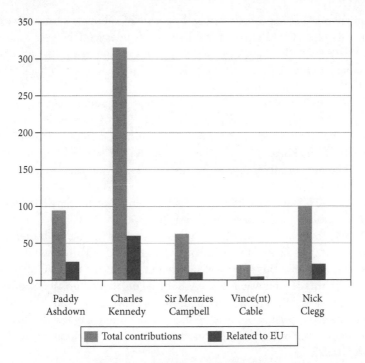

Fig. 3: Relation between Overall Contributions and Europe-Related Ones per Speaker

speeches relating to Europe, namely 24.5 %. His successor Kennedy only contributed to the debate on Europe during 18.6 % of his speeches, whereas the share dropped to 14.3 % during Campbell's term of office. With 15 %, the number slowly picked up in the interim phase headed by Cable, before it reached 21 % under Clegg. These last two figures rectify the impression that the salience has sunk steadily under the successive leaders.

In the following, all five party leaders will be considered individually in more detail. The results are grouped according to the following parameters: first, the overall mentions of Europe per speaker in the research period, and second, the mentions per parliamentary session per speaker. This allows for subsequent conclusions pertaining to the timing of the respective topic's salience.

6.1.1 Paddy Ashdown

Paddy (Patrick) Ashdown was the party leader of the Liberal Democrats from 1988 until 9 August 1999. While in office, he made oral contributions in

Parliament on 94 separate days during the period of Labour governments examined in this paper. On 23 separate days thereof, the interventions were concerned at least partly with the European Union or European countries. This amounts to 24.5 % of all interventions by the party leader being concerned with a European topic in the researched period.

In the parliamentary session 1997/1998, beginning with the State Opening on 14 May 1997 and ending with the Prorogation of Parliament on 19 November 1998, Paddy Ashdown made speeches on 65 occasions, of which 17 were related to Europe/the EU. This amounts to 26.2 % of all his interventions. The total number of sitting days in this session was 241, so Ashdown contributed on 8.9 % of sitting days.

In the parliamentary session 1998/1999, beginning with the State Opening on 24 November 1998 and ending with Prorogation on 11 November 1999, Paddy Ashdown made speeches on 29 occasions as party leader (until 9 August 1999), 6 of them related to Europe/the EU. This represents 20.7 % of his interventions. This share is visualised in Fig. 4. The total number of sitting days in this session was 149, so Ashdown contributed on 19.5 % of sitting days, which is significantly higher than in the previous session. This number is particularly surprising because he did not serve as party leader during the whole session, but only until 9 August 1999, when Charles Kennedy took over as party leader.

Parliamentary Session	Speeches Corpus 1	Speeches Corpus 2	Ratio (in %)
1997/98	65	17	26.2
1998/99	29	6	20.7
Total	94	23	24.5

■ EU-related ■ Not EU-related

Fig. 4: Share of Europe-Related Speeches Paddy Ashdown

6.1.2 Charles Kennedy

Charles Kennedy took over the post of party leader of the Lib Dems on 9 August 1999 and held it until 7 January 2006. He made 318 speeches in Parliament during this time. Fifty-nine of these speeches were concerned with Europe or the EU, some more pertained indirectly to these topics. This leads to an overall share of relevant speeches of 18.6 %, which is visualised in Fig. 5.

Parliamentary Session	Speeches Corpus 1	Speeches Corpus 2	Ratio (in %)
1998/1999	4	3	75
1999/2000	58	12	20.7
2000/2001	28	1	3.6
2001/2002	68	13	19.1
2002/2003	51	10	19.6
2003/2004	63	10	15.9
2004/2005	22	3	13.6
2005/2006	24	8	33.3
Total	318	59	18.6

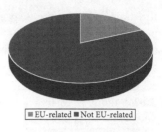

EU-related ■ Not EU-related

Fig. 5: Share of Europe-Related Contributions Charles Kennedy

6.1.3 Menzies Campbell

Sir Menzies Campbell was the elected party leader of the Lib Dems from 2 March 2006 until 15 October 2007. After Charles Kennedy had stood down, Campbell had acted as interim leader from 7 January until 2 March 2006; this period is also included in the analysis. Campbell made 63 speeches in Parliament during this time. Nine of these speeches were concerned with Europe or the EU or pertained to these topics. This is an overall record of 14.3 % of contributions (as per date/debate) relating to Europe, as shown in Fig. 6.

Parliamentary Session	Speeches Corpus 1	Speeches Corpus 2	Ratio (in %)
2005/2006	34	5	14.7
2006/2007	29	4	13.8
Total	63	9	14.3

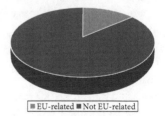

EU-related ■ Not EU-related

Fig. 6: Share of Europe-Related Contributions Menzies Campbell

6.1.4 Vince Cable

Vince (Vincent) Cable was the interim party leader of the Lib Dems in 2007 (15 October until 18 December) and made 20 speeches in Parliament during this time. Three of these speeches were concerned with Europe or the EU or pertained to these topics, which amounts to 15 %, visualised in Fig. 7. Four of these speeches were made in the parliamentary session 2006–2007 (1 on Europe), the other 16 in the parliamentary session 2007–2008 (2 on Europe).

Parliamentary Session	Speeches Corpus 1	Speeches Corpus 2	Ratio (in %)
2006/2007	4	1	25
2007/2008	16	2	12.5
Total	20	3	15

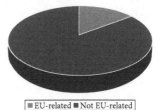

EU-related ■ Not EU-related

Fig. 7: Share of Europe-Related Contributions Vince Cable

6.1.5 Nick Clegg

After having won the leadership contest, Nick (Nicholas) Clegg became party leader of the Lib Dems on 18 December 2007. He held the position until 2015, which includes the rest of the covered research period (which ends formally with the formation of a new government after the general election in May 2010, but de facto already with the prorogation of Parliament on 8 April 2010). During this time, he made exactly 100 speeches in Parliament. Twenty-one of these speeches were concerned with Europe/the EU or pertained to these topics, representing a share of 21 % overall. This amounts to roughly every fifth speech.

In the parliamentary session 2007–2008, Nick Clegg made 39 speeches, 11 of them related to Europe/the EU. This amounts to an impressive 28.2 %, nearly a third of all interventions. The total of sitting days was 165. In the parliamentary session 2008–2009, Nick Clegg made 40 speeches, 7 of which were related to Europe/the EU. This represents a share of 17.5 %. The total of sitting days was 136. In the parliamentary session 2009–2010, Nick Clegg made 21 speeches, 3 of them related to Europe/the EU. This is the lowest share, namely 14.3 %. It was a "rump parliament", with the session only lasting from November until the following April, when the election campaign period for the general election 2010 began. The overall number of sitting days was, therefore, only 69.

Parliamentary Session	Speeches Corpus 1	Speeches Corpus 2	Ratio (in %)
2007/2008	39	11	28.2
2008/2009	40	7	17.5
2009/2010	21	3	14.3
Total	*100*	*21*	*21*

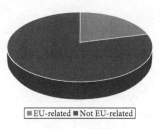

■ EU-related ■ Not EU-related

Fig. 8: Share of Europe-Related Contributions Nick Clegg

6.2 Types of Debates in Corpus Two

The speeches made by party leaders in Parliament can be classed into five different categories:

- contributions to debates concerned with a particular subject (titled as such in *Hansard*, e.g. 'Economic and Monetary Union')
- contributions to 'event-induced' debates (e.g. 'G8 Summit')
- speeches on the UK budget (also called 'Amendment of the Law')
- comments during the 'Debate on the Address', i.e. the 'Queen's speech', which contains the government programme for the new parliamentary session and is then debated in the House of Commons (HoC)
- questions to the Prime Minister (in the historic *Hansard*, PMQs are titled "Engagements". This is due to the convention that the first question asks after the PM's engagements for the day, and is only then followed up by another question)
- on one occasion, a Lib Dem leader moved a motion, namely on 'Farming and Fishing'

While speeches mentioning European policy during the event-induced debates, e.g., on European Council meetings, can be expected, it is interesting to see which other occasions are used to bring up European policy. The budget debates and the debates on the Address are subject to high media attention and can, therefore, be seen as especially relevant when it comes to agenda-setting. Furthermore, especially PMQs represent a prime opportunity for agenda-setting and drawing attention to certain topics: "UK Prime Minister's questions (PMQs) is potentially one of the most important means for the opposition to challenge the government on the major issues of the day" (Bevan and John 2016: 59). The format of PMQs can be defined as follows:

Prime Minister's Questions is a parliamentary convention whereby the prime minister answers questions in the House of Commons from members of parliament [including the leader(s) of the opposition, in addition to other backbenchers from all parties]. PMQs is perhaps the most public opposition platform, given its prominence in the media and that it follows a regular weekly cycle. (Bevan and John 2016: 61)

Confirming the importance of PMQs, Ryle concurs: "Prime Minister's Questions today provide a big political occasion […] when MPs […] can call the Government to account on what they see as the major issues of the day" (2005: 6). Giddings and Irwin confirm that "specifically Commons' Questions [are] the most famous aspect of scrutiny and accountability" (2005: 71). They describe Question Time as "a significant part of the battle between the main parties" (Giddings and Irwin 2005: 73); it is also the time "when the House is fullest" (Giddings and Irwin 2005: 76). When it comes to the Lib Dems' role in this famous ritual, they explain that "[t]he Leader of the Liberal Democrats gets two questions" (Giddings and Irwin 2005: 73). Bevan and John claim that the issues brought up by the opposition during PMQs also reflect the issues that are considered most important and salient in public opinion: "PMQs is one of the most public ways that MPs can express their concerns" (2016: 69). The questions are also usually quite topical; since 2002, a notice period of 3–5 days is sufficient (cf. Giddings and Irwin 2005: 74). Bevan and John confirm this: "the relationship between public opinion and PMQs [can be treated] as contemporaneous due to the close relationship between current events and PMQs" (Bevan and John 2016: 69–70). Refuting the criticism that PMQs have degenerated to a mere show, Bevan and John postulate that "the ritual and the drama of PMQs, despite appearing to be shallow and media focused, can help backbenchers and the opposition change the attention of government" (Bevan and John 2016: 80).

This shows that the speeches chosen for analysis are relevant not only because of their wide outreach to the public and their rhetorical sharpness, but also because they possibly had a real impact on government agenda-setting by highlighting issues such as specific decisions in European policy. To put it in a nutshell, it makes a difference if European policy is brought up by opposition party leaders during day-to-day debates or during special formats such as PMQs. The types of debates will, therefore, be included in the interpretation of results.

6.3 Topics Addressed by Lib Dem Party Leaders

After the quantitative results were calculated and presented, the subsequent content analysis of corpus two brought to light which topics the Lib Dem party leaders debated during the 13 years preceding their government participation in the coalition. The resulting list of categories was combined with a frequency count and is given in that order (starting with the topic discussed most often) in Tab. 3. The number of mentions is indicated as well. It is important to bear in mind that more than one topic can be addressed in a debate, so the mentions of topics exceed the overall number of debates concerned with European policy, namely 115.

The topic mentioned most often was the euro (49 mentions), followed by foreign and defence policy (30 mentions). It can thus be concluded that these EU policy areas have been deemed especially relevant by the Lib Dem party leaders. I will use these identified policy areas as categories for the organisation of Chapter 7, which presents the results of the in-depth textual analysis of Lib Dem rhetoric and arguments in parliamentary discourse on Europe.

Putting the topics addressed by Lib Dem party leaders into their historical context, it becomes clear that they reflect several important developments on the European level which took place in the researched period of time: the bovine spongiform encephalopathy (BSE) crisis, which is interlinked with the ongoing debate on the CAP, the debate on EMU, and the introduction of the common currency, the euro; the signing of European reform treaties and the (failed) European Constitution project as well as the 'Eastern' enlargement of the European Union. These events were subject to controversial discussion on member-state level and in this light, the debate can thus be expected to yield interesting results as to how conceptions of Europe are negotiated in this specific context.

Comparing these topic areas to the ones that New Labour put first on their government agenda in relation to European policy, namely jobs, completing the single market, competitiveness, environment, and international security (Wall 2008: 166), it becomes clear that interestingly, this choice of topics is not taken up one on one by the Lib Dem leaders' speeches, which focus primarily on the

Tab. 3: Topic Overview

Rank	Topic	Mentions
1	Economic and Monetary Union (EMU): the euro (independence of Bank of England) and the single market	49
2	Foreign and defence policy	30
3	EU treaties (including the EU Constitution)	25
4	Common Agricultural Policy (CAP)	17
5	Enlargement	17
	All Topics	*138*

above-mentioned topics. Environmental policy, crime and immigration, the EU budget, and European trade policy were also discussed by the Lib Dem party leaders, but the frequency analysis pointed to a low salience. These policy areas were, therefore, not included in the subsequent analysis steps.

Overall, it can be concluded from the quantitative content analysis that the Lib Dem leaders attempted to establish their own agenda with regard to European policy and focused on topics they deemed important. Obviously, they did not only respond to the agenda of the government, but they also highlighted other issues where they saw opportunities to sharpen their profile. A focus on the number of questions put during PMQs may allow further conclusions as to which topics they wanted the government to debate and justify publicly.

7. Qualitative Results

In the following part, the five topics debated most often have been used as chapter titles and chosen for a subsequent qualitative analysis. This analysis will take into account the specific policy area and its context since Critical Discourse analysts propose that there is a mutual relationship between language and society (societal context). The relevant context will, therefore, be briefly sketched out at the beginning of each subchapter and referred to in the following analysis.

7.1 A Tale of Two Currencies: Economic and Monetary Union

Early plans for a single European currency were already made in 1970 (European Commission: "History 1970–1979"). To maintain monetary stability, an exchange rate mechanism (ERM) was created in 1972. This can be interpreted as "a first step towards the introduction of the euro, 30 years later" (European Commission: "History 1970–1979"). While further provisions were laid down in the Single European Act, the actual introduction of the euro as the common currency of the European Union member states was decided on and codified in the Treaty of Maastricht, which established both the EU and the EMU (Economic and Monetary Union) and entered into force in 1993 (European Commission: "EU Treaties").

The United Kingdom, represented by John Major at that time, had secured an opt-out of the single currency. Nevertheless, the developments on the EU level went ahead and the topic became highly salient during the researched years: in 1999, the common currency was officially introduced (as bank money) and in January 2002, the euro coins and notes became available in the participating countries, also termed the 'Eurozone' (J. Schmidt 2011: 441). Wall summarises where the main parties stood on the single currency in the UK in 1997:

> In practice, both parties [CON and Labour] had promised a referendum on entry into the single currency and neither was ready to recommend membership. However, as the 1997 General Election approached, hostility to the single currency, and indeed the EU as a whole, grew in the Conservative Party while Labour's approach became more positive. (Wall 2008: 161)

Still, the Labour manifesto mentioned "'formidable obstacles' in the way of Britain joining [the EMU] in the first phase" and "emphasised the triple safeguard of the need for a favourable decision by Cabinet, a vote in favour in Parliament, and then a referendum" (Wall 2008: 162). Wall claims this was due to "lack of popular support" and a Murdoch press hostile to EMU (Wall 2008: 162).

The statement by the Chancellor in the HoC on 9 June 2003 said the 'five tests' had not been met yet and the press concluded that the UK would not join the single currency during the second Labour parliament (Wall 2008: 171). Additionally, "[t]he road show on EMU which was announced never happened" (Wall 2008: 171). Wall concludes that when the 2005 general election came, the good UK economic performance made it less likely that a EMU referendum would be won and that joining the euro as a principal concern had been super- seded "by the argument about the European Constitution, on which the Prime Minister had promised a referendum" (Wall 2008: 171).

The introduction of the euro put the Labour government under pressure to act; however, they had repeatedly emphasised their general readiness to intro- duce the euro, and their strategy to wait and see became a problem. A refer- endum on this issue was promised publicly, but its success was deemed far from certain and the decision to delay was taken accordingly (Ludwig 2011: 46–47). Ultimately, no referendum on the euro was held at all.

Meier-Walser claims that Blair was perceived as inconsistent because the government's strategy on the euro and EMU changed several times, and the gov- ernment under Blair tried to keep this subject out of public debate. The CON in opposition under William Hague, however, launched a campaign titled "Save the Pound" and tried to mobilise what Meier-Walser describes as deep-rooted fears of a European super state and the loss of national independence among the British public (2001: 26).

Wall concedes that the UK representatives in Brussels feared the Eurozone countries could coordinate policies without the UK in future, making it a group within the EU where the UK had no membership and influence. These fears did not materialise, however, which he sees as a reason that interest groups in the UK and government have seen euro membership as dispensable (Wall 2008: 172). The global financial crisis beginning in 2007 hit the United Kingdom and the Pound Sterling hard, but when the 'euro crisis' set in (in the wake of the global financial and economic crisis), calls for joining the euro quickly died out. It is especially interesting to discover in the speeches on EMU how the Lib Dems addressed this situation and the continuing evolvement of the single currency. Did they criticise the approach that Blair called "prepare and decide" but which was seen more as "wait and see"? How did they react to the changing circumstances and how did they justify their support for the single currency?

As Tab. 4 shows, the Lib Dem leaders debated issues relating to the possible introduction of the euro through to the problems in the Eurozone during the financial and economic crisis on 49 different occasions overall. Four instances of these were references to the independence of the Bank of England, which was

Tab. 4: Lib Dem Leaders' Speeches Mentioning the Single Currency

Leader	Date	Name of Debate
Paddy Ashdown	04.06.1997	Engagements
Paddy Ashdown	18.06.1997	European Council (Amsterdam)
Paddy Ashdown	29.10.1997	Engagements
Paddy Ashdown	15.12.1997	European Council
Paddy Ashdown	21.01.1998	Engagements
Paddy Ashdown	28.01.1998	Engagements
Paddy Ashdown	17.03.1998	Amendment of the Law (Budget)
Paddy Ashdown	29.04.1998	Engagements
Paddy Ashdown	05.05.1998	Economic and Monetary Union
Paddy Ashdown	20.05.1998	G8 Summit
Paddy Ashdown	17.06.1998	European Council (Cardiff)
Paddy Ashdown	08.07.1998	Engagements
Paddy Ashdown	21.10.1998	Engagements
Paddy Ashdown	04.11.1998	Engagements
Paddy Ashdown	24.11.1998	Debate on the Address
Paddy Ashdown	23.02.1999	Economic and Monetary Union
Paddy Ashdown	09.03.1999	Amendment of the Law
Charles Kennedy	20.10.1999	Food and Farming
Charles Kennedy	17.11.1999	Debate on the Address
Charles Kennedy	13.12.1999	Helsinki European Council
Charles Kennedy	16.02.2000	Engagements
Charles Kennedy	21.03.2000	Amendment of the Law (Budget)
Charles Kennedy	27.03.2000	European Council (Lisbon)
Charles Kennedy	17.05.2000	Engagements
Charles Kennedy	21.06.2000	European Council
Charles Kennedy	05.07.2000	Engagements
Charles Kennedy	12.07.2000	Engagements
Charles Kennedy	24.07.2000	G8 Summit
Charles Kennedy	11.12.2000	Nice European Council
Charles Kennedy	20.06.2001	First Day
Charles Kennedy	17.12.2001	European Council (Laeken)
Charles Kennedy	18.03.2002	European Council (Barcelona)
Charles Kennedy	17.04.2002	Amendment of the Law (Budget)
Charles Kennedy	22.05.2002	Engagements
Charles Kennedy	24.06.2002	European Council (Seville)

(*continued on next page*)

Tab. 4:   Continued

Leader	Date	Name of Debate
Charles Kennedy	03.07.2002	Engagements
Charles Kennedy	28.10.2002	European Council
Charles Kennedy	27.11.2002	Engagements
Charles Kennedy	16.12.2002	European Council (Copenhagen)
Charles Kennedy	09.04.2003	Amendment of the Law
Charles Kennedy	21.05.2003	Engagements
Charles Kennedy	08.11.2004	European Council, Brussels Summit (EC)
Charles Kennedy	16.03.2005	Budget March 2005
Menzies Campbell	22.03.2006	Budget March
Menzies Campbell	21.03.2007	Amendment of the Law (Budget)
Nick Clegg	20.10.2008	European Council
Nick Clegg	17.11.2008	G8 Summit
Nick Clegg	15.12.2008	EU Council/Afghanistan, India and Pakistan
Nick Clegg	29.03.2010	European Council

Total: 49 Debates

seen by many observers as a prerequisite for joining the euro. These references have thus been counted in that category as well. Overall, contributions were made during PMQs (16), during budget debates (8), in debates on European Council meetings (16), in debates on the government programme for the next parliamentary session (3), in debates on G8 meetings (3) and in debates which were directly concerned with Economic and Monetary Union (2). One further reference occurred during the debate on "Food and Farming".

While references to the euro during budget debates seem logical and not surprising, it is very interesting to see that the Lib Dem leaders chose to dedicate 16 questions during the valuable time of directly speaking to the PM to issues related to the euro. This shows that the euro was high on their agenda, and they saw it as a worthwhile opposition topic where they could sharpen their profile as a party with their own positions.

7.1.1 Paddy Ashdown

Paddy Ashdown addressed the euro in 17 speeches. The first instance was during Engagements in the first parliamentary session of the Labour government in 1997.

"Engagements" (04.06.1997)

Are not the first crucial decisions on monetary union now just weeks away and likely to turn on a choice between relaxation and delay? Which does the Government prefer? [...]
While I agree with the latter part of the Prime Minister's answer, does he agree that there is a very limited degree of flexibility allowed in the Maastricht criteria, not least on the timetable? Would it not be better if Britain were to accept that and lead the search for a pragmatic solution, and to show the way that that could be done through the leadership of his Government? [Official Report, 4 June 1997; Vol. 294, c.70–75]

Ashdown mentions the Economic and Monetary Union for the first time very early in the first in the parliamentary session 1997/1998, right at the beginning of Labour's first term of government. He addresses the progress of the decision process and describes the situation as pressing, with a characterisation of the coming decisions as "crucial" and the phrase "just weeks away", suggesting urgency and a high salience. This can be interpreted as a call for action, calling for the government to play a part. This is underlined by the direct question as to the preferences of the government. Ashdown portrays the decision as being a "choice between relaxation and delay", thereby implying that the EMU will come later than planned. He then reminds the PM that the big decisions, also concerning the timetable, are already laid down in the Maastricht treaty which allows for a "very limited degree of flexibility".

The alternative policy goals presented are more involvement in European decisions, indeed taking the lead in steps towards more European integration such as the introduction of the EMU, and not to accept delays. The Lib Dem leader also proposes to adopt a constructive approach in this regard and show leadership by presenting solutions. In the Lib Dem vision, the UK government should "show the way" and provide "leadership" on the EU level. The self-image of the UK that Ashdown propagates here is thus that of a strong, pragmatic country leading the other EU member states.

Values shining through in this argumentation are pragmatic and efficient decision-making, strong leadership, courage, and clarity (instead of dithering and waiting). It also includes reliability and observance of contracts – once the UK has signed the Maastricht treaty and thus agreed to its stipulated goals, it is no option for the Lib Dems to not honour these obligations. This is in line with the high UK level of compliance with European laws and of implementing guide lines, where other EU states have a rather poor record. It can be assumed that flexibility is also seen as a good thing, but it is not so high a priority such as working with what you have got. International cooperation (as opposed to conflict and domination) and consensus-seeking are also on the list, but the UK's role should be among the ring leaders; acquiescing into agreements reached by others is not what the Lib Dems argue for.

"European Council (Amsterdam)" (18.06.1997)

The next instance is a side remark on EMU among other results of the European Council at Amsterdam. Interestingly, Ashdown happily concedes that the government has done a good job – he acknowledges the "not unjustifiably long list of Government's successes at Amsterdam" [Official Report, 18 June 1997; Vol. 296, c. 320–321]. He then, however, proceeds to criticise the claim that the UK has rescued the EMU as "bizarre" [Official Report, 18 June 1997; Vol. 296, c. 320–321] and points out that the UK is not (yet) part of EMU and can, therefore, not speak too loudly on the subject. This is a criticism of the UK's perceived role as a 'know-it-all' commenting on developments from the side lines without participating fully themselves. From this accusation, we can deduce that the Lib Dem leader would indeed prefer the alternative policy of joining early in order to influence the EMU policies and decisions instead of being reduced to the role of outsider, and thus rather powerless spectator. Ashdown later openly and directly confirms the PM's attribution that he, Ashdown, is "a great proponent of EMU" [Official Report, 18 June 1997; Vol. 296, c. 320–321]. The self-image of being pro-European in a general sense means supporting European integration steps in order to head and shape the development, regardless of some details speaking against it, becomes very clear in these two words "I am [a great proponent of EMU]" [Official Report, 18 June 1997; Vol. 296, c. 320–321]. Values underlying this argumentation can be named as integrity (vouching for your convictions), and a general preference for big lines (at the expense of prudent wait-and-see).

"Engagements" (29.10.1997)

The next intervention is during PMQs on 29 October 1997, after the summer recess of parliament. Ashdown dedicates both his valuable questions to "monetary union", thus singling out the euro from other economic concerns:

> I will ask a question about monetary union. Is not the significance of the statement made by the Chancellor on Monday not as much its time scale as its clear and unequivocal expression of support in principle for the single currency and for Britain's joining it?
> The Prime Minister believes that the Government will take that decision later rather than earlier. I think he is wrong; I think it will come at him much faster than he believes. He may believe that the decision, to be driven by the national interest, may be taken after the next general election, but will he at least admit that if it is in the national interest for it to be taken earlier, there is nothing to prevent that happening?

[PM's response]
Does the Prime Minister not realise that it is illogical to say in one breath that this decision will be taken in the national interest and to say in the next that it will be driven by the electoral agenda? That makes no sense. Will the Prime Minister at least agree with the former Chancellor to this extent: that if the Government now set a clear and decisive lead on this matter, they have nothing to fear from a referendum, even an early one, because the decision to enter the single currency will enjoy such cross-party support in the House, and such wide support in the country, including from the Trades Union Congress and the Confederation of British Industry, that that referendum can be run as soon as the Government call it in the national interest? [Official Report, 29 October 1997; Vol. 299, c. 894]

Ashdown tries to elicit a statement from the PM whether or not the euro will be introduced in the UK. This is the first time that a referendum on the euro is addressed. Ashdown seems convinced that the opportunity is there and the referendum would succeed if the "Government call[ed] it in the national interest". The Government is portrayed as wilfully delaying the decision although there is a majority both in the political as well as in the public sphere for it. It is surprising that the Lib Dems would call for a referendum at all if that were true, since this effectively claims that a democratically elected government with a large majority in parliament needs to legitimise the decision via a referendum. This assessment sits awkwardly with the doctrine of national sovereignty.

Ashdown's claim that the government need only change their assessment of the status quo in order to proceed and convince everyone shows that he attaches a great deal of importance to public discourse and believes it can change everything. The Lib Dem leader portrays the delay as "electoral agenda" and defies the PM's claim that the moment for the introduction of the euro is not right. This is the first instance of the Lib Dem leader calling for a referendum on the possible introduction of the euro. From this moment onwards, the Lib Dems have repeated their calls for a referendum on the introduction of the single currency in the UK.

"European Council" (15.12.1997)

As for the rest, the Euro X, as the Prime Minister has said, is the key element of the decision. I am bound to say that the Prime Minister has made the best of a very weak hand, although the fact that his hand is weak is of his own choosing. He dealt the hand to himself; his own Government did so.
We have consistently said that, although we welcome the apparent decision in principle that a European single currency is a good idea and Britain should be part of it if the British people agree in a referendum, the Government have not yet made a clear declaration of policy on their intention to join, with a target date and policies consistent with

it. We have consistently said that, unless and until the Government do that, their own bargaining hand and influence in Europe will be weaker, and the consequences will be felt in investment and jobs in due course.

If the Prime Minister is to respond by saying that this is just a typical example of the Liberal Democrats' overblown enthusiasm for Europe, I would remind him— [HON. MEMBERS: "Yes, it is."] I remind the Prime Minister and Conservative Members that such a view is now the overwhelming view of the CBI, the TUC, many Labour Members and very many sensible and senior Conservatives.

Until and unless the Government do what they say they should be doing—setting a lead on Europe—the consequence for Britain in lost influence, investment and, ultimately, jobs will be greater than the Prime Minister wants it to be. I repeat what I have said before: I believe that the Government will be driven down the course by events rather than leading them, which is what they should be doing. [Official Report, 15 December 1997; Vol. 303, c. 24–25]

In this speech in the House of Commons occasioned by the European Council on 15 December 1997, the second call for a referendum on a European policy by a Lib Dem party leader issue is recorded in *Hansard*. The referendum is clearly given as a necessary prerequisite for the UK joining the euro, a policy decision the Lib Dems explicitly condone and seek to advance/bring about. Ashdown once again uses the word "welcome" and says that the single currency is "a good idea". The PM receives praise for his negotiating skills but is criticised for having marginalised the UK by the decision not to go along with EMU straight away (and is thus said to have "weak[ened]" his hand). This metaphor sets the perception of the relationship between the EU and the UK as a round of poker (or possibly another card game), where it is crucial to get a good hand and play it smartly in order to win and outsmart your opponent. This means that in a negotiation, only one can win while the other players will lose – and it depends on the players' skills and their hand if they win. The Lib Dem leader suggests that in making decisions before European council meetings wisely, the "hand" can be made stronger. This is an argument for making strategic choices to win room for manoeuvre in the future, i.e. agreeing to European projects to win goodwill and get a better "bargaining hand", instead of just reacting to what others propose. It seems that the negotiations are seen as a win-lose situation, where you have to give something away in order to get something else, and a win-win scenario is unlikely. In the British historical cultural context, gaming is an occupation for rich elites and playing fair is necessary in order to remain in high esteem in society. This will also become important later since this metaphor will reappear and the European "players" are often portrayed as cheating and tweaking the rules.

The finance ministers of the EU member states having joined the single currency in the first wave met in the so-called "Euro X committee", where they exchanged views and drafted legislation concerning the management and future development of what is now called the Eurozone. The Lib Dem leader argues that the UK should be part of this format even though they did not adopt the single currency in order to be able to participate in the talks, which was also the proclaimed goal of the government even though joining the single currency was still far from decided.

The Lib Dems insist on the idea of consistency and obviously prioritise this as a sign of trustworthy and good governance. Ashdown repeatedly tells his listeners that their case in favour of the euro under the condition that the "British people agree in a referendum" has been made "consistently" and that the Government's position lacks this quality. The government is also accused of not having made a "clear declaration" on where it stands on the euro. This opaque and lengthy decision-making process invokes weakness and indecisive leadership, which amounts to a severe criticism of the PM's stance and ability to govern.

Investment and jobs are also brought into the equation and serve to strengthen the impression that the PM mars the good opportunity to retain both in the UK with his dithering. The wait-and-see, pragmatic, piece-meal 'muddling through' with a steady eye on opinion polls is certainly not what the Lib Dem leader would like to see – they portray it as economically dangerous and deleterious to the national interest of preserving jobs and investment. Another possible explanation for Ashdown's criticism may be the fact that it makes it much harder for an opposition party to "attack" if the government policy is still in the dark. It is thus this manoeuvring which is decried as weak leadership.

The Lib Dem leader then proceeds with a rhetorical device named rebutting possible anti-theses which can be expected from the answer by addressing the general Europhile stance attributed to the Lib Dems as a party. The jeers by opposing MPs show that this is exactly what he could expect and since he addresses the CON MPs as well as the PM, the hecklers can be easily identified in his speech. He rebuts this by listing organisations supporting his view, ranging from business and unions to many members of the two biggest parties. This serves to underline the divisions over "Europe" right across the party lines. The adjective "sensible" indicates that the Lib Dem leader claims this to be a sensible policy for his party and that MPs using their brains and common sense agree with him and his party's stance, regardless of their own party allegiance. This shows that the Lib Dems seek to present their position as neutral and pragmatic, without the taint of any ideology and without fear from voters' feelings. This stance relies on politicians and voters making rational and logical choices, rather like a "homo oeconomicus", and dismisses elements or influencing aspects such as identity, emotions, and tradition as irrational and unimportant. The second qualification of those agreeing with the Lib Dems as "senior" further emphasises the weight and authority of those agreeing with the Lib Dem position and may also be understood as a warning to the two big parties: they may face backbench rebellions or outright splits if they do not adopt the matter-of-fact approach proposed by the Lib Dems. In hindsight, the first assumption has been proved wrong – the Lib Dems could possibly win the minds, but not the hearts of voters for their pro-European stance justified with cold economic logic. A split over Europe is a danger, however, that is still lingering for both the CON and Labour.

In the end, Ashdown sums up his argument and repeats that in his view, the way forward is to make a decision and stick to it; all the while demonstrating strong leadership, in this case in Europe. He also repeats that the PM is acting negligently in accepting "lost influence, investment and, ultimately, jobs" as a price worth paying for delaying a decision and reserving the possibility of changing his mind. Ashdown ends with the rather dark prediction that the British government "will be driven down the course by events rather than leading them, which is what they should be doing". This echoes H. Young's conclusion that "vacillation" when it comes to European policy is a "chronic disease" (1999: 471) that has affected British governments for the best part of the twentieth century. The clear alternative policy goal is to be a strong leader on the European level, which is coherent with the idea of a strong leader on the domestic scale by deciding to go along with European integration and then use this position to make demands or adjustments later.

"Engagements" (21.01.1998)

Is the Prime Minister aware that what he calls a patriotic alliance across parties on Europe in the national interest already exists? It consists of the Confederation of British Industry, the Trades Union Congress, the ex-Chancellor of the Exchequer and his Conservative friends, and the Liberal Democrats, and it believes—as it appears the Government do not—that we 1008 ought not to rule out the possibility of a referendum on a single currency in this Parliament if that is in the nation's interest. Will the Prime Minister join us?

[...]

I ask the Prime Minister to answer the question, which is whether he rules out a referendum on a single currency during this Parliament. Either that can be done in the national interest or it can be done according to the electoral timetable, but it cannot be done on the basis of both.

I do not, of course, expect the Prime Minister to agree with the previous Chancellor of the Exchequer but, even given the tensions between them, I do expect him to agree with the present Chancellor—and he has said that nothing should be ruled out in this Parliament. Does the Prime Minister agree? [Official Report, 21 January 1998; Vol. 304, c. 1007–1008]

This statement is a remarkable contribution in so far as for the second time, a community of pro-European British politicians and officials is named by the Lib Dem leader – and the Labour PM Blair is not among them (but is invited to join). Importantly, these like-minded people are described as an "alliance" – and one that is "patriotic". The values of solidarity and putting one's own country first (or what Ashdown calls the "national interest" here) are hereby emphasised and given as the motives underlying a justified cause the PM should join. The diversity of the members of this alliance is designed to lend it further credibility, making it appear to cross the narrow boundaries of vested interest or party ideology and to embody the common-sensical position of many, and many of them professionals. However, it seems that the focus of this alliance has shifted from the speech before; now, it seems, their common denominator is that they all want a referendum on the introduction of the single currency. The thrust of both questions during this session of PMQs is to push for a referendum – or at least to get the PM on record promising one or defending a contrary decision. Ashdown tries to establish an opposition between the national interest and the electoral timetable: he claims that the decision has to be made for the sake of the former, not the latter motive. This establishes a dialectic of power-hungry and self-interested (interested in clinging to power, anyway) politicians in government and the Lib Dems as pure-hearted opposition who take up the positions voiced by public organisations and interest groups.

In retrospect, this seems to indicate the exact cleavage becoming salient much later in the actual referendum campaign 2016, where other 'outsider parties' such as UKIP used this discursive strategy to collect votes from disenfranchised and anti-establishment voters. Obviously, the Lib Dem leader in 1997 is of the opinion that a referendum would result in a yes vote if properly advertised for, and that it would be beneficial to hold it soon. The campaign strategy would then logically be based on the claim that it is in the national interest to join the euro.

"Engagements" (28.01.1998)

> The Prime Minister might like to address a serious question. Does he rule out the possibility of a referendum on a single currency in this Parliament?
> [...]
> The question that I asked the Prime Minister was whether he rules that possibility out. His answer last week and today was so "majoristic" that it might have come from his predecessor. To the question, "Is it possible to have a referendum on a single currency during this Parliament?", there are three possible answers: yes, no or maybe. Which is it?
> [Official Report, 28 January 1998; Vol. 305, c. 343]

In the following PMQs, only one week later, Ashdown once again tries to get the PM either to commit to or rule out a referendum. In a clear attempt to distance his question and policy proposals from the style in which the CON opposition leader made his contributions to this session, the Lib Dem leader qualifies his own as a "serious" question and condemns the PM's evasive answers as resembling the style adopted by former CON leader Major – creating the impression that the Lib Dems oppose the political style followed by the Conservatives but oppose the actual policies of the government. His pushes for clarity and attempts (again, in vain) to elicit a 'yes' or 'no' answer from Blair. This can be seen as an opposition strategy; later, such statements are useful to hold the speaker to account and produce a "split-screen" image showing the promise-breaker. Additionally, the statement expresses frustration that the substantial politics do not change as much as hoped when it comes to Europe. The issue of giving the people a say retreats to the background in this criticism of handling the issue generally but is still present.

"Amendment of the Law" (17.03.1998)

On the occasion of the budget debate (regularly titled "Amendment of the law") in the House of Commons in March 1998, Ashdown mentions the independence of the Bank of England implemented by the government yet proposed by the Lib Dems. Since this is one of the prerequisites for joining the single currency, many observers interpreted this as a sign of preparation for entry:

> We applaud the Chancellor for adopting what has been our policy for years on a fiscal responsibility code and the independent status of the Bank of England—something that was in our manifesto, but not his, yet he adopted it three days after the election.
> [...]
> The Government's second mistake came not before the election, but after 1 May, when they injudiciously allowed themselves to be bounced into foreclosing the option of an early decision on Britain's entry into the single currency by a single Financial Times headline and an incautious phone call from a Westminster pub by the Chancellor's press officer. That the Government appear to have decided in favour of the single currency is a good thing; that they have decided to sit on the fence about when to enter it is not. I make the prediction that I have made before, and I make no apology for that: as soon as the rates are fixed on economic and monetary union on 1 May, the Government will be forced down the road by events and will have to take a decision in principle backed by a referendum before—not after—the next election. [Official Report, 17 March 1998; Vol. 308, c. 1123]

Ashdown returns to the issue of the single currency a little later in his speech and goes on about an incident reported in the media before and which he qualifies with the words "injudiciously" and "incautious", resulting in being "bounced into" a denial of any intention to join soon. This criticism is aimed both at the indiscretion or foolhardiness shown by communicating internal information in a public place and the apparent government policy to delay any decision on an entry date, even though a general consensus to join eventually seems to have been established at government level. It is intriguing to see that the Lib Dem leader welcomes this consensus but implicitly criticises the government's concern with public opinion and approval rates for their policy (which Labour could ignore, given their comfortable majority in parliament, but obviously, they did not deem it wise to use this power to go against the general trend in the population. The Lib Dems seem to advocate proper parliamentary sovereignty and a certain disdain for public opinion – if it is sensible and the top levels agree on this, it should be done – and the decision justified by a referendum which the Lib Dems are confident they could win (public can be persuaded according to their view). The referendum, however, seems to be locked into this line of argumentation and has become inseparable from any call to join the single currency.

Yet Ashdown appears impatient seeing this dithering and embarrassing handling of such a big issue by the government. He presents his prediction as a certainty and thus makes his proposed actions and timetable look plausible and without alternative should the government like to remain in control over events.

He refers to the scheduled date of 1 May 1998 when the next step of EMU would be decided and prophesies that the ensuing dynamic will "force[…]" government "down the road of events". He laments the lack of leadership and decisiveness (which arguably had become a pattern of British EU policy) and forecasts that the result will be the same as usual: the EU project will be a success or at least so important that the UK will eventually join and not have taken part in setting the course at the outset with all the loss of influence and the impression that the Brits are not in it with their whole heart strengthened.

It is sad to see the current Government, who are unquestionably more pro-European than any of their predecessors, still being led by events on Europe instead of leading them. It is sad indeed to see that, on the Government's timetable, even Greece will now be sitting at the top table deciding future economic policy in Europe while Britain is stuck in the waiting room outside. It not only a question of leadership: we are paying a real and painful price for that fatal mobile phone call from the Red Lion pub in Parliament square. Our industrial and export industries are bleeding because of the uncompetitive level of the pound; jobs are already being lost, and more—I fear, many more—will follow; interest rates are higher than they need to be, piling on the agony for our manufacturing sector; crucial investment is already beginning to go elsewhere; and much, far too much, of the genuine good will and enhanced influence that the new Government have won for themselves in Europe is being allowed to ebb away. [Official Report, 17 March 1998; Vol. 308, c. 1123]

Bringing in emotion and a judgement, Ashdown declares that "It is sad" and repeats this (anaphora). The emotional appeal makes the Lib Dems seem like a well-meaning wise outsider looking on the situation, as if they had nothing to do with it but are affected nevertheless. The Lib Dem leader describes Labour under Blair as "unquestionably more pro-European than any of their predecessors"; he then points out the conundrum that this apparent quality does not translate into action where the EMU is concerned. The word "still" marks this continuity of wait-and-see.

The example of Greece is used to point out that even a small, economically speaking unimportant newcomer to the community has now more influence on EMU than the powerful and financially savvy UK, the latter thus unnecessarily ceding their place to lesser countries (out of fear/indecisiveness). This is a rather snobbish point meant to appeal to a sense of self-worth and self-importance: taking their rightful place at the "top table" where important stuff gets decided is presented as the proper thing to do for a sovereign British government instead of fearfully looking to survey results and not daring to take part. The metaphor of Britain being "stuck in the waiting room" is another poignant hint as to the preferred self-image of the Lib Dems: the want the UK to be in the middle (or even better at the top) of important European policy decisions, not waiting in front of closed doors as non-members of the Eurozone.

He explains why his proposals are more sensible through enumerating the good things that are being and will be lost because of the government's indecision: leadership, economic advantages gained by a competitive currency, jobs, investment, and not least "much, far too much, of the genuine good will and enhanced influence […] in Europe".

The aim to retain all this seems, economically speaking, very common-sensical and is fundamentally opposed to the current government's actions, vividly characterised as "a real and painful price" and the government blunder of leaked information as "fatal"; the effects on the economy are that is "bleeding" and the manufacturing sector in "agony". Thus, this assessment of the status quo resembles the result of a terrible accident with severely injured victims – and it makes the government responsible for that not only look weak, incompetent, and careless but also criminally negligent where the economy and people as well as the international standing of the UK are concerned.

> As the Budget figures reveal, Britain has met all the main criteria for joining monetary union, so I urge the Government to adopt now a declaratory policy on EMU. They should set a clear target date for joining, follow policies consistent with that aim and announce that they are prepared to have a referendum on the principle of the single currency before the next election. The result would be immediately beneficial both to the

> Chancellor in his predicament and to the country in that it would bring a lower pound, lower interest rates, more inward investment and a real boost to the Government's influence and standing in Europe. [Official Report, 17 March 1998; Vol. 308, c. 1124]

Ashdown refers to figures which "reveal" that his point of view is correct, a rhetorical trick to make the proof appear neutral and objective (when it is highly dependent on calculation methods and interpretation of the meaning). The fact that it is the government's figures serves to make the Lib Dem claim more credible.

The main criteria he mentions are most likely the Maastricht criteria since Brown's own "economic tests" were only introduced later; the technical conditions are met, so he sees no point in waiting. Ashdown only urges the government to make a stand and say what they will do, not to jump now; thus, combining the virtues of setting a lead and being courageous but also the virtue of caution. And transparency as well as clarity and efficiency; without a proclaimed goal, no one can measure success or hold you accountable, so it is not surprising that the opposition wants more of that.

He outlines a clear alternative policy proposal: he proposes to set a target date for joining and then take all the necessary measures and let the economy prepare. The idea that insecurity is toxic for economic development is clearly visible in this line of argumentation. He argues that being clear and consistent would be better for all involved, mainly for the country. Here, a macroeconomic view is adopted: the country will benefit from lower interest rates, a stronger currency, and more investment. Thereby, he suggests that good economic figures will benefit everyone including the government. This supposed trickle-down effect is part of liberal economic theory and is seen critically by many today. But, last in the enumeration, Ashdown also argues that the UK's "influence and standing in Europe" are also important and should not be given away lightly! This is another supposed "soft-power" effect that is denied by the CON and does not chime with the hard-headed, realist (politically speaking) approach believed in by many CON members, in that everything is negotiable, and pursuing the national interest first is a legitimate and desirable goal (and the other states believed to act in this way, too).

> The hon. Gentleman was—uncharacteristically, perhaps—not listening to my speech as carefully as he might. I said that the Government should follow a declaratory policy; I did not say that we should enter the single currency now. We should set a target date of 2001 or 2002. We should follow policies consistent with that, by which time we can, no doubt, achieve convergence, and then hold a referendum on the principle before the next election. I do not know whether the hon. Gentleman agrees, but I believe that the Government will do that.

[...]
No. I have said this twice in simple English. The Government will be forced to take a decision and hold a referendum on the principle of joining a single currency before the next election. They can then join on their target date of 2001 or 2002. That is pretty simple. I should have thought that the hon. Gentleman could understand that without too much further assistance. [Official Report, 17 March 1998; Vol. 308, c. 1128]

In two intervening statements, the CON MP Bell attempts to paint Ashdown in the corner of wanting to join straight away and thus to portray him as an ideologically blinded politician insensible for other arguments, a portrayal Ashdown vehemently denies. His call is for a timely decision by the government which is then followed through, and his view is that the time for this will come soon enough, before the next general election (and thus material for the campaign of the opposition anyway). The values of strong leadership and taking responsibility for deciding on things you believe to be in the best interest for your country are underlying this call for a principled stand. But even the Lib Dems concede that this decision will be controversial and seen to believe that it can only be legitimised by a referendum (which they are confident can be won, though).

"Engagements" (29.04.1998)

In a regular take-up of the subject one month later, Ashdown dedicates both his questions during PMQs to EMU again and criticises the government's apparent non-action and indecision sharply by alluding to the national interest:

If a successful euro is important for Britain, why on earth are the Government still sitting on the fence about it? As the Prime Minister, with understandable justification, celebrates the first year of his party in office, will he spare a little time to reflect for a moment on the fact that Britain's industrial sector is now officially in recession; that the reason for that is an uncompetitive pound; that his Government's inability to face up to taking a clear decision on monetary union means that he can do nothing in that respect; and that the price is now being paid in lost exports, and will soon be paid in broken businesses and lost jobs?
[...]
Does the Prime Minister not realise that this is one of those issues in which the short-term interest and the long-term advantage coincide? He will be forced down the track faster than he now believes is likely because his Government, like the last, are being led by events in Europe, rather than leading them. What he should be doing is adopting a declaratory policy, setting a target date for entry into single currency, following policies consistent with that aim, and holding a referendum on the principle before the next election. If he did that, the pound would go down, interest rates would go down, investment would go up and the Prime Minister would not be placed in the position, in which he is going to find himself this weekend, of presiding over a European meeting in which

> Britain ought to be playing on the field, but is relegated to standing on the touchline.
> [Official Report, 29 April 1998; Vol. 311, c. 322–323]

The first question is actually a strong accusation: Ashdown claims that by adopting the euro, lots of economic problems could be avoided and jobs be preserved – and that the government loses this chance because of their "inability to face up to taking a clear decision". Weak leadership, indecision, and incompetence are thus ascribed to the Labour government, whereas joining the euro appears as some kind of panacea for all economic ills faced by the UK at the time, with the industrial sector in recession. When the PM retorts that economic policy is not only about short-term solutions, the Lib Dem leader exasperatedly explains that he is also convinced that the euro will be beneficial in the long term – an assessment later called into question by the euro crisis.

The tone of the second question especially indicates a certain level of frustration and makes it clear that Ashdown sees a continuity in British policy towards the EU – it is the same dithering and wait-and-see as always (this echoes the judgement of H. Young (e.g. 1999: 269) once again). He once again spells out clearly what he considers to be the better alternative to government policy: make a decision to join later, then prepare for it. His prediction that otherwise, events will force the UK government anyhow to act is a warning that might also be seen as a threat posed by cooperation among the other EU members. It seems the UK only has the choice to go along with the dynamic and try to shape it along the way or to be forced to stay outside. This is not a particularly positive image of the EU: it is depicted as a club moving pitilessly onwards, whereas the UK is in a position where it is either being carried along with the development or cast off.

A second metaphor taken from the field of sports shows that the Lib Dems prefer international cooperation to isolation: Ashdown makes his criticism clear by stating that dithering brings about situations where the PM, at this moment president of the European Council, is "presiding over a European meeting in which Britain ought to be playing on the field, but is relegated to standing on the touchline" [Official Report, 29 April 1998; Vol. 311, c. 322–323]. Ashdown thus clearly advocates staying on the field and try their best to win instead of quitting and living with the rule changes agreed by others.

All in all, it can be concluded that the Lib Dems argue in favour of joining the EMU as an important step in European integration, so their aim can be classified as pro-European. The justification, however, puts (macro-) economic rational thinking first, combining this argument with the national interest, and bargaining power in other European policy projects as a further pro-point. There is nowhere an "ideological" or emotional connection or conviction that the EU is preferable to the nation state. In their reasoning in connection with the EMU, they sound like the CON in the 1970s – 'let's join because it will benefit the economy'. The Lib Dems and some Tories could, therefore, be seen as good partners when it comes to EMU and the 'scare' campaign to stay in the EU in 2016 seems to align with the stance of a party that says economic necessities count in favour and staying outside would be stupid.

"Economic and Monetary Union" (05.05.1998)

In the next speech, occasioned by the Commons debate on Economic and Monetary Union on 5 May 1998, Ashdown qualify the decision on EMU as "historic". This underlines the importance he accords to the topic and while he agrees with the PM that it is right for Europe (a Churchill-like outside perspective on development on the continent), he criticises exactly this position by describing the UK's role in this context as a "sadness". Using the sports metaphor again, the UK is "actually a spectator at the sidelines" where it is hard to even see it in the role of umpire, not to mention the role of a "sponsor" that Churchill wanted the UK to be while the United States of Europe should be formed by the others. The role of spectator is a powerless one and certainly not what the Lib Dems see as an appropriate role for the UK. The desire to be a big player at least on the European level is clearly transported by this wording. It is also a criticism of the government and their make-believe version of the UK's third-way role of being a mediator between different positions but in the eyes of the Lib Dem leader this looks more like indecisiveness and isolation from the real game:

> I agree with the Prime Minister that the result was the right one for Europe. One should use the word "historic" sparingly in the House, but this genuinely was an historic event. The first sadness is that Britain, instead of being a part of it, was at best an umpire, but, as the Prime Minister well knows, actually a spectator at the sidelines. Is it not the case that, yet again, we shall in due course join an institution to which we did not belong when it was formed and which we have not effectively shaped? Is not the second sadness the sad position to which the official Opposition—an increasingly inappropriate term—have sunk? They have locked themselves into a corner, and locked themselves out of mainstream domestic politics and European politics as well. Is it not a sad reflection on the party of Europe, as the Conservatives once called themselves, that, instead of commenting on the big event, they comment on the small compromise? It is a little like treating the news of the victory over the armada with a complaint that Drake did not play a very good game of bowls. It is a preposterous position. [Official Report, 5 May 1998; Vol. 311, c. 569]

As becomes clear here, he goes on to criticise the CON and their discourse on Europe. He phrases a scathing judgement and paints them as losing their grip on European policy. Employing a combination of a further emotional frame introduced with "sadness" and of a hierarchy – he says they have "sunk" to this low. Ashdown effectively establishes his own party alongside Labour as "mainstream" on the upper end of the hierarchy and claims the CON MPs have isolated themselves to such a degree that even the label "Official Opposition" is becoming steadily less appropriate. He describes their predicament as having "locked themselves into a corner". This captures the idea that it will be hard for them to return to the political centre ground, where elections are usually won in the UK. Over their position on Europe, the Lib Dems present them as no alternative to the current government and instead create the impression that it is the Lib Dems who make a sensible policy proposal. Ashdown particularly points out that the CON have once called themselves the "party of Europe" (when Heath took the UK into the EC) and, by repeating the word "sad", criticises their focus on what is not perfect in the decision on EMU as small-minded and as if they could not see what is really important. In short, it is the Lib Dems that are pragmatically focused on the UK's economic well-being, while the CON MPs have lost the instinct allowing them to do just that.

The word "preposterous" used to describe their position in this context further adds to the impression that they are outside rational and adult consideration when it comes to European policy. This dimension of perhaps irrational fear or aversion is ridiculed by the Lib Dem leader and obviously not accepted as legitimate grounds for a policy position. The comparison to the victory of the armada serves to put EMU on a level with this decisive moment in British history and shows how ridiculous they find it.

> Of course the compromise was messy. Some may even say that that is a specious description of it. However, that will not make the slightest difference to such an historic event. Two questions must be asked about the compromise. First, will the euro have effective government and leadership? The answer is yes, not for 10 years, but for 12. Secondly, do the markets express their confidence in that? The answer is resoundingly yes.
>
> I shall make two further points to the Prime Minister. First, unhappily for his Government, who are more pro-European and could have much more influence in Europe, he is losing that by standing at the side and making the same mistake as the previous Government made, being led on Europe rather than leading on Europe. Secondly, for as long as he does that, Britain will lose trade, investment and influence. Is not the risk for Britain the fact that this weekend there was formed a soft but stable Europe, while we must continue with a high, volatile and unstable pound? [Official Report, 5 May 1998; Vol. 311, c. 569]

Ashdown nevertheless concedes that the EMU decision was a "compromise" and that it was "messy". By introducing this concession with "of course", however, he makes believe that this is the normal state of affairs and as such was to be expected. He goes on to claim that this fact "will not make the slightest difference to such an historic event". The EMU is for the second time described as "historic", eclipsing details and making them seem irrelevant. Ashdown says only two aspects are really important: "effective leadership" and the "confidence" of the markets. As Ashdown's phrasing makes clear, these are the values or goal states that the Lib Dem leader accepts as the benchmark against which to measure his own party's policy proposals – and that of others. If they are fulfilled, he supports it. This seems indeed to be the party of business; without ideology, but purely and rationally conforming to market needs.

Ashdown then repeats the attribute that Blair's government is "more pro-European" and makes a causal connection to having "much more influence in Europe" because of this quality. This assumption is then contrasted with the "unhappy" circumstance that the government do not capitalise and/or act on this. Ashdown puts this behaviour in line with the CON governments before that, establishing a British tradition (as it were) of "being led on Europe rather than leading on Europe". This shows up the values of strong leadership and making a mark, as well as making the most of a good bargaining position (self-interest). A further causal connection is established between not taking part in the EMU (not joining the euro) and losing "trade, investment and influence". This enumeration shows that economic advantage is at the forefront and that the position of the UK in relation to its partner is second to that. Together, these reasons do include hard macro-economic gains as well as a foreign policy clout, two principles that let shine through market liberal as well as realist view of the world. It is thus pure self-interest which could and should constitute the reason for Blair to join the euro.

Not joining the euro and being isolated from the Eurozone countries is described as a "risk" and the desirable adjective "stable" is associated with "Europe" while in the UK, a negatively contrasting picture is painted caused by a "volatile and unstable pound". Stability is what everyone wants, whereas to end the boom and bust of unchained capitalism is exactly what the Chancellor Brown wants to abolish but cannot attain while opposing the euro, according to the Lib Dem reasoning.

"G8 Summit" (20.05.1998)

> Does the Prime Minister agree that one could not have a more eloquent statement of the
> current state of the Conservative party [sic] than the contrast between the welcome to
> monetary union given by all the world's leaders at the G8 summit and the increasingly
> neurotic and isolationist speeches made by the leader of the Conservative party [sic],

which do good neither to his party nor to the country? [Official Report, 20 May 1998;
Vol. 312, c. 962–963]

In this paragraph from a speech on the outcome of the G8 Summit on
20 May 1998, Ashdown directly addresses the stance on Europe taken by the
CON and describes it as "neurotic and isolationist", a stance which is judged
as not doing "good neither to his party nor to the country" [Official Report,
20 May 1998; Vol. 312, c. 962–963]. This shows that the Lib Dem position is the
exact opposite, namely to be open-minded and cooperating, and above all that
they want the best for the UK, whereas the CON MPs are split and not interested in pragmatic and rational economic policy anymore but rather in other
matters (to be researched in more depth). This negatively depicted stance is rhetorically compared to the view of "all the world's leaders" and the Lib Dems,
therefore, shown to be in agreement with these authorities and experienced as
well as respected public figures whereas the CON MPs are inward-looking and
irrational.

The topic of the euro remains high on the agenda, being brought up again just
weeks later:

"European Council (Cardiff)" (17.06.1998)

Finally, the Prime Minister quoted with approval the comments of a German newspaper
that there had been an historic achievement on monetary union. Does he find anything
odd in the fact that monetary union had only a bit part in the concluding paragraph of
his statement? Monetary union was one of the most historic achievements of the presidency, but Britain presided over it rather than took part in it. The previous Government's
failure—and, I am bound to say, the timidity of this Government—on monetary union
means that Britain is outside Euro X exactly when the provisions for external trade, in
which Britain has a greater stake than any other European nation, are being drawn up.
As I have said before, the Prime Minister will have to grasp this nettle, and he will have
to do so sooner rather than later. If he followed, as we recommend, a declaratory policy
saying, "We will join," set a target date, held a referendum on the principle before the
next election and took the decision afterwards at a time of the Government's choosing,
the pound would go down, interest rates would go down, investment would come to
Britain rather than be at risk of going elsewhere, and Britain would be able to capitalise
on the Government's fresh and new tone, so that our influence in Europe would increase
incredibly, giving us a better deal for the future. Why can the right hon. Gentleman not
see that? [Official Report, 17 June 1998; Vol. 314, c. 374–375]

In this speech on the outcomes of the European Council meeting in Cardiff, at
the end of the six months of British presidency of the Council of the European
Union, Ashdown mentions the single currency last and criticises the fact that the

PM's statement had not focused on this issue enough, despite it being "one of the most historic achievements of the presidency". Ashdown implies that the government have their priorities wrong or are incapable of judging the importance of events correctly. He puts Blair in line with the CON governments before him and says they all failed to grasp the importance of being part of monetary union for the national interest. He names international trade and points out that the UK should be at the table to protect its own interests in this regard. The words "failure" and "timidity" paint a picture of incompetence and lack of strong leadership aimed at both big British parties. He laments that Britain is "outside Euro X", drawing a picture of a timid loser or outsider who does not dare to join a game played by his peers. And peers, the other "European nations" certainly are in the eyes and words of the Lib Dem leader: by saying "a greater stake than any other European nation", he expressly includes "Britain" in the imagined community of European nations, although he does not define which qualities exactly define the limits of this community.

Ashdown continues to define what others claim to be credit to the value of caution as negative character qualities such as fear and weakness and a supposedly traditional wait-and-see pragmatic 'muddling through' practiced by many British governments (see e.g. Hennessy 1996) as signs of a lack of leadership qualities and foresight. Saying that Blair "will have to grasp this nettle", however, does nothing to present European policy decisions in a positive light. The nettle as metaphor for a thorny or painful experience stands for the EU – and no one wants to touch it because they know it will hurt and sting whoever gets too close to such an unpleasant object. Taking up this conceptualisation of the matter, Ashdown presents EMU as a necessary but painful decision. This makes both the EU and decisions on integration as well as political actors who shy away from them in fear of getting hurt seem unpleasant – one as inherently stingy and the other as cowards. The additional prediction that this nettle-grasping will come "sooner rather than later" suggests a quality of unavoidable unpleasantness connected to EU policy decisions aimed at further integration. Ashdown could also refer to the fact that public opinion and rational advantages clash and argue that responsible politicians must listen to their 'conscience' rather than playing to the public, which could then be an admission that further EU integration is unpopular and could hurt voting chances. It also includes a criticism of populism, i.e. proposing what is popular against your better knowledge, which is aimed at both big parties.

He then repeats his alternative policy proposal: to accept the unavoidable and steer rather than drift in a direction, i.e. keep up apparent power and sovereignty. But he justifies his proposal with a suggested positive correlation of joining the euro and achieving desirable economic outcomes which he predicts will follow automatically: a weaker pound and thus better competitiveness of exported goods, lower interest rates which are supposedly good for consumers and trust in the economic situation, as well as retaining the UK's popularity as a place for FDI. Last in that list of desirable outcomes for the British macro-economic climate comes the better negotiation position within the EU. In this logic, accepting the euro is both rationally advantageous and the right thing to do if capitalist values are the foundation for good policy decisions as well as the necessary price (worth paying in the Lib Dem view) to retain a favourable place on the European level of governance. The use of the word "capitalise" in this context reveals the self-interested tone of this whole argument: it is not because the UK is part of a community but because they want to retain their clout in negotiations with the other EU member states. Joining the single currency is thus not presented as the right thing in itself but as a means to an end, namely serving the national interest of the UK first and foremost, with a focus on the economy and not necessarily on consumers or British citizens who are not mentioned in the whole debate. The interests of people (public opinion) who might not want to join for nostalgic or emotional reasons are thus dismissed as not legitimate to take a decision, and representing them is portrayed as populist. The same dilemma is still present today – whom do MPs serve, economic interests or voters' preferences?

The use of the word "declaratory policy" expresses the wish for clarity and accountability. The call for a referendum on the "principle", i.e. whether the UK should join with the decision on the exact timing left to the government is repeated and has become a firm part of the Lib Dem's proposals on how to deal with the matter. It remains unclear how such a referendum is justified in itself other than to counter the impression and insinuation that the Lib Dems disregard the opinion of a majority.

"Engagements" (08.07.1998)

Surely the issue that should worry us today is not so much the job prospects of a couple of cadet new Labour insiders, but the jobs of tens of thousands of people across the country that are now placed in jeopardy as a result of the rising pound and rising interest rates. Does the Prime Minister not realise that he could take a decision today that would relieve the pain immediately: he could come off the fence on the single currency, set a target date—subject to a referendum—and give the economy, the country and industry the lead that they so desperately need?

[...]

The Prime Minister has given that answer before. It did not wash then, and it does not wash now. If he took the decision that I have suggested, the pound would come down tomorrow, interest rates would come down next week, investment would keep coming into this country over the next decade, and Britain would have more influence in Europe right through into the next century. Why does he not realise that, on this occasion, long-term interest and short-term advantage coincide? He will have to take such action soon; why not take it now? [Official Report, 8 July 1998; Vol. 315, c. 1068–1069]

In his two questions at PMQs on 8 July 1998, Ashdown brings up endangered jobs in the UK and describes the rising pound exchange rate as well as interest rates as the cause for this. He claims that the decision to join the single currency would stop or even reverse these two developments and reproaches the PM of not using the instrument at his disposal. He wants the PM to "come off the fence", thereby suggesting he sat on it and is indecisive and cannot even bring himself to come down either side when British jobs are at risk. The insecurity surrounding the question whether the UK would join or not hurts the economy first, according to the list the Lib Dem leader presents. Furthermore, it is also the country which suffers "pain", and the industry. These impersonal entities are humanised (real people do not feature in Ashdown's intervention) and described as "desperately need[ing]" a "lead". Clearly, it is not people he is primarily concerned with, or if he is, it does not become apparent by his choice of words. Macroeconomic benefits to certain sectors as well as "the country", an imagined community that seems strangely devoid of life in this instance here, seem enough to legitimise his proposed actions. The causal chain of setting a target date, holding a referendum, and then reaping the benefits for all concerned is discursively established: "the pound would come down tomorrow, interest rates would come down next week, investment would keep coming into this country and Britain would have more influence in Europe right through into the next century". This chain of events is described as doubtlessly effective and the inactivity of the PM seems, therefore, inexcusable. Ashdown says these consequences will naturally follow and predicts even the moment in time that the results will manifest themselves, making them seem even more probable and within the grasp of all listeners. It seems as if he could predict the future and as if macro-economics were not multi-faceted and complex but a very simple machine – it is enough to tweak one single screw to get a desired result and fix anything wrong.

The referendum is not presented as a risk but as a further simple step down the line. Obviously, Ashdown thinks it will be won easily should the government decide to back entry into the single currency. It is questionable, therefore, why the Lib Dem leader insists on having one at all – he does not seem to think that it is a truly open decision where both outcomes are possible but sees it merely as a pacifying exercise to engender the apparent support by the public. He seems to suggest that the result can be heavily influenced by a cross-party campaign in favour of the euro like in the in/out referendum in 1975. Why parliamentary sovereignty is not enough to make a decision that apparently has only positive consequences both in the short and long term is not explained and it seems probable that they have taken up this demand for a referendum as a reaction to surveys suggesting low public support for the single currency in the UK and also to counter the claim that the Lib Dems do not have the British interests at heart first.

Ashdown ends with a repetition of the prediction that a decision will have to be taken at some point soon and that waiting thus is not helpful but only strengthens the impression that the government are weak and indecisive.

"Engagements" (21.10.1998)

> Beneath all the sound and fury and the Government's flawed economic forecasts, are not these the human facts? Whatever the situation may have been in the past, most observers now believe that some 300,000 manufacturing jobs are in jeopardy, and one of our greatest industries—agriculture—is now experiencing its deepest crisis for 50 years. Will the Prime Minister at least start by acknowledging those facts?
>
> [...]
>
> Instead of indulging in the blame game, the Prime Minister could do three things now. Will the Government consider them? First, the right hon. Gentleman could tackle our exchange rate problem by making a clear commitment to the single currency. [Official Report, 21 October 1998; Vol. 317, c. 1273–1274]

After the summer recess, Ashdown criticises economic incompetence at the government level by accusing them that they have either disputed, refused to see, or were unable to see serious problems in the manufacturing sector and in agriculture, which he describes as "one of our greatest industries". The pronoun "our" touches again on a feeling of being a community and that a part of this community (and an important one at that) is in danger. This makes it a question of solidarity and loyalty to help them and take all possible measures to achieve this end. By the use of the words "deepest crisis", the situation is dramatised and importance thus added. The Lib Dem leader addresses the single currency again as a remedy for job loss and "our exchange rate problem", describing the country as a community that has a joint problem to solve or suffer from. The inaction of the PM appears thus as disloyal to the community.

I think it is possible that exactly such a rhetoric, i.e. framing the strength of the pound as a problem and suggesting that it is more beneficial to "hide" behind the (economically speaking) weaker members in a currency union which could have given ammunition to the likes of UKIP, who insist that British strength is something positive and not a "problem" but a source of pride and a natural result of their superiority to other economies. The question of competitiveness is thus approached from different angles: one by "rational" economic hard-headedness and opportunistic motives, the other more by emotions and the desire to uphold a reputation regardless of consequences. This indicates that different values stand behind the policy proposals of future Remainers and Brexiteers and that these differences were visible in the discourse 18 years before. In addition, it makes the government seem indifferent to the plight of British people working in manufacturing and agriculture and instead only interested in staying in power, which may have contributed to distrust in elites coming to the forefront in the referendum campaigns.

"Engagements" (04.11.1998)

> The Prime Minister says that the Government's policy on the single currency is clear, but on Monday the Trade Secretary described when we would join the single currency and on Tuesday the Cabinet enforcer rushed round saying that we should wait and see if we join the single currency. Which is the Government's policy?
> [...]
> The Prime Minister must answer for his policy. Let me remind him that one of his Cabinet Ministers has said "when" and another has said "if". They cannot both be right. When will the Government realise that this is the most important decision facing our country? The Government cannot abandon leadership in favour of a policy of nods and winks. For as long as they do, the Cabinet will remain confused, the country will remain without a lead and British industry will continue to suffer. [Official Report, 4 November 1998; Vol. 318, c. 864]

In close temporal succession, the issue is brought up again and Ashdown points out inconsistency in the government's communication about a possible entry into the single currency, namely the difference between "when" and "if". Referring to the collective responsibility of the cabinet, Ashdown says the PM is responsible for ensuring a consensus. This shows how dangerous the topic is and that it can split governments as it did in the past. This is the opposite of "clear" and is likely to engender insecurity which makes it harder to plan ahead.

Additionally, he vents his frustration at this unclarity by describing the single currency issue as the "most important decision facing our country". This makes the government seem undecided and passive to a dangerous point and shows how highly the Lib Dem leader values strong leadership, which he accuses the PM of having "abandoned in favour of a policy of nods and winks". The consequences are drastically outlined in an enumeration putting the split cabinet as the first problem, a country without leadership second and the British industry last, implying that all ills can be traced back to the government's problems to find a common position. Making a decision on the euro is thus presented as the solution to many problems which are only caused by not deciding in the first place, making the government to blame twice. The community of the country is thus blighted by a "confused" governing elite, by the absence of leadership and by a "suffer[ing] industry", which are all negative. In this intervention, it does not become clear, however, that in fact it is not so much making a decision but making the one the Lib Dems think the right one is what matters to Ashdown. The referendum is also not addressed here, which strengthens the impression that it is really more about the government deciding than about all voters deciding. I think the insistence that leadership is important puts the responsibility but also the power and competence at the door of the elected politicians in government, not "the people".

"Debate on the Address" (24.11.1998)

On the economy, the key, as the Prime Minister said last week, is stability—how to create it and how to preserve it. The Government have made good early progress towards monetary stability by granting independence to the Bank of England last year, as we have long recommended. Good, but are they prepared to back that up with the measures necessary for fiscal stability and exchange rate stability?

Next year will be tough for the economy, especially for manufacturing and for manufacturing employment. The question that the Government must answer is whether they are prepared to hold their course, as they have said they will, and whether they can sustain their commitment to the golden rule when the economy gets rougher and the decisions get a lot tougher. Crucially, will the Government now give the lead that the country so desperately needs on the issue of the single currency – adopting a declaratory policy, setting a target date for joining and pursuing a policy that enables us to do that? That is not, as the hon. Member for North Durham (Mr. Radice) pointed out, just a matter of the enthusiasm of the Liberal Democrats. There is now a wide view across industry that what the country needs is a lead. Only yesterday, as the hon. Gentleman noted, 114 senior business people, including the leaders of 20 of the FTSE 100 listed companies, issued a statement calling on the Government to give the lead on the euro that they and the country are calling for.

The position that the Prime Minister has adopted is no different from that of his predecessor. We sit on the fence. We do nothing. We wait until the time is ripe. That is the old formula for a lack of leadership, rather than giving the country a clear direction. I understand that it would mean taking a risk – perhaps even a risk with some of the Prime Minister's newspaper-owner friends, but that is what leadership is about. It means giving the country a clear lead on a big issue. The Government are failing the country when they fail to do that.

[…]

I strongly welcome that. It should make it all the easier for the Government to come clean and set the lead. I have no doubt that that is what they believe and that is the direction in which they are going, but they cannot lead the nation by stealth. They must make sure that they set a direction for the country. In so far as the Prime Minister and his Government agree with the hon. Gentleman and me, I find it perplexing and bewildering that they cannot set that lead. I can put it down only to timidity on the issue, which I think is not the characteristic for which the Government would want to be recognised.

[…]

To be fair, the Government's manifesto was that they would decide according to the nation's interests. Fine. I know of no cogent case in support of the country's future interests which requires us not to join a single currency. That is evident now. If the Prime Minister would like to describe circumstances which he can foresee in which he will take a decision not to join, I will agree that he should sit on the fence and look longer. But I do not believe that such a case can be made. [Official Report, 24 November 1998; Vol. 321, c. 41–44]

With a new parliamentary session having begun, Ashdown's next intervention referring to the euro is in the 'Debate on the Address', the speech given by the Queen outlining the government's programme for the next year. Ashdown links general questions pertaining to the economy with the decision to join the single currency.

The first point is stability, and the independence of the Bank of England, interpreted by many observers to be a sign of preparation to join the single currency, is lauded by the leader. While acknowledging this as a "good early start", Ashdown says there is plenty more to do if the government is serious about stability. He predicts hard times for the manufacturing sector and repeats his words nearly one to one, in an effort to drive home the message and make it stick in the minds of all listeners, when he asks once again "will the Government now give the lead that the country so desperately needs on the issue of the single currency – adopting a declaratory policy, setting a target date for joining and pursuing a policy than enables us to do that"? The use of the pronoun "us" establishes a discursively established 'imagined community', which is equalled to the whole "country" and qualified as "desperate"; in this way, the Lib Dem leader frames the issue as a problem concerning everyone. With all being in the same boat, the alternative actions the Lib Dem leader proposes naturally appear to be in the national interest, in that he knows how to save the country in times of desperate need.

Addressing criticism voiced by a Labour MP, Ashdown seeks to rebut the claim that arguing in favour of joining the single currency is a "matter of enthusiasm" for his party by citing others with the same opinion as back up: he says 114 "senior business people" support his view that a decision would be beneficial. The seniority and their competence in economic matters is underlined to lend credibility and urgency to Ashdown's proposal and show that they are compatible with a hard business head, countering the word "enthusiasm" which implies emotion and an ideological blindness and thus makes his proposals appear less valid because less rational. It becomes clear that no one wants to be caught having or believed to have any emotional involvement with European integration, and that only business figures constitute a legitimate reason to go along with further European integration. Interestingly, it is business people "and the country" which are said to call for a decision on the euro – not to join, but to have clarity on the future developments – as if business people were somewhat apart from the rest of the country, an elite understanding the economy.

Ashdown aligns Blair's European policy with that of the Major government and proceeds to condemn both as indecisive dithering and poor/weak leadership: "We sit on the fence. We do nothing. We wait until the time is ripe". The repeated use of "we" as an anaphora at the beginning of each of these three sentences again creates the impression of the same old story over again (further strengthened by the words "old formula") but also implies that the country is a big community inclusive of its politicians. This is interesting because it shows a total identification of government and people as everyone living in the country is bound by these decisions. An alternative is drawn up and qualified as "clear" and courageous because deciding also means taking a risk. Ashdown thus portrays taking a risk and going against the Eurosceptic 'Murdoch press' as showing moral fibre and strength, qualities arguably necessary for good leadership, and claims the PM lacks these qualities and values, which means in the eyes of the Lib Dems the government "are failing the country".

Responding to an intervention by Labour MP Bradshaw defending the government's policy approach, Ashdown repeats that the "Government [should] come clean and set the lead". This implies that they are either too scared or timid to lead or that they have something unpleasant to hide; both options reflect badly on the government. Ashdown then paints the picture that the Labour government want to join but do not dare to openly defend this position, leading Ashdown to make the remark that they "cannot lead the nation by stealth". Again, this choice of words has a connotation indicating criminal intent or at least a lack of honesty. In this dilemma between assumed personal preference for joining and a public display of reserve, Ashdown admits that the government's handling of the issue is "perplexing and bewildering", i.e. that he cannot understand or find reasonable grounds to deny your better knowledge and convince everyone else that your choice was right. Public opinion or doubt thus is dismissed as no legitimate reason to delay a policy decision. He says that "they cannot set the lead", invoking an image of incapability. The only logical conclusion to Ashdown is "timidity" on the government's side – a quality he himself describes as negative and shameful.

Ashdown ends with the concession that the national interest is what was in Labour's manifesto and that this is important, but he does not accept the reasoning that following the national interest and joining the euro are mutually exclusive, a fact that obviously needs to be established through discourse because there are others disputing it or presenting an alternative interpretation. Citing the value of rationality again and dismissing all other arguments, Ashdown claims that "no cogent case" can be made that establishes this mutual exclusivity. This places all opponents of the single currency in the camp of people not able or willing to use their brain to produce a logical coherent argument.

"Economic and Monetary Union" (23.02.1999)

A debate expressly dedicated to Economic and Monetary Union on 23 February 1999 is the next instance where the euro is naturally addressed by all speakers, including the Lib Dem leader:

> There is a rule of thumb about Government statements in the House, which is that the longer the statement, the more opaque the policy. That is a bit of what we heard earlier. I am reminded of a comment from a Minister earlier today when he was asked whether entry was a matter of when or if. He said that the Government's policy was that the two words are now interchangeable. I do not know precisely what that means. [Official Report, 23 February 1999; Vol. 326, c. 187]

First, Ashdown points the finger at conflicting messages coming out of different cabinet members, showing up the fact that collective responsibility is not achieved on the subject of joining the single currency. This unclarity and division is duly criticised.

> The statement was very significant. Is not the truth simply that today the Government have crossed the Rubicon in favour of the euro? I greatly welcome that, even though the Government have crossed the Rubicon only by the tiniest millimetre. I welcome it even though the Government are trying to pretend that they have not crossed the Rubicon. I welcome it because now the Government will have to defend their position—something that they have not done before. [Official Report, 23 February 1999; Vol. 326, c. 187]

The Lib Dem leader then proceeds to comment on the statement by the PM itself and describes it as "very significant". He explains this attributed importance by implying that finally the real intentions of the government have become clear. The central metaphor he employs throughout his speech is the image of crossing the Rubicon. The phrasing "inch[ing] across the Rubicon" is not the strategically smartest one if joining the single currency is to be portrayed as desirable, since it means "to do something extreme that cannot later be changed and whose effects cannot be avoided" ("Rubicon"). This metaphor does not create an especially inviting atmosphere and may involuntarily exactly describe how the government sees it: as a momentous decision with unknown but unavoidable consequences when taken. From the viewpoint of the Lib Dem leader, it is, however, the courage and will to power demonstrated by Julius Caesar when he crossed the now metaphorical river to become emperor himself that is needed when it comes to European policy in the UK. These qualities are not demonstrated by the government in his opinion, which is why Ashdown gives only a concessional "welcome" to their policy decisions. In a threefold anaphora, he begins every sentence with such a discursive welcome and then qualifies it twice with the words "even though", when the shortcomings in the process are voiced. He critics the slow pace and lack of decisiveness as well as the perceived unwillingness to stand up for the decision. By using the words "truth" and "pretend" to indicate that the government do not openly communicate their policy decisions, Ashdown implies that they have not been honest and frank before, which reflects badly on the Labour government. Additionally, he justifies his third welcome with the accusation that they have not "defend[ed] their position" in the past, but which they will have to do after this statement in his view. This underlines the importance of public discourse that Ashdown believes in, and it also shows that he favours a top-down approach of representative politics in the case of the euro. The government should make a decision and then defend it publicly, in the tradition of parliamentary discourse so traditional to the UK.

> The statement has two levels: the level that one sees, and the level that one is supposed not to see. The level that one sees is the perfectly sensible statement about measures to be taken in preparation for the euro. We welcome those measures, which are sensible, realistic and practical. I am glad that they will be debated and voted on in the House.
>
> The level of the statement that we are not supposed to see is the continuation of the Government's policy of leadership by stealth. They move forward a millimetre at a time, but sooner or later they arrive at a point from which they cannot go back. That point has been arrived at today.
>
> I have a question for the Prime Minister. Today he has been attacked by the Tories, and tomorrow he will be attacked by the Tory, Euro-sceptic press. Does he then leave the position undefended, or does he leave it to others—such as the CBI and the other organisations that he has just mentioned—to defend it for him?
>
> All those organisations have shown more leadership on the issue than the Government, but the Prime Minister cannot leave it to them. The Government will have to defend their position: they can follow a policy of stealth, but they cannot win a referendum by stealth. Unless the Government are prepared to come forward and argue the case for the euro, they risk this decision, the most important that Britain has to face, being lost by stealth. [HON. MEMBERS: "Hear, hear."] That response shows what that lot on the

Conservative Benches want to happen. That is the policy that the Government are currently following.

Is it not a tragedy for Britain, as this country faces the most important decision that it
will face in the next two or three decades, that the Government take the view that they
want to join the euro but try to pretend that they do not, and that the Tories take the
position that they want to get out of Europe but try to pretend that they do not?

I have a single, specific question for the Prime Minister, which will reveal his intentions.
He has told us that he wishes there to be a referendum early in the next Parliament,
which means that the necessary legislation must be passed in this Parliament. Does he
understand that? [Official Report, 23 February 1999; Vol. 326, c. 187–188]

Proceeding with his speech, Ashdown then claims that there are two sides to
the statement: the openly communicated part of the statement is welcomed and
described as "perfectly sensible" (sensible is repeated) and "realistic and practical". With this praise, the Lib Dem leader clearly demonstrates which values he
condones as an acceptable basis for political decision. Next, however, Ashdown
addresses the alleged subtext of the statement. Once again, by phrasing this "a
level one is not supposed to see" and later specifying "we are no to see", Ashdown
implies that the Labour government is trying to hide important facts from a
group, "we", which might include the listeners – MPs as well as voters who might
follow the debate online, on TV or as a live audience, but seems more likely to
mean everyone not in government, thus establishing a divide between members
of government and the rest of British citizens. This frame is further emphasised
by the phrasing "leadership by stealth" that is repeated here and adds a clan-
destine and criminal element to the lack of transparency bit. This portrayal of
the governing elite as deliberately trying to dupe voters or even lie by omission
leaves a negative impression and might propel a further estrangement and distrust among voters. As an opposition strategy, this might be understandable, but
the danger is that dishonesty is associated with every politician in power, which
can backfire.

Although the Lib Dem leader has always argued in favour of making a commitment to join, he criticises the slowness he perceives in the government action,
and thus reveals that he prefers swift and efficient decision-making as a sign of
strength and good governance. He then claims that even by inching forwards,
a point of no return has been reached with this statement. Then he predicts the
impending attacks by opponents of EMU. Both seem not very positive or inviting
prospects. He frames the CON and parts of the press that sympathises with their
"Eurosceptic" views as the enemy (or main opponent) says the decision must
be "defended". This metaphorical realm of conflict and fight stands for the discursive battle of words to establish and ensure the hegemony of the respective

point of view and points out inner-British conflict lines and cleavages. The CON is described as completely and uniformly Eurosceptic, which is intended as an offence or negative ascription to "that lot on the Conservative benches". Furthermore, it is a sweeping judgement of parts of the press that Ashdown portrays as a mouthpiece of the former and thus not independent or objective but basically political actors (see e.g. Daddow 2012).

The values of bravery and courage and backbone are implied in the question if the Blair government will leave it to business organisations to "defend" his position and thus making him out to be a coward if he does so. The issue of a referendum on joining the single currency is brought up again here and the need for a public campaign is highlighted, where taking a stand in order to win support for the decision to join is portrayed as essential. Otherwise, he paints a scenario where the referendum is "lost by stealth". This prediction will arguably come true 17 years later. This "risk" he speaks of concedes that there is vocal and large opposition on the topic but also shows that the Lib Dem leader believes the main discourse actors to be newspapers and opposition politicians when it comes to influencing voters. This basic assumption of the nature of the political suggests that it is a question of winning the debate and that pro-Europe discourse in public, i.e. making a compelling argument in favour of the EU, will sway voters in favour of the euro. This implies that voters are not independent and do not really have a mind of their own but that they will vote on a principle of European integration on the basis of who makes the better campaign. A desire to emulate the 1975 referendum, where the campaign to stay within the common market succeeded in making up lost ground in the last months leading up to the vote and achieve the desired result, can be perceived here.

The last paragraph uses exaggeration to emphasise and drive home his message, appealing to pathos when Ashdown describes the current situation as a "tragedy for Britain". This imagined community of all dwellers in the country who are in the same boat and would all be negatively affected by what Ashdown claims is being in the middle between indecisiveness of the Labour government and the thinly disguised desire to exit the EU altogether discernible in the CON. This results in a stand-off in the face of "the most important decision that [this country] will face in the next two or three decades". This goes to the heart of the debate of 17 years later; parts of the CON had obviously advocated this position already in 1999. The fact that the CON leadership denied this, though, shows that at this time it was not part of an acceptable discourse.

The aim of the concluding dramatic "single, specific question" to the PM, provided the latter follows through with preparing for a referendum in the next parliament like he said, is to "reveal his intentions". This once again paints the PM as not open but cagey and possibly dishonest, but at least not willing to clearly say what his plans are unless pressed by the opposition. With the contingent element that Labour must win the next election to implement a referendum in the next Parliament, Ashdown aims to show that the PM has announced a goal but does not really mean to reach it, showing him again as not to be trusted and that his words might be empty.

"Amendment of the Law" (09.03.1999)

In the last mention of the single currency during his term of office, occasioned by the budget debate in March 1999, Ashdown claims that the government have finally decided to join but still try to dispute that fact. The necessity of a referendum to legitimise this decision is at this stage presented as natural and unquestionable so that it even goes without saying here. In essence, Ashdown says he knows better and the government try to keep the public in the dark but cannot fool the Lib Dems. He then goes on:

> As I told the Prime Minister a couple of weeks ago, we welcome the fact that the Government have inched across the Rubicon on joining the euro, even though they still try to tell us that they have not; but, once again, the Government will the end but do not will the means. Why is the commitment to join the euro when conditions are right not followed by the policies to make them right? That is what a Government should do if they are governing and leading the nation. A change of gear is not enough if no one is driving the car. [Official Report, 9 March 1999; Vol. 327, c. 200–205]

In this part of the debate, Ashdown reminds the listeners of the Rubicon metaphor again and claims that "once again", implying a pattern of behaviour, the government "will the end but not the means". This is to say that the goals of both Labour government and the Lib Dems converge but that the former are not courageous and proactive enough to use their power to bring the goal about. Ashdown suggests that it is easy and the government must just follow the course of action he recommends. He does not accept the reason that economic conditions are not conducive but insists on the government's ability, should they "will" it, to change these conditions and thus reach the goal. A referendum is not mentioned, and it really seems that the Lib Dem leader believes in executive as well a parliamentary power which should govern the country. Using strong words in the end, Ashdown finishes his paragraph on the single currency with the scathing remark that "a change of gear is not enough if no one is driving the car", thus disputing that the current government do exactly this and that the "nation" is without governance and leadership at this time. This is the first use of the word "nation" meaning the United

Kingdom, thus establishing an imagined community that needs and deserves a powerful leader. Ashdown constructs the question of joining the euro as a debate on leadership and power, and the relation between governing and governed.

7.1.2 Charles Kennedy

In this first speech by Charles Kennedy as new leader of the Lib Dems in which the single currency is addressed, the main topic of the debate is actually agriculture:

"Food and Farming" (20.10.1999)

> The second much broader issue is that of the single currency. I am glad that Britain in Europe campaign was launched last week and that it has a healthy degree of cross-party support, which is important. The Government must recognise, however, that there has been a significant change in grass-roots farming opinion on this matter. My view is based on discussions that I have had in the past couple of years. Because of the strength of the pound over the past period, the increasing perception among the agricultural community in this country is that a commitment on the part of this country to a single currency would be in the long-term interest of UK agriculture.
> [...]
> I appreciate that the Minister is constrained by the policy of the Chancellor, the Foreign Secretary and the Prime Minister, who from time to time seem to have the same policy on this issue. None the less, I hope that he will acknowledge that there will be real long-term benefits to British agriculture if we are coherently and sensibly part of a single trading currency zone within Europe.
> [...]
> No one who has considered the issue sensibly would argue that the single currency is the panacea for all ills in the agricultural sector or elsewhere. Of course it is not. It is a technical as well as a political and a constitutional judgment. On balance, it brings merits and benefits and that is why I am in favour of it for agriculture, as for other things.
> [Official Report, 20 October 1999; Vol. 336, c. 444–450]

Kennedy mentions the "Britain in Europe campaign" and expresses his support for it by acknowledging his "gladness". The fact that he addresses the "healthy degree of cross-party support" aims critically at the principle of collective responsibility, which is violated by ministers pulling in different directions. The split over the euro is thus not only a problem for internal party cohesion, but also a government problem in that cabinet is not united. The "cross-party support" that Kennedy welcomes is thus an attempt to build a consensus round this controversial issue and simultaneously a concession that other ways and means outside of parliament are needed to organise support for Europe because the fault lines in this regard are not represented by the party system any more. Therefore, traditional politics are not able to generate a sensible decision because party allegiances and splits block the process.

Kennedy legitimises his own position by saying he talked to farmers and thus establishes a connection to ordinary people with real concerns, the currency directly affecting their livelihoods. He characterises them as a coherent group, the "agricultural community in this country", and indicates that they are well aware of changed circumstances. Unabashedly, Kennedy says he picks up on this "changed perception", demonstrating that he is responsive to people's concerns which in turn duly influence his behaviour as a politician. Moreover, he claims that the discourse about it matters. Kennedy styles himself as a real representative of the people who is responsive and truly advocates voters' wishes. Moreover, he claims that the strong British currency hurts their chances when exporting to the world market – yet this is a mainly macro-economic argument since it neither primarily applies to consumers in the UK nor to exports to the EU common market where prices for some agricultural products are still fixed at this point in time (Roederer-Rynning 2015: 197). Thus, the case for joining the euro is subtly made but also the rightful place of the UK as a strong trading power who can compete in the global marketplace is defended.

Kennedy proposes that there will be positive outcomes of a decision to be "part of a single trading currency zone within Europe". The emphasis is on the benefits for trade and the word "Europe" is used, not the more accurate concession that only some EU member states adopt the euro at this point. The connection through trade is thereby further underlined. This alternative proposal is justified with the adverbs "coherently and sensibly" which also transports the values as coherence and common sense, i.e. pragmatic and objectively beneficial decisions as opposed to ideological reasons. He predicts "real long-term benefits to British agriculture". The argument is hence centred around British macro-economic interests and not even individual British people or groups of people anymore, and no values like European solidarity or togetherness are mentioned. The line of argumentation is unashamedly self-interested.

In the last paragraph, he repeats the adverb "sensibly", thus really focusing on pragmatic, hard-headed decision and shaking off any claim that the Lib Dems just love Europe. Hence, Kennedy refutes the impression that he is not aware of risks or disadvantages but presents the case like an accountant who has done the sums and decided on this completely cold-blooded and rational basis. Tellingly, Kennedy describes the decision to join the euro as a "technical, as well as a political and constitutional judgement". Politicians thus seem like external experts who simply have to decide on the basis of figures which way to turn. All emotions or reservations are thus brushed aside as belonging to the realm of emotion and illogical qualms because it is only the balance that counts in the end – and it is tipped in favour of the euro. The Lib Dems present themselves as the true party of business indeed, and the euro as a technical project not inspiring anything emotional or solidarity i.e. the feeling of connectedness with others but a purely rational and calculated business arrangement or investment. This line of argumentation treats all feelings as non-legitimate sources for political decisions and denies their importance; a strategy which was also adopted in the remain campaign, with the well-known results.

"Debate on the Address" (17.11.1999)

Another huge omission from the Queen's Speech was mention of an issue of great importance for the United Kingdom, now and for the future—the single currency. Liberal Democrat Members have stated our position on the issue, and—to be fair— Conservative Members have stated their many positions on it. However, we need the Government to give the country a lead on it. A single currency preparations Bill would help the country to prepare sensibly for the euro, if the British people decide in a referendum that they want it. The Government's policy is to prepare and decide. That is fine, but first they must prepare. Britain in Europe is one thing, but Britain's long-term interests in Europe are another and they are suffering as a result of indecision and timidity at the top. [Official Report, 17 November 1999; Vol. 339, c. 32–38]

In this part of the 'Debate on the Address' opening the new parliamentary session 1999/2000, Kennedy criticises that the government did not put the single currency into the Queen's Speech by describing it as a "huge omission", a hint that the government did not want to draw attention to it by letting it slip under the table. Kennedy leaves no doubt as to the level of importance he attaches to this "issue of great importance for the United Kingdom, now and for the future". He points out that the Lib Dems stand united behind their policy proposals, and voices a negative side remark to the apparent disunity and indecision within the CON on the issue. He repeats his call for a stronger leadership: "we need the Government to give the country a lead on it". The use of "we" could include all MPs, or all British voters, or all British people, who depend on the government taking action. He clearly spells out his alternative means-end premise: a "single currency preparations Bill", depending on the condition that a nation-wide referendum will be held. Kennedy claims that this "would help the country prepare sensibly for the euro", explicitly letting the value of sensibility shine through. Policy decisions should, therefore, allow sensible, foresighted actions by business people as well as establish an economy-friendly climate where businesses can plan. He says all living in the UK, "the country", are affected and have to prepare for it. It appears, however, as if he means mainly businesses, because for consumers it does not make much of a difference. The Lib Dems thus adhere to the view that macro-economic positive trends are the basis for the well-being of the entire society.

The referendum is mentioned in passing, not even an entire sentence, yet it consistently crops up in the alternative policy proposals by the Lib Dems. It seems that this part has become firmly established as a consensus and that even though they are in favour of joining, they obviously judge a referendum neces-sary and thus degrade the parliamentary majority of Labour as insufficient to make a policy decision here. This begs two important questions pertaining to the reason for the Lib Dem calls for a referendum on the single currency: does this mean that the decision is just too far-reaching and important or do they sub-scribe to the view that the public is not well represented in the current political system in the UK? Both options are equally possible, but both would undermine the current political system in the UK which rests on the legitimacy of elected MPs forming a majority in Parliament.

Finally, the Lib Dem leader says that "Britain in Europe is one thing, but Britain's long-term interests in Europe are another and they are suffering as a result of indecision and timidity at the top". He claims to be the political party leader whose only agenda is to serve the "long-term interest" of the UK, which implies that the other party leaders also have other motives. As opposition party without participation of government for decades, this is maybe an easy point to make. Kennedy also implies that the cross-party "Britain in Europe" campaign is a good thing, but not nearly enough.

"Helsinki European Council" (13.12.1999)

> On the issue of the withholding tax, the Prime Minister said, tellingly but not altogether revealingly: "I have made it clear that we will not permit that". What does that mean? Does that mean, as far as the eurobond market is concerned, that he will be willing to exercise a British veto, come Oporto in June? It would be helpful if he would clarify that issue. Finally—
> [...]
> Will the Prime Minister none the less acknowledge that the mood music in terms of the summit was that Britain is clearly not playing the central leading role in Europe that it should? It cannot and it will not until Britain and the British Government are more unambiguous about our commitment to the single currency, and about being fully plugged into the European project as a whole. [Official Report, 13 December 1999; Vol. 341, c. 28–29]

In his statement on the Helsinki EU Council meeting results, Kennedy focuses his question on the "eurobond market" and a possible British veto at the next EU council, due to concerns about the withholding tax. This shows how anxious the Lib Dem leader is to not antagonise the UK's European partners. If the UK does not take part in further integration steps, at least it should not put obstacles in the others' way by "exercis[ing] a British veto". Kennedy clarifies his line of argumentation that being on good terms with the other EU member states and to at least appear to support the "European project" where the UK is not fully taking part yet is the only way to achieve the government's goal of occupying a "central leading role in Europe". Put simply: it is in the long-term national interest to go along with European integration because it will ameliorate the UK's bargaining power and influence. This means accepting some things against the short-term inclination of voter or party members or at least take a risk by joining the single currency, even if this may go against the public mood or surveys saying this might be an unpopular decision. This course of action is justified by the promised outcome of gaining more power in the future. Clearly, the Lib Dem leader sees the EU as the main power option for the UK's future, thus excluding nostalgic "we are the great nation that has once governed the empire and will do fine on its own" but acknowledges that the UK will need strong partners to matter in a multipolar world. Interestingly, the "special relationship" with the USA is not mentioned and the only sensible choice they see is to go along with the European Union. Nevertheless, their aim or standard is that the UK "should" play a central leading role. So, if it can no longer rule the waves along with many countries on its own any more, at least the UK should be at the top table of the only viable power bloc option open to them.

In order to achieve this goal, Kennedy says the government should convince the European partners that they are fully on board and stop being "ambiguous" about the policy concerning the single currency, i.e. to become a reliable partner and full-scale member of the EU to then take the lead. The values brought up here include rational behaviour and power politics, the national interest, and being a leading power.

"Engagements" (16.02.2000)

Has the Prime Minister seen the reports in today's press that the entrepreneur James Dyson, who is to commit a significant sum involving a substantial number of jobs, is likely to invest that sum in China, Hong Kong and Malaysia because of the strength of the pound and the uncertainty over the Government's commitment to the euro? Does the Prime Minister not recognise that, if we are losing investment opportunities of that kind, the Government need to make the case for the euro and promote the cause of Europe more strenuously?

[...]

Surely the Prime Minister must engage more seriously, given the serious campaign that
has been launched by the leader of the Tory party. If ever there was a case of dodgy
goods falling on to the back of a truck, that is it.
Does the Prime Minister not recognise that sentiment is slipping away from the sensible
pro-European case, and that those of us in all parties who have shared a platform—
including the former Tory Chancellor, the former Tory Deputy Prime Minister, himself,
myself and others—must redouble our efforts to make the case, and to win in our vital
national interest? [Official Report, 16 February 2000; Vol. 344, c. 942]

During PMQs, Kennedy mentions the example of well-known British businessman James Dyson's decision to invest overseas instead of at home and puts
it down to the strength of the pound and uncertainty over the euro, both of
which he attributes to the government's policy regarding the single currency. He
concludes that in order to retain direct investment in the UK, business leaders
must have transparency over future currency conditions in the UK. Kennedy
argues that the government must "make the case for the euro and promote the
cause of Europe more strenuously". This argument seeks to align rational pro-
business policy and the national interest with joining the euro and, maybe more
importantly, sell this decision to the public by making the case for it and pro-
moting it. The discourse reality that Kennedy establishes here implies that elites
understand business rationale and must, therefore, act accordingly to preserve
jobs for their voters, and that they must explain what they do and why they do
it to voters, i.e. take the issue of democratic accountability seriously. This ideal
of being in contact with voters is combined, however, with the rather patriarchal
belief that voters will demurely accept decisions when their betters tell them they
are for the best.

Kennedy introduces urgency by drawing attention to the opposing forces in
action, led by William Hague and his "save the pound" campaign. He claims
that they are "serious" about trying to sway public opinion against the "sensible pro-European case". This highlights his preference for "sensible", rational
decision, like a businessman, as opposed to irrational, emotional campaigns
which he qualifies as "dodgy" in the metaphor of stolen goods falling on a truck,
a clear reference to the bus tour of the "save the pound" campaign. He calls for
a cross-party campaign to counter this narrative which he is obviously worried
might be successful if left unchallenged. The voters are seen as sheep following
the most confident guide, or rather running scared of an uncertain way ahead
even if it led to greener pastures.

The use of the word "vital" as an attribute to "national interest" again injects
urgency into his call for action, conjuring up the image of a danger that needs to
be faced by (former) allies and fighters for the European cause, and says those

"must redouble their efforts". In short, Kennedy sees leadership as telling the voter why a certain decision is crucial for the sheer survival of the UK, mostly in economic terms, but possibly also regarding power and influence on the global scale. He concludes that the Lib Dems can, therefore, not leave this important matter to others determined to wreck it. So, while the government appears inactive and weak, the Tories are portrayed as irrational and dangerous because they do not have the national interest at heart.

"Amendment of the Law" (21.03.2000)

In a week that has seen the massive problems with Rover, the country will be amazed that the Budget did not touch on the priorities of the wider economic context: the strength of the pound and the failure to give a lead on British entry to the euro. That is hitting manufacturing—Longbridge, obviously, in particular—and surely the Government must accept their share of the responsibility, however the management of BMW may have acted recently.

The uncertainty created by the fence-sitting on the euro is deterring inward investment and pushing up the value of the pound. That, coupled with high interest rates, which are twice those of our European competitors, constitutes a double whammy. It is worth recording that since last November, the trade deficit has doubled, rising from £10 billion to £20 billion. It is a remarkable Budget that makes no reference to any of those facts. [Official Report, 21 March 2000; Vol. 346, c. 883]

In the budget debate of 2000, Kennedy then connects the strength of the pound and the crisis of a well-known British car manufacturer (in the hands of the German brand BMW at the time) to the "failure to give a lead on British entry to the euro". He, therefore, not only directly links the two economic developments but also puts the blame on the government, basically accusing them of failure to assist the economy in danger and thus weak leadership, inaction, and economic illiteracy, or, even worse, carelessness even when British jobs are in danger.

He also insinuates that the Labour government are shying away from "accept[ing] their share of the responsibility" for the crisis at Rover and try to cover up this failure by not mentioning either this or any other problems facing the economy, i.e. trying to bury evidence of their own incompetence. Once again, the Lib Dem leader presents deciding to join the single currency as the cure to remedy economic problems within the UK, and mainly in the manufacturing sector.

Among the further problems Kennedy attributes to the government's "fence-sitting", i.e. not committing to either joining or not joining, are uncertainty in the economic climate and determent of inward investment. The strength of the pound at the time is also repeated, which according to Kennedy resulted in the doubling of the trade deficit. High interest rates add their bit to the "double whammy" hitting the British economy. The economy is clearly portrayed as a victim of a series of unfortunate events and the Labour government does nothing to help in the words of the Lib Dem leader.

"European Council (Lisbon)" (27.03.2000)

> The Prime Minister is right to say that, where Britain takes a lead, we can benefit in Britain and Europe benefits with that. Where the Government is still not taking a sufficient lead is on the issue of the euro. Given the generally positive response that he had at the weekend, will he and his colleagues redouble their efforts so that we make continuing constructive progress in Europe, and do not disappear up the cul de sac that the Conservative party [sic] is offering? [Official Report, 27 March 2000; Vol. 347, c. 27]

In the statement on the European Council meeting in Lisbon, only days later, Kennedy repeats the Lib Dem argument that "where Britain takes a lead, we can benefit in Britain and Europe benefits with that". This remarkable order shows that Kennedy uses the patriotic or even imperial tone that where the British dominate, others will benefit, like birds eating the breadcrumbs of a mighty leader. It also shows a UK-centred approach that has nothing to do with idealist pro-Europeanness but is about rational and utilitarian profit-maximisation which can be achieved by the proxy or means of European cooperation. This is at least what it looks like, it could also be possible that such a pro-Europeanness is disguises as rational "national interest" politics because this is deemed a more useful or successful narrative. This is underlined by the goal the Lib Dem leader gives out, namely making "continuing constructive progress in Europe". The double use of "we" in this context is interesting because it constructs an imagined community of pro-European British people who are united by the same goal. This should appeal both to voters and also to other MPs who share this view and might feel included in this deictic "we".

The CON's European policy receives a rhetoric slap by being described as a "cul de sac" and thus no alternative for anyone wanting to progress or indeed go somewhere at all. Following their means-goal premises would result in the imagined community of British citizens to "disappear", a prediction which others have repeated both in the run-up to and in the wake of the Brexit referendum called by the CON in 2016.

"Engagements" (17.05.2000)

> When the Secretary of State for Northern Ireland said last night that as long as we remained outside the euro we could not protect our industry against an overvalued pound, was he on-message or off-message?

[...]

As the Prime Minister has had some time to think about the position since the Chancellor's statement, can he give the benefit of his analysis, as of today? When does he expect us to meet the Chancellor's economic criteria, and does he hope that we will meet the Government's criteria? Is it not about time that he began to give a real national lead? *The Prime Minister:* There are really three positions on the single currency. One is to rule it out as a matter of principle. The second is to say that we will join immediately. The third is to say that whether we join depends on the economic conditions being met. But the timing depends on the economic conditions. Unless the right hon. Gentleman believes that we should join now—

Mr. Kennedy indicated dissent. [Official Report, 17 May 2000; Vol. 350, c. 326–327]

On 17 May 2000, Kennedy uses both his questions to the PM during Engagements to point out conflicting messages coming from cabinet members concerning the euro and to criticise an apparent lack of transparent communication as well. The description of the status quo and the tool to remedy the situation mirrors the Lib Dem assessment and relies on three assumptions: that the pound is overvalued at the point of speaking, that this hurts the British industry sector, and that joining the euro is the only way to remedy this situation by bringing the pound exchange rate down. The Lib Dem leader uses the statement by a government member as a confirmation for the accuracy of his own policy proposals but mainly uses the incident to flag up discord within the cabinet because of the unclarity concerning the question of joining – or not joining, as it were.

He takes this up and demands a concrete timetable from the PM, as well as questioning the PM's own preferences and thus implying that the "five economic tests" are only a political excuse to avert making the decision. Kennedy obviously suspects that instead of shaping the future development in a way that makes meeting the tests and thus joining the single currency more likely, the government hides behind an economic reality they present as fixed and uninfluenceable. The Lib Dem view that the primacy of politics means influencing the development according to one's own preferences, the PM portrays the economic conditions as something of a natural context and the way of politics as acting according to these contextual factors. This touches on fundamental questions concerning the understanding of politics: should there be a primacy of politics or of the economy? Is it the visions and goals of an elected government that take precedence or is it the will of the people as expressed in opinion polls? It seems that the Lib Dems go for parliamentary sovereignty but make liberal economics a principle that good governance needs to respect in any case.

The answer by the PM tries to counter this 'discourse reality' by describing a different set of policy proposals to choose from that does not include the Lib

Dem alternative. Instead, he presents Labour's version as a third-way option, an outcome of rational and pragmatic reflection taking the economy into account, and the other two options as undesirable; either not joining "as a matter of principle", which would fall into the category of "Hard Euroscepticism" represented by the CON at the time, or "joining immediately" as a policy goal resulting from an idealist pro-Europeanism, which is how he sees the Lib Dem approach. Labour seeks to position itself as taking into account both arguments and coming up with a balanced solution that avoids "principle" and "ideology" but simply looks for the best solution for all concerned. Kennedy tries to rebut this view and get the audience to register that he objects to being put in the latter category and denies that he wants to join immediately, thus fighting against the ascription that the Lib Dems ignore economic conditions because their love for the euro makes them blind.[4]

"European Council" (21.06.2000)

In the next instance, which is the Lib Dem leader's comment on the results of the European Council meeting in June 2000, Kennedy repeats the causal chain of supporting or participating in European integration:

> Finally, on the euro, if the message—largely credible—of the summit was that, where Britain engages rationally and positively, effective influence can be exerted, does not the same argument apply to the development of the eurozone and our participation in it? Given that our influence is virtually nil because we do not subscribe beyond the position already adopted by the Government, whose words have been mixed words of late, does the Prime Minister recognise that those of us who favour increasing engagement in the argument are worried that the headcase tendency wants to take this country out of Europe? Membership of the euro is but a fig leaf for that argument. The danger is that the prepare-and-decide policy espoused by the Government is beginning to look very much like the wait-and-see policy of the right hon. Gentleman's predecessor. Will the Prime Minister at all costs resist the temptation to follow his predecessor's lead, which we know ended in tears? [Official Report, 21 June 2000; Vol. 352, c. 343–344]

---

4   It is interesting to see that Labour apparently feel they have to fight on both sides: against the 'right', with their principled Euroscepticism, and against the 'left' with their over-enthusiasm for European integration. In this line, their "wait and see" politics could in truth be perceived by themselves as a third-way style attempt to reconcile these two opposites. This could then, in turn, be perceived as half-heartedness by others and make it hard to stand up for this solution because it implies that both other sides are right to a degree. This lukewarm support for and cautiousness about the euro was arguably not enough to convince doubters.

Kennedy equals "effective influence" within the EU. He qualifies the necessary engagement as "rational[…] and positive[…]". He argues that this must hold true then for the question of the single currency as well, meaning that when the UK commits (even only in principle or for a later date) to join, they could influence the nature and architecture of the Eurozone, whereas staying outside or waiting means no such influence can be exerted. Once again, the point is that joining is only advocated because it would suit the national interest, a form of calculated power politics, or at least strategic pragmatism. In this regard, Kennedy laments that "our influence is virtually nil" at the moment of speaking because there is no clear commitment to joining. Whom he includes in the group designated with the pronoun "our" is open, but obviously more people than just the government which can travel to Brussels and try to get their position heard in the appropriate places. The community the Lib Dem leader imagines is clearly limited, however, and excludes any other European governments or citizens because he refers to different and also contrary influences which go against the British interest and which need to be countered or corrected. To do this, more power is needed on the European level and especially within the Eurozone group according to the Lib Dem leader.

Continuing, Kennedy remarkably describes the resistance against joining the euro as a "fig leaf" for a bigger "tendency to take this country out of Europe", thereby linking opposition to further European integration steps to opposition to the EU as a whole. This and the fact that he verbally puts himself in a group of people "who favour increasing engagement" show that he sees being pro-European as equal to supporting EU projects, even if "only" for the self-interested reasons shown above. He also admits that he is "worried" about the increasing acerbity of the debate and campaign positions, which he claims are getting more radical. This is also a criticism of the CON, which he effectively accuses of campaigning for a "Hard" Eurosceptic policy but passing it off as a "Soft" Euroscepticism, which refers to rational and reasoned opposition against certain aspects of the EU on the grounds of logical arguments. He thus expresses his worry that the debate has left the realm of logic and finding the best solution for the UK but that it is more about fundamentals, about principles which cannot be reconciled but will result in a rift.

The Lib Dem leader ends his statement with the likening of Labour's policy on the euro to that of the CON PM Major's – and not to an advantage. He gives the outlook that the current government's policy might "end in tears" like that of John Major. Surprisingly, he says that this path constitutes a "temptation" which needs to be "resist[ed]" thereby framing what he terms "wait and see" as a comfortable choice, probably because it is easier to do nothing and react to developments than to develop a coherent strategy and defend a controversial decision which risks also the split of the party and/or cabinet.

"Engagements" (05.07.2000)

> While I acknowledge the welcome level of investment that has been recorded today, what does the Prime Minister make of the opinion that was expressed to him and the Foreign Office by our ambassador in Japan? The ambassador said that there is a perception among Japanese business men that, unless this country gets firmly on track for membership of the euro, additional future investment will entail unnecessary costs and doubts. Does the Prime Minister agree with his ambassador's analysis?
> [...]
> On the euro, Richard Branson wrote this morning: outside the Euro...we will be much poorer both as a nation and as individuals. Did the Prime Minister notice that? Does he disagree with Mr. Branson as well as his ambassador in Japan? Is he not in danger of allowing his "prepare and decide" policy to slip into the "wait and see" policy that had such disastrous consequences for his predecessor? [Official Report, 5 July 2000; Vol. 353, c. 326]

During PMQs in July 2000, Kennedy repeats his point that the "prepare and decide" mantra by the Labour government is just the same as the "wait and see" favoured by Major. He departs from the assumption that Major toppled over inner-party conflict on Europe and uses this negative example as a warning: this time, he specifies the consequences as "disastrous". He also uses this assumed causal link between indecision on European policy and loss of power as a legitimisation for his assumption that a change in policy approach would lead to a different, positive result.

The Lib Dem leader quotes the British ambassador to Japan, a senior and distinguished civil servant, as someone sharing his point of view to make it appear objectively correct. The claim is that not only the Lib Dems see the delay in deciding on joining as resulting in "unnecessary costs and doubts" regarding trade relations and foreign investment within the UK. Furthermore, famous and successful businessman Richard Branson is quoted to lend even more credibility and force to the Lib Dem proposals. These authorities are brought up to highlight that the current government policy is not rational and not in the interest of the country, epitomized by its economy. Interestingly, this is the first time that in the list of beneficiaries, the imagined community of a "nation" is mentioned first but is also followed by "individuals". This is one instance of trying to move the discourse from a macro-level to every single member of it. Content-wise, the claim is that everyone and the nation as a whole would be negatively affected in terms of money, i.e. become "poorer". This is an argument that once again only targets people's pockets, not their hearts and minds. The values or discourse reality behind this is that if you are rich, you are intelligent and competent to tell others about complex economic causalities – but also that you are right and assumed to be convincing because all people strive to maximise their own financial gain or at least do not want to lose any of their money. This is the typical 'homo oeconomicus' logic. Also, there is an idea of progress hidden in this argument: joining the euro and thus participating further in EU integration goes hand in hand with the promise of accumulating wealth, whereas staying behind means losing out on this steady increase in wealth.

"Engagements" (12.07.2000)

In the following PMQ session, Kennedy says that "Whatever view the Conservatives may express on the euro, the Liberal Democrats, in acknowledging that it is both inevitable and desirable, certainly agree with the Foreign Secretary—very happily so" [Official Report, 12 July 2000; Vol. 353, c. 863]. Using the word "inevitable" is not a very positive way of phrasing this since it denies any other options, similar to the word *alternativlos* in German political discourse. The Lib Dem leader hereby tries to present his view as the only credible one and reinforces this message by quoting the agreement with the Foreign Secretary, seeking to increase his credibility by apparent cross-party consensus. The attribute "desirable" which is added to this allegedly inevitable development seems not very convincing, rather like a honeyed trap or the soothing resignation into something one cannot change anyway. This argumentation might spark instinctive protest in a society where values like freedom are important. However, the Lib Dem leader seems to think that rational submission to one's destiny is a virtue to be followed regarding the single currency. Kennedy underlines his agreement with the Labour government member and also the difference between the CON, whose arguments he dismisses as insubstantial or plainly wrong ("whatever they say"), and the former two parties.

"G8 Summit" (24.07.2000)

My second question concerns the report, not referred to in the statement – it may be accurate, or it may be inaccurate – that the Prime Minister was at pains to reassure his Japanese hosts that he intended, in a future Parliament, to move as quickly as possible towards a referendum on the issue of a single European currency and to take a positive stance on such a referendum. Is that report accurate? If so, what comments did the Prime Minister's opposite numbers make? [Official Report, 24 July 2000; Vol. 354, c. 768]

When Kennedy's intervention in the debate on the "G8 Summit" turns to the euro, the main issue is again a lack of transparency over the government's concrete plans on how to proceed with a referendum asking the public whether to join the single currency. By bringing up an unconfirmed report whose accuracy is doubted by himself, the Lib Dem leader puts it on the official record and thus lends it credibility or at least brings it more attention. This shows that he seeks to highlight the government's failure to communicate clearly and beyond doubt and also insinuates that he is more open and honest with partners abroad than with the British MPs or British voters. While in principle, judging from the speeches they made before, the Lib Dems are in favour of the course of action discussed here, Kennedy nevertheless uses this as an opportunity to show the government in a bad light and to cast doubt on their motives when it comes to a referendum on the single currency and a concrete timetable for it. This does, arguably, not serve the cause to generate support for the policy and rather plays into populist extreme right or left claims that the government does not have the nation's best interests at heart but that the PM cooperates with foreign powers to generate economic advantages for the business elite.

"Nice European Council" (11.12.2000)

In his comment on the PM's statement on the Council meeting, Kennedy asks rhetorically:

> Does he concur with Chris Patten that, to use his word, it would be 'barking' to deny the people of Britain a referendum on a single currency while imposing one in respect of the treaty of Nice? That position is completely illogical. [Official Report, 11 December 2000; Vol. 359, c. 356–357]

This short intervention pertaining also to the single currency touches on the deeper issue of public support and legitimate decision-making power when it comes to committing the UK to further EU integration steps. Who has the right to decide these things? Is parliamentary sovereignty or direct democracy the leading principle? And is a referendum needed because there was, by way of a new treaty, a further step towards "ever-closer union" or because joining the euro represents such a fundamental change in domestic politics or on the constitutional level, handing over a significant sovereign right to the EU? It becomes clear that European policy and the referendum question are now deeply entangled, regardless of which actual policy area is concerned and regardless of the actual scale of the integration step. It seems there is a general unease with proceeding on any terms, a position that has left the realm of reason or rationality, described in Kennedy's comment with the words "barking" [mad] and "completely illogical".

The people who are the alleged victims or affected recipients of such a mad decision are termed "the people of Britain", imagining a community of people that are duped by their government. It is also remarkable that Chris Patten, the former CON MP and minister who was the British European Commissioner at the time, is quoted as an authority. With his EU office, he is supposedly well-informed on the best way for the UK to engage effectively with the EU, and the fact that he goes against the line of his former party is sure to be registered. But this instance might be interpreted quite differently by listeners who are suspicious of his loyalties now that he works in Brussels. The Lib Dem leader quotes a figure of authority, an expert, but he might not convince everyone that this is for the British national interest.

This passage shows that for the Lib Dems, European policy decision should be based on rational reasoning, and the option which is best for the British economy should be chosen by voters in a referendum. At the same time, people from the (political) elite tell them which option is best beforehand. This world-view completely ignores any other motives to make a political decision. They also claim to not understand the position that a referendum should be held for every further step of European integration to take heed of public opinion or surveys indicating unease with the EU, but qualify it as "mental". Thus, it does not even need to be taken seriously but can be easily dismissed because the people advocating it are obviously not capable of making a sane decision. Eurosceptic opposition to any further deepening of the EU is thus disqualified as an illegitimate position, deviating from the norm of rational pragmatic thinking. The fact that the government is associated with it in the Lib Dem leader's discourse makes this criticism bear very heavy.

"First Day" (20.06.2001)

May I raise a specific point about the politics of the euro, the single European currency, which does not feature in today's Queen's Speech? A couple of years ago, the Prime Minister, the Chancellor, myself, the former Deputy Prime Minister—now Lord Heseltine—and the former Chancellor all sat together in the Prime Minister's study the day before we launched the Britain in Europe campaign, and a very good, positive discussion we had, too. But, as is so often the way in party politics and cross-party politics, nothing has happened since the launch. We have had a mixture of mood music from the Cabinet, not least the Chancellor and the Prime Minister. We have had good cop one day, bad cop another.

On that issue, which will be a paramount issue in the politics of this Parliament, we must not repeat that mistake. The Prime Minister will have to follow on from the rather courageous speech that he made during the election campaign, setting out a constructive and rational case for Europe in general and the single currency in principle. That case will have to be made on an all-party basis to turn round public opinion in this country. Although the issue does not feature in today's Queen's Speech, it is an issue of principle and priority for this Parliament and, I hope, for this Government. [Official Report, 20 June 2001; Vol. 354, c. 61]

After Labour had won the second general election in a row in 2001, the government programme for the new parliament was discussed in the "First Day" debate in the House of Commons. In his contribution, Kennedy points out that the euro was not mentioned in the Queen's Speech, an omission from the official government programme he has criticised before and which he repeats in the last sentence of his statement. The euro is termed "the single European currency"; interestingly, the word "European" is mentioned in this context for the first time whereas before, it was only the referred to as the "single currency". Kennedy reminds the listeners of the cross-party "Britain in Europe" campaign that was launched one year previously and laments that "nothing has happened since the launch". With this, he admonishes that its efforts need to be revitalised. The problem and reason for this inactivity is attributed to the indecision and disunity among the government itself: "a mixture of mood music from the Cabinet" – a metaphor that brings in an emotional aspect and criticises the absence of collective responsibility. This is either weak leadership or the PM has not decided on his own preference or the issue of joining. It could also imply that the single currency is considered a matter of conscience by government members, not as a factual question. In the latter case, an interesting twist would be added since many Cabinets have been split over Europe and even in the actual in/out referendum in 2016, cabinet members campaigned on either side. It would mean that European integration cannot be debated on the same level with other political decisions but that the realm of the private and emotional is touched by it. This would be a further hint at the importance of identity in this context.

The second comparison Kennedy makes, namely "good cop, bad cop", points to the perception that the PM and Chancellor do not agree on the issue and appear to follow entirely opposite strategies. However, the popular concept of TV productions where two very different cops (have to) work together usually implies that both ways are crucial to solve the problem or catch the criminal in the end. In this case, the strategy would actually be a popular and usually successful strategy to approach a given challenge. The Lib Dem leader also highlights the theatrical and performative quality in this aspect of governing while at the same time deepening the impression that they treat the issue without enough respect or fail to see how serious and urgent it would be to address the question of to join or not to join. This is the aspect that he seeks to criticise; the Cabinet should act as a single body, which in the British political system is also supposed to speak with one voice. In this case, playing "good cop one day, bad cop another" would refer to the conflicting and unclear message by the government which has still not made clear when and if is their policy that the single currency should be joined. This would also introduce a normative evaluation in that "good" is associated with a clear decision in favour of joining, whereas "bad" is the delaying of any such decision or the obstructing of progress in the "join" direction. This then reflects the values and preferences of Kennedy.

In the next part, Kennedy terms the question of joining the euro one of "paramount" importance and an issue of "priority and principle" in the new Parliament. He further emphasises that a decision should be taken by describing the duality portrayed above as a "mistake". This clear judgement is the basis for the alternative policy proposals he puts out: make the case for Europe publicly and on an all-party basis to "turn round public opinion in this country". This is the first time he acknowledges that surveys show a majority of British voters do not want to join the euro, but he insists that this circumstance can be changed. This line of argumentation bears a strong resemblance to the situation in 1975, when public opinion before the first in/out referendum showed support for leaving at over 50 % only months before the actual vote, and the result was the opposite as a result of a massive cross-party campaign for staying in. This experience that public opinion can be influenced to support their case if the proponents believe in their case and credibly and vocally make the case for it leads Kennedy to the assumption that the exercise can be repeated. The values he favours become apparent in his praise for the PM's "rather courageous speech" in favour of the EU and his verdict of it being "constructive and rational".

"European Council (Laeken)" (17.12.2001)

Half a year later, still no decision has been made. During the House of Commons debate in December 2001 on the next European Council meeting, Kennedy brings up the timetable for the decision to join the single currency again and comes to an assessment of the government's strategy expressed with the word "over-caution": "Could the Prime Minister modify his over-caution on the euro by giving the House a clearer idea of any possible time scale vis-à-vis a referendum?" [Official Report, 17 December 2001; Vol. 377, c. 28]

He also implicitly criticises that there is no clarity and brings up the referendum as a natural step towards the eventual decision to join. His remark shows impatience and shows that he thinks clarity and transparency are important values in politics. In his view, opportunism and 'muddling through' are not acceptable. Instead, he urges a quick decision, i.e. what he perceives as efficient governance.

"European Council (Barcelona)" (18.03.2002)

> Does the Prime Minister acknowledge that, in the politics of this summit and increas-
> ingly in the politics of British involvement in the European Union, welcome and vital
> as that is—we obviously strongly support it—the fact that we do not have a clear time-
> table for a referendum on our participation in a successful single European currency
> is holding us back from making the diplomatic contribution that we could make in
> Europe?
> When that referendum campaign comes, we will want a broadly based coalition
> of interests, which will involve some Conservatives, the Government, the Liberal
> Democrats, the CBI and the TUC. To be seen cavorting with the likes of Berlusconi,
> given the response that that has elicited from John Monks, is not helping to build that
> long-term coalition for the referendum. [Official Report, 18 March 2002; Vol. 382,
> c. 26–27]

Taking the next Council meeting in Barcelona as an opportunity to mention the
euro once again, Kennedy starts out with making a self-description of his party
as a pro-European group ("we") who "obviously strongly support" the "welcome
and vital" "British involvement in the European Union". This shows that the
self-image and ascription of the Lib Dems coincide and that the use of the word
"obviously" suggests that the Lib Dem leader does not want any criticism of the
government's handling of EU policy to be misunderstood as opposition to the
EU itself.

He urges the PM to accept his view that making a decision on joining the euro
is necessary for the UK to play a full role in the EU and make "the diplomatic
contribution that we could". The use of the pronoun "we" in this case refers to the
UK delegations and office-bearers interacting with EU institutions, and includes
the listeners in an imagined community whose potential is not being used to the
fullest but held back by Labour's indecision or unclear timetable. Kennedy says
this precludes an adequate contribution not only on the limited scale of a single
summit and the issues debated and decided there but also in a more general way,
negatively affecting the whole relationship – if this can be read from the statement that criticises mostly the negative effects on the British position.

The referendum is presented as the compelling next step on the way to
deciding to join the euro; clearly, the Lib Dem leader no longer sees this as a
competence of the government but an issue that requires further legitimisation
by a popular vote. Consequently, he issues a repeated warning that the campaign for the desired outcome to join the euro needs cross-party support.
Interestingly, he once again uses the word "we", and in this case, it might refer to
all people in the UK advocating to join, thus expressing a clear social cleavage
along the pro-euro/anti-euro line. He enumerates whom he sees as part of this

community and makes an explicit concession that "some Conservatives" will take part. This shows a nuanced assessment but also makes the perceived split in that party apparent. The Labour Party is not explicitly mentioned but subsumed under the term "Government", while his own party, the Lib Dems, are enumerated as a united organisation, as are the CBI and the TUC. This list only contains elite/political organisations; this circumstance highlights the top-down approach favoured by Kennedy. By not mentioning public opinion at all, the impression is created that their views do not count for much but that it is the job of these "enlightened", rationally thinking people at the top to bring about a beneficial result – he says the single currency is "successful", making it illogical not to join from a purely rational point of view) – which will enhance the "diplomatic contribution" in further EU-UK interactions. The whole exercise thus seems a call to the elites to get themselves a stronger mandate so they can have a better position in future negotiations. The national interest is the nodal point here.

The final criticism is that the PM is not helping this "long-term coalition for the referendum" by meeting unpopular and perceived as irrational and corrupt Italian PM Berlusconi, as the latter obviously stands for the negative aspects of the EU. An association with him might thus deter potential British pro-Europeans from supporting or making the case for the EU publicly to avoid the impression of siding or agreeing with Berlusconi.

"Amendment of the Law" (17.04.2002)

There was one crucial issue on which the Chancellor chose not to dwell. He made only a teasing reference to the euro, rather than displaying leadership on it. As he well knows, the Liberal Democrats have long argued that it is high time we set a proper timetable for getting this country, post-referendum, into the single European currency. The reason why we must do so is precisely that to which the Chancellor and, indeed, the Conservative leader referred—the weakness of the manufacturing base caused by the strength of the pound.

One day we have got to win a referendum, but if we at least lay down clear guidelines and a timetable, that in itself, with the Government expressing an aspiration, would do much to reduce the value of sterling in the interim and stop the haemorrhaging of jobs right across the manufacturing sector.

We are very disappointed with the failure to show leadership and the conflicting smoke signals that the Chancellor and the Prime Minister all too often give out on that issue, but the Conservatives cannot with any intellectual or political rigour decry the decline in our manufacturing base while saying that they will positively deny the people a referendum and not join the euro at all. On that basis and policy prescription, the Conservatives cannot offer anything approaching a solution to the problems that have so badly afflicted the manufacturing sector. [Official Report, 17 April 2002; Vol. 383, c. 599–602]

In the next budget debate ('Amendment of the law'), Kennedy picks up the euro and refuses to let the Chancellor Brown get away with only mentioning it in passing: he once again terms it a "crucial issue" and accuses the government of not "displaying leadership on it". The word "teasing reference" he uses to express the, too short in his view, mention of it shows that he reproaches him with not taking the euro seriously enough or even take it for a game. He repeats the consistent Lib Dem line of argumentation that a "proper timetable for getting this country, post-referendum, into the single currency". He presents it as a no-alternative option by using the words "we must to do so", again including the whole country or at least its governing elites in the process and making a call for action simultaneously. He also gives a reason for his policy proposal: the strong pound which he says is the cause for trouble in the manufacturing sector. The fact that both the real and the shadow Chancellor referred to this and he can thus claim to depart from a joint acknowledgement of the status quo as problematic, he claims his solution strategy is the only one that would work. He unashamedly states that his goal is, therefore, to "get this country [...] into the single currency". It is a national economic problem and Kennedy claims here that the euro represents the means to reach this end. As a consequence everyone not using this means is a fool or at least responsible for the continuing problems. The referendum appears as a useless or low priority formality because the Lib Dem leader is bent on making everyone see that he is right and his preferred result is the only good one. He justifies this by saying he only wants to save the jobs in the manufacturing sector with it.

Kennedy then continues to address the referendum in more detail in the next paragraph, though. He concedes that "we have to win a referendum" at some point, using "we" to indicate that he counts himself among the politicians who will be campaigning for a yes vote. This imagined community of the sensible and positive ones is not a nation, but only a part of it – an interesting conception showing that when it comes to European policy, the Lib Dem leader draws clear boundaries between those in favour of doing what it takes to further the national interest and those willing to exploit negative human character traits to achieve the alleged opposite. He goes on to lay out a chain of events he says are causally related: announcing a timetable for a referendum and supporting a vote to enter the single currency would be enough, in his prediction, to demonstrate that entry was coming. This would result in a lower exchange rate of the pound. Kennedy implies that in this case, a weaker currency would help to bring prices for British products down in other countries and make them more affordable, which Kennedy hopes will result in selling more goods, resulting in lessening the negative trade balance at the time. Without explaining this economic context, which he thus makes appear as natural, common-sense and universally known, the Lib Dem leader directly jumps to the number of jobs in the British manufacturing sector, which he claims are "haemorrhaging". This vivid metaphor, together with a latter description of the sector being "badly afflicted", conveys the image of a severely wounded body and losing jobs would thus be tantamount to losing blood – with the injured person in danger of dying completely if too much blood is lost. This introduces urgency and accuses the government of non-assistance to a dying person – or a business sector in their "care" as politicians responsible for the economic policies. Kennedy's criticism is thus directed at Brown for not playing along and at Blair for not exercising his authority. Consequently, he brings in an emotional aspect when he concludes: "We are very disappointed with the failure to show leadership", basically portraying the Lib Dems as the wise and rational onlookers on a dispute costing lives because attention of the responsible people is diverted from the real problems. The Official Opposition receives a similar discursive slap: Kennedy says since they oppose the euro and a referendum on it, they cannot claim to be concerned with manufacturing sector either. Thus, only the Lib Dems appear to have the national interest at heart, or at least manufacturing workers' interests. The argumentative strategy used by Kennedy to delegitimise the policy proposals by Labour and CON are to describe both as lacking "intellectual or political rigour". The aim here is to make preparation for entering the single currency seem as the only possible remedy that may stop jobs from being lost in the UK.

"Engagements" (22.05.2002)

On a different issue, does he agree with his former policy director, the hon. Member for South Shields (Mr. Miliband), who this week signed a parliamentary motion that puts forward his view that the five economic tests for sterling's entry into the single currency have already been met?

[...]

Then here is the ideal opportunity for the Prime Minister to clarify what the Government's policy actually is. Given the conflicting signals over the past week coming from the Treasury and No. 10, has the Prime Minister ruled out introducing legislation in the Queen's Speech this autumn to enable a single currency referendum?

The Prime Minister: The position is entirely clear, as it always has been. We believe that if the economic tests are met and passed—that assessment has to be made before June 2003—we will put the issue to people in a referendum. That is clear, and it is different from the policy of the Conservative party [*sic*], which is against the single currency for

good, for ever and at any point in time, and the policy of the Liberal Democrats, which
is to enter the single currency even if the economic tests are not met and it is not in the
economic interests—
Mr. Kennedy: indicated dissent. [Official Report, 22 May 2002; Vol. 386, c. 286–287]

In PMQs on 22 May 2002, Kennedy references a motion signed by Labour
members claiming the five economic tests, the condition for considering joining
the euro, "have already been met". He picks out David Miliband, a former government minister, and stresses the latter's position as policy advisor to Blair. This
naturally puts pressure on the government as it shows their own MPs and among
them even senior members and confidants of the PM himself are not convinced
by the alleged objectivity of this condition. The tests are thus in danger of being
"unmasked" as a discursive make-believe to gloss over serious political disagreement at the heart of government. Kennedy draws attention to the fact that "conflicting signals" have been given out by the PM and his Chancellor and tries to
make the PM give a guarantee, a promise for which he can be held accountable.
It becomes clear that Kennedy is mainly concerned with preparing for a referendum – he asks whether appropriate legislation will feature in the coming
Queen's speech, thus trying to force the PM to commit to a clearer timetable than
the rather vague one in place now.

The PM's response is the "usual" one: he presents the economic tests as the
prerequisite and then makes out that the CON and Lib Dem policy proposals
on the euro are two extremes in which Blair chooses the third way, reconciling
both arguments with pragmatic hard-headedness when it comes to economics.
At least he volunteers the promise that an assessment will be made "before June
2013". Again, Kennedy registers his disavowal of this discourse reality in such a
pronounced manner that the official record shows he "indicated dissent" with
this description by the PM.

"European Council (Seville)" (24.06.2002)

On the central issue of the single European currency, however, does the Prime Minister
agree that the debate needs to be led in this country? It can be led only by the Prime
Minister and the Government, and the absence of a positive lead leaves us in the weakened position in which we saw ourselves as an EU member state last weekend in Spain.
[Official Report, 24 June 2002; Vol. 387, c. 616]

In his speech on the European Council in Seville, Kennedy qualifies the "issue
of the single European currency" as "central" and highlights that the Lib Dems
accord it a high priority, even though the Labour government might seek to
convey the impression that is was not of much salience. He draws attention
to "the debate in this country", which underscores the central role he accords

to public discourse when it comes to justify policy decisions. He accuses the PM of not having "led" and not leading the debate, and tries to get the PM to acknowledge that this needs to be done. In other words, Kennedy attributes the development of public opinion at the time as the result of the missing guidance in the right direction, implying a moral judgement. He then claims that the role of guiding wise men lies with the PM and his cabinet: "It can be led only by the Prime Minister and the Government". This is a direct call for action and also a plea for them to accept responsibility. As an opposition party leader of a third party in a majority government, Kennedy obviously feels he lacks the resources to sway public opinion in a direction he approves of himself, and to underline the urgency of his call for the PM to help, he claims that the "absence of a positive lead leaves us in the weakened position in which we saw ourselves in as an EU member state last weekend in Spain". The double use of "we" points to an imagined community which includes either every British person, or the representatives thereof who are the government. The Lib Dem leader clearly includes himself as well, which could mean he thinks the pro-European forces in British politics are the only group or community that matters in this respect. This is likely since he purports that only those can remedy the "weakened position" and make the UK stronger in Europe again. This quote also shows that Kennedy has a second imagined community in mind, namely that of "EU member states" which includes the UK and in which the latter should play a strong role. This can only be achieved with clarity on the euro, he argues.

This shows that the ideal conception behind Kennedy's calls for action is a UK that is a leader among the other EU member states, maybe comparable to the ideal that the UK is the leader of the Commonwealth members. This means that despite being for an integration and adoption of EU projects, the Lib Dems still favour a special, distinguished role of their own country in the community.

"Engagements" (03.07.2002)

Does the Prime Minister agree that the single European currency debate deserves better than being reduced to gross caricature, playing on people's fears and prejudices, of the type that we have seen in the already notorious broadcast issued today by the no campaign?

[…]

The Prime Minister may dismiss the matter lightly, saying that a joke is a joke, but the fact is that, for many communities in this country, this broadcast has generated considerable offence. What action will he take to sanction the Labour MPs who lent their names and their presence to this deplorable piece of advertising? [Official Report, 3 July 2002; Vol. 388, c. 218–219]

The next instance, during PMQs only a few days later, is occasioned by the publication of an anti-euro broadcast, which Kennedy sharply criticises. The fact that some MPs belonging to the governing Labour Party have "lent their names" to the "no campaign" is obviously perceived as treason or at least unhelpful rebellion by Kennedy and he demands that they be "sanction[ed] by the PM, probably also to ensure future party discipline in voting behaviour. It shows that the apparent split or diverging opinions within the Labour Party is perceived by Kennedy as a threat that needs to be addressed – otherwise, his policy objective of taking the UK into the single currency would be seriously endangered. Additionally, a majority of public opinion would be much harder to win in a possible referendum campaign if the governing party introducing the subject did not speak with a united voice on the issue. It also highlights that the benefits are not as clear to many other MPs and British voters as the Lib Dem leader portrays them in his speeches, or that other aspects play a major role in people's decision-making regarding the euro.

In order to remedy this situation, Kennedy portrays the MPs' actions in campaigning against the euro as morally flawed by using both his questions at PMQs to discredit the intervention as "reduc[ing the debate] to gross caricature, playing on people's fears and prejudices", the broadcast itself as "notorious" and a "deplorable piece of advertising". These adjectives and the accusation of populist methods and negative campaigning are designed to make the criticism appear in a bad light since they use illegitimate tools to further their goal, and thus do not act in the interest of the people but use their fears to manipulate them into backing their negative opinion of the euro. Instead of purporting a positive message in this instance, Kennedy thus condemns the actions of his political opponents regarding the single currency. He also cites "many communities in this country" which have been offended by the broadcast, thus portraying his own position as one winning support, too, and the others of not playing fair. And he accuses the PM of not doing enough to protect their interests against rhetoric appealing to the dark side in everyone, thus leaving the field to negative and destructive forces seeking to dominate the discourse.

"European Council" (28.10.2002)

Will the Prime Minister acknowledge that our country would have greater leverage, not least on agricultural reform, if we were seen to be more of an active participant at the top table in Europe, especially as we are the fourth largest economy in the world? Are we not in danger of missing the boat at the formative stage of the single currency in the same way as we did at the outset of the establishment of the CAP? Did the Prime Minister have bilateral discussions on the single currency with other Heads of Government over the weekend? In that context, when will the next bilateral summit between France and Britain take place, and what items does the right hon. Gentleman propose to discuss with the President of France? [Official Report, 28 October 2002; Vol. 391, c. 547–548]

Commenting on the outcome of the European Council in October 2002, Kennedy uses a rhetorical question to renew his claim that in matters European, generally "our country would have greater leverage [...] if we were seen to be more of an active participant at the top table in Europe". Coupled with the hint that "we are the fourth largest economy in the world", this statement leaves no doubt as to where the UK's rightful place should be: among the leading member states, wielding large influence on decisions and shaping the development of EU institutions and policies. This position is justified by the economic might generating pride and importance and lending the tools and weight to shape the world according to one's own wishes. The use of the word "leverage" also implies that negotiating partners are to be forced into complying with the UK's wishes and that "greater leverage" is thus a desirable asset in interaction with the other EU member states.

Although he mentions the CAP as a pertinent example, Kennedy then points out parallels between the UK's unhappiness with and inability to change this policy when he continues with the metaphor of "missing the boat". He claims that the problems with CAP arose from the fact that the UK was not at the negotiating table during "the formative stage" and thus says the UK could have intervened and changed the policy according to their own preferences. His argument is an analogy and thus uses the widespread frustration with the CAP in UK government circles to underline the urgency of his alternative policy proposal to join the euro rather sooner than later to avoid a second unpleasant situation like this. In the remainder of his intervention, Kennedy brings up the question of future meetings with "other Heads of Government" of EU member states concerning the single currency and singles out the French President among them. It is likely, therefore, that Kennedy considers the French president a crucial figure on the way to more British involvement in the single currency. These questions demonstrate that the Lib Dem leader is not willing to let matters rest and is determined that the UK should take their rightful place among the leaders of the EU. This shows that he believes British influence to be so far-reaching that once they decide to take part, they are strong enough to change policies to make them conform to their taste, rather than the apparent fear voiced by others that the UK will be drawn into something that infringes on their sovereignty without any chance to influence this destiny.

The Lib Dem version of events is thus more up-beat about the power and influence wielded by the UK than that of the CON in particular, but also simultaneously more pessimist that insisting on fundamental changes later will be futile. However, at least the picture of the UK in Europe is that of a country that has a choice and the power to create and modify, thus what Kennedy terms an "active participant". The Lib Dem leader thus advocates values of openness and pride in their own national interest and the confidence to seek to implement it in cooperation with the other EU members. The repeated use of the pronouns "we" and "our" in this speech indicate that Kennedy sees the aspects of this national interest as something all British politicians, himself included, should pursue and advocate, while the responsibility of having the appropriate talks with the French president is decidedly placed with the PM himself.

"Engagements" (27.11.2002)

> The fact is that the percentage of investment in the European Union that comes to Britain was 28 per cent. four years ago, 20 per cent. last year and currently stands at 16 per cent. How low must it go before the Prime Minister takes action, particularly by setting a timetable for a referendum on entry into the single currency? [Official Report, 27 November 2002; Vol. 395, c. 308]

In the next PMQ session, Kennedy tackles the issue of a falling share of EU investment in the UK, i.e. what the UK gets from being an EU member states in terms of FDI. This could also be termed the economic and financial benefits that the UK gets from being a member. Kennedy portrays the current situation as an undisputable problem by using the word "fact" and quoting numbers, a rhetorical device to make his statement appear rational and objective.

After the status quo has thus been characterised as flawed and in need of a remedy, the Lib Dem leader asks in a rhetorical question what more is needed to make the PM take action to address this undoubtedly bad development. The remedy Kennedy suggests is, once again, "setting a timetable for a referendum on entry into the single currency". This demonstrates again how confident Kennedy is that such a referendum can be won, once it is called, and that the consequences of taking the UK into the euro would be a brighter economic outlook for the UK. This economic, rational, numbers-based argument resembles the one many academics claim has been the basis for the UK joining the EC in the first place, namely the realisation that it would do better economically inside than outside, and that such a decision needs to be legitimised in a referendum whose outcome can be swung according to the government's and political elite's wish. A clear historic analogy to 1975 is thus apparent in the Lib Dem's view on the euro. The fact that economic benefits are quoted as the reason to join the euro points to a "pragmatic", self-interested pro-European stance. More investment into the UK is given as a sufficient reason without translating it into tangible benefits for potentially listening voters such as jobs, maybe because it is deemed common knowledge or because it is not seen as necessary to explain. This discourse is then focused on an elite or the government in particular where macro-economic figures stand alone as a reason for action and do not require values or policy results to legitimise the alternative policy proposal brought forward by the Lib Dem leader. The government, on the other hand, is portrayed as inactive and slow to do something about the economic situation of the UK, thus neglecting what he sees as central British interests.

"European Council (Copenhagen)" (16.12.2002)

> Would not Britain's hand in Europe be strengthened more generally if we showed greater political resolve on the single European currency? Increasingly, we risk 543 marginalising ourselves, as well as suffering domestic economic disadvantage, due to continuing uncertainty about a referendum and about the Government's long-term political commitment on the issue. [Official Report, 16 December 2002; Vol. 396, c. 543]

The line of argument that joining the euro equals increased bargaining power on the EU level is repeated in Kennedy's comment on the next EU Council meeting in Copenhagen in the form of a rhetorical question: "Would not Britain's hand in Europe be strengthened more generally if we showed greater political resolve on the single European currency?" This quid-pro-quo approach is rather utilitarian, foregrounding the question: how can we maximise our influence? And then the measures to achieve this goal should be taken, as this hidden call for action in this alternative look on the issue presents. The metaphor of holding a "hand" (of cards) conjures up the image of EU cooperation as a game of poker where everyone seeks to get the best cards to trump the others, and the winner takes all. This is the opposite of consensus-style European politics and resembles closely the British political culture where there is almost always a clear win-lose situation. It implies that strength is necessary to win advantages. And it implies that the other EU member states all play for themselves and not for a common goal or solidary cooperation. Trust also seems to be acknowledged as an important factor in this game: by saying that "uncertainty about [...] the government's [...] commitment" is a problem, Kennedy introduces the values of reliability. Maybe he even advocates to play with an open "hand" and to let the others know which strategy one pursues.

To illustrate the contrast between this positive scenario included in their alternative policy proposal, Kennedy uses the words "marginalising ourselves", "suffering domestic economic disadvantage", and "uncertainty", which paint a dark scenario should the PM not listen to the Lib Dem proposals. In addition, the blame is also accorded to the Labour government in power and their "long-term political commitment" to joining the euro called into question.

Again, he says "we" all the time – and thereby includes the Lib Dems in a community of sensible people who want the best for the country. It seems that on the euro, he really is for cross-party cooperation. A justification or simply different discourse reality could be that there simply is no alternative to their own proposals on the euro that the Lib Dem can accept as in the national interest or sensible, and consider the euro as above party politics. This would lend an inevitable nature to the issue of joining.

"Amendment of the Law" (09.04.2003)

> As a country, we should be doing more to prepare our way for entry into the euro. We certainly look forward with considerable interest to the statement at the beginning of June to see whether white smoke emanates from No. 10 or No. 11, depending on what is going to happen—
> Lembit Öpik (Montgomeryshire): Or both. [Official Report, 9 April 2003; Vol. 403, c. 294]

A further instance of the UK imagined as a "country" by Kennedy can be found in the Budget debate of April 2003. Here, he insistently uses the first person plural. He draws attention to the still missing decision on the euro and voices a call for action: "As a country, we should be doing more to prepare our way for entry into the euro". He also highlights the promised test if the economic conditions have been met, the prerequisite set by Blair on Brown's initiative. This perceived conflict between PM and Chancellor is highlighted, too. The metaphor of an election of a new pope, indicated to spectators by white smoke from the chimney, brings up the question of leadership in the sense that there can only be one pope, i.e. one leader setting the policy for the UK. In the event of choosing a new pope, the election process takes place behind closed doors and can take hours and hours, even days. This idea of a lengthy power struggle where all 'bishops' allowed to vote have to find a consensus and a decision is only taken when everyone is happy or persuaded is applied to the UK context: the addresses "No. 10" and "No. 11" are used as metonyms for the holders of the two most powerful offices of the British executive, the Prime Minister with his office in Downing Street No. 10 and the Chancellor of the Exchequer in the Treasury in No. 11, right next door.

The euphemistic formulation of "look[ing] forward with considerable interest" indicates the inherent criticism at the long time the decision has not been taken for, and the importance the Lib Dem attach to it. Strong and effective leadership and the will to take risky or unpopular decisions if they are "objectively" good for the country belong to the values allegedly absent here but favoured by Kennedy. This view and criticism is increased by his party friend's interjection that white smoke may emanate from both chimneys, thus mocking the idea that even after such a long fight, the two most prominent Labour cabinet members will probably still not be able to come to an agreement. It becomes clear that he considers this behaviour irresponsible, probably independent of the actual issue at stake but even more so since they think it is a vital one to make a clear decision when to hold a referendum on joining the euro and campaigning in favour of that proposition.

"Engagements" (21.05.2003)

> May I ask the Prime Minister a question of which his right hon. Friend the Member for Hartlepool (Mr. Mandelson) helpfully gave me notice? If he does not agree with his right hon. Friend's description of the Chancellor, will he take this opportunity to disavow it? [...]
>
> Is not the Prime Minister's real problem not the economic circumstances, but the political conditions of the Chancellor? The more he allows himself to be boxed in by the Chancellor's conditions, the more his policy will be characterised as dither and delay, just like John Major's.
>
> *The Prime Minister*: I profoundly disagree with the right hon. Gentleman that the economics are irrelevant. There are three positions on this European debate. What he has effectively said, and the Liberal Democrats have said for six years is that Britain should join the single currency immediately, irrespective—
>
> *Mr. Kennedy*: indicated dissent. [Official Report, 21 May 2003; Vol. 405, c. 1006]

In the next relevant instance, PMQs on 21 May 2003, Kennedy refers to the remarks by Peter Mandelson, the former Northern Ireland secretary for Blair, concerning an alleged conflict between Blair and Brown over the euro. They were apparently made off the record the day before but found their way into national newspapers (e.g. Wintour et al. 2003: "Mandelson") and were taken up by the opposition parties on PMQs that same day. Kennedy obviously is of the opinion that Brown is the cause for the delay in setting a date for a referendum on entry into the single currency. The official statement on the question whether the economic tests were met was announced for 9 June 2003. Kennedy insinuates that the disagreement with Brown stands in the way of a decision that the Lib Dems would like to see by asking a rhetorical question and describing the PM as powerless and ineffective in dealing with inner opposition, saying he lets "himself be boxed in". Kennedy vents his frustration that his proposed political actions are opposed not by the Official Opposition, but by a member of the "pro-European"

Labour government. He expresses this by warning the PM that more inaction and indecisiveness (i.e. weak leadership and inability to impose his will) will lead to an impasse faced also by Major, whose government is said to have toppled over weakness on European policy (UK Government: "John Major"). He once again terms this "dither and delay", characterising both PMs as lacking courage and a vision, respectively, the will to fight for what they believe is the right way forward. The values of strength and dominance clearly shine through, and it seems this is thought even worth the risk of a split party or cabinet. The Labour strategy to wait for the right moment and take into account public opinion (surveys) is deemed weak and opportunistic and costing the country chances of more prosperity.

The PM's response tries to frame Kennedy's proposals as a denial of the importance of economics in the decision whether to join or not to join, which the latter rejects. This has been recorded in *Hansard* although he had no official speaking time left, meaning that he made it very clear that he did not agree with the discourse reality or version of events put forward by the PM, who repeated his view that the CON stand for absolutely not, the Lib Dems for absolutely yes and only Labour for a balanced, third-way style deliberation which has yet to come to a conclusion. Instead, Kennedy wants to have it on record that his party stands for economic rationality without consideration for petty let alone emotional arguments. It is interesting to see that here is a live dispute about which version of events is more pragmatic and rational, and in the end of course more convincing to voters.

"European Council, Brussels Summit (EC)" (08.11.2004)

> If the type of economic liberalism and greater economic flexibility, to which he alluded in his statement and which were discussed at the summit, are achieved, will he perhaps, on a future occasion, see scope for doubling up a referendum on the constitution with one on the single currency? [Official Report, 8 Nov 2004; Vol. 426, c. 575]

This short excerpt from Kennedy's comment of the EU Council meeting in Brussels in November 2004 highlights the Lib Dem preference for "economic liberalism and greater economic flexibility". The Lib Dem leader seems to doubt, however, that they will be easily achieved in the EU, carefully phrasing it as a conditional clause. Or maybe he just doubts that the government would assess such a circumstance correctly in order to avoid admitting the economic argument does no longer serve as an excuse for not making a final decision on entering the euro. However, in such a case, he puts forward the idea of "doubling up a referendum on the constitution with one on the single currency", thus demonstrating that even the proposed EU constitution will not let him be diverted from pushing for a UK decision on entry into the single currency. It is interesting to see that the Lib Dem leader here unquestionably advocated holding a referendum for each important step on the way to closer EU integration. It seems that they really believe a referendum would focus on a single item of policy and obviously they accept the fact that a referendum would be a prerequisite for implementing such big steps in European policy. Moreover, Kennedy suggests it is likely that both referendums can be won.

"Budget March 2005" (16.03.2005)

> I want to acknowledge that the Chancellor's Budget statement is taking place against a fortunate backdrop for our country. Ours is one of the largest and most successful economies in the world. We are generally doing well. Of course part of the reason for that, on which I know the Chancellor now agrees, is that when he first came to his high office, he implemented Liberal Democrat policy on giving operational independence to the Bank of England. [Official Report, 16 March 2005; Vol. 432, c. 274–277]

In the Budget speech on 16 March 2005, Kennedy mentions the independence of the Bank of England again, repeating that it was their idea (by labelling it "Liberal Democrat policy") and claiming that is at least partly because of this that the economy is doing well at this moment in time. It is interesting that he uses the pronouns "ours" and "we" here to demonstrate that he and his party feel very much part of the country as a community pulling together to achieve this result in this moment of economic strength, and thus also demonstrates that he sees himself as having played a part in this success.

7.1.3 Menzies Campbell

Campbell did not address the euro directly but mentioned the independence of the Bank of England twice, on 22.03.2006 and on 21.03.2007, both times during the budget debate, respectively. He insisted that the good economic figures presented by the Chancellor were in part due to the Lib Dem proposal to make the Bank of England independent and vies for acknowledgement from the government that the Lib Dems had it right.

7.1.4 Nick Clegg

Nick Clegg mentioned the single currency four times during his years as Lib Dem leader in opposition. The first three instances happened one after the other over a period of only two months at the end of 2008, while the last one was shortly before the general election in 2010 that would return a hung parliament and ultimately result in the Lib Dems sharing office with the CON in a coalition government.

"European Council" (20.10.2008)

> It was significant that President Sarkozy invited the Prime Minister to the eurozone meeting. The eurozone group will obviously be the forum at which many discussions about the future regulation of our financial services sector will take place. What arrangements has the right hon. Gentleman made with the Government of Sweden— and the Czech Republic, which will hold the EU presidency next year—to have further access to the eurozone group so that he can participate in those discussions next year, too? [Official Report, 20 October 2008; Vol. 481, c. 28–29]

The first mention was during a parliamentary debate on the results of the European Council in October 2008. Clegg highlights the importance of the Eurozone in deciding the "future of our financial services sector". Interestingly, the pronoun "our" suggests an identification regarding politics and the City of London. The impression of extreme closeness between the two is created, whereas 'normal' people suffering from turmoil in the financial world are not mentioned. Clegg urges the PM to safeguard further access to the Eurozone meetings to ensure the UK interests can be protected or at least the latest information be learned without delay, implying that this will be the most important political task in the months and years to come with the financial crisis beginning and new regulations appearing unavoidable. It seems that for Clegg, the EU or more precisely the Eurozone leaders are the enemy or the actors to be watched lest they should meddle and interfere in a negative way in British affairs, and not the banks and lack of regulations and checks which have caused the crisis. Values and goals underlying the proposal to secure access to the Eurozone meetings are being in the know/the first to know, importance, protecting one's own interests on a macro-economic level, being in the middle of action although one has an opt-out for the area of economic and monetary union.

"G8 Summit" (17.11.2008)

> British exports, of course, will be boosted after the recent fall in the value of the pound after a long period of over-valuation. In my opinion, the shadow Chancellor was well within his own rights to talk about the falling pound, even if he made almost no sense at all. Does the Prime Minister agree that this sudden desire for currency stability is a bizarre U-turn from a party that once referred to the euro as a 'toilet paper currency'? [Official Report, 17 November 2008; Vol. 481, c. 28]

The second mention of the euro by Nick Clegg only four weeks later, at the occasion of the G20 summit, puts the single currency in a good light: Clegg associates it with stability. Clegg attacks the position presented by the CON Shadow Chancellor of the Exchequer and implies that they were not concerned about currency stability before but wanted to keep the pound on a matter of principle. This contrasts a rational, no-nonsense but also pragmatic and opportunistic approach by the Lib Dems, namely advocating to adopt the euro if it brings the UK benefits, with the allegedly erratic and emotional as well as vulgar approach followed by the CON leader.

The derisory comments aimed at the CON highlight their supposed inconsistency by using the words "sudden" and "bizarre U-turn". This shows that the Lib Dems construct the CON as the main political opponent when it comes to European policy. Clegg seeks the assurance of agreement from the PM in rejecting the CON's policy on Europe, marking them as being on the same page. The contrast allows an inference to the underlying values: The Lib Dem leader highlights values such as rationality, far-sightedness, and cold-blooded self-interest but also consistency and reliability as positive and locates them within his own as well as the governing party. He clearly condemns and despises populist techniques such as using colloquial language to appeal to emotions and parts of the population that are distant from the elite discourse. This is expressed in his repetition of the CON's description of the euro as a "toilet paper currency". This kind of talk is deemed unworthy of a serious politician by the Lib Dem leader, it seems. In retrospect, the absence of emotion from the Lib Dems leaders' argumentative strategy, thus leaving this aspect to be addressed solely by Eurosceptic discourse, may have "alienated" non-voters even more, since they could not connect with the macro-economic reasoning of the Lib Dems.

"EU Council/Afghanistan, India and Pakistan" (15.12.2008)

> Already, in some places one can no longer buy a whole euro for a pound. Does the Prime Minister recognise that many eurozone economies could surge ahead of Britain, under his leadership, leaving us once again as the sick man of Europe? [Official Report, 15 December 2008; Vol. 485, c. 821–822]

In this short mention of the euro and the development of the euro-pound exchange rate at the dispense of the pound during the debate on the most recent EU Council as well as other matters, Clegg voices concern about the UK's economic performance overall. The Eurozone countries' economic performance is used as a benchmark against which the UK has to measure up; the idea that the UK might be overtaken (others "could surge ahead of Britain") is clearly a negative scenario and a call for action from the government. Clegg's argument is that the UK can only retain a top position in relation to other European Union countries when they join the single currency. The comparison to fellow EU members and the choice of words imply a race or sports competition scenario.

In such a scenario, there is only one winner and losing is coupled with shame and failure. This is the opposite of an imagined community based on solidarity where everyone profits from good economic performance of any member state through shared prosperity within the single market. It also implies that the UK belongs at the top of the league and must not be left to become "once again the sick man of Europe", an experience that is obviously undesirable and associated with illness and ill-functioning. This serves to underline the clear call for action directed at the PM and also to demonstrate that the Lib Dem proposal to join the single currency has been the right one since it would now guarantee economic growth and currency stability in a time of crisis. It emerges that Clegg seeks to convince the PM to adopt a different policy this time, not simply to obtain his approval or agreement. However, with the euro crisis setting in towards the end of 2009, even the Lib Dem calls to join the euro fall silent.

"European Council" (29.03.2010)

> On the bail-out for the Greek Government, as the Prime Minister knows, instability in the eurozone can and will rapidly turn to instability across the European Union, which will affect us too. Given that, I found the lack of details about the potential Greek bail-out a little concerning. Yes, Greece has not yet formally asked for help, but we have a deal on the table that is meant to calm the markets' nerves but gives us very little in the way of detail. The Prime Minister is frowning, but can he tell me what will be the exact role of the IMF in this deal? How will the burden be broken up between the other eurozone countries? What is the maximum level of support likely to be given to Greece in the event that it asks for help and, crucially, what conditions will be put on Greece in return for this support? [Official Report, 29 March 2010; Vol. 508, c. 515]

The last mention of the euro by a Lib Dem leader in opposition takes place on 29 March 2010, shortly before the next general election which would return a hung parliament and eventually result in a Lib Dem participation in government for the following five years. This time, it is the euro crisis which Clegg addresses. He spells out a clear interconnection between the UK and the other EU member states, but now in a negative context: instability in the Eurozone is portrayed as contagious and resulting in deleterious consequences for the UK. It is also interesting to observe the order in which Clegg explains this to listeners: first, there is one member state, Greece, then the Eurozone is affected, which in turn has an effect on the whole EU and only as the last step, Clegg says, "it will affect us, too". This use of the pronoun "we" establishes an imagined community where the UK or all British people are on the receiving end of negative developments spreading within the union. This is the opposite of solidarity or perceiving oneself to be in the same boat in a good way. The consequences of the euro crisis are described as a "burden" which the other countries have to shoulder, and Clegg shows himself concerned with the details of the deal on the table. This leads to the conclusion that the Lib Dem leader sees the Eurozone countries as distinct from the UK and only cares if the consequences potentially affect the UK, too. The role of observer is confirmed and presented as necessary to avert involvement. Membership in the EU is described as dangerous and values underlying this are caution, prudence, and far-sightedness to protect one's own interests. Alternative political action he calls for are, therefore, obtaining much more information and closely watch the actions of others – probably to be able to interfere should stability in the UK be threatened further.

7.1.5 Summary

Speeches addressing the common currency were numerous; the euro was the topic most often addressed in the Lib Dem discourse on Europe. As the instances analysed in this chapter show, the Lib Dem leaders debated the possible introduction of the euro in the UK as well as the decisions taken by the Eurozone countries with fervour over large parts of the research period, especially in the first parliament; from 2003 onwards, however, a steady decline in the topic's salience can be perceived. In 2008, there was renewed interest in this policy domain, coinciding with the beginning of the global financial crisis and the ensuing eurozone crisis.

The main thrust of the speeches was consistently in favour of joining the single currency, but they nevertheless adopted the argument that this decision must be based on economic soundness and pragmatic reasons. Interestingly, the call for a referendum to legitimise the decision to join the euro came up quite early in the debate and was repeated with increasing urgency. It was, thus, especially intriguing to dissect the reasoning behind this claim, which is consistent with the Eurosceptic demands from parts of the Conservative Party as well as UKIP. If the Lib Dems are indeed a Europhile party and referendums count as a sign of Euroscepticism, then the argumentation structure and underlying values are paramount to understand.

Many instances showed that the Lib Dem leaders were anxious to present their policy proposals as pragmatic, rational, and in the national interest. Every other motive such as "enthusiasm" about Europe or European integration was denied; instead, their position was backed up by economic predictions and figures. The question whether the Lib Dems are really pro-European and more so than any other party can, for the debate around the single currency, thereby not be confirmed entirely. If they are, they seek to disguise it, which leads to

the conclusion that over many years, only numbers adding up and solid economic advantages for the UK appear to count or are perceived as valid reasons.
Euroscepticism cannot be attributed to them, but the argumentation tactics
resemble the CON's tone and also New Labour's talk of "economic tests" that
needed to be met. The line of argumentation that joining the euro equalled an
increased bargaining power on the EU level, and that the UK needed to join the
single currency to protect the national economy and specific industry branches
from disadvantages, confirms this interpretation.

The Lib Dems presented themselves as rational, efficient, and trustworthy,
and claimed to fight in an emotionless way for joining the euro. This can be
defined as a pragmatic and even opportunistic approach by the Lib Dems,
namely advocating to adopt the euro if it brings the UK benefits such as a more
favourable currency value that could make British exports more competitive,
also at the expense of less economically strong EU members. This was confirmed
by the use of metaphors for this decision which included "to grasp this nettle"
and "to cross the Rubicon" as well as competing in a race with both other EU
member states, which implied that a hard-headed cost-benefit analysis had been
conducted and the price was worth paying.

According to the Lib Dem leaders, the UK could only retain a top position
(speaking in terms of macro-economic performance) in comparison to other
European Union countries when and if they joined the single currency. The
Eurozone countries' economic performance was used as a benchmark against
which the UK had to measure up; the idea that the UK might be overtaken
(others "could surge ahead" of Britain) is a metaphor taken from the world of
racing or other sports competitions. Losing to the other Europeans, thus cast as
rivals not fellow team players, would clearly be negative.

While neither Campbell nor the interim leader Vince Cable addressed the
euro, suggesting that it was not very high on the agenda any more by then, Clegg
referred to the issue repeatedly. Strengthening the impression that it is only
the national interest the Lib Dems seem to be interested in, he argued that the
changes to European laws in the domain of finance in the context of the global
financial crisis could negatively impact on the UK's financial sector. Therefore,
he called for access to Eurozone meetings which he described as crucial for the
UK. It became clear that at this point in time, the Lib Dems no longer proposed
to join the currency, but to influence the rules to protect national British economic interests.

Still, Clegg associated the euro with stability, but after 2008, under the impression of the euro crisis gathering momentum, the issue was dropped. It was
even turned into the opposite when the eurozone was portrayed as a source of

instability that could threaten the UK as well. It became very clear that as long as the eurozone countries prospered, the Lib Dems would have liked to profit from membership of a currency favourable to worldwide exports; as soon as the currency was under severe pressure, they changed their tune and warned of the Eurozone as a source of contagious economic trouble instead.

In the case of the single currency, the Lib Dems clearly sided against the CON and criticised Labour for not following through with their "pro-Europeanness". A referendum was called for but apparently only as a make-believe since the Lib Dem leaders consistently claimed the government could win it if they only defended the decision to join publicly instead of avoiding the issue, which according to them ceded the power to determine the regime of truth in the discourse on the euro to the Eurosceptic Official Opposition.

7.2 "Bandying about a Euro-Army": Foreign and Security Policy

To put the following speeches into context, the most important developments in this policy area in the UK will be shortly summarised. Pine sees a change in foreign policy orientation in the late 1960s: "Retaining influence with the US was still a key aim of British foreign policy, [...] but there was in these years a recognition that the influence could only be obtained through British membership of the EC" (Pine 2007: 180–181). After the Western European Union (WEU) council in Rome in 1968, closer collaboration in foreign policy matters ensued (Pine 2007: 178–179). After the UK had become a member of the then EC, both the Single European Act (SEA) and the Maastricht treaty enhanced cooperation among members in the domain of foreign policy and defence (European Commission: "EU Treaties"). In the Maastricht treaty, the WEU was mentioned for defence and "the positions and obligations of NATO members were also explicitly recognised" (Wall 2008: 169).

However, even under New Labour, Wall sees a certain wariness when it comes to the domain of foreign policy: "At Amsterdam, Tony Blair was cautious on Foreign Policy and Defence. Foreign policy was excluded from the new arrangement for enhanced cooperation" (Wall 2008: 168). Blair's approach changed, however, and during his term of office as Prime Minister the policy domain became increasingly important: "In due course, European defence was to become the area where Tony Blair moved British policy further than any of his predecessors" (Wall 2008: 169). Wall claims this was the "area where Britain could demonstrate leadership" to compensate for not joining EMU (2008: 169). The first instance of this changed stance was the declaration on increased cooperation by Blair and

Chirac at Saint Malo in December 1998; however, as an insider, the former diplomat Wall concedes that the UK would always put NATO and the USA alliance first when it came to foreign policy (2008: 172).

This can be seen when on "nine eleven" 2001, airplanes crashed into the World Trade Center and Pentagon, resulting in the "war on terror" proclaimed by the US President Bush. PM Blair promised him full UK support then, with the operation 'Enduring Freedom' beginning in October with the invasion of Afghanistan to fight the Taliban and Al Quaeda (J. Schmidt 2011: 441). The war in Iraq, beginning in 2003, marked a further decisive point in the domain. Later in 2003, a "joint headquarters to run European defence" was proposed by France, Germany, Luxembourg, and Belgium. Blair had to balance this with the US interests against the background of the divisions over the Iraq war (Wall 2008: 172). Chirac's offer to cooperate more closely among France, Germany, and the UK was put to the test in the area of defence when the CFSP wording on the Constitutional treaty was negotiated (Wall 2008: 174) – the UK insisted on a veto when it came to defence decisions but agreed to the European headquarters idea and made the US accept this deal, too, in an attempt to ease the strain on the relationships to EU members not supporting Iraq.

The following 30 speeches were related to European and foreign and security policy:

Tab. 5: Lib Dem Leaders' Speeches Mentioning Foreign and Security Policy

Leader	Date	Name of Debate
Paddy Ashdown	18.06.1997	European Council Amsterdam
Paddy Ashdown	09.07.1999	NATO Summit
Paddy Ashdown	24.11.1998	Debate on the Address
Paddy Ashdown	10.02.1999	Engagements
Paddy Ashdown	08.06.1999	Kosovo/Cologne European Summit
Charles Kennedy	13.12.1999	Helsinki European Council
Charles Kennedy	27.3.2000	European Council (Lisbon)
Charles Kennedy	25.11.2002	NATO Summit (Prague)
Charles Kennedy	16.12.2002	European Council (Copenhagen)
Charles Kennedy	24.03.2003	Iraq and European Council
Charles Kennedy	04.06.2003	G8 Summit
Charles Kennedy	23.06.2003	European Council
Charles Kennedy	15.12.2003	European Council
Charles Kennedy	14.06.2004	G8 Summit
Charles Kennedy	30.06.2004	NATO Summit/Special EU Council
Charles Kennedy	08.11.2004	European Council/Brussels Summit

Tab. 5: Continued

Leader	Date	Name of Debate
Charles Kennedy	20.12.2004	European Council
Charles Kennedy	24.03.2005	European Council, Brussels Summit
Charles Kennedy	20.06.2005	EC Budget
Menzies Campbell	19.06.2006	Brussels Summit (EC)
Menzies Campbell	12.03.2007	European Council
Vince Cable	17.12.2007	European Council (Brussels)
Nick Clegg	17.03.2008	European Council
Nick Clegg	19.05.2008	National Security Strategy
Nick Clegg	21.05.2008	Engagements
Nick Clegg	23.06.2008	European Council
Nick Clegg	15.12.2008	EU Council: Afghanistan, India and Pakistan
Nick Clegg	11.03.2009	Engagements
Nick Clegg	23.03.2009	Spring European Council
Nick Clegg	23.06.2009	European Council

Total: 30 Debates

7.2.1 Paddy Ashdown

Ashdown made five references to foreign policy, beginning with the first European Council meeting (in Amsterdam) after Labour won the election in 1997.

"European Council Amsterdam" (18.06.1997)

> I think that the Government misunderstand the process now in place for the integration of European defence and foreign policy. I do not think that the Prime Minister was right to say that NATO has not previously appeared in a treaty text in the way that he described. I note that the former Prime Minister, the right hon. Member for Huntingdon (Mr. Major), is nodding. If my memory is not wrong, NATO appeared quite explicitly in the Maastricht text, which said that nothing undertaken under the treaty should prejudice the importance of NATO. No one I know in Europe wants to get rid of NATO. However, building a second European pillar—which, over time, must mean the WEU being integrated into the European Union—will not undermine NATO; it will strengthen it. [Official Report, 18 June 1997; Vol. 296, c. 320–321]

He mentions the "European defence and foreign policy" – correctly called the Common Foreign and Security Policy (CFSP) – and says the "Government misunderstand the process now in place for the integration" of said policy. He refers to the PM's claim that it was his government's achievement to include a NATO safeguard in the council communiqué, while Ashdown insists that NATO has always been recognised in the EU treaties and its predominance has never been doubted. He cites from the Maastricht treaty text to underline his reasoning. For this assessment, Ashdown receives nonverbal confirmation from Blair's CON predecessor Major, which lends it more authority.

The Lib Dem leader proceeds to claim that "[n]o one I know in Europe wants to get rid of NATO", thus refuting the discourse that the EU threatens or wants to replace the Transatlantic defence alliance. The making out of a choice between the EU and the USA as both possible but mutually exclusive defence partners is described as inaccurate; Ashdown claims that European integration in the policy area of foreign and security policy (what is termed the "second European pillar" since it is ruled by intergovernmental agreements rather than the truly supranational regime for CAP, etc.) "will not undermine NATO; it will strengthen it". He expresses the preference of cooperation with all international partners and not a one-sided approach which means the UK would have to choose. This includes keeping all options open and also keeping a balance of powers and interests rather than committing oneself to one ally. This pragmatic approach is reminiscent of an earlier, "typically British" strategy to assure a balance of powers but not committing to alliances. Ashdown makes the argument that the proposed developments must result in "the WEU being integrated into the European Union". He, therefore, frames the EU as the rightful and logical organisation into which the efforts and policies of the Brussels Treaty powers can successfully merge. The history of the WEU includes the idea of forming a "Euro army", proposed by the French government in 1952, which failed, however. The main point is that Ashdown portrays European integration to include foreign and defence policy as something positive that will enhance NATO and thus the UK's security partnerships and security itself. This statement will remain the only one addressing the EU and security policy in this first parliamentary session under Blair as PM.

"NATO Summit" (09.07.1999)

My second question relates to the general progress in Madrid. That progress was sensible, but short-term. We still lack a strategy. Let me give the Prime Minister an example. The armed forces of Romania, which has been excluded from NATO, are by general consent both more 941 efficient and more under civilian control than those of, say, Poland and the Czech Republic. Are we now going to draw up general criteria that will be applied in the consideration of future entrants?

Does the Prime Minister accept that there is a necessary but growing divergence between the long-term strategic aims of the Americans in NATO and the Europeans in NATO? The Americans see NATO as a global institution, perhaps with implications for their policy on the middle east, while we see it as an institution concerned with security in Europe. [Official Report, 9 July 1997; Vol. 297, c. 940–941]

In the debate on the 'NATO summit' in July 1997, Ashdown points out that there are differences in the shape of the national armies of EU membership candidate countries Romania, Poland, and the Czech Republic. He says it makes no sense to include the latter two while denying entry to the former. Ashdown sees this as a strategic problem and pushes for "general criteria" to make access less dependent on political but "objective" reasons. It could also be seen as a call for more concentration on making Europe more secure by taking in every European state with an acceptable army, which in the case of Romania would also overlap with arguing for EU membership of this country.

The more interesting comment comes directly after that: "there is a necessary but growing divergence between the long-term strategic aims of the Americans in NATO and the Europeans in NATO". This is a prime example of a binary opposition and shows that Ashdown is not content with following the US lead in the area of defence and security policy. Ashdown continues to explain where the main difference lies: "[t]he Americans see NATO as a global institution, perhaps with implications for their policy on the middle east, while we see it as an institution concerned with security in Europe". In this assessment, a rational approach is advocated that is opposed to claiming the US and the UK have a special relationship and relying exclusively on American support in times of conflict. He obviously sees the need and the opportunity for a distinct European approach based on cooperation and advocates a more confident stance by the members of the EU towards ensuring their own security. This confidence placed in the imagined community of Europeans, in which he includes the UK political elite or at least his own party using the pronoun "we", stands in contrast to CON calls for sticking with the Americans and also Tony Blair's ultimate choice to back the US in all major decisions in the area of security policy.

"Debate on the Address" (09.07.1999)

> Who knows, perhaps we shall also work constructively with the Government on European issues, such as the formulation of a common foreign and security policy—if the Prime Minister is serious about that. [Official Report, 24 November 1998; Vol. 321, c. 41–44]

In this short excerpt from the 'Debate on the Address' in the next parliamentary session, on 24 November 1998, Ashdown enumerates the policy areas where the Lib Dem and Labour goals overlap and where the government can thus expect support from the second largest opposition party. Among them, albeit last in the list, are "European issues, such as the formulation of a common foreign and security policy – if the Prime Minister is serious about that". The way Ashdown phrases this, the way he adds this last subclause, and the way he introduces this last item on the list with "[w]ho knows, perhaps we shall" indicate that the Lib Dem leader is wary about how realistic the announcement of the second government programme in the Queen's speech is. The verbalised reservation casts a shadow of doubt on the PM's credibility as well as his sincerity.

Content-wise, it is interesting that the Lib Dem leader singles out the CFSP as the one issue worth mentioning explicitly where European policy is concerned. This shows the importance that the domain of foreign and security policy has in the eyes of the Lib Dem leader. It also reveals their own preference for cooperation. Foreign policy and defence belonging to the realm of "high" politics, typically classed as an inherently national prerogative; the fact that they still argue for more cooperation shows that they trust in the other European member states as like-minded.

"Engagements" (10.02.1999)

> The Government say that they are in favour of an international regime for arms control. Good. Does the Prime Minister find it odd, though, that, less than two weeks ago, when the Germans in the European Council proposed that we publish the European report on arms sales, the Government declined to support them? Will he now give an undertaking that, when the Germans return on 18 March with a European code for arms brokers, the Government will support them this time? [Official Report, 10 February 1999; Vol. 325, c. 314–315]

This is an interesting side mention of foreign policy during PMQs in so far as the Lib Dem leader criticises the lack of support for a German proposal in the EU council to agree on common rules in the area of arms trading. Ashdown reminds Blair of his promise to pursue an "ethical" foreign policy and calls on him to support a "European code for arms brokers" expected to be proposed by the German government. It can be seen that the Lib Dem leader is all for cooperation with the other European member states where policy aims coincide. An obstruction of a joint decision which cannot be justified by the British national interest being touched is clearly not a valid way to behave according to Ashdown. He thus expresses the values of keeping one's word – integrity, reliability, sincerity – and obviously has no problem to accept proposals by other EU countries when they are in line with moral principles both Labour and the Lib Dems say they stand for. The danger of embarrassing details about British arms sales coming to light is not accepted as a justifiable excuse not to support partners on the way to a better world. This shows that the repute of the UK is not of much concern to Ashdown but that he is rather interested in following through with the policies promised. He puts moral values before protecting possible dirty secrets.

"Kosovo/Cologne European Summit" (08.06.1999)

During his statement on the European Summit on 8 June 1999, Ashdown takes up the debate on the future state of Kosovo ('Kosovo/Cologne European Summit'):

> In the Balkans, the devil lies in the detail, and there are four brief questions that I wish to ask by way of clarification. First, will the Prime Minister confirm that the interim status of Kosovo will be, de facto if not de jure, as an international protectorate or trusteeship? Will he tell us who the sponsor of that will be? Will it be the United Nations, the Organisation for Security and Co-operation in Europe or the European Union? [Official Report, 8 June 1999; Vol. 332, c. 469–470]

The very interesting choice of the word "sponsor" recalls the famous Zurich speech by Winston Churchill, in which he said the UK was to be the sponsor of a "United States of Europe". Now it is the European Union of which the UK is a part. This is a hidden concession that the UK alone is no longer in a position to play a prominent role in global politics and it is indeed now dependent on larger organisations to exercise this kind of influence. This is a rational, matter-of-fact assessment of changed circumstances and does not show a nostalgic hankering for the former status of the UK as a world power. The order of possible "sponsors" of an independent Kosovo is the UN, followed by the OSCE, and the EU. The UN is the largest organisation, so the order is of diminishing size. The EU is the smallest organisation in terms of members, but its focus has been on the economy. It is telling that the Lib Dem leader now brings it up as a possible forum that could take over the role of protective force in the Balkans. It shows that Ashdown believes the EU is capable of managing this task more effectively than the UK alone.

7.2.2 Charles Kennedy

Charles Kennedy made 14 mentions of foreign policy in connection with the EU.

"Helsinki European Council" (13.12.1999)

> I welcome what was said and the steps that will be followed, as a result of the Helsinki summit, in respect of the Russian position. The Government deserve support, as do the efforts of the European Union. Does the Prime Minister concur that that matter is an important test of the EU's ability to manifest a more constructive and coherent foreign policy approach to such a significant neighbour as Russia, which currently is behaving in such an outrageous fashion over humanitarian issues?

On defence, will the Prime Minister acknowledge that—despite all the hokum and nonsense about a European army—among those who take a more sensible and constructive interest in the matter, there will be a welcome for the modest but significant step towards the establishment of a European rapid reaction force? That is not least because it bolts us further into NATO and bolts a European component into NATO, which is essential for our long-term interest. [Official Report, 13 December 1999; Vol. 341, c. 28–29]

In his first speech that connects foreign policy and the EU, Kennedy refers to European policy with regard to Russia during the 'Helsinki European Council' debate. In a supportive move, he claims that both the UK government and the EU "deserve support" in their dealings with Russia, referring to the latter's war actions in Chechnya. The order suggests that first, the Lib Dem leader sees the national governments as the responsible actors which have the duty to step in, and then the EU follows as a further political actor with a responsibility to at least declare its opposition when the values it should represent are disregarded by others. However, Kennedy emphasises that only an actor as big as the EU can take a credible stand faced with big and powerful countries like Russia. It could thus also be argued that the contribution serves to show that both the national and the EU level are equally important to respond to foreign policy challenges.

The second important aspect is defence cooperation on a European level. Talk about the idea that a joint European army should be introduced is described as "hokum and nonsense". This is an appeal not to believe that such a European army will be introduced. Interestingly, the Lib Dem leader seems intent on denying that military cooperation is discussed at EU level. One reason could be that public opinion or a consensus among the British political elite prefer defence to be a very national domain. The army is also connected to the monarchy, and according to Anderson, it is at the very heart of a nation as an imagined community to be ready to die for it. Patriotic feelings are thus possibly considered tantamount for soldiers, and military cooperation has therefor tight limits. To fight and possibly die for Europe is apparently unthinkable and even the leader of the allegedly "most Europhile of all British parties" distances himself from the mere idea by dismissing it as "nonsense". The army is, at its core and chief belonging, exempted from calls for European integration.

Kennedy tries to assuage any possible fears or reserves concerning a "euro army" by separating discursively a "sensible and constructive" approach on the subject from an (implicitly) irrational one. Emotional arguments are thus discredited as illegitimate. He then says what is "sensible" in his eyes: he confirms support for a "European component in [...] NATO", which he says is "essential for our long-term interest". This shows that to justify actions in the policy field of defence, the national interest is also invoked by the Lib Dem leaders.

"European Council (Lisbon)" (27.3.2000)

> In regard to the Balkans in general and to Kosovo in particular, the Prime Minister speaks about the need for "enhanced economic assistance". Will he clarify whether there has been further, more detailed discussion about that? On television yesterday, Chris Patten said, for example, that the issue is either greater contributions from member states, or a rearrangement of existing budgets within the European Union. Can the Prime Minister give us some further flesh on those bones? [Official Report, 27 March 2000; Vol. 347, c. 27]

The Balkans and the future of Kosovo are a further focus of Lib Dem concerns in the foreign policy domain, and in this case, it is the EU budget that might be affected. Kennedy brings up the question of financing foreign policy objectives during the debate on 'European Council (Lisbon)', which is apparently something needing separate discussion after the objectives as such have been agreed. It sounds as if Kennedy would not be too happy – at least he demands more information – about any possible "greater contributions from member states" to the EU budget to finance common foreign policy missions like "economic assistance" to Kosovo after the Balkan war. It seems that paying more money to Brussels is a toad to swallow even for the Lib Dems. A TV appearance of the British EU Commissioner at the time, Chris Patten, is cited as a source for these rumours. This topic is not taken up again, however, in the years to come.

"NATO Summit (Prague)" (25.11.2002)

> Does the Prime Minister share my curiosity? We just heard the argument that greater coherence and integration of NATO – a wider NATO – and, at the same time, greater coherence and integration of the defence realm in Europe are bad ideas, but if that is the case it is puzzling that countries are queuing up to join both organisations. Instead, they see the success and future stability that such membership and cooperation can bring. Can the Prime Minister say a little more about the comparative funding? The Americans are always unhappy about the European contribution to defence—there is nothing new about that—but does he anticipate that countries that may not have contributed as much per capita as we would like can do more in that direction? [Official Report, 25 November 2002; Vol. 395, c. 39]

A positive view of NATO and the EU is rendered in the 2002 speech on the 'NATO Summit' in Prague. Kennedy uses the claim that "countries are queuing up to join both organisations" to rebut the CON's criticism of "greater coherence and integration of the defence realm in Europe", which their leader has described as "bad ideas" in the contribution before Kennedy's. The attractiveness of the EU to countries outside the union is an interesting means of portraying the EU in a positive light (thereby legitimising the Lib Dem support for most of its policies and membership as such) in a seemingly neutral way, presenting a third party's views on it instead of praising the EU (NATO) as such themselves. This distancing can be seen in several other instances and is intriguing since the Lib Dems obviously deem it prudent or feel the need to rely on "objective" arguments to be in favour of the EU. It is not a consensus but needs constant justification. Any emotional or 'irrational' attachment or sympathy for the EU is denied. Another noteworthy aspect in this line of argumentation is that the UK should be content with something other countries covet – a singular or special position for the UK is thus denied or assumed to be unimportant. Instead, it is the wisdom and choice of others that should be accepted as a benchmark against which to measure the benefits of an EU policy change, i.e. more integration also in the domain of defence. This shows that the Lib Dems believe that at this time, the UK cannot 'go it alone' any more, and cooperation with others is a sensible way forward.

A second issue is the funding of NATO (and EU spending on foreign policy). The 2 % spending quota agreed upon in the NATO contract is adhered to by the UK, but not by many other European members – and the "Americans are always unhappy about the European contribution to defence". It becomes clear that NATO is meant here, and in the following sentence, Kennedy uses the pronoun "we" to indicate a community, probably with the US position (as in the special relationship) or with the Prime Minister. The British position is obviously to adhere to the quota, and their goal must thus coincide with the US aim of getting the other member states to comply and spend more. Not doing this could be (and is) perceived as disregarding solidarity. While it is NATO addressed here, the paying habits of European NATO members have repercussions on the EU foreign policy cooperation. If the other EU and NATO members are perceived as unreliable partners and free riders relying on both US and British troops if a war breaks out, the argument for more and deepened cooperation on FP and defence within the EU is weakened.

"European Council (Copenhagen)" (16.12.2002)

Does the Prime Minister agree that it does not help intelligent discussion of matters European in this country to speak in a completely misleading fashion, bandying about such shorthand terms as "Euro army"? In fact, there is a strategic and sensible basis on which NATO and the EU can co-operate when they want to do so or whereby they can pursue different or varying agendas when that is the most sensible course. Does the right hon. Gentleman agree that that message from the summit, following the most recent NATO discussions, is welcome and must be the sane way forward? [...] Finally, I welcome the Palestine conference, which the Prime Minister has announced today, but will he underscore the need for Europe to be seen to be contributing to restarting the middle east peace process? [Official Report, 16 December 2002; Vol. 396, c. 543]

Kennedy opens his speech in the 'European Council (Copenhagen)' debate with a rhetorical question deploring the way the "discussion of matters European in this country" is conducted by certain people, a thinly disguised attack of the CON's rhetoric on Europe. He refers to the entire discourse on Europe, and he is obviously of the opinion that the term "Euro army" is unpopular. This is why he criticises it as a "shorthand term" and the way it is used as "misleading" and "bandying about", suggesting that people who do cannot be trusted and they do it in a careless way or because they are determined to manipulate the public. Kennedy thus claims that CON MPs simplify and escalate complicated matters with the aim of confusing or influencing voters. This would run counter to the probable Lib Dem policy aim to support European cooperation in the domain of foreign and defence policy.

Interestingly, the Lib Dem leader frames NATO and the EU as two entities and formulates the condition for cooperation between them as follows "when they want to do so". This denies a blind following of US interests in the domain of foreign policy, which can be seen as opposition to Blair's nearness to Bush which would result in the British involvement in Iraq the following year. In order for the EU to be a credible counterpart to NATO and to be able to undertake their own missions, cooperation between EU member states and their military is necessary. The idea that the EU could then pursue a "different" agenda than NATO is a surprising goal to be named.

That he says the outcome of the summit is "the sane way forward" implies a medical diagnosis of everyone disagreeing or proposing an alternative as insane, which condemns any reasons brought forward to justify it as illegitimate.

The words "intelligent" and "sensible" as well as "sane" are thus used to condone his proposed course of action, whereas the discourse of political opponents (very likely the CON) is described as misleading. This implies that the opposite characteristics of being stupid and even insane applies to the political opponents and their way to portray policy proposals relating to the EU. This reveals Kennedy's values and moral judgement: political ideas should be measured and evaluated according to the standard of intelligence, rationality, logic, and saneness. Anderson's concept of an imagined community and emotions are completely disregarded.

He claims, however, that "Europe" has an obligation to support peace in the Middle East. He does not justify this claim, so this task falls to the audience. The Lib Dem leader's words could be interpreted as arguing for a purely self-interested obligation to keep the peace in a geographically not too far away region, or indeed as implicitly advocating a moral and historically aware foreign policy which takes into account that Palestine was a British protectorate.

"Iraq and European Council" (24.03.2003)

By entrusting the reconstruction of Iraq to the UN, does he agree that we would have the opportunity to begin the reconstruction of the international order, which has suffered so much damage diplomatically in recent weeks, and of the European Union, to which he referred in his statement? [Official Report, 24 March 2003; Vol. 402, c. 26]

The war in Iraq is the cause for Kennedy's next intervention related to foreign policy and the EU: he calls for the "reconstruction of the international order [...] and of the European Union" during the debate on 'Iraq and European Council'. This shows that he thinks both need such reconstruction and have been damaged in the course of this war. This reference to the split among EU member states regarding the decision to join the "coalition of the willing" to invade Iraq is telling; all 52 Lib Dem MPs having voted against the UK's entry into war with Iraq in the division on 18 March 2003 [Official Report, 18 March 2003; Vol. 401, c. 858–911], Kennedy obviously does not agree with the way the UK government chose to disregard European unity, mainly with Germany and France who refused to join the war, for the sake of the transatlantic alliance.

"G8 Summit" (04.06.2003)

Will he rule out taking military action against Iran? Does he see further potential for the development of a common European front on this issue?
It is correct to welcome the movement, such as there was, towards rapprochement among the nations that were in disagreement with our country and, primarily, with the United States over what has taken place in Iraq, although there is a great deal further to go. Does the Prime Minister acknowledge that the Germans and, perhaps to a lesser extent, the French bridle somewhat at the sight and sound of the American President arriving in continental Europe and remonstrating with those who, in a candid and upfront international way, chose to take a different view from his own and that of his Administration of what took place in Iraq? [Official Report, 4 June 2003; Vol. 406, c. 163–164]

In the next speech, during the debate on the 'G8 Summit', the more critical and independent stance towards the US president and his foreign policy is confirmed, which is a clear distancing from Tony Blair's America-friendly foreign policy. Kennedy seeks to obtain assurance that no military action would be taken against Iran, and voices the hope that "a common European front on this issue" can be developed. The metaphor clearly refers to military strategy and portrays finding a position towards the treatment of Iran as a battle in itself, and one where the Europeans are seen as one party and the US possibly as the opponent. This is followed by a critical comment on "what has taken place in Iraq". Kennedy points out that invading Iraq was and is a controversial issue which has damaged UK and US relations with other "nations". It is very interesting to see that Kennedy refers to nations rather than countries where defence issues and military actions are concerned.

Kennedy moves on to explicitly mention Germany and France as the two main opponents of the Iraq war in the EU. Interestingly, Germany as a NATO and EU member is mentioned first and Kennedy claims the Germans "bridle" as a reaction to the US rhetoric that criticises their decision not to join the war. The verb is used in its meaning 'to show anger' but it also recalls the idea that there is a rider trying to force its will on a horse. The metaphorical allusion might not have been intended but captures the relationship between the European countries and the US in the area of defence quite well. It might be that the Americans pay most into NATO and implicitly guarantee Europe's security but expect support and loyalty in return. This relationship principle was followed by Blair but objected to by Schröder and Chirac, who did not (also because popular opinion in both countries was against a war in Iraq). Kennedy shows sympathy with these latter two countries' positions in describing their opposition to the US position as "candid and upfront international" (all positive values endorsed by the Lib Dems). The description lends legitimacy to a sovereign and independent decision on a country's foreign policy, especially when it comes to military action, and implicitly condones the "different view" taken by these two countries, even when it is in opposition to the UK and the US. Here, a clear confession to the sovereignty of countries is formulated and the position of the Lib Dems becomes clear: like Robin Cook, foreign secretary and architect of the "ethic foreign policy" advocated by Labour, who resigned in protest against the decision to invade Iraq without a UN mandate, the Lib Dems are not in favour of this war and Kennedy expresses this in his speech by citing the values of international cooperation and "candid" talk, i.e. honesty and transparency. It also becomes clear that the preference of the Lib Dems is to gain a common position with the other EU members, especially with France and Germany, instead of prioritising UK-US relations. In a subtle way, namely by asking the PM to acknowledge the anger of the most important European partners in the EU, Kennedy expresses his preference and implicit alternative policy proposal to align foreign policy with them rather than relying solely on the US.

"European Council" (23.06.2003)

Later in the same month, the issue of foreign policy in the context of an EU Constitution is discussed by Kennedy during the debate on the latest 'European Council':

In an article in last wee's [*sic*] The Wall Street Journal, the right hon. Gentleman referred to foreign and security policy and mutual solidarity, as it is described. That goes to the central issue, which the Prime Minister may want to address. The right hon. Member for Wells argued: Since this solidarity requirement will be enshrined in a constitution, it will be legally binding. Does the Prime Minister agree that it is incumbent on him, the Foreign Secretary and all those involved to make the case for a strengthened conduct of EU external relations based on the institutions of the Union, which remain emphatically intergovernmental under these processes? Does he also agree that that will provide sufficient safeguards for independent foreign policy making by member states, including any British Government coming before the House of Commons?

In that respect, the proposed Foreign Minister role is to be welcomed, as is the solidarity shown over Iran and the middle east peace process. Does the Prime Minister agree that if that solidarity could be extended to Iraq it would assist the cause against weapons of mass destruction?

The proposed intergovernmental agency for defence issues, not least research and procurement, is to be welcomed. Many a Committee of the House has examined this area, and we all know about the excessive wastage on procurement measures over the years. [Official Report, 23 June 2003; Vol. 407, c. 712-713]

The speech is an example of the role of the House of Commons as a debate forum where important print publication headlines are discussed, in this case an article by the PM published in *The Wall Street Journal*. The idea that the solidarity principle will be "legally binding" in the domain of foreign and security policy is something that the Lib Dem leader opposes – supranational elements in the EU competence for foreign and security policy are obviously the limit to his pro-EU stance, and he insists that this policy area must "remain emphatically intergovernmental". He argues that EU member states should be able to decide on and make their own, independent foreign policy. The justification he gives is implicit but clear: on foreign policy decisions, the British government shall remain accountable to the elected MPs, the (factual, since the monarch's role is only symbolical) sovereign in the UK. It is interesting that the House of Commons is explicitly mentioned, as if the House of Lords did not count. As leader of a third party in opposition, this position is understandable – the lower chamber is the only chance for his party to vote against and criticise policy decisions made by the government. The decision to invade Iraq is certainly a relevant background to this demand; if the EU had the power to command security policy, national opposition would hardly matter or make a difference.

The idea of solidarity in the sense of a coordinated foreign policy among EU member states on an intergovernmental premise is welcomed, however. The examples of Iran and the Middle East peace process are mentioned in favour, but in the same sentence Kennedy draws attention to the lack of solidarity in the case of Iraq. By formulating this as an asset, he implicitly criticises the failure to secure the cooperation of many EU member states, and calls into question the easy reach of the target to deprive Saddam Hussein of the supposed weapons of mass destruction. The concession that it would be easier if other EU members worked alongside the UK to achieve this is a further hint that the "punch above one's weight" maxim when it comes to British foreign policy is not shared or advocated by the Lib Dem leader.

The third point is research and procurement in the domain of defence. While Kennedy once again stresses the preference for "intergovernmental agency", he nevertheless acknowledges the benefits to be had from cooperation, with the aim to save money (synergy effects, economies of scale). The British processes are criticised with the judgement that the procurement of weapons was characterised by "excessive wastage". In conclusion, Kennedy reveals that not even the Lib Dems are prepared to let the EU take over a supranational competence for foreign and security policy and instead advocates an intergovernmental approach, which allows every member state an effective veto or opt-out of common decisions. On the other hand, Kennedy stresses the advantages of cooperation, conceding that policy objectives might be reached more easily and effectively together than alone and that money can be saved by pooling resources and processes in the area of defence.

"European Council" (15.12.2003)

> May I at least welcome the progress that was achieved on defence matters and draw attention to the fact — the Prime Minister has referred to this — that that has involved a compromise with the American Government and that that understanding between our country, the rest of the European Union and the Americans is to be broadly welcomed and built upon? [Official Report, 15 December 2003; Vol. 415, c. 1326]

In the next speech, occasioned by the next 'European Council' half a year later, Kennedy takes up the dilemma of choosing sides in the area of foreign policy over Iraq and welcomes the "compromise" with the US, the UK and "the rest of the European Union". The fact that a compromise was necessary highlights the divergent positions and interests between the US and the European powers. The order of the enumeration of the parties in this compromise is also telling: "our country" comes first, strengthening the idea of a community indicated by the pronoun "our", and then "the rest of the European Union" is mentioned. This order suggests that the UK is very much part of the EU and that the other members are paramount or come before the US in their closeness, but also set the UK apart from the "rest" in that it is mentioned first. When it comes to foreign policy, the UK is thus seen and presented as an independent actor whose interests should be considered first in the British parliament. The "Americans" come last in the enumeration, which strengthens the impression of a certain distance. Nevertheless, international cooperation ("understanding") is a value that the Lib Dems fully endorse and thus Kennedy repeats that the furthering of such understanding is "to be broadly welcomed".

"G8 Summit" (14.06.2004)

In the debate on 14 June 2004, occasioned by the G8 summit, Kennedy closes his speech with a reference to Iraq and repeats his view that cooperation on an EU level is necessary and should be pushed for by the British government:

> Finally, on Iraq, at the European Union summit in a few days' time—I appreciate that there are certain other items on the agenda—will the Prime Minister take any opportunity to explore the EU's contribution to the work of the Quartet in respect of the middle east peace plan? [Official Report, 14 June 2004; Vol. 422, c. 525]

This insistence on EU engagement and involvement in the quest for peace in the Middle East shows the importance Kennedy attributes to the EU in the domain of foreign policy. As one of the four powers making up the so-called "Quartet", the influence the EU can wield if the member states agree on a common stance is also demonstrated. Together with the UN, the EU is a power bloc that can contribute to negotiations, next to world power USA and Russia. No single EU member state is part of the Quartet, which is a concession that in the domain of foreign policy, the UK can do more as part of the EU, and is not as powerful and influential on its own. It does confirm the international outlook of the Lib Dems and their support for the idea that the EU has an obligation as well as an interest in the Middle East and should engage in the peace process.

"NATO Summit/Special EU Council" (30.06.2004)

> Was Sudan discussed, either formally or on the margins, at either the European summit or the NATO summit? The Prime Minister did not refer to Sudan in his statement, and it may be that the issue did not arise. [...] Was the matter discussed as a result of the European Union position on placing monitors in that country? [Official Report, 30 June 2004; Vol. 423, c. 290–292]

In the following speech, Kennedy briefly touches on foreign policy by bringing up the question of Sudan, where a civil war had been raging on in the Darfur region since February 2003, in relation with the summits discussed on the floor of the House. It shows that both NATO and the EU and their summit meetings are seen as potential occasions for the PM to talk about foreign policy with other European leaders. Kennedy follows up this question with a critical reference to the fact that the EU had declined to place monitors in Sudan or intervene in any other way prior to the debate. It seems that the UK should, according to the Lib Dems, always be in the know about such decisions and be a part of discussions about foreign policy on a global scale. Furthermore, it shows once again the preference for cooperation on foreign policy issues within the framework of the EU as well a moral dimension that justifies intervention in cases of ethnic conflicts with civilians dying and condemns inaction, similar to early Labour 'ethic' foreign policy guidelines.

"European Council/Brussels Summit" (08.11.2004)

If, as he suggested a moment ago, further discussions among the three European powers – the United Kingdom, France and Germany – will be taking place over the next few days, is he hopeful that he will be in a position to ask the President to endorse the strategy of these three countries in regard to Iran later this week in Washington? [Official Report, 8 November 2004; Vol. 426, c. 574–575]

The agreement between the "European powers", which Kennedy names as "the United Kingdom, France and Germany" in the next speech in regard of foreign policy, is presented as powerful and preferable to the alliance with the US and their position. This time it is about the strategy regarding Iran. The order in which these European powers are listed is also significant: it is the UK first, doubtlessly revealing the belief in British predominance in foreign policy, followed by France with its big army and the second nuclear power in the EU, and Germany in third place, probably less because of its military importance but because of its political and economic clout within the EU. It also seems that Kennedy is wary of Bush and the US foreign policy and he also doubts that the PM will even dare ("be in a position") to ask for the European position to be considered by the mighty American president.

"European Council" (20.12.2004)

The Prime Minister properly referred to Iraq. Will he give us some indication of the Government's current thinking on possible requirements for the deployment of more British troops in Iraq? Did he have a chance at the summit to speak to his Polish opposite number about Iraq? Poland confirmed only last week that it will pull out 1,700 troops – approximately half its force – from Iraq in February. [Official Report, 20 December 2004; Vol. 428, c. 1924]

Iraq continues to be the main topic in the area of foreign policy. During the debate on 'European Council', Kennedy asks after a possible increase of the number of British troops in Iraq. The connection to the EU level comes afterwards: Kennedy brings up the announcement that Poland plans to repatriate half their troops. The question implies that this will have an impact on British troops on location (debunking the idea that the UK can act alone in foreign policy, especially when it comes to military engagements). Moreover, he seems to be calling for coordination with other EU and NATO members or at least to acknowledge the desire to align policy decisions with them when the occasion (in this instance the regularly held European Council) arises.

"European Council, Brussels Summit" (24.03.2005)

> The Prime Minister did not mention the ongoing troop commitment in Iraq in his statement, but it is unlikely that some discussion of it did not take place, certainly at the margins, with some of his opposite numbers in the EU. Given that several of the allies have either withdrawn their troops or have indicated a willingness or a timetable to withdraw them, did he discuss those matters with any of his counterparts at the summit? In that context, will he take account of yesterday's all-party Defence Committee report, which acknowledges an ongoing British presence in Iraq, perhaps even at present levels, into the next calendar year? Will not withdrawal of further European Union countries maintain that position or indeed require our troop numbers to be increased? Did he discuss those matters with any of his opposite numbers? [Official Report, 24 March 2005; Vol. 432, c. 1019–1020]

Some three months later, Kennedy again foregrounds the issue and also criticises that the PM chose to leave out "troop commitment in Iraq" from his speech. Kennedy wants to hear something about consultations with "some of his opposite numbers in the EU". In the context of a parliamentary speech, the word choice "opposite number" – a term repeated in this speech – can be interpreted as a reference to the traditional seating arrangement in the House of Commons, where each cabinet member has their opposite number of the Shadow cabinet as their main political opponent. The metaphorical meaning of the term implies that EU leaders can be perceived as political opponents ready to take over if the ones in power show weakness. However, an interpretation suggesting that the government need their opposite numbers' support because the issues at stake are so crucially important for the country is more convincing, since the Lib Dem leader obviously pushes for cooperation among the UK's and other EU governments. The synonym "counterparts" possesses less of a competitive connotation but suggests a complementary quality, thus supporting the latter interpretation. Kennedy specifically refers to "other EU countries" and their decisions regarding troop numbers in Iraq as relevant for the UK.

Kennedy criticises the absence of the topic of Iraq in the PM's statement and decides to foreground the issue himself. Again, the "opposite numbers in the EU" in relation to Iraq are mentioned (the term is used repeatedly, as well as "counterparts") in the next speech to do with foreign policy. Countries that are members of the European Union are also described as "allies", and Kennedy expresses his concern that those have withdrawn or will withdraw troops from Iraq. Implicitly, a desire to act together with them instead of being the only country deploying more troops or maintaining their number becomes clear – the Lib Dems obviously favour cooperation in the domain of foreign policy instead of going it alone. The constant probing if the PM has consulted other EU leaders underpins this conclusion: dialogue with EU leaders on the issue of defence is rated as important.

The fact that Kennedy brings up the possible increase of British troops in Iraq as compensation for troop withdrawals from "further European Union countries" also shows how closely he monitors their actions and that he perceives them to have a direct impact on UK policy decisions. A factual acceptance of increased integration in the domain of foreign policy is discernible, but also the feeling that the British have more responsibility than other EU countries to bring the situation in Iraq to a reasonable end.

"EC Budget" (20.06.2005)

The last discursive connection between British foreign policy objectives and the EU by Kennedy as party leader is made during the 2005 budget debate, when he asks the PM: "[i]n that regard, does he agree that, especially in the Balkans, the prospect of EU membership is a great driver for positive change as well as for regional stability?" [Official Report, 20 June 2005; Vol. 435, c. 528] He thus claims a positive causal connection between the prospect of becoming an EU member and consolidation as well as convergence with EU standards "especially in the Balkans". The two desirable consequences "positive change" and "regional stability" are attributed to EU enlargement (this link will be more fully debated in the chapter on enlargement policy) which is remarkable in that only years ago there was a war there. To rebuild the region and ensure long-term peace and prosperity, the Lib Dem leader obviously favours the EU as the best option to achieve this. This is one of the instances where enlargement or the prospect of enlargement are constructed as foreign policy tools, which confirms that the Lib Dem leader sees the EU as an attractive organisation and the benefits of membership as a powerful incentive to comply with its prerequisites such as the rule of law and democracy. The moral dimension thus clearly comes to the fore and the Lib Dems can be seen as pro-Europe in that they both welcome the EU's basic principles and the certainty or confidence that others see it as something desirable and will go to some length to achieve membership. This expresses the comfortable position of a UK party who is already a member (and, as he implies, an important one) of this powerful and attractive organisation: they should now use the prospect of joining to influence others. This is faintly reminiscent of the patronising but also missionary sense of bringing good principles to others and letting them enjoy the benefits of the Commonwealth, for example. Whereas war and ethnic conflict belong to an uncivilised past, the future belongs to peaceful trading inside the European Union. This belief in the power of attractiveness is underlined by Kennedy's emphasis that the prospect of joining can be "a great driver" and thus a decisive factor in bringing about the desired stability in the Balkans.

7.2.3 Menzies Campbell

Menzies Campbell only shortly addresses foreign policy in two different speeches, both during debates on European Council meetings (in June 2006 and March 2007).

"Brussels Summit (EC)" (19.06.2006)

> Was there any discussion of rendition and possible breaches of international law? Does he accept that, however welcome negotiations with Russia about security and energy might be, they should not absolve Russia from legitimate criticism of its human rights record, its restrictions on non-governmental organisations and its attitude towards freedom of the press? [Official Report, 19 June 2006; Vol. 447, c. 1070–1071]

In the debate on the 'Brussels Summit (EC)', he addressed the issues of "rendition and possible breaches of international law", which refers to allegations that British intelligence was involved in the abduction and torture of people. This shows that when it comes to upholding international law and human rights issues, the other EU member states are considered as proponents by the Lib Dem leader. Campbell also mentions the dilemma of cooperating with Russia on an economic and political (energy and security) level while still exerting pressure on it for the non-respect of human rights and the freedom of opinion and the press. This highlights a moral-based and normative value-laden approach to foreign policy, which would be in line with Labour's proclaimed "ethical" foreign policy. The way Campbell chooses to foreground the difficulties in achieving this when dealing with Russia shows that he harbours doubts that decisions are always made on the basis of ethical considerations, though. He seems to think that the other EU leaders can contribute something favourable in this direction to British policy, otherwise he would not choose to foreground the issue after the PM has returned from a European summit.

"European Council" (12.03.2007)

> In the discussion of the Mecca agreement and a Palestinian Government of national unity, can the Prime Minister tell us what practical steps, if any, were considered to maintain the momentum of that agreement as a contribution to the middle east peace process? [Official Report, 12 March 2007; Vol. 458, c. 27–28]

In the second speech, the Middle East peace process is mentioned by Campbell, and he voices the expectation that the EU leaders should agree on concrete measures to support the process in the wake of the Mecca agreement. Once again, cooperation based on deliberation and a choice to participate is favoured by the Lib Dem leader, but this is coupled with the expectation that EU countries will cooperate where it would benefit common policy goals. To achieve peace in the Middle East is obviously such a consensus topic in the view of Campbell. This shows once more the underlying assumption that in a team, EU member states and the UK as one of them can achieve more than when acting alone.

7.2.4 Vince Cable

The interim party leader made one reference to foreign policy in connection with the EU.

"European Council (Brussels)" (17.12.2007)

> He was absolutely right not to attend the EU-Africa summit. The European Union has a travel ban on Mugabe, and the Prime Minister was absolutely right to take a principled stand on that. The only doubt that I am left with is why, given his strong position on human rights, he did not take a comparably strong position on the King of Saudi Arabia. I suspect that Mr. Mugabe will be wondering whether the only way to get on the right side of the Prime Minister's principled view of foreign policy is to have some oil. [Official Report, 17 December 2007; Vol. 469, c. 602–604]

Cable makes his only reference to the EU in the domain of foreign policy during the debate on the 'European Council (Brussels)'. He highlights the Lib Dem's support for an "ethical" foreign policy by affirming his party's approval for a "principled stand" on Zimbabwe's leader Robert Mugabe over human rights. He, therefore, condones the boycott of the whole EU-Africa summit, where the policies towards this important continent are streamlined among EU members. While he terms the decision not to attend "absolutely right", he also raises doubts as to how coherent this "principled stand" is and if the same standards are applied when British trade interests are touched. Implicitly, he blames the PM that oil is more important to his government than human rights.

On balance, in his condoning the individual decision of Blair not to join all the other EU leaders or foreign ministers, Cable expresses the opinion that the EU does not follow an ethical foreign policy and if the moral advantage is on one's side, acting against all the others is right. In a way, this shows that there is a belief that the UK can still 'go it alone' and that it is morally superior to all other EU members (not to speak of the likes of Mugabe). It could also be read like a schoolmaster's reaction: in order to teach one African leader a lesson, all others are punished with him. He sends the message that all other issues that might be discussed at the summit are not as important as the UK keeping a clean slate on the moral record.

In the same speech, he also refers to Kosovo and possible refugees which may result in a need to do more peacekeeping operations. This shows that security in Europe is seen as an issue that should be discussed at the EU summit and thus attributed high relevance to the EU as a forum for coordinated foreign policy efforts in the area of peace and stability in Europe and managing the consequences of war and destruction, namely refugees. In retrospect, this is a truly "pro-European" position because even today many EU member states insist that they will not accept refugees according to a solidary EU mechanism but will decide each for themselves. It becomes apparent that although the PM brought this issue up at the EU Council and NATO is involved, too, British troops are still considered an exclusively British issue.

7.2.5 Nick Clegg

The last leader of the Lib Dems in opposition, Nick Clegg, mentioned foreign policy eight times in an EU context. Five out of these were occasioned by European Council meetings, two mentions were made during PMQs (Engagements) and one was during a specialised debate on the "National Security Strategy".

"European Council" (17.03.2008)

I am grateful to the Prime Minister for his statement. As European summits go, the conclusions were workmanlike; largely welcome, but fairly unremarkable. I wonder whether that is in part because of the issues that were omitted. Notwithstanding the Prime Minister's words about Tibet today, will he explain why there was no discussion among EU Heads of State last week on Tibet? Does he not think that it is precisely the actions of the Chinese authorities in Tibet that should be the subject of discussion between European leaders?

I know that the Prime Minister is extraordinarily reluctant to do anything, it seems, to annoy the authorities in Beijing, but will he none the less confirm today that he will follow the lead of President George Bush and of Chancellor Angela Merkel and meet the

Dalai Lama on his forthcoming visit to London to express solidarity with the Tibetan people? [Official Report, 17 March 2008; Vol. 473, c. 623]

The first speech is concerned with the outcomes of the European Council meeting of March 2008. Clegg describes the outcome as "workmanlike; largely welcome, but fairly unremarkable". This sounds critical and the preceding addition "as European summits go" implies a repeated, general quality of European policy decision made during the regular meetings, thus the criticism is more generally aimed at the functioning of the EU and not just at the particular summit outcome in question. It seems Clegg would like European politics to have more glamour and ceremony instead of just getting on with the work. The adjective "unremarkable", which Clegg explains is due to "the issues that were omitted", also suggests that he would prefer more bold statements in the domain of foreign policy, like taking a stand on Tibet in the face of Chinese pressure on EU member state governments. This would imply controversial decisions as a result of a unanimous (because intergovernmental) process, which seems highly unlikely. Nevertheless, Clegg uses the examples of the US president and German chancellor Angela Merkel as a benchmark to which the PM should measure up and thus also "express solidarity with the Tibetan people". The values of human rights, the right of self-determination of the people enshrined in international law and also courage to own up to one's principles build the basis for this judgement and alternative policy proposal.

"Does he not think that it is precisely the actions of the Chinese authorities in Tibet that should be the subject of discussion between European leaders?" This rhetorical question highlights Clegg's expectations of the EU to be a forum where these values are upheld by at least discussing a country encroaching on them in the meetings of heads of government. Oddly, in this instance the national level is backgrounded and the EU as a value community seems to be the place in the spotlight. But only single countries like the US and Germany are named as examples to be emulated – which makes the tendency less pronounced. And the fact that the PM is criticised by the leader of an opposition party in the HoC is also a sign that accountability for foreign policy is deemed important by the Lib Dem leader and that he is not unhappy to be able to do so instead of criticising a majority decision by many EU countries' leaders who would not listen to him.

"National Security Strategy" (19.05.2008)

Does the Prime Minister agree that many of the threats he has enumerated—terrorism, climate change, cross-border crime—cannot be dealt with by the United Kingdom on its own, and, indispensably, we can deal with them only as full and committed members of the European Union? I noted that in his statement he referred to the EU only third after the United States and NATO as a crucial forum in which many of the collective

security threats will be tackled. Does that attach enough significance to the extent
to which our membership of the EU affords us a certain safety in numbers? [Official
Report, 19 March 2008; Vol. 473, c. 933–934]

The international perspective and need for cooperation within the framework
of the EU is emphasised by Clegg once more in the next instance, the debate
on the 'National Security Strategy', where terrorism and cross-border crime,
which Clegg terms "collective security threats", are debated. He draws attention
to his view that EU-wide cooperation is necessary to combat these phenomena.
Engagement within the EU is thus presented as doubtlessly following conclu-
sively, as the forum where they can be tackled together with like-minded countries: he says the challenges "cannot be dealt with by the United Kingdom on
its own, and, indispensably, we can deal with them only as full and committed
members of the European Union" and urges to PM to accept this view. It is a clear
concession that the UK cannot hope to fend for itself according to the opinion of
the Lib Dem leader and that the PM should recognise this and act accordingly.
A rational assessment of the status quo and unemotional action that is required
present the alternative policy proposed by the Lib Dems. Cooperation with
others is acknowledged as vital to the UK's foreign policy interests by Clegg. The
word "indispensable" is also interesting in this context, since it tries to persuade
listeners that the EU is without alternative and leaving it or excluding the domain
of foreign and security policy would be either impossible or hugely disadvanta-
geous to the UK. This can be seen as a not so very indirect criticism of the CON's
insistence on the UK's (former) glory as world power, on which role the contemporary policy should be built, and makes these claims appear as an illusion.

The criticism aimed at Blair's apparent priorities assigned to cooperation with
the US and working within NATO, putting the EU in third place when it comes to
finding partners to advance the goal of tackling these challenges shows clearly that
Clegg disagrees with this assessment and views the EU as paramount and deserving
to be named in first or second place. He also terms the EU a "crucial forum" to further strengthen this point. The last rhetorical question is especially revealing: "Does
that attach enough significance to the extent to which our membership of the EU
affords us a certain safety in numbers?" It is a concession that the UK cannot hope
to fend for itself and that the only chance for self-preservation and achieving policy
goals on the international level lies in cooperating with others.

"Engagements" (21.05.2008)

I am grateful to the Prime Minister for that reply. That being the case, does he share my
concern that much of our defence expenditure continues to be misallocated on cold war
priorities? For example, we are committed to spending £6 billion on the Eurofighter but

are failing to deliver enough of the right kinds of armoured vehicles to our troops on the ground in Afghanistan. Will the Prime Minister commit to undertaking the first strategic defence review in 10 years to ensure that our troops are properly equipped for the new kinds of conflict that they now face? [Official Report, 21 May 2008; Vol. 476, c. 315]

The next instance where foreign and security policy is brought up is in the Engagements session. Clegg's questions are concerned with the UK "mission in Afghanistan" and the spending review of defence expenditure. Clegg presents his view of the fallacies of the priorities where money is allocated to and says that at the time of speaking, "much of our defence expenditure continues to be misallocated on cold war priorities". More precisely, he criticises spending on the Eurofighter. This is the reference to a European dimension since the Eurofighter is a joint production in the UK, Germany, Spain, and Italy. Clegg, however, is not happy about it. In fact, he suggests that the national interest would be better served if the British soldiers in Afghanistan got more "armoured vehicles". This alternative proposal suggests that European cooperation on defence and weapon construction is less important than the armament of British soldiers on the ground while they are on mission in a foreign country. Clegg effectively says that the world and the challenges have changed and a major strategic overhaul of defence and security strategies is needed. The fact that he brings this up again in the Engagements session and uses up his valuable questions to the PM for it when a special debate has been held only 3 days previously shows how much importance he attaches to the topic. It seems that when it comes to choosing between cooperating with the European partners or the requirements of British soldiers, the Lib Dem leader will prioritise the latter.

"European Council" (23.06.2008)

On the issue of Zimbabwe, I welcome the Prime Minister's commitment to working in the European Union and the United Nations. I hope that the international community will consider all the options available, including the case for stopping foreign currency remittances into Zimbabwe, restricting electricity supplies from South Africa and Mozambique, and encouraging the Southern African Development Community to take more action. However, does the Prime Minister agree that there are more things that he could do now, here? Will he, for instance, consider allowing asylum seekers who are fleeing Mugabe's brutal regime to live and work temporarily in the United Kingdom, until such time as Zimbabwe is more stable and they can return home? [Official Report, 23 June 2008; Vol. 478, c. 30–31]

Mugabe is the subject of the next intervention by Clegg. He "welcome[s] the Prime Minister's commitment to working in the European Union and the United Nations". This flags up a preference for international cooperation and the mention of the EU before the UN shows that Clegg thinks this forum more important. Moreover, he puts forward the view that the UK can deal more effectively with the situation when acting in concert with the other EU member states and then also together with the wider international community in the framework of the UN. The word community would refer to shared values and the boundaries stop short of Zimbabwe, which has breached human rights and is thus excluded from the community (at least discursively in the speech by Nick Clegg). Clegg also calls for more action, and indeed urges unilateral measures from the PM – but not to punish Mugabe, instead he calls for help to people "fleeing Mugabe's brutal regime to live and work temporarily in the United Kingdom" by letting them "live and work temporarily in the UK". A certain special responsibility for the people living in the former British colony and Commonwealth member Zimbabwe (formerly part of Rhodesia) can be perceived in this call for the UK to do more, and mostly in the idea of offering people fleeing the regime shelter in the UK until "Zimbabwe is more stable". A certain remembrance of empire mentality with the concept of a stable 'mother country' helping out when the unruly 'child' is going through a phase may be read into this alternative policy proposal.

"EU Council: Afghanistan, India and Pakistan" (15.12.2008)

In the winter of the same year, Clegg voices a strong normative judgement: "He has given the wrong leadership on the Congo. Why, instead of encouraging EU leaders to send EU troops, has he encouraged them not to send them?" [Official Report, 15 December 2008; Vol. 485, c. 821–822] The question directed at the PM makes it clear that a reinforcement of British troops in Congo is considered desirable and necessary by Clegg, leading him to this outspoken condemnation of the PM's policy as "wrong" and calling his leadership instincts or decisions into question. Interestingly, Clegg refers to "EU troops" that could be sent by "EU leaders". This contribution to the existing UN forces there is considered necessary by Clegg to reinforce the latter in the deteriorating situation in Congo where massacres have been happening since 2003. The fact that Clegg refers to "EU troops" discursively establishes a power that is able to send troops, thus the EU is painted as a full-blown actor with military power and troops, like a state in its own right. Another possible interpretation is that Clegg uses the term as a shorthand for all military available to the national leaders – and in this case, the term would designate a group with a common characteristic – namely that the EU member states can agree on foreign policy goals that are worth pursuing together, which would make the EU a value community and a safeguard for human rights abused in states abroad. This resembles the idea of the US as world police and accords similar influence and responsibility to the EU. This would explain why the Lib Dem leader argues that discouraging the EU member states to send troops was a "wrong" decision.

"Engagements" (11.03.2009)

> I am sure the Prime Minister will agree that today's announcement from President Sarkozy that he will reverse General de Gaulle's legacy and rejoin NATO is hugely significant, but does he also agree that it offers an enormous opportunity for Britain, along with France, to lead European defence cooperation, which has been held back by tensions surrounding the Atlantic alliance?
> [...]
> I welcome the Prime Minister's response, but my main concern is that he may still miss the full opportunity available to him. If he could commit Britain to working fully with France and others on European defence—which, frankly, we have not done before now—he would be in a stronger position to ask them to commit more money and troops to Afghanistan. Does he recognise that there is a good bargain to be had, which would be of enormous help to our overstretched service men and women for many years to come? [Official Report, 11 March 2009; Vol. 489, c. 290–291]

On 11 March 2009, Clegg uses both questions during PMQs to put foreign and security policy on the agenda. This time, this is occasioned by France's decision to rejoin NATO. France as a NATO ally is welcomed, which can be read as a concession that France is an important partner in foreign and security policy (as the second nuclear power in the EU and a large military together with a similar history of colonialism) and to have them in the framework of NATO makes things easier for the UK because they do not have to negotiate the "tensions surrounding the Atlantic alliance" when they want to engage on joint projects any more. In the second question, however, the national interest is ruthlessly foregrounded and Clegg postulates that "there is a good bargain to be had", effectively making the case to "commit Britain to working fully with France and others on European defence" and using the good will generated by this to ask them to "commit more money and troops to Afghanistan" in return. The rationale is that of a give-and-take approach and to 'use' engagement within the EU and participate in integration only when the deal generates a desirable result for the UK, namely furthering their foreign policy objectives. It becomes clear that engaging in the EU is not, in this case, propagated by the Lib Dems as something positive and desirable in its own right, but merely as a means to an end.

"Spring European Council" (23.03.2009)

"The eastern partnership with countries such as Georgia and Ukraine is also welcome, not least because of Russia's sometimes belligerent attitude towards its neighbours" [Official Report, 23 March 2009; Vol. 490, c. 27]. In this short passage taken from Clegg's speech on 23 March on the outcomes of the EU Spring Council, the focus is on foreign policy in Eastern Europe. Clegg endorses the EU leaders' decision to establish formal partnerships with countries bordering on or close to EU territory even if they are not (prospective) EU membership candidates within the framework of the European Neighbourhood Policy. Obviously, he thinks that this association with the EU will improve the security of Ukraine and Georgia and afford them protection from Russian attacks motivated by expansionism. (With hindsight, this did not work out as planned.) This policy endorsement reveals that an association with the EU is considered more effective by the Lib Dem leader than, e.g., the protection promised by the UK as a single country.

"European Council" (23.06.2009)

> Finally, the summit text included declarations on Pakistan and Afghanistan. It is vital that there is adequate security in Afghanistan for the elections in August, and that Britain continues to play its role in Helmand province. In that context, will the Prime Minister confirm recent reports that he rejected the advice of his military commanders that there should be an increase in British troop numbers in Afghanistan? Can he not see that it would be the worst of all worlds to ask our troops to do their very difficult job in Afghanistan without committing enough resources for them to do that job properly? [Official Report, 23 June 2009; Vol. 494, c. 666–667]

In the last intervention on foreign and security matters linked to the EU level, Clegg focuses on the outcome (final statement) of the European Council in the debate on 23 June 2009. Although he refers to the joint statement issued by all participants at the end of the summit, the whole speech is only concerned with British troops and the resources they arguably need. Clegg criticises PM Blair for ignoring expert advice from military commanders – instead, the Lib Dem leader advocates increasing the number of British troops in Afghanistan in order to reach the policy goal of enabling free elections there, for which "adequate security" is "vital". The word vital is to be taken literally in this context. It is telling that when it comes to deploying or repatriating troops, the opposition politician Clegg addresses the PM directly, as the issue of defence is still a national concern and accountability rests with national leaders. Clegg is obviously of the opinion that the UK has a special responsibility in Afghanistan and that reducing troops to save money or avoid political discussion is not to be condoned. In conclusion, it can be stated that in the domain of foreign and security policy, the rational, *homo oeconomicus* logic is not applied by the Lib Dems. Instead, other factors are foregrounded and rated more important than in other political domains.

When it comes to the lives and safety of British soldiers (even if deployed in wars which the Lib Dems opposed), the pattern of argumentation changes and deviates from the usual cost-conscious and strictly rational or "sensible" rationale. This is confirmed by the use of the pronoun "our" [troops] to designate British soldiers serving abroad; Clegg includes them in the imagined community of British people who deserve to get "enough resources" to complete their "very difficult job".

7.2.6 Summary

The domain of foreign and security policy was the second-most debated topic in relation to Europe in corpus two. Concerning the argumentative structure of their contributions, the Lib Dem leaders' speeches in this policy area emphasised the importance of NATO (and, to a lesser degree, WEU) as primary safeguards of British security interests. Thereby, they accepted the dominant discourse and consensus that the transatlantic alliance should take precedence before EU cooperation in this area. However, they also made it clear that their primary concern was security in Europe, thus distinguishing a common European interest from the US-American approach. A belief in the "common" of a common foreign and security policy with other EU member states could thus be discerned in the Lib Dem speeches. They implied that these countries could be trusted, and a pooling of resources would, therefore, make perfect sense. They dismissed the wish for national significance exemplified in a sovereign foreign policy citing the rational assessment that the UK alone was in a weaker position than as part of an alliance or coordinated defence policy of a large organisation such as the EU. Although foreign policy and defence belong to the realm of "high" politics, typically classed as an inherently national prerogative, the Lib Dems consider the sharing of sovereignty as a price worth paying.

They stressed the possible positive outcomes of cooperation, e.g., when it came to a "European code for arms brokers", thus insisting that the EU brings an ethic or moral element into the domain of defence policy. The attractiveness of both NATO and the EU was repeatedly highlighted, and the Lib Dem leaders argued that this justified their endeavour to further integrate in the realm of defence policy. They dismissed the claim that the UK can punch above its weight or 'go it alone' in matters of foreign policy, instead adopting a rational and 'emotionless' approach. Feelings of national significance or nostalgic memories of a UK as a world power were dismissed as irrelevant. The Lib Dems apparently saw these emotions as superfluous and not worth to be addressed by a serious politician.

It can be concluded that the Lib Dem leaders advocated cooperation, even sharing sovereignty with the other European member states where policy aims in the areas of cost efficiency and peace-keeping coincided. When it came to defence spending, however, a community between the UK and the US as reliable contributors to the NATO budget was imagined, and other EU members were thus implicitly criticised for free-riding. The British army was exempted from calls for European integration. Equally, a higher EU budget for the CFSP was at least questioned, so the main aim seemed to be saving money (e.g. in the area of arms procurement) while maximising the impact of foreign policy through the pooling of resources.

In the months leading up to the UK commitment to the Iraq war, a change in tone could be perceived: In order for the EU to be a credible counterpart to NATO and to be able to undertake their own missions, cooperation between EU member states and their military was considered necessary. The idea that the EU could then pursue a "different" agenda than NATO was a surprising goal to be named. This became more pronounced when the UK joined the Iraq war, and there was the ensuing breach with France and Germany. The Lib Dems were against the Iraq war and expressed unhappiness about the close ties between Blair and the US president, calling for a more critical and independent stance. While Iraq dominated since 2003, the case of Iran was another example where the Lib Dems preferred policy coordination in the framework of the EU to following the US line. Similarly, conflict and peace in the Balkans and the Middle East were further topics on the Lib Dem agenda. Here, a high relevance was accorded to the EU as a forum for coordinated foreign policy efforts in the area of peace and stability in Europe and managing the consequences of war and destruction, namely dealing with the refugees.

However, the Lib Dems argued in favour of national sovereignty when it came to war and rejected a solidarity clause in the European Constitution which could force the UK into entering a war. So, while the same provision was accepted when it comes to NATO, a similar duty to stand by EU member states was rejected by the Lib Dems and they insisted that the "EU external relations remain emphatically intergovernmental". In the end, the UK government must be accountable to the HoC. Supranational elements in the EU competence for foreign and security policy were obviously the limit to their pro-EU stance.

Referring to identities, the word "community" was used in a very wide sense to refer to global communities with shared values. The boundaries were drawn to exclude Zimbabwe, which had breached human rights and was thus excluded from the community (at least discursively in a speech by Nick Clegg). This highlights a moral-based and normative value-laden approach to foreign policy where human rights are important. The Lib Dems took care of presenting their approach as "sensible", "sane", and "intelligent", and criticised other contributions to the discourse as "misleading" and stoking fear.

In conclusion, the Lib Dem leaders expressed a general preference for deepening cooperation with the EU in matters of foreign policy. This was presented as complementary to NATO, yet over the research period, a tendency towards emphasising distinct European security interests could be noted. While it was 'yes' to solidarity and joint projects as well as cooperation, however, the 'security' aspect, i.e. actual defence policy and military deployments, was excluded from the calls for more integration. A clear and resounding 'no' to a legally enforceable obligation to execute majority decisions in the policy area of foreign and security policy has to be seen against this background. When it came to the lives and safety of British soldiers (even if deployed in wars which the Lib Dems opposed), the pattern of argumentation changed and deviated from the usual cost-conscious and strictly rational or "sensible" line of argumentation. This is confirmed by the use of the pronoun "our" [troops] to designate British soldiers serving abroad; Clegg includes them in the imagined community of British people. When it came to their needs, he ruthlessly advocated taking advantage of strategic opportunities to get concessions from other EU countries such as France.

Coming back to Anderson's argument that the military aspect is a prime example of the strength of the national element and that in order to die for a country, the abstract concept of a nation has to be translated into an imagined community of fellow nationals, the Lib Dem position emphasised this line of reasoning: Factual gains (in money or efficiency or effectiveness) were not enough to legitimise the giving away of competences allowing to deploy national, i.e. British, soldiers. The idea that such decisions which affect the life and death of British citizens could be made somewhere else than in the HoC was unacceptable to the Lib Dem leaders. This shows that in this area, their priorities were not saving money or other "rational" motives, but it was about a national matter, whose control and accountability was attributed to British institutions but not the EU ones.

7.3 EU Treaties and the EU Constitution

EU treaties are a sensitive subject in British politics, not least because each codified step towards European integration touches on the issue of sovereignty. Giddings argues that "[i]nsofar as sovereignty can be taken to mean the ability to act independently or unilaterally, there is no escaping the fact that accession to the European Community has meant its diminution" (Giddings 2005b: "Westminster" 215). This means that from 1973 onwards, "the Diceyan view of parliamentary sovereignty" (Giddings 2005b: "Westminster" 215) was strictly speaking no longer applicable. Some argue that this was the case only from the introduction of the Single European Act onwards, but Giddings states that "to accommodate Diceyan theory it can be argued that as these restrictions [of Parliament's legislative competences] were self-imposed, they could be, as it were, self-removed" (Giddings 2005b: "Westminster" 215–216). It could be argued that with the Treaty of Lisbon of 2009, which includes Article 50 formally allowing members states to exit the EU, this element of sovereignty was officially recovered. Ironically, this state was not meant to last very long since the next British PM, David Cameron, called the referendum which paved the way towards this unprecedented move, and on 29 March 2016, his successor Theresa May triggered the Article 50 process which continues to riddle British politics ever since.

Looking back, EU treaties signed or at least discussed during the research period were the Treaty of Amsterdam, right at the beginning in 1997, and the Nice Treaty. However, the proposed EU Constitution was the most important treaty project; alternative names or descriptions of the EU constitution are "intergovernmental conference" and "convention", referring to the meetings or bodies negotiating a common text. Blair had promised a referendum on the European Constitution but changed his mind on this in spring 2004, for fear of a blockade in the House of Lords by the CON members and a parliamentary vote thus possibly (and embarrassingly) lost shortly before the election (Wall 2008: 183). Wall concludes that this "was already enough of a challenge" (2008: 171), meaning the EU Constitution debate superseded and blotted out the one about the euro. Wall also states that with an unsympathetic press and Blair almost single-handedly addressing European policy in public speeches in an attempt to swing public opinion, "the Constitutional Treaty risked becoming almost as much of an incubus for Tony Blair as the Maastricht Treaty had become for John Major" (Wall 2008: 182). When the Constitution Treaty was vetoed in two referendums in the Netherlands and France, "[i]t fell to the British government, in its Presidency of the EU in the second half of 2005, to try and pick up the pieces of the Constitution debacle" (Wall 2008: 183). Ultimately, the Treaty of Lisbon was the compromise, containing much of the text of the former Constitution treaty.

A manual search of all speeches resulted in 25 speeches where EU treaties were discussed by Lib Dem leaders:

Tab. 6: Lib Dem Leaders' Speeches Mentioning EU Treaties

Leader	Date	Name of Debate
Paddy Ashdown	18.06.1997	European Council Amsterdam
Paddy Ashdown	17.06.1998	European Council (Cardiff)
Charles Kennedy	11.12.2000	Nice European Council
Charles Kennedy	17.12.2001	European Council (Laeken)
Charles Kennedy	23.06.2003	European Council
Charles Kennedy	05.11.2003	Engagements
Charles Kennedy	15.12.2003	European Council
Charles Kennedy	20.04.2004	Europe
Charles Kennedy	21.06.2004	European Council
Charles Kennedy	03.11.2004	Convention on the Future of Europe
Charles Kennedy	08.11.2004	European Council/Brussels Summit
Charles Kennedy	23.11.2004	Queen's Speech
Charles Kennedy	17.05.2005	Queen's Speech
Charles Kennedy	15.06.2005	European Constitution
Charles Kennedy	20.06.2005	EC Budget
Charles Kennedy	22.06.2005	Proportional Representation
Menzies Campbell	19.06.2006	Brussels Summit (EC)
Menzies Campbell	03.07.2007	Constitutional Reform
Vince Cable	22.10.2007	Intergovernmental Conference (Lisbon)
Vince Cable	06.11.2007	Debate on the Address
Vince Cable	17.12.2007	European Council (Brussels)
Nick Clegg	27.02.2008	Engagements
Nick Clegg	17.03.2008	European Council
Nick Clegg	23.06.2008	European Council
Nick Clegg	23.06.2009	European Council

Total: 25 Debates

7.3.1 Paddy Ashdown

Ashdown made two references to European treaties and, therefore, institutional change on the EU level in total.

"European Council Amsterdam" (18.06.1997)

> That having been said, does the Prime Minister agree that the summit is marked not by the work it did, but by the work left to be done? Is it not true that there is a great deal of work to be done, perhaps at some future intergovernmental conference – surely there

must be one – to prepare the way for enlargement and to complete the process of institutional change? Surely the right hon. Gentleman cannot be satisfied with the progress
in, for example, the democratisation and accountability of the European institutions and
in other areas that need to be dealt with before Europe can move forward. That is important, and I hope that the Prime Minister will agree.
We should dispose of the leftovers of the Maastricht treaty and move on to the new
agenda of creating a people's Europe, which is less about the Europe of political elites
and more about the Europe that delivers what people in Europe want. It is only through
that that we can bind Europe's institution and move forward sensibly in the process of
integration. [Official Report, 18 June 1997; Vol. 296, c. 320–321]

In the first speech, in the debate on 'European Council (Amsterdam)', Ashdown
decides to focus first on the failures and omissions, i.e. the issues that could not
be resolved and the policy areas where no decision could be agreed upon in the
Treaty of Amsterdam. The long negotiations for this treaty had been concluded
earlier on the same day, triggering this Commons debate. Ashdown anticipates
a "future intergovernmental conference" as a means to an end – an agreement
on the constitutional issue should "prepare the way for enlargement and [...]
complete the process of institutional change". The word "complete" points to the
idea that the process of European integration should be finished at some point,
that there is a future state of the EU that can and should be considered as an end-
point of integration.

The enlargement of the EU is the policy goal that, in the argument of Ashdown,
necessitates the constitutional change; the latter is not advocated as something
positive in itself. In calling for improvement of the EU institutions, Ashdown
acknowledges current problems he sees in the EU at the time of speaking, such as
an unsatisfying level of "democratisation and accountability". The lack of these two
qualities is described as an obstacle for progress. Very clearly, Ashdown identifies
the issues holding back this progress in his opinion: the "leftovers of the Maastricht
treaty". This refers probably to the unresolved questions of the future make-up of
the European Commission and the voting procedures for majority votes, which
could not be agreed upon during the negotiations and had been deferred.

The direction he would like to see pursued is to "move forward sensibly". The
vision he would like to attain is a "people's Europe", a "Europe that delivers what
people in Europe want". In laying out this vision, Ashdown implies that in the
present state, the EU is not doing just that, and he also explicitly terms the status
quo a "Europe of political elites". A certain populist element is apparent here, with
the pitting of 'elite' versus 'the people'. However, Ashdown advocates change that
he obviously thinks can be attained and the vision realised with the government's
support, i.e. a renewal and reform from the inside instead of a radical overthrow
(which has later arguably been chosen with the pro-Brexit vote in 2016). This

seems to tie in well with the British mentality of seeking gradual reform while avoiding revolutions. Nevertheless, a constitution or somehow agreed separation of powers between the EU and the nation states is deemed necessary to "bind Europe's institution [sic]". This image conjured up with the word "bind" is something whose form needs to be compacted, or which needs to be tied down or restricted because it would spread otherwise. It could also refer to a rule-free space where no one is bound by law. Additionally, the word "sensibly" is an appeal for a rational and logical policy, i.e. one based on benefits for the UK and the tradition of pragmatically deciding whatever is best for the national interest.

"European Council (Cardiff)" (17.06.1998)

> I want to touch on three areas. The first is institutional. Does the Prime Minister agree—there was a hint of it in his statement—that the time has come for a much clearer definition of those powers that will be held at the centre of the European institutions and of those that must ultimately remain with the nation state? [Official Report, 17 June 1998; Vol. 314, c. 374–375]

In the second instance, speaking of the 'European Council (Cardiff)' Ashdown argues that the relationship between the institutions of the EU[5] and the member states needs to be much more clearly defined. The metaphor or "centre" versus "nation state" is interesting in that it establishes a centre-periphery analogy with Brussels as the centre and the negative connotation of the periphery applying to the nation states that are members of the European Union. He also says some powers "must ultimately remain with the nation state", thereby suggesting that they are in danger of being taken away. The need for codification or at least a clear definition of the respective powers accorded to each of the institutions and the member states themselves implies a difference between them, as if the member states were apart from European Union institutions and not an integral part of them such as in the Council of Ministers and with parliamentarians chosen from the member states in the European Parliament. The main point of criticism is then probably aimed at the European Commission, which represents a supranational element in the make-up of the EU. The idea of an "ever-closer union", which David Cameron tried to exclude from the wording of the Treaty on European Union during the re-negotiation preceding the in/out referendum in 2016, is clearly discernible in the argument. The Lib Dem position towards this principle expressed here is far from an enthusiastic endorsement of

---

5 Possibly, this is also menat to include other organisations such as the European Court of Human Rights and the Council of Europe since he says "European", not "EU".

a continuously progressing integration but rather a warning and a proposal to define the respective powers to prevent the supranational EU institutions from 'spreading', i.e. gradually acquiring more and more competences. This development is seen very critically by the CON at the time (whose leaders use terms like "European superstate"), but it is surprising to see the Lib Dem leader to argue along similar lines – or not even consciously argue but implicitly express the same unease about European integration without clear boundaries. The question of the *finalité*, the end-point or goal of the European integration process, thus becomes an issue for the European discourse of British political parties as early as 1998 and by outspoken Eurosceptics as well as by self-proclaimed Euro-friendly political actors. The fear that the nation state will be compromised is thus a pervasive feature of those parties' discourse and could in part be attributed to the national parliament as the only forum where the opposition parties play a role, and thus can exert any kind of influence or control over developments and decision on the European level.

7.3.2　Charles Kennedy

Charles Kennedy mentions this subject 14 times overall.

"Nice European Council" (11.12.2000)

> For Opposition Members who wanted the Nice summit to succeed, it is with a sense of relief, but not rapture, that we look at the outcome. It is good that an outcome was achieved; the alternative would have been a disentanglement of Europe. The Government should be complimented on maintaining the British veto in areas on which Labour and the Liberal Democrats agreed previously. [Official Report, 11 December 2000; Vol. 359, c. 356–357]

The first mention is occasioned by the Treaty of Nice and the Commons debate about it on 11 December 2000. Kennedy discursively creates a group of Europe-friendly MPs on the opposition benches ("opposition members who wanted the Nice summit to succeed"), which refers to the divisive and controversial nature of European integration. Moreover, it also points to the split within the CON where this topic is concerned, implying that some of their MPs would rather see European integration fail. Kennedy brings in an emotional element when he quotes "relief" and denies "rapture" as reactions to the outcome. He then proceeds to give a qualified welcome to the fact that there was some kind of agreement and thus a result of the summit, which he defines as a positive sign. Interestingly, he paints a very bleak picture of "the alternative" – namely "a disentanglement of Europe". The compromise that was achieved thus assumes a vital quality. Therefore, the argumentation structure presents a choice between moving forward of the path of integration and failure of the whole project. The option of preserving the status quo is denied, which means that the Lib Dem leader only accepts two kinds of positions: being in favour of the EU, which in this logic automatically means supporting further integration or at least signing further treaties on the one hand, and on the other hand a refusal of the latter and in consequence being against the EU as a whole or at least willing to take the risk of seeing it fail (due to a lack of progress). This is a binary that does not allow for nuances and makes for a justification to paint both the CON leader in a corner and justify Lib Dem support for the Nice treaty.

The second comment on the outcome is quite surprising given the self-styling of the Lib Dem leader as a pro-EU figure in the sentence before: "[t]he Government should be complimented on maintaining the British veto in areas on which Labour and the Liberal Democrats agreed previously". British vetoes in certain areas are welcomed, i.e. the Lib Dem leader admits that there are policy areas where integration steps are perceived as potentially unwelcome and threatening by both "pro-EU" parties in Westminster. A veto right is a defensive weapon against legislation decided on by a majority of other EU member states and the insistence on preserving it shows a certain degree of distrust or suspicion that future decisions might need to be blocked in the national British interest.

The comment also shows that the Lib Dems agree with the governing Labour Party on many aspects of European policy, suggesting a rather different relationship than that of opposition party to government. The CON is painted out of the important consensus across party lines on something as fundamentally integral to the British political system as membership of the European Union; indeed, Kennedy makes it appear as just one more policy area where the Official Opposition holds entirely different views and would seek unwelcome and irresponsible change should their turn in government come.

"European Council (Laeken)" (17.12.2001)

> In welcoming the Prime Minister's statement and the outcome of the summit, I wish to point initially to the fact that too many of the European Union's detractors over the years have been able to make their cases precisely because it has not had an adequately defined constitutional settlement for the member states. The work that will now be undertaken on that matter is therefore to be welcomed. We will end up with a document that sets out what the EU should be doing and what it should not get involved in. Any sensible, candid friend of Europe—in this party, we are certainly that—would give a broad measure of welcome to such a development. [Official Report, 17 December 2001; Vol. 377, c. 28]

In the next speech where Kennedy brings up a possible EU constitution, one full year later, commenting on the outcome of another European Council meeting (Laeken), he starts with a positive message of welcome extended to both the outcome and the PM's comments on it. He proceeds to condemn a group of other (political) actors as "the European Union's detractors" and argues that anti-EU arguments could only thrive in the past due to the absence of a clear reference document setting out the powers and the limits to the powers of the EU.

How this should convince anyone opposed to the EU to adopt the Constitution remains doubtful. It can thus be assumed that the Lib Dem leader addresses the government and other 'friends' of the EU in a bid to exclude Eurosceptics from the debate. The Lib Dem support for the Constitution then comes across as an attempt to withdraw the basis for fearmongering from the EU's opponents by putting it all above board, in a rational way; he basically claims that the absence of a constitution allowed for irrational fears of the EU and its potential power.

He predicts that the result will be "a document that sets out what the EU should be doing and what it should not get involved in". He thus claims that both the competences and the limits and boundaries to the EU's powers will be clearly allocated and limited; Kennedy refers to both in equal measure. Maybe Kennedy hopes that the (irrational) fear of the unknown or vague can thus be alleviated. It is interesting to note that the constitution is portrayed as something static, like a concluding document for a long process which defines the final status – laying down once and for all what remains the power of the nation state and what is the realm of EU competence. This appears like the opposite of "ever-closer union" and seeks to denounce predictions that the EU will try to aggregate more and more powers over time, in a never-ending process which is interpreted as a threat to nation-states by some British Eurosceptics.

Describing himself and his party (members) as "sensible, candid friend[s] of Europe", Kennedy contrasts this assessment with "the European Union's detractors" as the political opponents. He portrays Euroscepticism as destructive instead of constructive attempts for reform. He claims the vagueness of the EU treaties (and probably also the still wide-open question of *finalité*) are a breeding ground for fears (which he calls irrational, not justified in the least). All fears are dismissed as invalid reasons for political actions and decisions and the politicians using these fears in a state of uncertainty to promote their own goals are equally criticised. It is remarkable that he welcomes the constitution with the justification that there must be "an adequately defined constitutional settlement for member states". The Constitution is thus framed as a protective tool to serve the member states – against both fearmongering politicians seeking to overthrow the EU and the EU itself stopping the latter from appearing threatening by reigning in its powers.

"European Council" (23.06.2003)

My right hon. and hon. Friends and I certainly welcome the acceptance of the Convention's proposals in principle, and it is worth reminding ourselves that, not that many years ago, it would have been unthinkable that 15 existing member states and 10 accession countries could reach even this degree of consensus for sensible cooperation over the development of the EU.

There will be an intergovernmental conference later in the year, albeit that we do not know how long it will last, and I gather that the Government now acknowledge that there will be an opportunity for a further debate before the recess on the Convention proposals.

We obviously welcome that, but do the Government acknowledge that it would assist the House's capacity to discuss these matters in even more detail if they were to publish a White Paper outlining with more specific intent their approach to the forthcoming negotiations and their position on the relevant articles?

It was good to hear the Prime Minister make the positive case, where appropriate, for the relevant extensions to qualified majority voting and for the relevant applications of that process, and to begin to destroy some of the myths attached to that by opponents of the process.

The Government have described the proposals as they stand as a "good basis" for discussion. Surely, a dividing line must be drawn between what is a good basis for the ensuing discussion and allowing the unravelling of the basis of the Convention proposals, which is what some of the wreckers want to happen. Does the Prime Minister acknowledge the inherent dangers in that? [...] Equally welcome is the fact that taxation policy is to remain within the ambit of nation states, Governments and Parliaments.

On asylum, immigration and cross-border crime, not much progress seems to have been made on the first two. The Prime Minister said that the European Commission will report back on the pilot projects that did not command unanimity. What is the time scale for that report back, and what force will it have?

The whole point of a constitution for Europe is to codify the relevant levels of responsibility and competence. That should satisfy Euro-supporters and Euro-sceptics alike. In the House and in the debate in Britain, we must identify and make clear the difference between reassuring those who are constructively sceptical about aspects of Europe and those diehards who can never be satisfied. The leader of the Conservative party [sic] talks about a false debate. Is it not important that for the first time we have a voluntary exit clause for EU member states, which will place an obligation on each and every political party in British politics to make it clear whether it would ever wish to avail itself of such a clause?

In so far as the Convention moves us forward towards a Europe that is more democratic, more accountable and more transparent, it is to be welcomed. As a country, only inside Europe can we continue to make that case constructively—not increasingly destructively outside it. [Official Report, 23 June 2003; Vol. 407, c. 712–713]

The speech on the European Council meeting where the Convention's draft for
a European Constitution was accepted by the EU member state leaders is concerned with the Constitution only. Kennedy says he speaks for all the Lib Dem
MPs when he welcomes the "acceptance of the Convention's proposals in principle" and points out that it is the fact that a common denominator has been
agreed between so many states is worth something; the Lib Dem preference for
"consensus" enabling "sensible cooperation" becomes very clear. International
cooperation and seeking general agreement as to the future development of the
EU are deemed important, something that is diametrically opposed to the political culture of the UK where opposing views are fought about and the more convincing one wins without accommodating the other side.

Kennedy points out that the process of finally agreeing to a convention draft
document will be of an intergovernmental nature, which seeks to allay fears of
a supranational element that does not consider member states' views should
they differ from the rest. He also points out that parliamentary scrutiny on the
UK will be respected, with debates on the proposals in the HoC previewed. The
Lib Dem leader says: "we obviously welcome that", underlining the Lib Dem's
respect for the British parliament and its powers and procedures, which may be a
pre-emptive statement against accusation of unpatriotic views when it comes to
European policy, but is really not surprising for a third party whose main influence is wielded in the parliament at home (they had only 10 MEPs at the time).
Thus, the call for more transparency and better, more detailed opportunity to
comment on the government's stance on "relevant articles" of the Convention
is not surprising, either. It amounts to a demand for a more planned and clear
approach as opposed to a 'muddling through' by the government, some sort of
'make it up as you go along' approach without proper involvement of parliament,
which needs time.

Kennedy offers qualified support for majority voting in some areas on the
EU level, something he calls "relevant" twice, and praises the PM's communication on that subject which he terms "destroy[ing] some of the myths attached
to [QMV] by opponents of the process". The opponents are clearly British
politicians or other actors seeking to defend national sovereignty by fighting a
transition from intergovernmental decision-making where every leader as representative of his country's interests must agree to a proposal to QMV, meaning
some countries could be outvoted by a majority. The "opponents" consequently
want to keep a kind of veto right on many issues whereas the Lib Dems agree
with the PM's stance that QMV makes EU decisions more efficient and not every
single member country's national interests have to be respected – in view of the
enlargement, this is a provision to prevent any scenario where one out of 25

members could stop a consensus from being agreed upon. Politicians who prefer the opportunity for the UK to block unwanted developments at the price of such possible stalemates are classed as "opponents" who make up "myths" by the Lib Dem leader, which shows a rather fierce opposition between supporters of more supranational integration and those who reject this. The idea that other countries could decide something which goes against British interests but is nevertheless legally binding for every EU member state, including the UK, raises accountability and sovereignty issues for some – but these concerns are brushed aside as irrelevant by the Lib Dem leader. He obviously thinks the risk a low one and the big picture more important than details. Kennedy goes even further and attacks critics for supposedly wanting the "unravelling of the basis of the Convention proposals" and calls them "wreckers" (probably of the Constitution). The presence of political actors pursuing this goal is described as bearing "dangers" which Kennedy urges the PM to recognise. It is interesting that the discourse on the Constitution takes centre stage itself. Kennedy argues that the failure of the Constitution is not an acceptable option, and concerns voiced by opposition parties (however founded or not) are, therefore, a threat that he calls on the PM to address.

However, Kennedy goes on to address one point made by such a man, the CON MP and Convention member Heathcoat-Amory, thereby accepting that it is worth discussing. The domain of foreign policy seems excluded from the argument he just made and Kennedy supports an independent British foreign policy making, arguing that the Constitution should not bind the UK to any unwanted solidarity requirement and parliamentary scrutiny needs to be guaranteed in that regard (he does not oppose the NATO solidarity clause, however, so the line of argumentation is not really logical here and seems addressed to sceptic listeners fearing a blank cheque to EU member states for military action. A historical reference to the First World War dynamics at work in Europe might be the cause, for most members of the EU are NATO members too and it would, therefore, not make a real difference, but the impression of an automatic triggering of alliances shall nevertheless be avoided. Although he welcomes the position of an EU foreign minister, Kennedy obviously prefers foreign policy to be governed by intergovernmental principles, not by supranational ones. This could also be seen in more detail in Chapter 7.2. on foreign policy.

Another area where national precedence over the EU is welcomed by Kennedy is "taxation policy", where "nation states, Governments and Parliament" are to remain in charge according to Kennedy. He, therefore, does not support tax harmonisation and obviously does not deem it necessary to offer an explanation for this position. Since the budget is one of the crucial prerogatives of the British parliament obtained in a long historical struggle, however, it can be assumed that it is clear to every MP and British voter that these rights should remain untouched or at least that the Lib Dem leader assumes this is the case.

After having set out all these assumptions, Kennedy offers his view on why a constitution is needed after all: "The whole point of a constitution for Europe is to codify the relevant levels of responsibility and competence". This assessment presents the Constitution as a rather uncontroversial aim which also lays down the principle of subsidiarity. Kennedy thus adds the following to his statement: "That should satisfy Euro-supporters and Euro-sceptics [sic] alike". This is a rather clever discursive trick to make any attempt to let the Constitution fail as unreasonable and not effective. What follows is a harsh criticism of hard Euroscepticism as according to the definition by Szczerbiak and Taggart (2008: 240-241) in the UK political arena: "In the House and in the debate in Britain, we must identify and make clear the difference between reassuring those who are constructively sceptical about aspects of Europe and those diehards who can never be satisfied". This is a distinction mirroring Szczerbiak and Taggart's definition of hard and soft Euroscepticism almost exactly and shows very clearly that while Kennedy is ready to engage with soft Eurosceptics interested in real improvements or with legitimate concerns about European integration whereas he absolutely refuses to give in to "diehards who can never be satisfied". He effectively claims that there is a group of politicians and other members of the public (in "Britain" – which shows that he has accepted public opinion and the quality of the public discourse and debate as important, too) that are not interested in debating alternative ways of preserving British interests within the EU but only want out of the European Union. This is made even clearer when he claims that the case for reform of the EU can only be made and achieved by staying a member and coming up with pragmatic solutions instead of arguing "increasingly destructively outside it" which he accuses hard Eurosceptics of at the end of his speech. He even points out that the Convention proposals contain an exit clause and that the possibility of an exit would make it necessary for each party to take a stand and declare their position on the EU once and for all, meaning mostly the CON (foreshadowing the in/out referendum in 2016).

However, the idea that Lib Dems and government politicians should "reassure[...]" "those who are constructively sceptical about aspects of Europe" expresses a power and knowledge gap (like a doctor reassuring a patient or parent reassuring a scared child) and does not really accept concerns as legitimate or possibly more convincing or right, but rather as a lack of information that can be provided by those in the know – a rather arrogant or at least patronising approach.

In the last part of the speech, Kennedy describes the goal or vision the Lib Dems pursue, namely "a Europe that is more democratic, more accountable and more transparent". He claims the Constitution represents a step in this direction which justifies his support for it but also can be read as a concession that the EU is not perfect at the moment and definitely would profit from reform addressing an assumed democratic deficit and improving the lack of transparency in decision-making. He repeats the claim that reform and once again refers to an imagined community: "As a country, only inside Europe can we continue to make that case constructively", implying that the whole country is a community and should/needs to act as one single actor to achieve reform. This excludes all Eurosceptics who do not want to do this but rather leave the EU altogether from the community or at least accuses them of splitting the community.

"Engagements" (05.11.2003)

> May I also express my best personal wishes to the leader of the Conservative party [sic]? I want to raise an issue on which he and I share considerable common interests, if not common instincts: the Government's European policy. Yesterday, the Chancellor remarked that some of the measures in the proposed European Union constitution would lead to tax harmonisation and a federal state in Europe". Does the Prime Minister agree with the Chancellor?
>
> [Answer by PM]
>
> Yes indeed, but the Foreign Secretary keeps describing the proposed constitution— he has done so repeatedly in the House on many occasions—as a tidying-up exercise. Yesterday, however, the Chancellor warned that it could lead to fiscal federalism. With that difference of emphasis between the Foreign Secretary and the Chancellor, with whom does the Prime Minister agree? [Official Report, 5 November 2003; Vol. 412, c. 791–792]

In the next mention, the constitution is subject of Kennedy's questions at PMQs. Being called directly after the CON leader, he points out the shares "common interests, if not common instincts" on the UK European policy. This makes the self-perceived rift between the two main opposition parties in the area of European policy very clear and shows that the Lib Dems seek to differentiate themselves from the CON and not from the governing Labour Party. Nevertheless, Kennedy then picks out a controversial point in the Constitution and uses his two PMQ questions to draw attention to the possible impact on British tax rates and the eventual consequence, the *finalité* of the European Union that is foreshadowed or envisaged in the Constitution. These are "tax harmonisation and a federal state in Europe".

The spectre of a tax-controlling super state which would factually hollow out the British parliament, robbing it of its primary power and domain to control the budget of the government, is raised. While both terms are attributed to the Labour Chancellor at the time, Gordon Brown, it becomes clear that the Lib Dems object to both and Kennedy demands clarification from the PM. This shows up a split in government – their communication is clearly not streamlined but the two most senior cabinet members present very different assessments of the Convention. While the Foreign Secretary has been insisting, according to Kennedy, that the treaty can be seen as a "tidying-up exercise", a formulation which seeks to downplay the importance of the Constitution and denies any symbolic value attached to it, making it a rational argument only concerned with content, the Chancellor sees the EU headed towards "fiscal federalism" with the Constitution and thus discursively imbues the Constitution with a high and worrying density of regulations that could lead towards a state of affairs that is undesirable for the British. The fact that this is seen as a threat by the Lib Dems is underlined by the use of the verb "to warn" that replaces "to remark" in Kennedy's second repetition of the claim that the Constitution contains provisions for tax harmonisation. The Constitution is thus framed as potential danger and Kennedy does not accept an evasive answer but seeks a final clarification from the PM as to whether Blair sees it the one way or the other. This could also be an attempt to get the PM to deny any danger which would strengthen their own position of supporting the Constitution. It shows a sense of unclarity and mixed messages sent about the Constitution by cabinet members; this may further confuse voters and makes it clear that a lot here is about interpreting facts and fears about a potential future development, not about facts and events themselves. The fact that "tax harmonisation" seems to be such an undesirable development shows that the British parties care more about parliamentary sovereignty then about European solidarity (tax harmonisation aims at reducing competition between member states in order to avoid a "rat race" that would benefit some countries while others paid the price by losing company headquarters, for example).

"European Council" (15.12.2003)

May I stress to the Prime Minister that the Liberal Democrats remain firmly of the view that there remains the need for a constitution – a codification of European operating procedures – not least because of the welcome enlargement that is now in front of us and that those who seek some comfort from the difficulties of the weekend overlook the much bigger picture? Those of us who were Members of Parliament at the time remember the Monday after the weekend when the Berlin wall came down and all those countries of central and eastern Europe that had been under the tyranny of the communist regime in the Soviet Union suddenly began to experience liberation. That was the big picture and the big prize for Europe, and we must not lose sight of the fact that, despite the political difficulties that were encountered at the weekend, the constitution will give effect to an enlarged Europe. That is a pivotal point, which those of us who are of a pro-European slant are correct to emphasise.

Does the Prime Minister agree that the spectre that has been raised during the weekend of a two-speed Europe – a two-tier Europe – is not in Europe's interests and is certainly not in British interests? That being the case, will the Prime Minister tell us how that sense of two-tierism will prejudice his ambitions on behalf of the Government for our country to remain at the heart of Europe? Finally, will he confirm that it remains the Government's intention to secure a decent and deliberative outcome to the Convention process, arriving at a workable constitution for an enlarged EU? That is in British interests, and it is profoundly in European interests as well. [Official Report, 15 December 2003; Vol. 415, c. 1325–1326]

In the next speech concerned with the Constitution, Kennedy stresses that the Lib Dems are united on that matter and that his comments reflect a unified party line at the beginning. This remark coupled with a repetition of the verb "to remain" – he says the Lib Dems "remain firmly of the view that there remains the need for a constitution" begs the question if he perceives a slackening of support and waning resolution either among his own MPs or the government when it comes to the British acceptance of the Constitution. He proceeds to define what the Constitution means, offering his assessment: it is described as "a codification of European operating procedures". This interpretation is in line with the foreign secretary's stance of downplaying the importance of the constitution in so far as it does not mention any symbolic value and apparently no new content – listening to Kennedy, the constitution is thus a mere transcript of procedures already in place, making them transparent but not adding anything substantial to them.

The speech argumentatively connects the Constitution with the enlargement of the European Union (which will be more widely discussed in Chapter 7.5.) by offering this "welcome" development as a reason for the Lib Dem support for the constitution. Kennedy claims that "the constitution will give effect to an enlarged Europe". He presents the constitution as something of a firmly mandatory character, something that is needed for enabling enlargement (an example of making a policy appear as without alternatives if a commonly agreed on goal is to be reached). This claim is underlined discursively by calling it "a pivotal point" which all pro-European British politicians "are correct to emphasise". This moral judgement involves an imagined community of "those of us who are of a pro-European slant", creating an in-group and an out-group pitched against each other among British politicians characterised by their attitude towards Europe. It is also "those who seek some comfort from the difficulties of the weekend", which saw the failure of the EU Council meeting which was supposed to produce agreement on a constitution for the enlarged EU and settle a conflict over voting powers among the member states (BBC 2003), who seem to belong to this morally superior group of constructive politicians who "overlook the bigger picture" that the transition from former Eastern bloc countries to EU members will be achieved, instead of enjoying the possible failure of the constitution and in conflict among EU member states. Kennedy thus transports the view that the details of the constitution's content are less important than a general ability of the member states to agree on a common path and to solve conflicts of interest peacefully with the grand strategic goal in mind.

The last paragraph comes back to the disagreement among member states and the proposal that some states could adopt and agree on the Constitution while others opt out or join later because no agreement was reached in the negotiations leading up to the summit meeting. Kennedy terms this proposal a "spectre", something threatening and wholly undesirable, and establishes the presupposition that the construct of a "two-tier" or "two-speed Europe" is not in "Europe's and certainly not in British interests". Once again, the EU and "Europe" are used synonymously here. Kennedy himself does not explain why exactly, but calls on the PM to elaborate on the incompatibility of the Labour policy goal of "being at the heart of Europe" with a multi-speed Europe. It is surprising because a) the UK already has quite a few opt-outs from European integration steps and has been quite happy with this and b) Kennedy seems to assume that it will be the UK that falls into the second class or tier, as opposed to other countries. Implicitly, the acknowledgement that a Eurosceptic majority among voters might block the UK's role at the top table in favour of being a second-tier member who does not keep up with the rest is apparent here and that such a development is highly likely. Thus, the Euro-friendly Lib Dems must oppose a two-tier Europe to secure their goal that they share with Labour, namely to move the UK to a top position in the centre of EU power. This "ambition" is only attributed to the Government but obviously shared by the Lib Dems. The imagined community "our country" is portrayed as deserving a top spot and play first fiddle in the EU. The idea of trading importance in the EU for a higher degree of national sovereignty is not described as desirable or even possible. This can be classed as a case of "punching above one's weight" or seeking to uphold appearances of being an equally important member in the EU as, say, in the UN's Security Council – a top vote among European powers.

Kennedy ends his intervention with a call for the PM to ensure there is "a decent and deliberative outcome to the Convention process" and that the end result will be a "workable constitution for an enlarged EU". The priorities are made clear again: it is reaching a consensus and enabling good processes adapted to a much larger EU, which is a policy aim the Lib Dems support (again, see also Chapter 7.5 on the issue of enlargement for more details). He claims that this is in the national as well as international interest, while the order in which interests are presented is clear: it is "British interests" first, although Kennedy goes on to say that it is "profoundly in European interests as well".

"Europe" (20.04.2004)

We certainly welcome the Prime Minister's confirmation today that in due course there will be a referendum of the British people on the proposed European constitution. We welcome that, whatever the ultimate motives that led the Prime Minister to his overdue decision. I can only express the hope, at the outset, that the co-ordination of a European referendum campaign will be a bit more slick and polished than the co-ordination that led to today's announcement in the House of Commons.

Does the Prime Minister agree that when the referendum comes it must be based on an unloaded, unbiased question which will be subject to confirmation by the Electoral Commission, and that it is best decided after due parliamentary consideration? Does he agree, or at least acknowledge, that one of the subtexts of the dispute, or debate, about timing in which he is now engaged is that—while the other European member states have their own processes, which mirror or will act in parallel with ours, and that is obviously outside the Government's control—the timing of the next British general election is of course in the hands of the Prime Minister himself? The general election is the only race in the world in which a principal competitor also holds the starting pistol. When it comes to an issue as important as the timing of a referendum on a fundamental matter concerning Britain's role in Europe and the related timing of a general election—if ever there was a case for fixed-term Parliaments, this must surely be it.

It is clear from the exchanges so far that when the referendum comes it will set its own pace and develop its own character. Does the Prime Minister agree that, whatever the expressions of public support over the past year to 18 months, one thing that comes through loud and clear in every analysis of public opinion is that a great percentage of people repeatedly say that they want more unbiased, factual information on which to base their final conclusions about Europe? This campaign must represent the opportunity to provide that.

Does the Prime Minister also agree that, in one of the great missed opportunities of recent years, those of a Eurosceptical or Euro-hostile disposition have been allowed far too much of the running, and that therefore the more quickly the pro-European forces can co-ordinate and make a positive case based on the facts, the better it will be? Does the Prime Minister now propose to move quickly to re-establish a pro-European British campaign, drawn from all political parties and, indeed, from outside formal party politics itself? Does he acknowledge that if the referendum campaign, whenever it comes, were hatched, controlled and spun from No. 10 Downing Street, that would not command the confidence or its participants and would not persuade the British public of the desired outcome?

Does the Prime Minister acknowledge that his negotiating position between now and June will be strengthened by today's announcement? Does he acknowledge that that applies particularly to his ability to guarantee the red lines—which, as he knows, we support—especially the maintenance of the national veto over matters concerning constitutional changes, defence, taxation, spending policies, social security and the like? Given his strengthened negotiating stance, will he, between now and June, push for further improvements in the treaty? Not least, will he stress that European Union action should be limited to specific objectives that make sense in the context of nation states, that there must be more enforcement of consistency in regard to EU rulings and laws across member states, and that there should be more decentralisation to local communities throughout Europe?

Finally, what discussions does the Prime Minister envisage will take place to decide what will be the umbrella organisation for a pro-European campaign to be registered with the Electoral Commission? Assuming that his Government are in power administering the proposed referendum, will he apply collective Cabinet responsibility or will he take the view of Harold Wilson in the 1970s that it can be suspended?

Surely this is an historic opportunity to settle at last an issue that has bedevilled two generations of British politics and each and every successive Government of whatever political persuasion across those generations. At the end of the day, it will come down, to use the phrase of the leader of the Conservative party [sic], among those of us of all political persuasions where Britain's future engagement in Europe is concerned, to being between those who want to live and let live and those who will increasingly be exposed as wanting, where Britain's future in Europe is concerned, to live and then let die. [Official Report, 20 April 2004; Vol. 420, c. 161–163]

In the debate entitled "Europe", Kennedy makes a long speech and starts it off with applauding the PM's decision to hold "a referendum of the British people on the proposed European constitution" and calls it "overdue". It seems the Lib Dems have well and truly accepted a referendum as the legitimate option to ensure the constitution's acceptance among the British – this shows that the monarch in Parliament as the sovereign is no longer seen as able to decide and have that decision accepted. In fact, this marks up a perceived crisis of the British political system and dire need for constitutional reform according to the Lib Dem leader, which is consistent with Kennedy's further demand to introduce fixed-term parliaments so the general election date will not interfere with a referendum. In this context, he terms the constitution as concerned with a "fundamental matter concerning Britain's role in Europe", thus attributing a high salience to the constitution and also charges with significance the entire relationship between the UK and the EU.

Moreover, he criticises the way the referendum was announced by the government and expresses his hope that "a European referendum campaign will be a bit more slick and polished" – this draws attention to the fact that a least keeping up appearances of an orderly, serious procedure is deemed very important by the Lib Dem leader. This is a sign that Kennedy assumes the style in which the campaign is conducted and the perceived professionalism of the campaign will be highly influential on the outcome. Connected to this, he also calls for an "unloaded, unbiased question" and "parliamentary consideration", which shows how concerned he is that the campaign should not be perceived as subjective in any way. It also shows that he factors in the issue of distrust in political elites. Addressing (British) public support of European policy, he comes back to this more explicitly when he quotes polls saying British voters "want more unbiased, factual information on which to base their final conclusions about Europe". Kennedy calls for the campaign to deliver on this wish. This flags up again the distrust of voters in information provided by politicians, perhaps coupled with the fear of being manipulated. This might lead to the conclusion that the Labour strategy to marginalise the issue in public debate (see e.g. Daddow 2011a: *Britain and Europe* 6) was not effective in reaching the goal to ensure public support for the EU Constitution. The fact that Kennedy speaks of "final conclusions about Europe" makes it clear that he sees the referendum indeed as something that will settle the matter for a long time, with a yes-vote giving a strong mandate for continuing European integration to future British governments.

In this speech, Kennedy takes a verbal swing at "Eurosceptical or Euro-hostile" political actors and other influential figures in the UK and argues that they have been allowed to dominate the discourse on Europe over "recent years". This assessment serves a justification for his call for action, asking the PM to "re-establish a pro-European British campaign" as a means for "pro-European forces [to] co-ordinate and make a positive case based on the facts", and this rather sooner than later. It is an implicit criticism that public debate has been shunned by Labour and thus been dominated by newspapers and Conservative politicians arguing against Europe, which acknowledged the importance of public opinion when it comes to British European policy and highlights the absence of an established consensus between mainstream parties and the majority of voters on this issue. The specific description of a needed "positive case based on the facts" also implies that other actors have not been telling the truth and have indeed produced 'fake news' on the issue of Europe, and with an invariable aim to discredit the EU, not informing about both benefits and problems.

What the Lib Dem leader then says, however, indicates a worrying distrust in British political structures and official government communication by himself as leader of the third-largest party in the HoC: he demands a campaign that is perceived to be neutral, and this excludes a government initiative according to Kennedy.

> Does he acknowledge that if the referendum campaign, whenever it comes, were hatched, controlled and spun from No. 10 Downing street, that would not command the confidence or its participants and would not persuade the British public of the desired outcome?

This is a surprisingly blunt vote of distrust against the government and accuses them of misinforming the public and even supporters of the referendum within the highest levels of politics and society, so that neither citizens nor other politicians will believe them. This can indeed be classified as a populist message unworthy of the Lib Dems but also an important clue where the main problem lies (and it may not be Europe but a crisis of the political system which no longer enjoys the trust and respect). To remedy this, Kennedy calls for a campaign similarly structured to the one in 1975 instead, where a cross-party platform was strengthened by supporters from domains such as sports, entertainment, and business as well as interested citizens, as the documents of the campaign in the parliamentary archives in Westminster impressively show.

An interesting return to a more realist world view when it comes to states negotiating with each other is shown by the argument that the decision to hold a referendum gives the PM more power in the negotiations on the final constitution text. The rationale is clear: the fear of losing a referendum in the UK and thus a failure of the entire project makes it more likely the other member states will give in to more UK demands. This line of argumentation assumes that the decision will be a rational one about the actual content of the constitution, though, and also that the government knows and demands exactly what a majority of the British voters want. It is a classic win/lose scenario that uses pressure or even blackmail to obtain more favourable results for oneself (the UK) at the expense of the rest of the EU, at least according to the Lib Dem leader. He effectively calls on the PM to use the referendum to pressurise the other negotiation partners into concessions for the UK. He explicitly says that he supports British vetoes – he says "national" and thus extends the privilege to other member states as well – but the main thrust of the argument is clear in that it expresses distrust in and rejection of supranational decision-making in those areas. This applies to a number of policy domains: "constitutional changes, defence, taxation, spending policies, social securities and the like" –which is indeed a quite comprehensive list and reveals a large number of policy domains in which the Lib Dems support national sovereignty over EU competences. Subsequently, Kennedy demands that the PM should push for "improvements in the treaty" that safeguard these interests. The formulation is also telling: in insisting on those exemptions from EU influence, the Lib Dem leader supports "red lines" that he hopes the PM will be able to "guarantee". With these words, Kennedy describes a large part of policy domains as a threatened area that the British government must protect from unwelcome interference by a foreign power, namely the EU. It is not mentioned that especially the large member states are always involved in EU decision-making and the European Council and Council of the EU are both EU institutions that consist of national government members, without whom nothing can effectively be decided. This impression is further strengthened by the rhetorical question: "will he stress that European Union action should be limited to specific objectives that make sense in the context of nation states"? The heavy emphasis on the idea that the constitution should mainly serve as a bulwark against the EU gaining more competences and having power to decide on matters the Lib Dem leader considers inappropriate for it to do so is unexpected from the self-proclaimed pro-European party and stands in contrast to the sharp criticism of Eurosceptics earlier in the same speech. In fact, Kennedy reveals his own ambition to "persuade the British public of the desired outcome" – how this differs from government "spin", which he criticised earlier, remains unclear, unless we read this passage as an effective accusation that the government lie and spread false facts.

Kennedy also calls for "more consistency" of EU law, addressing the issues of (a lack of) certainty of justice and the power of the European courts to interpret and create new laws in a legal system *sui generis* (which is not popular with many British political actors and voters) and "more decentralization to local communities", stressing the supposed absence or not insufficient applicability of the subsidiarity principle and addressing the fear of a centralising super state named EU (albeit this sounds more like the CON's view!) and positioning himself as defender of the less influential parts in the UK (itself a highly centralised state, despite changes introduced with devolution).

Moreover, he seems interested in knowing whether Blair will "apply collective cabinet responsibility" or emulate the example of Harold Wilson, who had suspended the principle in 1975. This is a further remarkable hint that the relationship between the UK and the EU is seen as such an extraordinary topic that abandoning one of the defining principles of the British political system seems justified, namely that of collective cabinet responsibility. Whereas inner-party disagreement might have prompted Wilson to suspend the principle in order to avoid a rebellion and break-up of government, the fact that the Lib Dems call for such an exception points to both the continuing existence of such disagreements within the Labour Party and/or to the nature of this decision which should be

decided according to the conscience and personal conviction of each MP even if
they are government members. This is remarkable because the issue of British-
European relations thus acquires the status of a matter of personal belief, not one
of rational argument and party line (which is possible on every other subject – at
least no such exceptional procedure is demanded for any other policy domain
(if we ignore the fact that the Lib Dems also call for proportional representation,
which might give us a clue as to where their belief in referendums to achieve
their goals stems from; as a third party, they cannot hope to achieve that in parliament against the majority of the two beneficiaries of the system. However, this
is not the same as a policy area where parties can normally formulate a position
and let the voter decide – in the case of Europe, this legitimisation does not seem
enough even to the Lib Dems.) As it happened, Cameron later decided to emulate Wilson's example and failed miserably to achieve the desired result, with the
fiercest opposition against his position coming from his own cabinet members
(Glencross 2016).

The importance Kennedy accords to the referendum is made clear towards the
end of the speech: "Surely this is an historic opportunity to settle at last an issue
that has bedevilled two generations of British politics and each and every successive Government of whatever political persuasion across those generations". This
assumption serves as a further justification of Lib Dem support for a referendum
on the constitution and makes it clear that for the Lib Dems, it is about much
more than just the treaty itself, but about a general approval of British involvement in the European integration process which will establish a consensus and
make it redundant to fight about each and every step along the way. He portrays
the decision as a binary pole with egotistical, cold-blooded defenders of a national
sphere who are happy to let the European project go to shame at one end and
the tolerant and cooperative politicians who prefer to come to an arrangement
with the EU that is beneficial for both sides on the other. This comes close to
a choice between good and bad and the listeners may feel compelled to choose
sides. The use of the metaphorical phrases "live and let live" versus "live and then
let die" to illustrate the two different poles introduces a vital element into the
debate and makes the position of hard Eurosceptics seem inhumane and rejecting
solidarity – first profit from a situation and then turn away when the tables turn.
In terms of values, the latter behaviour can be morally judged as bad and unsympathetic. It also says a lot about the importance of the UK for the EU according to
the Lib Dem leader: the UK is obviously seen as on a par with the rest of the EU as
an 'other', a rival with which one has to circumvent. If the British should vote no in
a referendum, this is presented as handing a deadly blow to the EU. The parallels
to the 2016 debate surrounding the in/out referendum are obvious.

"European Council" (21.06.2004)

The next speech is made after the constitution treaty was signed by Blair and the other 24 EU member states and the ratification process needs to get underway.

May I, on behalf of my right hon. and hon. Friends, give a general welcome to the fact that this compromised treaty was agreed and unanimously endorsed by 25 member states and Governments over the course of the weekend? Will the Prime Minister acknowledge that, given the welcome and historic enlargement of Europe and the triumph of democracy, and of socially fair market democracy at that, the model that operated for a Europe of six was simply not applicable to a Europe continuing to develop with a membership of 25?

Does the Prime Minister agree that this constitutional treaty should be seen as a mechanism? It is not a moral crusade, although listening to some of those opposed to it, one could be forgiven for thinking otherwise. Indeed, in the minds of many of us, including those who support Europe, much of the conduct in and around this weekend's summit was a rather poor advert and a persuasive argument that further reform of the way in which Europe goes about its business is long overdue.

Does the Prime Minister agree that the new threats facing Europe, particularly global terrorism and climate change, as well as long-standing problems such as reform of the common agricultural policy, will be given better effect in a collective way as a result of the procedures outlined in the treaty? Will he indicate specifically the prospects under the provisions in the treaty for tackling the CAP – such a long-running source of frustration for successive Governments and this country as a whole?

We surely deceive ourselves by the allure of semi-detachment as a country from Europe or, far more so, of outright isolationism. Therefore, those who are sceptical as well as those who are enthusiastic about Europe should surely welcome a treaty that sets out the competences of the wider European Union and how they can be fairly adjudicated in the interests of both the individual European citizen and member states and Governments who make up the wider Europe.

Will the Prime Minister acknowledge that none of us can deny the growth of Euroscepticism both in this country and throughout the EU? Political elites have run ahead of their domestic public opinion for too long. That is why the referendum has become so essential. The Prime Minister spoke in his statement of the new responsibilities of national Parliaments under the treaty to shape and have a greater input into European legislation. Does he agree that however long it is until the referendum in Britain, from now until such time the Government could make – the Leader of the House is with us today – specific proposals to put more of our handling of European business in this House, centre stage, in order to explain and demonstrate to people the relevance of what Europe is doing and the way in which, as parliamentarians from across the spectrum, we attend to it? Do the Government have any proposals in that respect?

Finally, on the issue of the referendum, we have had so many false dawns and false starts with this Government, as the Prime Minister well knows. Will he acknowledge today that, having put his signature to the treaty and given that he is having to try to sell it to the British public and that trust in him and his Government is not what it was several years ago, the campaign for the referendum, if it is to be successful, will have to be broadly based, cross-party and involve significant persuasive voices from those outside formal party politics? Will he acknowledge that a referendum campaign that is seen by the public in this country to be spun from No. 10 Downing street would not be won? Although there is scepticism about Europe to be overcome, there is also scepticism about the Government that can undermine the case that needs to be made. The battle is now joined. I hope that, across the political spectrum, we shall be able to make a constructive, pragmatic and principled pro-European case. We look forward to the spectacle of some of the very strange bedfellows who will face us. [Official Report, 21 June 2004; Vol. 422, c. 1086–1087]

In the speech on the 'European Council', Kennedy emphasises the unity of the Lib Dems when it comes to support for the EU Constitution, which he terms a "compromised treaty". While "compromised" is usually a negatively connoted word, in this case it might be meant as a compliment for the many EU members to have found common ground. Kennedy stresses the dynamic character (a need to adapt to changing circumstances) of the EU polity structures, in so far as it is an ongoing process. The enlargement is presented as driving this change to a significant degree. The fact that 25 states agreed to a single treaty is celebrated as something remarkable by Kennedy, showing his preference for cooperation and consensus rather than competition or conflict between states. The Lib Dem leader offers an ex-post legitimisation for his party's support for the constitutional treaty in advancing the view that "the model that operated for a Europe of six was simply not applicable to a Europe continuing to develop with a membership of 25". The treaty is thus framed as a necessary corollary to keep up with previous developments, a means to adapt to a changed situation and to allow for efficiency and efficacy. It seems like an 'I've always said so' moment, indicating that Kennedy feels confirmed by the developments which seem to have proven him right.

However, he downplays the importance of this perceived political victory when he then asks for the PM's agreement, saying that "this constitutional treaty should be seen as a mechanism". This sounds like a technical, rational, and pragmatic solution for a problem that denies any symbolic content which could warrant emotional responses. The constitution is also called "the treaty" very often in this speech, as if Kennedy was trying to avoid the use of the word "constitution". The turning against opponents and critics of the treaty (he refers to the CON) for trying to frame the debate on the constitution with just these factors contributed to making it look like "a moral crusade". This points to the existing split in British politics when it comes to views on the constitution, and Kennedy rejects this wholeheartedly as inappropriate. However, he also criticises any undignified behaviour on the part of continental European leaders, which obviously does not correspond to British values like fairness and politeness. He, therefore, concedes that more reform of the procedures of European cooperation is needed. It is possible that he has a British standard of etiquette and manners in mind to which the EU (which is personified with the sentence "the way Europe goes about its business") does not conform yet. It seems he claims that the lack of style is a reason for many British observers to reject the EU; this points towards a cultural clash rather than a disagreement over policy content or institutional structures.

Addressing the actual content as far as policy areas are concerned, Kennedy emphasises the potential benefits of cooperation and his view that the constitution will enhance the cooperation of member states, notably in the policy domains of terrorism (security policy) and climate change (environmental policy), describing these two challenges as "new threats" that he claims the EU can face in a better way now the treaty has been agreed (this anticipates the success of the ratification phase which was still outstanding at this point in time). Besides, he concentrates on the CAP as a problem to be solved and voices his hopes that the PM will push for reform here using the new procedures agreed in the treaty. The Lib Dem position on CAP is analysed in more detail in Chapter 7.4.

"We surely deceive ourselves by the allure of semi-detachment as a country from Europe, or, far more so, of outright isolationism". With this sentence, Kennedy addresses all British listeners as an imagined community, and although the aim is to unveil the idea that outside of the EU the grass is greener, this is countered by his use of the word "allure", which concedes that the idea of keeping one's distance or breaking it off entirely seem quite attractive to the British community he mentions at the start of the sentence. It is the tone of a wise man speaking to his not so clever and experienced compatriots, explaining to them what is real(istic) and what is a mirage, a dream. In this understanding and avuncular tone of a sympathetic and well-meaning advisor, Kennedy elicits the impression that it is understandable to want to leave but unfortunately not possible or sensible. The word semi-detachment may also be read as a curious cultural reference to a common form of dwelling that is the dream of many British families who cannot afford a detached house – the same order of preference applies, with a generally accepted assessment that a flat, i.e. sharing a house with others is less desirable than having at least half a house to oneself, with the ultimate aspiration of owning a detached home all by oneself which may then fittingly seen as one's "castle" (see e.g. Kamm and Lenz 2004: 136). All this strengthens the impression that the Lib Dem leader tries to convince his listeners that it is a necessary, but not quite agreeable decision to participate in European integration. This can be considered as foreshadowing the Brexit decision in so far as he acknowledges the existing wish for isolation.

He calls, therefore, on both groups – he describes them as "those who are sceptical [sic] as well as those who are enthusiastic about Europe", making this once again a choice between ratio and emotion – to accept that factually, they both stand to gain something from the treaty because it will fix and regulate the relationship between and seek to balance the interests of "both the individual European citizen and member states and Governments". Interestingly, these two are presented as different stakeholders, and the idea that only the constitution will ensure that the competences of the EU "can be fairly adjudicated" does not shine a positive light on the status of the EU before the treaty. Once again, Kennedy uses the word "Europe" when he means "EU", interchanging the terms at leisure or equating them (whereas Brexiteers have later tried to define them as separate in the referendum campaign).

In a surprisingly outspoken way, Kennedy then admits that "none of us can deny the growth of Euroscepticism both in this country and throughout the EU". The last information puts the British situation in an EU-wide context, thus avoiding the impression that the problem is restricted to the UK or that Euroscepticism is a specifically British phenomenon at all. He accuses political elites to be the cause of Euroscepticism because they did not listen to their voters and "have run ahead of their domestic public opinion for too long". The expression "run ahead" implies a hierarchy between someone who is better and able to run faster who does not respect the lesser ability of his fellow runners although they can only win as a team (that is what Kennedy suggests). Kennedy presents the referendum as the only solution to close this gap and claims: "[t]his is why the referendum has become so essential". He attempts to establish a monocausal chain of events, with the political elite as the origin of the problem (notwithstanding the fact that he himself is part of the elite and did not mention the public or voters a lot in the discourse on Europe). This laying the rise of Euroscepticism at the feet of the government bears resemblance to the rather populist arguments advanced by the CON and UKIP. It suggests that the referendum is seen as a tool to re-establish the connection between people and elite, implying that basically MPs as the sovereign of the UK have failed to convince voters that what they do is acceptable and calling into question the legitimacy of the government majority in making decisions on behalf of all British citizens. This is effectively a vote of no confidence in the political system to deal with the "Europe" issue.

Kennedy further claims that voters do not "trust" the PM and his party as much as they used to (speaking when Labour's second term was drawing to a close), and he repeats this alleged trust crisis when he claims that "a referendum campaign that is seen by the public as in this country to be spun from No. 10 Downing street [sic] would not be won" and again when he says "there is scepticism about Europe to be overcome, there is also scepticism about the Government that can undermine the case that needs to be made". That is heavy stuff from the mouth of a self-proclaimed pro-European and believer in parliament. It paints the picture of a political system in crisis because it no longer commands the trust and respect of voters, and pictures the government support as an obstacle on the way to reaching the policy goal. This uncommonly harsh attack on the government when it comes to European policy may be an indicator of just how critical the level of Euroscepticism is in the eyes of the Lib Dem leader, but also a mark of self-importance – the Lib Dem leader claims that the success of the referendum rests on the condition that the campaign "will have to be broadly based, cross-party and involve significant persuasive voices from those outside formal party politics", which presumably is an undisguised advertisement for an important part in the campaign for the Lib Dems. Besides prophesying that the government will lose the referendum otherwise, the list of needed supporters also reveals an acknowledgement that British voters' trust in the political establishment as a whole is so low that they need help from other parts of society in order to win. The fact that Kennedy wants to persuade voters, together with the expression that the PM "is having to try to sell" the treaty to the "British public", however, does not sound much different to the supposed government spin; Kennedy does not say "convince" but persuade.

The metaphorical imagery for the two sides of the expected campaign, i.e. when Kennedy says: "the battle is now joined", depicts the decision on Europe as a fight and the persuasion of the public as the battleground that needs to be won (over). He sets out the rules and strategy for this discursive fight he deems appropriate for his camp, namely to "make a constructive, pragmatic and principled pro-European case". From the political opponents of the constitution, Kennedy expects a "spectacle" however, and the alliance with "very strange bedfellows who will face us". This is probably meant to include the UKIP members and supporters. This imagery depicts the political debate over which kind of relationship with the European Union is appropriate not as a serious and adult exchange of views but a coming fight in a circus where the battle lines are clearly drawn, and compromise or consensus is not an option. This is a typical set-up of a British political culture of having to win a debate and impose the dominant view on the opponent (majority system). It does not seem advisable to me, however, to try and extend this debating style to a nationwide discussion if the risk of a split society is to be minimised. The discursive demeaning of the proponents of the opposing view as "strange" is not very gentlemanlike, either. It seems the Lib Dem leader sees style and manners as more important as the actual positions of the constitution critics.

He also says parliamentary scrutiny of European legislation has to be improved and calls for new rules for debating European issues not mostly in committees, as is was the case at the time, but rather in the HoC, "centre stage, in order to explain and demonstrate to people the relevance of what Europe is doing and the way in which, as parliamentarians from across the spectrum, attend to it". This is a criticism which implies that not enough has been done on that score. Kennedy personifies the EU or "Europe" as an independent actor that "is doing" things, and that MPs "attend to". This is a construction that pits the EU against national parliaments and does not explain the interrelations, but nevertheless acknowledges that the whole political spectrum may express their opinion (which might be designed to avoid the impression that the EU is a government project only). The verbs "explain" and "demonstrate", however, remind one of a school lesson or another academic context of some sorts, where in this case the MPs have the knowledge and impart it on their less clever voters. While the proposal might acknowledge that the public have a role and a right to be informed, this does not sound as if Kennedy thinks they are on the same level and a gap in power and knowledge is still there.

"Convention on the Future of Europe" (03.11.2004)

> Staying on the subject of referendums, we would all agree that one of the lessons of the north-east campaign is that the more positive campaigning is done in advance, the better it is when the decision is reached. As all parties in the House are committed to a referendum at some point on the European Union proposed constitution, when is the Prime Minister himself going to get out, with cross-party support, and begin positively to make the case for that constitution? [Official Report, 3 November June 2004; Vol. 426, c. 302]

After the summer recess, Kennedy comes back to the ratification of the constitution through a referendum in the UK in a debate on the 'Convention on the Future of Europe'. He suggests that "the more positive campaigning is done in advance, the better it is when the decision is reached". In a very direct way, he asks the PM to start campaigning for the constitution, effectively calling on him to exert his authority and influence to reach the outcome he knows is desired by himself as well as the Labour leader. He states that since an all-party consensus has been reached that a referendum should be held on this question, the PM can now use his energy to "begin positively to make the case for that constitution". Kennedy implicitly accuses the government of not having done this before, which makes the referendum appear in a rather controversial light as it is clearly only seen as an ex-post legitimisation of a government position already taken. This debate is the first one to be entitled "Convention on the

Future of Europe", the name of the official body convened to work out the draft constitution.

"European Council/Brussels Summit" (08.11.2004)

> Finally, on the issue of the constitution and the referendum pertaining to it, the Prime Minister has said that it is the Government's position that there should be a referendum in due course. Will he confirm that the Government, irrespective of what might happen in referendums that may precede one here, will proceed with a referendum, come what may, in this country? If the type of economic liberalism and greater economic flexibility, to which he alluded in his statement and which were discussed at the summit, are achieved, will he perhaps, on a future occasion, see scope for doubling up a referendum on the constitution with one on the single currency? [Official Report, 8 November 2004; Vol. 426, c. 574–575]

Only a week later, Kennedy once again addresses the constitution in his statement on the outcome of the European Council meeting as the last point and rhetorically asks the PM for a confirmation that the UK referendum will go ahead regardless of developments in other countries (meaning a possible no vote from France or the Netherlands). This question shows that the Lib Dem leader does not see the referendum as merely concerned with the content, namely the ratification of the constitution, but rather as a general vote on British involvement in European integration. He basically insists on holding the referendum for the sake of having a national decision in the UK which would end debate, not merely because the constitution needs to be ratified. Bearing in mind the earlier comments on how controversial the issue is in British politics and that the Lib Dems want a final decision on this, his concern is understandable. For the government, however, a no vote in a prior referendum means an excuse not to hold a risky poll themselves that they might equally lose – which would damage their power and authority considerably and possibly trigger a general election. Kennedy knows this and senses the possibility that the referendum might be axed to spare the Labour government a possible defeat, which would not be nearly as risky for an opposition party like the Lib Dems.

The second point he mentions is economic and monetary policy, linking support for the constitution with support for the introduction of the euro (which further underlines his interpretation that a yes vote in any referendum on European policy or treaty basically equates to a general yes to Europe and all integration steps that entails). The ideological position he declares is support for "economic liberalism and greater economic flexibility", which in this case culminates in the support for the UK joining the single currency, which has been discussed in more detail in the Chapter 7.1.

"Queen's Speech" (23.11.2004)

In his comment on the Queen's speech some days later, Kennedy mentions that they are still waiting on "any European referendum" from the Blair government. The point in time suggests that the constitution is meant and that the Lib Dem leader would like to hear a fixed date. He then warns the government that using "Eurosceptical language to justify a pro-European move" [Official Report, 23 November 2004; Vol. 428, c. 36] in such a referendum campaign would not lead to success. With his argumentation, the supposed importance of discourse is reinforced, and the government accused of making a mistake in appropriating the same "language" as the political opponents of the EU Constitution. Seeing how they themselves have talked about Europe, however, it can be concluded that this warning does also apply to the Lib Dems themselves. The main point is that the issue is framed as two competing discourses and not two competing positions, which confirms the relevance and appropriateness to the approach chosen here to analyse the Lib Dems' position.

"Queen's Speech" (17.05.2005)

Kennedy continues to argue along these lines in the next instance, which is the Queen's Speech debate after Labour won the third general election in a row, one year later:

> We must go out and make the positive case for Europe and ensure a yes vote in whatever referendum comes down the track. The pro-European parties secured 58 per cent of all the votes cast in the election. That is very encouraging, but we must be prepared to build on it. [Official Report, 17 May 2005; Vol. 434, c. 54]

Kennedy here calls on a group he counts himself a part of to "go out and make the positive case for Europe and ensure a yes vote in whatever referendum comes down the track", and this group consists most likely of the "pro-European parties" he refers to a little later. This construction of an in-group against any party Kennedy might deem anti-European is more remarkable since this assessment counts the CON out, thus framing them as an outright anti-European party.

The issue at stake is a referendum on European policy, and Kennedy constructs the election result as an "encouraging" sign that a majority of British voters would vote in favour of more European integration. This constructs the general election as an expression of voters' views on Europe, although the MORI poll in May 2005 found that only 9 % saw European policy as the most important issue (Ipsos MORI 2006). This means the Lib Dem leader ignores other issues that have more likely decided the election outcome such as crime (40 %), the

NHS (36 %), immigration (27 %), and education (26 %) (Ipsos MORI 2006). Therefore, the claim that European policy was the most salient issue and, therefore, main reason for voting for a particular political party can be refuted and must be seen as a rhetorical device to justify Lib Dem strategic goals.

The wording "whatever referendum" expresses a certain weariness since a referendum was announced on the euro, on the constitution, and on the treaty of Nice so far and was never actually held. Still, Kennedy states that "we must be prepared to build on [the election outcome]", again referring to a group of pro-European politicians. This call for action in order to convince the public to vote yes in a European referendum shows that he acknowledges that there is still a considerable scepticism and a successful referendum outcome (successful in the eyes of the pro-European parties) cannot be taken for granted.

"European Constitution" (15.06.2005)

> Returning to the European issue, obviously, and given the exchanges that have just taken place, it would be only fair minded of me to pay tribute to the right hon. and learned Gentleman, the leader of the Conservative party [*sic*], for the principled stand he took over the endorsement of the Maastricht treaty. We remember that in this House and therefore wonder what we have been listening to today.
>
> Given the rejection of the treaty in the referendums in France and Holland, surely we have to accept that this constitutional treaty is no longer viable. That being the case, does the Prime Minister agree that what we need is not just his pause for reflection but a formal moratorium on significant treaty revisions, so that the European Union can demonstrate to the citizens of Europe that under its existing responsibilities it can carry out the tasks that it needs to carry out?
>
> [...]
>
> Does the Prime Minister accept—I am sure that he does—that the key challenge is to bring Europe closer to its citizens, but that a number of significant reforms can be begun here and now without significant treaty revision? For example, will he over the next few days be arguing the case for the opening up of the deliberations of the Council of Ministers, so that instead of meeting behind closed doors to make European law, we can see the discussions, in exactly the same way that we do in this House? In terms of this House and its procedures, has he given consideration to the all-party recommendations of the Modernisation Committee about scrutiny here of European conduct, so that we have better accountability from our Ministers when they go to the Council? [Official Report, 15 June 2005; Vol. 435, c. 255–256]

In a rare endorsement of any (even former) CON's position on European policy, during the debate on the 'European Union Constitution Treaty', Kennedy applauds Major for his "principled stand he took on the endorsement of the Maastricht treaty". Tellingly, this instance is well in the past and the current stance of the CON leader is criticised, but he obviously sees Major's behaviour as exemplary and to be emulated by the current government leader Blair (and also by the CON and its leader, making this both a call for action and a jab at the Official Opposition). He then addresses the context and reason of the debate, namely the "rejection of the treaty in the referendums in France and Holland" and says these votes have to be respected, meaning the constitution "is no longer viable". He accepts defeat and says "we", which includes presumably all British MPs. In a surprising move probably designed to appear respecting the wishes of European citizens and taking their obvious concerns expressed through the no vote seriously, he then calls for a "formal moratorium on significant treaty revisions". Contrary to his former argumentation that the enlarged EU cannot operate in the original framework, though, he justifies this by the supposed need for the EU to "demonstrate to the citizens of Europe" that it still works and delivers even without the constitution. This shows that the Lib Dem leader relies on output-legitimisation to establish popular support for the EU and that he wants to avoid the impression that the failure of the constitution means a failure of the European Union. In effect, though, he thereby contradicts his own claims that the constitution is necessary and reveals the urgency emphasised before as modifiable.

In a reprise, Kennedy argues that "the key challenge is to bring Europe closer to its citizens". In pushing for action to achieve this goal, Kennedy openly admits that he sees deficits on that score which he thinks should be addressed. He calls on the PM to push for specific measures to achieve more transparency which effectively call for the EU procedures to emulate those of the UK and the Westminster model, "so that instead of meeting behind closed doors to make European law, we can see the discussions, in exactly the same way that we do in this House" (again, this is put as a question but meant as an appeal). Interestingly, when it comes to democratic procedures, the Lib Dem leader puts the UK forward as a model whose standards other organisations should aspire to reach. This call for immediate reforms is made in defiance of the failed referendums on the constitution, and Kennedy stresses that he thinks this is possible "now without significant treaty revision". He claims that these changes would be significant without the fuss about big treaty changes, which amounts to a demand of a more flexible and dynamic organisation that is able to change gradually, without major hiccups, instead of the current process of accruing problems that are supposed to be solved in a huge wrench (the British preference for gentle, organic evolution over radical alterations (Kamm and Lenz 2004: 217) might be traced back in history, where the story of glorious revolutions and reforms have prevented a radical system change whereas in France and also in Germany change was accompanied or achieved only by violent upheavals).

Kennedy ends his intervention with a call for "better accountability from our Ministers when they go to the Council", something with has been proposed by the Modernisation Committee of the House. Effectively, he says that the Westminster model would also profit from reforms, and the PM should go ahead with them to set a good example. The overall aim is clear, though: more accountability, more transparency, more closeness between governed and governing and more democratic legitimisation. It seems the Lib Dem leader sees room for improvement in both organisations but that the EU has definitely more catching up to do in his eyes. A general distrust or need for control of people in power is expressed here, which is maybe not surprising coming from a small opposition party.

"EC Budget" (20.06.2005)

Naturally, those of us in the fundamentally pro-European camp feel a degree of pessimism about the present state of affairs. However, as Britain takes on the presidency of Europe it is our responsibility, as the Prime Minister will undoubtedly agree, to try to build a new consensus and a new sense of optimism about the European project. Surely, the Council was right to call for a much broader debate among member states during this "period of reflection" over what happens to the constitutional treaty. Does the Prime Minister agree that being pro-European in no sense precludes being pro the reform of European institutions for the better, and that the two in fact go hand in hand? [Official Report, 20 June 2005; Vol. 435, c. 528]

A further interesting self-description of the Lib Dems and a group of like-minded parties and/or individuals is made by Kennedy in the debate on the 'EC budget': "those of us in the fundamentally pro-European camp". The metaphor brings to mind a camp of soldiers in a hostile environment ("Camp"). There is also a degree of variation admitted between the levels of pro-Europeanness, with Kennedy counting everyone in who shares the fundamental conviction that the UK should stay in the EU and brushing aside potential disagreement over details.

Then, he brings in an emotional dimension and expectation, making the pro-European politicians human in this honest and open admission that their hopes for the future are dampened and that they "feel a degree of pessimism". Trying to inject new energy into this and shrug off the negative feelings, he reminds the listeners that the context of the UK's "presidency of Europe" (an interesting generalisation of the six-monthly tenancy of the presidency of the Council of the European Union) warrants new courage. He continues in a statesman-like tone to flesh out his rallying call: "it is our responsibility, as the Prime Minister will undoubtedly agree, to try to build a new consensus and a new sense of optimism about the European project". In the imagined community indicated by the pronoun "our", he addresses all listeners including MPs and the interested public when he informs them about his view on the necessary action now: the building of a new consensus is a reference to further discourse and debate that is needed within all member states including the UK; optimism is again an emotional aspect which implies that the EU integration process needs more than just rational reasons and self-interested negotiation positions but conviction and a vision that the members want to achieve, so that they can overcome setbacks and not give up. He reminds listeners that since the UK is a member and has now an official leadership role for six months, it is incumbent on them to do something constructive even though Kennedy accepts the need for reflection before further action can be justified. The values called up here are resolve, courage, solidarity, and determination.

He then offers his own definition of "being pro-European", which probably is a reaction to accusations that the Lib Dems uncritically support the EU, and argues that it "in no sense precludes being pro the reform of European institutions for the better". This is a very interesting clarification of the self-perception and serves to better understand the verbal Lib Dem leader's contributions to parliamentary discourse. Although rhetorically asking the PM to agree to a position is part of the ritual form of communication on the floor of the House (see e.g. Chilton 2004: 92), Kennedy seeks confirmation and validation and thereby exposes that the definition is still controversial and not universally agreed upon.

"Proportional Representation" (22.06.2005)

> May I come back to the Prime Minister, and indeed to the excellent first question that he was asked? Now that one referendum appears to be off the agenda, may I make a constructive suggestion for another? [Official Report, 22 June 2005; Vol. 435, c. 793]

The last occasion on which Kennedy mentions the issue, he only briefly refers to the called-off referendum on the European Constitution after it had already been rejected by France and the Netherlands and uses the opportunity to "make a constructive suggestion for another [referendum]", namely one on proportional representation. This shows that the Lib Dems consider referendums a good way of attaining their own policy goals but also that they are also interested in domestic power issues and not only in Europe, so the leader has no qualms to try and make the best of one missed opportunity and use the time and resources saved for another Lib Dem policy goal. This shows that either the Lib Dems place no trust in the government or that as a third party, they deem they have better chances of securing their goals by circumventing parliament which is geared towards a two-party system, or both. Most certainly, it shows that they are pragmatic enough to let it be and turn to other issues when the European integration process is in crisis.

7.3.3 Menzies Campbell

Campbell mentioned the constitutional framework of the EU twice.

"Brussels Summit (EC)" (19.06.2006)

> The Prime Minister is right to accept that a union of 25—soon to be 27—cannot operate within a framework designed for six. In the meantime, what practical steps can be taken for reform and does he remain committed to a referendum if there are any proposals for constitutional change that would significantly alter the relationship between Westminster and Brussels? [Official Report, 19 June 2006; Vol. 447, c. 1071]

Campbell lends support to the PM by voicing a moral judgement: the "PM is right to accept that a union of 25 – soon to be 27 – cannot operate within a framework designed for six", he says in the first of two speeches concerned with institutional change of the EU. Besides establishing that there is something such as a right/wrong binary when it comes to European policy and aligning his view to that of the government leader, Campbell thus seeks to convince his listeners of the presupposition that institutional change is necessary for the functionality of the enlarged EU and, therefore, the debate on it must continue even after the originally proposed European Constitution has failed. Acknowledging implicitly that to establish such a new framework will take time after the constitution has been derailed by the failed referendums in France and the Netherlands, Campbell calls for immediate "practical steps [...] for reform" as well as a long-term search for a new set of rules to govern the enlarged EU. This is an example of pragmatism coupled with long-term pro-European goals.

The second important point he makes is that the legitimacy for institutional change within the EU can only be achieved by a referendum in the UK, and it is noteworthy that he extends this demand to a general level in that he seeks the PM's confirmation that a referendum would be held "if there are any proposals for constitutional change that would significantly alter the relationship between Westminster and Brussels". This is not exactly the demand for an 'in/out referendum' but comes very close to the subsequent 'referendum lock' decided on by the CON-Lib Dem coalition government in 2010 (The Conservative Party and Liberal Democrats: "Coalition Agreement"). It is an expression of the acknowledged fear of the EU 'taking over' that is obviously also taken into consideration by the Lib Dems at this point and as a result they seek to limit ever-closer union as an unstoppable and automatic process constituting European integration. The assumption that only the CON called for a halt of further integration without public endorsement can thus be designated as false; as early as in 2006, the Lib Dem leader's policy proposals reveal that even the self-designated "friends of Europe" have noted the unease among British voters and incorporated it into their own positions.

"Constitutional Reform" (03.07.2007)

> Finally, will the Prime Minister accept that if the public are to be properly engaged in the matters that he has outlined so comprehensively today, a constitutional convention would be the best and most effective way of ensuring it? [Official Report, 3 July 2007; Vol. 462, c. 824]

In the second speech, roundabout one year later during the debate on 'Constitutional Reform', Campbell draws attention to the public's role in the Lisbon treaty debate and calls for a new "constitutional convention" as the "best and most effective way of ensuring" that the public was "properly engaged", implying that they are not in the process underway which would result in the Lisbon treaty. After the first convention's proposal had failed to be adopted by all EU member states, Campbell nevertheless expresses his preference for a "proper" engagement of many actors, not a renegotiation at the top level (government leaders) behind closed doors. The expression of doubt and distrust and the prediction that the "public" will not have their due say in the process is a critical assessment of the EU's processes and decision-making, which is surprising for a self-proclaimed Euro-friendly party and its leader. It is also worth noting that at this point, the parliamentary procedure of legitimising government decisions is obviously deemed insufficient by the Lib Dems; this might be due to their minority position in Westminster but might also hint at a greater problem among voters, namely eroding trust in the representatives and the feeling that a more balanced range of different views must be allowed to enter the debate about the EU and its future structure. This would move European policy away from a "simple" issue to be decided by the government commanding a majority in the HoC at a given time but a fundamental issue concerning everyone, which should thus be debated and decided on a much broader level.

7.3.4 Vince Cable

Cable made three references in total to the Lisbon treaty. His position on the Lisbon treaty seems to differ slightly from Campbell's in that he welcomes it and does not criticise or indeed refer at all to the way it was agreed. However, there is still concern about the legitimacy of a new treaty so closely resembling the rejected EU Constitution:

"Intergovernmental Conference (Lisbon)" (22.10.2007)

I welcome the statement. We believe that the treaty is necessary. It is in the British national interest that the European Union should work efficiently and effectively, but there remains the issue of legitimacy. We believe that there should be a referendum. The public should decide whether Britain should remain a committed member of the European Union. A great deal has changed since the Harold Wilson referendum in 1975. There has been a pooling of sovereignty through Mrs. Thatcher's Single European Act, John Major's Maastricht treaty, Tony Blair's Amsterdam and Nice treaties, and now this treaty. The time has come for consultation with the British public on the cumulative effect of those treaties, because there is anxiety about national sovereignty, and that has to be addressed through public debate. [Official Report, 22 October 2007; Vol. 465, c. 26–27]

The first intervention during the debate 'Intergovernmental Conference (Lisbon)' can indeed be considered a key speech, explaining explicitly how the Lib Dem position themselves in the ongoing debate on the Lisbon treaty. The result is clear: "[w]e believe that the treaty is necessary", he says. It is the explanation he offers for this position that is startling, however: solely the British national interest is quoted as the main reason for the Lib Dems to support the treaty, and efficiency and effectivity are singled out as necessary characteristics in the EU's working in order to safeguard that same interest. One can read this as an acknowledgement that at the moment of speaking, this desired state of affairs is not achieved, but also that the treaty of Lisbon can fix this.

Cable makes a concession, though: "there remains the issue of legitimacy". Cable offers a truly remarkable policy proposition to solve the "issue of legitimacy" the European Union suffers from when it comes to the British public's support: "[t]he public should decide whether Britain should remain a committed member of the European Union". Suddenly, the Lib Dem position has evolved from supporting the Lisbon treaty to basically demanding an in/out referendum, although he phrases this a little more carefully in adding the adjective "committed" in the demand. This is the first time that such a referendum is part of the Lib Dem demands or propositions when it comes to alternative policy proposals in the domain of European policy. Parliamentary sovereignty is also called into question by the statement "the public should decide". In order to justify this policy proposal, the steps of European integration since the UK joined the EU are enumerated and presented as a "cumulative effect" that the "British public" should be consulted about. The change of the EU "since the Harold

Wilson referendum in 1975" is attributed to treaties signed by former PMs. This stock-taking reads as follows: "[t]here has been a pooling of sovereignty through Mrs. Thatcher's Single European Act, John Major's Maastricht treaty, Tony Blair's Amsterdam and Nice treaties, and now this treaty". The last item is the treaty of Lisbon under discussion at the time. The conclusion Cable draws from the treaties is a "pooling of sovereignty" – a development for which he holds the CON and Labour politicians who were in government responsible. It seems the Lib Dems seek to appropriate the role of defender of the people, listening to their fears whereas the former and current PMs did not take public opinion very seriously when it came to European policy decisions. No positive consequence of European integration is mentioned, nor the fact that the PMs in question were all democratically elected leaders of government with a majority in parliament. The rhetoric here resembles populist Eurosceptic claims much more than expected.

Cable cites this seemingly threatening pooling of sovereignty as a reason for the policy change in favour of an in/out referendum: "there is anxiety about national sovereignty, and that has to be addressed through public debate". It seems the Lib Dems do not longer believe in parliamentary procedures to be sufficient to address and allay fears of losing national sovereignty and sees the only way to remedy this in a "public debate" as opposed to parliamentary debate. It is an acknowledgement that when it comes to European policy, a majority in the HoC is not sufficient but the electorate needs to agree, too. The split between government policy and public opinion seems to have become so wide that the Lib Dems leave the path of supporting the PM and envisage to convince voters directly.

"Debate on the Address" (06.11.2007)

> One of those issues, Europe, will be at the centre of the legislative programme. We believe that there should be a referendum on the issue of British membership of the European Union. The details of the treaty are important, but more important is the cumulative effect of three decades of widening and deepening the EU, and the fact that nobody under 50 has had an opportunity to express a view on Europe through the ballot box. We can have as much legislative scrutiny as we wish, but the fact is that, unless the British public are persuaded of the need to sign up to the European project, this issue will continue to poison British politics. That is why we want to go out and campaign for the European Union, and we want the Government to do the same in the context of a referendum. [Official Report, 6 November 2007; Vol. 467, c. 35]

In this speech on the government programme for the new parliamentary session ('Debate on the Address') proposed by the Labour government, "a referendum on the issue of British membership of the European Union" is demanded again by the Lib Dem leader Cable. The repetition adds rhetorical force and makes it clear that there is no way back for the Lib Dems; they cannot go back on their word to vote for such an in/out referendum any more. The risk they take with this is that a less pro-European government might not campaign for remaining and that the referendum is lost despite a pro-campaign. It seems that the Lib Dems have come to the conclusion that European integration is so controversial in the UK that they maybe want to raise the stakes to ensure a victory. They seem to believe that many object to single steps of European Union but not membership itself, and rely on a rational decision which takes the benefits of membership into account and weighs them against a possible desire to slow integration down.

Thus, Cable makes the referendum about more than "the details of the treaty". He repeats the expression "cumulative effect" and qualifies it further: "the cumulative effect of three decades of widening and deepening the EU, and the fact that nobody under 50 has had an opportunity to express a view on Europe through the ballot box". Denouncing every election held in the UK since 1975 as meaningless when it comes to European integration, the Lib Dem leader makes it sound as if for over 30 years, no democratic legitimacy for government decisions could be claimed.

And as leader of the then third-largest opposition party, he refers to anti-European public opinion when he basically admits to the failure of parliamentary sovereignty and procedures in the domain of European policy: "[w]e can have as much legislative scrutiny as we wish, but the fact is that, unless the British public are persuaded of the need to sign up to the European project, this issue will continue to poison British politics". The expression "to poison British politics" is of paramount importance in the short speech and shows that even the Lib Dems are obviously at their wits' end when it comes to resolving the controversial positions towards European integration and to bridging the destructive gap mostly between the public and pro-European parties. Still, Cable probably also refers implicitly to fundamental disagreement between government and opposition parties, as well as within political parties. The absence of a nationwide, cross-party consensus is thus described as the central problem British politicians need to solve.

The proposed in/out referendum is then presented as a means to clear the air and bring the public (back) on board. The Lib Dem leader seems to believe that a cross-party campaign is necessary to swing the public mood and that they can indeed successfully turn it around and achieve the desired result in a referendum. This renders the alternative explanation that the Lib Dems really only want to listen to the people more carefully less convincing; the word "persuade" adds to this impression. It seems that the Lib Dems see a referendum as an opportunity to make their voice heard and persuade more voters that membership of the European Union is beneficial to the UK, not as a chance for them to make their voice heard when expressing opposition to EU membership.

"European Council (Brussels)" (17.12.2007)

> The other meeting that the Prime Minister did not attend, of course, was the signing ceremony, and I am puzzled about the reasons for that. Either he could not organise his diary, which would be incompetent, or he could not make the effort, which would be discourteous. Alternatively, he was trying to send the conflicting signal that he did not like the treaty that he had agreed to. Whether it was duplicity, incompetence or discourtesy, it reflected badly not just on him but on the country as a whole. [Official Report, 17 December 2007; Vol. 469, c. 602–604]

In the last speech referencing EU treaties, Cable talks about the signing ceremony of the Lisbon treaty, at which Brown, who had succeeded Blair as PM by that time, was not present. This is criticised by Cable and he offers three possible explanation to listeners: "duplicity, incompetence, or discourtesy". Obviously, all three are not very flattering as they represent the exact opposite of qualities a good leader should possess, and the last also of a quintessentially British value. The order may be seen as significant as well; the motive mentioned first appears most likely to the listener.

The reproach of duplicity is a strong condemnation and implies that the PM's convictions and his European policy are not in line, which makes him appear dishonest and inauthentic. This ties in with populist ideas of a dishonest elite and weakens the PM's reputation by calling his motives into question. For a party proclaiming to support the Lisbon treaty, this is a remarkable discourse strategy (especially since the PM has already signed it) because it invites further speculation about the desirability of the treaty and the PM's potential doubts are discussed, possibly giving rise to more speculation on the subject. Although the PM is criticised for his lack of showing support of the treaty, listeners could take away a feeling of general negativity towards the issue.

The connection to the PM's handling of a European policy situation to these negative characteristics is interesting because they contrast rather starkly with the usual welcoming of the PM's decisions in this policy domain by Lib Dem leaders. It seems the Lib Dems are gearing up and seek to sharpen their own profile by taking a more critical view on government actions. Another central aspect of the criticism is the generalisation from PM to "the country as a whole", whose reputation has suffered, according to Cable, from the PM's no-show. The standing of the UK among its EU partners is thus considered important by Cable, and he chooses not to refer to public opinion in the UK, which might not welcome the treaty unreservedly given that a large majority of over 80 % would have preferred to have a referendum on the Treaty of Lisbon (Open Europe 2007). The symbolic message that others in Europe might take from the absence of the PM worries Cable and shows his preference for a full role of the UK in the EU; he is not satisfied with half-heartedly taking part.

7.3.5 Nick Clegg

Nick Clegg made four references to the European Constitution or related issues.

"Engagements" (27.02.2008)

> It is good to be here. It is a shame that the Prime Minister seeks to defend clapped-out 19th century procedures in this House, which are preventing the British people from—
> [Hon. Members: "Oh!"] [Speaker issues warning]
> Of course I will be careful, Mr. Speaker. I was talking about procedures, not people—procedures that prevent the British people from having a say in this Chamber, which is what they want. [Official Report, 27 February 2008; Vol. 447, c. 1085–1086]

Having only been elected some weeks before, Clegg used his first question during PMQs as Lib Dem leader to criticise the PM's decision not to hold a referendum on the treaty of Lisbon and using an old "trick" to push this decision through to crush resistance from the House of Lords very sharply; so sharply indeed that he is interrupted by MPs registering their protest and the Speaker decided to intervene with a word of caution (in order to safeguard the protocol). Clegg responds to the ruffle form the Speaker with the explanation that he did refer to "procedures that prevent the British people from having a say in this Chamber, which is what they want". With this, Clegg styles himself as defender of the public will against a despotic PM who, according to Clegg, does not stop at using every tool at his disposal to prevent "the British people from having a say". In a curious contradiction, Clegg qualifies this further with the words "in this Chamber", which constructs a conflict between parliamentary sovereignty versus a public opinion that is supposedly ignored by the government. It seems that Clegg shares the critical stance towards the British political system his predecessors brought up in the context of the Lisbon treaty. Clegg does not voice trust and respect for the PM's decision, based on Labour's parliamentary majority at the time, but accuses the government of wilfully going against the wishes of "the British people". This 'them vs us' (in this case the elite versus the people) logic resembles populist claims from other quarters of the political spectrum. It is remarkable that the Lib Dems seem to have evolved into sharp critics of procedures even when the result corresponds to their proclaimed support for the Lisbon treaty.

It seems Clegg believes that a contrary public opinion will have to be addressed sooner or later, and the Lib Dem position that a referendum on the Lisbon treaty or even EU membership is absolutely necessary has been strengthened further.

"European Council" (17.03.2008)

I strongly agree with the Prime Minister that there is a pressing need to move towards a fully integrated and competitive energy market in the single market. In particular, the EU needs the powers to take action against monopoly energy providers in markets such as France and Germany. Does he agree that the new Lisbon treaty would give the EU precisely those powers further to liberalise the EU energy market, and that that is just another example of the benefits that the treaty would bring the British economy, which the Conservative party [*sic*] is so keen to deny the British people? [Official Report, 17 March 2008; Vol. 473, c. 623]

Clegg uses the example of the energy sector to illustrate the benefits of the Lisbon treaty. Clegg advocates more powers to the EU when they suit the Lib Dems' economic preferences for liberalism, using the example of "monopoly energy providers in markets such as France and Germany" – a clever connection is made to problematic circumstances in the two main rival countries within the EU, with France named first and Germany second. Thus, the support for the Lisbon treaty is justified with safeguarding British economic interests and as a means to force other EU members to adhere to fairer practice. The subtext here is that the EU can act as a guarantor of free market principles if more powers and competences are transferred to the EU level, and that upholding these principles (introducing more competition) is a good thing. A sense of urgency is conveyed when Clegg claims there is a "pressing need" to "implement" a fully integrated and competitive energy market in the single market". A progress in European integration is thus portrayed positively, yet at the same time the status quo is denounced as unsatisfactory. The negative reviews focus on rivalry with other EU members, which are not seen as partners but offenders against liberal principles. The EU is described in a positive way, as a keeper and defender of liberal ideology, and it is thus considered worthy of support by the Lib Dems. Listening voters are expected to agree with the presupposed hypothesis that free markets are good for everyone in order to follow the argument – at least Clegg does not mention benefits for consumers from any of the proposed measures explicitly. It is also remarkable that in his statement, British energy firms are excluded and no mention of possible action against them on the basis of the Lisbon treaty is made, giving the impression that either all is well in the UK and British firms virtuously comply with free market principles – possibly to avoid the impression that UK firms are targeted by the EU and told what to do – an assessment the Lib Dem leader obviously fears would not be a popular opinion in the UK at this point in time. As it stands, the statement only presents the Lisbon treaty as conferring powers to the EU, so it can "take action against [...] providers in Germany and France".

"European Council" (23.06.2008)

> Compared with other six-monthly European Union summits, last week's was not a hugely significant one. In truth, it was more about catching up with fast-moving developments than about setting the pace for the future. Rather than being their master, the summit was in many ways a slave to events, whether the aftermath of the Irish vote on the Lisbon treaty or the unscheduled spat between the French President and the Prime Minister's good friend, the EU Trade Commissioner.
> On the Lisbon treaty, the Prime Minister is right, of course, that we need to respect the need for the Irish Government to consider their next steps before October. However, as a supporter of the treaty, I none the less worry that we might soon make the best the enemy of the good. Uncertainty beyond October would genuinely raise the spectre of a paralysed European Union, unable to deliver concrete benefits to European citizens. So will he give some assurance that the treaty's fate, whatever one thinks about it, will be sealed one way or another in October and that we will not be pitched into months of further uncertainty about the treaty? [Official Report, 23 June 2008; Vol. 478, c. 30–31]

Clegg describes himself as a "supporter of the treaty" and advocates a pragmatic approach to save it even after the Irish "no" vote in their referendum some days before. He criticises a lack of agency on the part of EU member states' leaders, including the PM, by describing the summit meeting as a "slave to events" and "catching up" when it should be "setting the pace for the future", thus dismissing uncertainty and disagreement at the EU top levels about how best to proceed as incompetent. In short, he attributes a lack of leadership and a strategic vision to the leaders once again, which renders them unable to deal adequately with the setback that is the Irish referendum outcome rejecting the Lisbon treaty. Moreover, rivalry with France is mentioned once again in a side remark on a disagreement between the French president and Peter Mandelson (at this point Trade Commissioner in Brussels but a close ally of Tony Blair and to be business secretary in Brown's cabinet). This situation is claimed to equally show that no one is really in control of the situation.

Respect for Irish sovereignty and the referendum decision is expressed, but Clegg then calls for a swift decision nevertheless, one way or the other. He, thereby, implicitly criticises the announced period of reflection and the EU's attempt to save the treaty a third time after both the constitution and the Lisbon treaty in its original form were rejected in referendums in different countries. 'Make the best the enemy of the good' is a saying that expresses Clegg's preference for a compromised deal instead of not agreeing on anything at all, which would make the last years spent on institutional debate a waste of time. He once again terms himself a "supporter of the treaty" but apparently objects to the way the issue is handled – he advocates certainty, mainly because he is worried that the economy will continue to suffer. Economic worries and uncertainty are clearly deemed worse than burying the treaty – the Lib Dem leader makes this priority clear, bringing the argument back to the EU needing to deliver "concrete benefits to European citizens". The spectre is thus paralysis according to Clegg; if the EU is only legitimised by output, as he has argued before, this is indeed worrying, for then it becomes hard for the self-proclaimed pro-European party to justify their stance. In talking about the "treaty's fate", he personifies the document.

"European Council" (23.06.2009)

> I welcome the Prime Minister's saying that the Irish have received the reassurances that they sought on the impact of the Lisbon treaty. Does he agree that if the Lisbon treaty is finally ratified this autumn, Europe should then get on with tackling the problems that really matter to people—climate change, the economy and crime—and that any attempts by any future UK Government to reopen the terms of membership would be self-indulgent and self-defeating? [Official Report, 23 June 2009; Vol. 494, c. 667]

The last intervention on the subject comes one year later. Clegg brushes aside the ongoing debate on the Lisbon treaty by listing "problems that really matter to people – climate change, the economy and crime". The ratification of the treaty and thus further integration and consolidation are not that important to "people" (whether he refers to citizens of the UK only or EU citizens in general remains unclear) according to Clegg. This is exactly the opposite of what the Lib Dem leaders had been claiming for the three preceding years, namely that the Constitution and Lisbon are so important that the British people should decide on them, come what may. It, therefore, seems like an attempt to bring policies instead of polities to the centre of attention again and focus on outcomes in policy areas rated important by EU citizens. It can also be seen as an attempt to provide output legitimacy for the EU; he seems to believe it had better produce results in the three areas mentioned instead of focusing too much on institutional issues. The rationale is that the EU is not an institution that can be accepted for its own sake but one that constantly needs to justify its own existence by addressing policy issues the Lib Dems (as self-proclaimed speaker of the people and their concerns) consider important. The obvious unease with the Lisbon treaty (for example among the Irish, whose worries he mentions but brushes aside as dealt with) is skated over in this statement and Clegg makes the issue appear like an unnecessary political squabble by elites who have lost touch with the real concerns of the people.

In a surprising move at the end of the speech, Clegg links the debate on Lisbon with British EU membership in general and rhetorically asks the PM to agree to his claim "that any attempts by any future UK Government to reopen the terms of membership would be self-indulgent and self-defeating". In retrospect, this statement has assumed more meaning than Clegg had probably intended and may ring true for many readers. It is not clear why he brings up membership at this point, however, and why the Lib Dem stance on the necessity of an in/out referendum in the UK has changed so completely.

The sense that the issue of constitutional change and membership need to be concluded once and for all and that the EU needs to get on with business is overwhelming, so the pending second Irish referendum is brushed aside as a mere formality that is not even worth mentioning; Clegg seems to assume that the Irish will accept the treaty now they have "received the reassurances they sought" (and true to this stance, the referendum result in October 2009 is not mentioned either).

7.3.6 Summary

Overall, the Lib Dem position on treaty change was supportive, in that they advocated the signing of all the proposed EU treaties in the research period, namely the Treaty of Amsterdam, the Treaty of Nice, the EU Constitutional Treaty, and the Treaty of Lisbon. The overall goal of seeing the UK at the "top table" in Brussels was translated into advocacy of treaty acceptance; the Lib Dem leaders argued that opt-outs would mean a loss of influence. This general support was carefully framed as purely rational and being in the British national interest, not as a general, fixed position of the party. Any emotional elements in the discourse, be it fears by Eurosceptics or alleged enthusiasm on the part of the Lib Dems, was firmly rejected, and no references to a European identity or solidarity with other EU members states were made.

The Lib Dems advocated the EU treaties as opportunities for reform; there was an idea of progress by treaty change inherent in their line of argumentation up until 2004, with the bleak alternative to reaching agreements on such treaties described as a "disentanglement of Europe". Continuous reform was thus presented as the only way to go and cooperation between EU member states was valued. On the Treaty of Amsterdam, the Lib Dems made it clear that they saw it as an interim result on the way to a European Constitution and complained that it did not provide for a "people's Europe"; even as early as 1997, there is criticism of the current state of affairs in the EU's institutional make-up focusing on a lack of accountability and a democratic deficit. Here, the UK is evoked as a model for openness and transparency compared to the EU. The second policy goal they put forward was to arrive at a point where the EU could be enlarged as soon as possible; the institutional changes effected through further treaties were discursively constructed as prerequisites for the EU enlargement.

Yet there was also an emphasis on the need for national parliamentary scrutiny of the proposed treaties as well as a certain wariness of alleged centralising tendencies within the EU which became apparent in the Lib Dem discourse, expressed by calls for a very clear definition of where the powers of the EU institutions began and ended. Thus, while the EU Constitution was advocated, it was framed as a safeguard for national powers from being grabbed by EU institutions, with veto rights in certain policy areas declared essential. Equally, the now infamous "Article 50" allowing member states to leave the EU was highlighted as a further such safeguard, although the intention was certainly not to push in that direction. The move towards more decision-making by QMV was also only partly supported, and the veto rights of the British government were confirmed as needed. The domains of foreign policy and taxation (which they feared could lead to "fiscal federalism") were equally firmly defended against anything but intergovernmental coordination. On the other hand, other MPs who opposed treaty change were classed as irrational fearmongers who did not have the British national interest at heart.

The idea of a 'two-speed Europe' was rejected as counterproductive – obviously, the Lib Dems were aware that the UK was unlikely to participate in a group of member states moving faster towards European Integration than others, and their own bargaining position in such a scenario would suffer. The question of the legitimacy of a European Constitution was answered with a call for a nationwide referendum on its acceptance, based on "unbiased, factual information" which should equally help to address the Eurosceptic discourse in the UK and a perceived gap between political elites and the public. Nevertheless, especially Kennedy emphasised the need for a powerful pro-EU campaign to persuade voters.

After the EU Constitution had fallen through in two referendums outside of the UK, this line of argumentation became increasingly urgent; the Lib Dems insisted that a referendum in the UK was still needed to address the domestic Euroscepticism but that a "moratorium" on treaty change was necessary to demonstrate the EU's responsiveness to public opinion, and conceded that "pessimism" had grown among pro-European parties. By 2006, it became clear that a referendum to legitimise any further treaties was now considered inevitable by the Lib Dems while they continued to identify the need for reform; this made a 'yes' vote crucial for them. In October 2007, after the Treaty of Lisbon had been agreed and Gordon Brown had not held a referendum on it, even the holding of an in/out referendum was backed by Cable, highlighting how fundamental the issue of legitimacy for any further EU treaty was considered by the Lib Dems then. Obviously, they thought it the best option to clear the air and get the question of the legitimacy of European integration settled once and for all, hoping to counter both British parliamentary opposition to European policies and public scepticism about European integration with a 'yes' vote in such a referendum. A growing impatience could be noted when the ratification of the Treaty of Lisbon was also delayed, and especially Clegg claimed that the EU needed to provide advantageous policy outcomes to its citizens instead of the treaty debates taking up the entire energy of the project. With the ratification finally achieved, Clegg argued that no future UK government should try to change the "terms of membership", which of course David Cameron did nevertheless in 2015/2016 as soon as he had won an absolute majority and could govern without the Lib Dems.

7.4 "A Long-Running Source of Frustration": The Common Agricultural Policy

In 1985, a disease called mad cow disease was discovered for the first time in Kent. In 1992, already more than 37,000 cows died of BSE. In the meantime, 17 EU member states had banned the import of British beef, which meant heavy losses for British agriculture (J. Schmidt 2011: 375). In March 1996, the European Union officially banned the export of British beef into all other EU countries because of BSE (J. Schmidt 2011: 397). The BSE crisis can thus be expected to be one of the issues addressed in the speeches.

In October 2002, Chirac and Schröder "fixed between themselves the budget for agriculture up to 2013" (Wall 2008: 179) without consulting the UK government. They also made their approval for enlargement dependent on this deal. Blair argued against this and sought to save the "big package of CAP reforms which the Commission had put on the table" (Wall 2008: 179) in the European Council. One year later, he succeeded when the Agricultural Council agreed the reform package Blair had insisted on, including the move to the single farm payment which was "one of the most significant reforms so far achieved" (Wall 2008: 180). It can be concluded that CAP was a bone of contention mostly between France and the UK. In June 2005, the European summit failed to produce an agreement because Schröder and Chirac demanded a stop to the British budget rebate, a demand Blair only wanted to accept if the CAP was reformed profoundly in return (J. Schmidt 2011: 446). This highlights once again the high level of importance accorded to this policy area by both the French and the British governments. The Germans tended to side with France, but mainly because their cooperation was much closer and also strategically motivated.

As Tab. 7 shows, the Common Agricultural Policy was discussed in the following 17 debates:

Tab. 7: Lib Dem Leaders' Speeches Mentioning the Common Agricultural Policy

Leader	Date	Name of Debate
Paddy Ashdown	15.12.1997	European Council
Paddy Ashdown	17.06.1998	European Council (Cardiff)
Paddy Ashdown	21.10.1998	Engagements (PMQs)
Charles Kennedy	20.10.1999	Food and Farming
Charles Kennedy	21.03.2000	Amendment of the Law (= Budget)
Charles Kennedy	24.06.2002	European Council (Seville)
Charles Kennedy	28.10.2002	European Council
Charles Kennedy	13.11.2002	First Day
Charles Kennedy	16.12.2002	European Council (Copenhagen)
Charles Kennedy	04.06.2003	G8 Summit
Charles Kennedy	21.06.2004	European Council
Charles Kennedy	24.03.2005	European Council, Brussels Summit
Charles Kennedy	20.06.2005	EC Budget
Charles Kennedy	19.12.2005	EC Budget
Menzies Campbell	10.05.2006	Questions
Menzies Campbell	25.06.2007	European Council
Vince Cable	22.10.2007	Intergovernmental Conference (Lisbon)

Total: 17 Debates

7.4.1 Paddy Ashdown

Ashdown referred to the CAP in three separate parliamentary proceedings. The first is during the debate on the PM's statement following the European Council.

"European Council" (15.12.1997)

> Secondly, I welcome the commitment made at the summit to substantial reform of the common agricultural policy. It is right to say that that is in the interests of Europe and its consumers in particularly, although I agree with the leader of the Conservative party

[*sic*] that "You ain't seen nothing yet" when it comes to the lobbying that we are likely to get from farmers when the process starts. It is very easy to give—indeed, our recent history is littered with—commitments to reform the CAP. It will be judged in the end by actions not words.

Since it seems that we are using this statement as a peg on which to hang comments on BSE, I recommend to the Prime Minister four actions, which I hope he will consider. First, I recommend that he reconsiders the ban on bone-in beef. I know of the legal advice that he has received, but it would be quite adequate to advise the public of the risk and let them make their own judgment.

Secondly, I recommend that we exercise as rigorous control on beef coming into this country as we do on British beef consumed in this country. Thirdly, I recommend that the Prime Minister reconsiders compensation. I know that that requires some Government commitment, but the state of farming is such at present that that is necessary. Finally, let the Government use their influence on supermarkets in particular, so that country of origin is labelled on beef. [Official Report, 15 December 1997; Vol. 303, c. 24–25]

Reforms of the CAP are only second to enlargement in the list of European policy decisions that the Lib Dem leader "welcome[s]" in his speech. Interestingly, Ashdown chooses to foreground the benefits he expects from these reforms for "Europe and its consumers", thereby adopting an international or at least pan-European perspective. It is not only the British, but all member state nationals who should profit from EU decisions, and falling prices as a consequence of more competition is obviously thought of as positive and reforms to that effect to be condoned. This corresponds to a clear conception of the UK as one more member of a European Union that should seek to generate advantages for all nationals of its members states alike. In a surprising alignment with the CON, though, Ashdown expects "the farmers" to protest against reform. While he might primarily target his remarks at French farmers burning tyres and blocking roads, British farmers are also included in this sweeping definition of one pro-fessional group across all EU member states. So, it can be concluded that the Lib Dems do not support British farmers when this means supporting protec-tionist measures by the EU at the same time. The priority is thus very clearly on liberal economic norms and values including worldwide competition in the agricultural sector at the expense of many small farms in the EU. Ending his comments on CAP reform, Ashdown casts doubt on the PM's words and says verbal commitments are not enough; actions are needed, too.

"European Council (Cardiff)" (17.06.1998)

At the House of Commons debate on the outcomes of the European Council in Cardiff which concluded the six-month period of the British presidency thereof, Ashdown assesses the government's performance in a tepid way:

In overall tone and initial intention, much in the British presidency over the past six months—culminating, of course, in Cardiff—can, we believe, be welcomed. It has been a pleasure to have a British Government who have taken a more constructive attitude, which has won Britain new chances. The Government's agenda—reform of the CAP and the common fisheries policy, cost cutting, institutional reform and jobs—has been right. Measured against the initial hype, however, the outcome has been more disappointing than we should have liked. [Official Report, 17 June 1998; Vol. 314, c. 375]

The description of the status quo is that the PM made an effort – and succeeded in amending the "overall tone and intention" in the area of European policy. Ashdown praises the PM's mindset which he terms a "constructive attitude" – in Ashdown's logic, this is the way to win "Britain new chances", i.e. an increased room for manoeuvre to further British interests on the EU level through accumulating goodwill. The underlying view of international cooperation is decidedly non-realist and instead one where goodwill is repaid with concessions from the other side, not a world where every state seeks to exploit signs of weakness to maximise their own benefits. This is why the Lib Dem leader condones the approach the Labour government have taken. Their agenda is equally welcomed, with the "reform of the CAP and the common fisheries policy" first on the list, followed by "cost cutting". This underscores the importance Ashdown accords to this policy and also reveals the source of the criticism of CAP: This policy does not conform to Liberal values of a free market. It is thus not surprising that when it comes to assessing the actual outcomes of the lauded constructive approach, the judgement is negative, indeed "more disappointing" than "we" – and in this case Ashdown is probably referring to the Lib Dems as a party – "would have liked". While expressing disappointment with the slow progress, the Lib Dem leader nevertheless obviously believes that the EU is capable of reform where they think it is needed, and the best option to achieve certain policy goals such as the creation of more jobs. It is to be noted, however, that the whole list contains only one such policy area, and the rest of the list is concerned with policies and structures in need of reform. From a Europhile perspective, it can be concluded that the Lib Dem leader expresses a critical view but ultimately sees the EU as a good thing.

"Engagements (PMQs)" (21.10.1998)

The third mention occurred during PMQs in October 1998, where the CAP is third in a list of urgent calls for action to the PM: "Thirdly, he could ensure that our farmers in Britain enjoy the same financial package and advantages as every other farmer in Europe" [Official Report, 21 October 1998; Vol. 317, c. 1273–1274]. It is clear that the workings of the CAP at the moment of speaking do not seem satisfactory to the Lib Dem leader – the EU policy is portrayed unfair because British farmers do not receive the same amount of money as other European farmers. At this point in time, the single farm payment – which would level this difference eventually – had not yet been introduced (Roederer-Rynning 2015: 206). The word combination "our farmers in Britain" expresses an identification or at least solidarity with this particular group of voters and the Lib Dems appear to fight for their interests which are neglected by the Labour government in power and the EU, likewise. The underlying values in this argumentation are fairness, solidarity, and some sort of caring patriotism, i.e. standing up for fellow Brits when they are treated unfairly by others. The EU is thereby portrayed as an outsider, a non-British organisation that needs to be tightly controlled lest it should cheat or overcharge a professional group in the UK. As an opposition party, the Lib Dem position also puts the government in power under pressure – for who would want to appear unpatriotic or too weak to protect some poor wronged farmers suffering from unfair policies made outside the country?

7.4.2 Charles Kennedy

Overall, Kennedy debated CAP eleven times during his time as party leader.

"Food and Farming" (20 October 1999)

In the first and longest intervention on the subject, Kennedy addresses CAP in the context of a thematic debate on "Food and Farming" on 20 October 1999. The Lib Dem leader actually proposes the motion which kicks off the debate, which shows what a high degree of importance the party accords to the subject:

> I beg to move,
> That this House notes with dismay the plight of British farmers whose incomes have plummeted to record lows in the last four years, as a result of higher costs and lower farm gate prices producing rapidly increasing losses, despite continually high supermarket profit margins and costs to consumers; further notes that the extra costs imposed through regulation and public health protection that fall directly on the industry should more properly come from the public health budget; deplores the failure of the Government to provide an adequate response to this national food crisis; and therefore calls on the Government to recognise that its latest financial package is insufficient to tackle the fundamental restructuring of UK and EU agriculture policy, necessary for a secure future for British farmers, consumers and the countryside. [Official Report, 20 October 1999; Vol. 336, c. 444]

Kennedy employs a rich vocabulary to paint a vivid image of a catastrophic state of affairs: it is the "plight", incomes "plummeted to record lows", "rapidly increasing losses" and "extra costs imposed through regulation" which result in a

"national food crisis". This verbally created scenario resembles the situation after
the war, when there was a real food crisis with shortages, rationing, and hunger –
which seems a bit overblown in a rich European country where obesity is much
more of a problem than an alleged lack of food availability.

It is noteworthy that only British people are of interest; it is, therefore, the
national interest which constitutes the main reason for acting. Contrary to a
liberal economic outlook, Kennedy identifies the following actors and factors
to blame: supermarkets and the Government as well as regulations and laws.
In a direct attack on the Labour government, Kennedy judges their measures
to counter the crisis to be a "failure" and the financial resources committed to
solve the problem as "insufficient". He comes to the conclusion that the roots of
the problem lie in "UK and EU agriculture policy" which needs, according to
Kennedy, a "fundamental restructuring". CAP reform, therefore, becomes the
method to achieve the goal of "a secure future for British farmers, consumers
and the countryside". While the CON has not even lodged an amendment on
the order paper for the debate, as Kennedy scathingly remarks, and seemingly
do not share his view that agriculture is "such an important issue", the Lib Dem
leader insists that urgent action is required to amend the situation and reach the
proclaimed goals. It is indeed remarkable that the Lib Dems position themselves
as the only protector of these interests and voter groups and tout a concern for
the countryside when traditionally, the conservation of traditional landscapes
and livelihoods as well as securing a future that is not too different from the past
and the present is a domain of the CON.

> We should also be seen to be debating and discussing the issue because there is a
> much wider public policy that goes beyond the immediate difficulties that are being
> confronted. On a European level, there is a broad agreement among member states,
> the United Kingdom included, and the Government, with all-party support, that we
> must seek and achieve further reform of the common agricultural policy, and that there
> will have to be a further emphasis or shift in the balance of approach away from direct
> sector support in terms of prices and price maintenance and towards environmental
> husbandry and countryside management. [Official Report, 20 October 1999; Vol. 336,
> c. 445]

Referencing the role of parliament as a public forum for debate and thus also
for agenda setting and addressing the concerns of voters across the country,
Kennedy then moves the debate on to the broader picture and links the current
situation with the EU. He cites an imagined community of EU "member states"
where it is telling that he feels the need to explicitly confirm that in this respect,
the United Kingdom is included in this community, and also points out that not
only the Government agrees but that they have "all-party support", which is also

sufficiently rare when matters European are concerned to mention it explicitly. The policy goal on which there allegedly exists such a broad consensus is to "seek and achieve further reform of the common agricultural policy". Listeners may ask themselves why this has not happened if everyone agrees on it. Kennedy goes into more detail and explains which elements he wants to overhaul particularly urgently: abandoning "direct sector support in terms of prices and price maintenance", i.e. the direct and open implementation of a protectionist regime of artificially high prices for certain products, and moving on to "environmental husbandry and countryside management". Thus, Kennedy makes it clear that the Lib Dems disagree with the price mechanism that basically turns a whole sector into some kind of planned economy but seeks to focus instead of preserving the environment and traditional forms of landscape and living.

> Is there not a great contradiction? If the family farm as a base unit within this country continues to implode, what will happen? More and more amalgamations will take place. We shall end up with a structure of family farming that will be more like that in North America than in the UK at the moment. We shall not then have the custodians of the countryside who for generations have been working, managing and looking after it to deliver the very environmental and countryside objectives that as a country and as a European Union we want to see achieved. It is surely of fundamental importance that in tackling the farming crisis we put it in a broader context and get across to the Government, and the Government get it across to the decision makers and policy makers at a European level, that unless something is done with even more urgency to redress the catastrophic state of income and the depressed state of morale among our fanners [sic], we shall thwart the longer-term policy that we all think is a sensible way in which to move. [Official Report, 20 October 1999; Vol. 336, c. 446]

Continuing his speech, Kennedy launches into a lament over the loss of the "family farm as a base unit within this country", firmly linking this institution with the national self-image and the idea entertained of the British as an imagined community. Tradition and a stake in the country, an emotional connection to the country(side) are presented as inherently and typically British, and thus not an economic sector but the heart of the British community with its way of life is under threat, illustrated with the word "implode" suggesting a burnt-out old star or an obsolete structure which lacks support to stay upright any longer. Economic necessities of upscaling to survive in a capitalist and competitive market environment ("amalgamations") are made out to be a negative development to be feared and countered. Kennedy interestingly picks "North America" as a counterpart, as the "other", against which British and European identity must be defended lest they should become too alike to make out a difference any longer.

Appealing to emotions and pathos as well as a sense of tradition, Kennedy paints a picture of a rural idyll where farmers are "custodians of the countryside who for generations have been working, managing and looking after it" – this sounds more like a line by the Earl of Grantham in Downton Abbey about 90 years before than a Lib Dem leader mapping out his vision of the future of agriculture. However, this is exactly the strategy Kennedy employs; and in a surprising move, he links the EU and includes it in the imagined community sharing the same goal of preserving this pretty picture by using the pronoun "we". While the UK still comes first, this enlargement of the community sharing the same values and goals for the future as opposed to American circumstances. The EU is further presented as a place where this vision can be defended more effectively than on the national level; indeed, by the order in which he cites the actors he wants to take measures indicates that the EU is seen as the higher and more powerful institution. Summing up, Kennedy revisits the dramatic scenario he painted in his opening paragraph by reminding his audience of the "catastrophic state of income" and the "depressed morale among our farmers" to press for urgent action.

> We welcome the package with which the Government have come forward but what further policy objectives should they as an Administration within a UK context be pursuing? […] First, there should be a Government-funded calf disposal scheme. That is surely essential given the difficulties in that sector. Secondly, there should be a national ewe cull scheme. Given the efforts made recently by my party colleague, Ross Finnie, in his capacity as a Scottish Agriculture Minister, and given the rebuff that he suffered at the hands of the European Commission, I shall be grateful if the Minister or whoever responds to the debate will give some further indication of what further discussions, if any, have yet taken place with the Commission to see what else can be achieved. [Official Report, 20 October 1999; Vol. 336, c. 447]

Further on, Kennedy offers support for the Government's financial aid to British farmers but proceeds to list very specific additional measures he thinks should be introduced and paid for by the government; he justifies the call for such interventions with the "difficulties in that sector" which make such financial aid "surely essential". The word "essential" indicates a matter of urgency and that no alternative can provide the survival of farms. Kennedy paints the EU Commission as the opponent of the Scottish Lib Dem Agriculture Minister, saying that he "suffered" a "rebuff" by them while trying to help British famers. Kennedy, therefore, lays the task to push through these British interests on the European level at the door of the government.

At this point, Kennedy takes two interventions which bring up the issue that in Scotland, the Lib Dems currently back a ban of beef on the bone, which Kennedy rebuts with the information that they base their decision on medical advice but are in favour of lifting the ban as soon as it is safe to do so. He adds that devolution means different parts of the UK can have different policies in place, which he fully condones. Interestingly, he uses strong words against the French policy to block British beef imports from entering their country:

> The Minister can speak for himself in due course, but I do not think that he feels that the Scottish Parliament, by any of its efforts or activities, is undermining the legitimate legal recourse, which we strongly support, that he is pursuing against the quite unacceptable activities of the French with regard to British beef. [Official Report, 20 October 1999; Vol. 336, c. 447]

The judgement is harsh and leaves no doubt as to what Kennedy thinks about the French policy: he refers to it as "quite unacceptable activities" and uses the generic "French" when identifying the perpetrator. This is a case of imagining a British "us" versus a French "other", which lets the Lib Dem leader unite Scots and English discursively against a common enemy. Furthermore, the Lib Dems "strongly support" suing the French government before the European Court of Justice because they are in breach of EU law. This is still to do with the BSE crisis, but while British beef has been given the all-clear and can be sold and bought across the EU once more (with the exception of beef on the bone), France still refuses to lift the ban. According to EU law, every product that may be sold in one member state automatically receives the licence to be sold in every other member state since the famous 'Cassis de Dijon' decision of the European Court of Justice from 1979. France is deliberately defying this rule with the claim that they do not want to risk their citizens' health on any account. With France being an, if not the main, opponent on CAP reform, this ban calls forth unusually sharp words from the British side, and the Lib Dems, though considered pro-Europe, make no exception here, which supports the hypothesis that their Europhile profile is pragmatic rather than euphoric and can, therefore, be classified as soft Euroscepticism according to the definition by Szczerbiak and Taggart (2008: 240–241).

Kennedy then takes a further intervention centred on the claim that richer farmers get more EU funding than smaller ones, neither have British fishermen received as much. While Kennedy guarantees his support also for British fishermen in all parts of the country, he points out that the current debate is not the place to do so.

Moving on, Kennedy addresses the issue of food imports:

> The second issue is that of importation. It is crazy that we load regulations and standards on ourselves and our domestic producers, which we cannot impose, on an equivalent

basis, on some of our European competitors who provide lower quality importation products. Because of insufficient labelling, those products are then passed off to British consumers. That is a daft state of affairs. We have asked the Government repeatedly to do something about that. They need to move with more alacrity. [Official Report, 20 October 1999; Vol. 336, c. 448]

Again, with a surprising choice of words, he condemns national UK policy in this sector by calling it "crazy" and adds criticism of the EU regulations on top, saying they produce a "daft" situation with different standards allowed within the EU. Kennedy claims that this puts British farmers at an alleged disadvantage. He also argues that unilaterally setting high standards for food productions harms British famers because they cannot compete with European competitors who only conform to lower standards (and, therefore, supposedly sell at a lower price). While this is an understandable criticism which ultimately leads to the call for more European legislation, i.e. it is a criticism that there is not enough regulation on the EU level to ensure the same standards across the whole single market, it is nevertheless telling how Kennedy chooses to support his claim: he describes not lower prices and a resulting advantage for other European producers, but instead points out that these are "lower quality importation products". This implies a negative "other", assuming that everything produced in the UK is automatically of a superior quality. The negative impression of the European competitors as "others" is strengthened when Kennedy proceeds to describe the process of selling their goods in the UK as being "passed off to British consumers". This wording suggests that there is a dishonest, unfair element in the practice of simply selling agricultural products from the continent in the UK when they are not explicitly labelled as having a non-British origin. To be fair, it has to be recognised that Kennedy avoids over-generalisation by pointing out this practice is only followed by "some of our European competitors" and by calling for mutually applicable rules on an "equivalent basis", not a discrimination against non-UK products. However, still a decidedly negative impression is created by the word choice used, which is accompanied by Kennedy's description of the EU labelling regulations as "insufficient". The EU is portrayed as an institution which is too weak or too slow or just not interested in providing a fair economic environment for the UK to trade in, along with the government which receives a verbal slap for not having acted on the situation fast and effectively enough.

The Lib Dems show themselves to be guardians of British economic interests – by insisting that everyone conform to their high standards and stop selling inferior foods to unsuspecting British citizens. This is an implicit admission that EU regulation of the agricultural sector is the way to ensure a fair trading environment – the opposite of a liberal economic model, where state regulation is seen as negative interference with market forces. Far from criticising CAP and the single market as protectionist and over-regulated, the Lib Dem leader actually calls for the government to engage at EU level to push through more regulation. Values underlying these policy goals are international cooperation, fairness, and freedom for a distinctly British community of "ourselves and our domestic producers" which allegedly suffer from regulations "load[ed]" on them. The 'other', European producers are portrayed as (ab)using their freedoms created by the absence of more regulation to cheat British consumers. This is an argument containing contradictions and on balance purveys a negative image of a generic European "other". With food being a sensitive issue that concerns all people directly and daily, this is a policy area where negative emotions and fears can easily be stirred up and used politically, especially in an environment where foot-and-mouth disease and BSE have created insecurity and fear amongst consumers anyway.

Taking an intervention from a fellow Liberal Democrat, Kennedy confirms the voiced criticism of too lax EU controls of which foreign producers get a licence to sell their products in Europe, with the example of Thai chicken farms with a questionable use of antibiotics:

> *Mr. A. J. Beith* (Berwick-upon-Tweed): Has my right hon. Friend noted today's press release about chicken imports from Thailand? It says that EU inspectors approved a number of chicken factories there without visiting them, and that the potential use of antibiotics in Thailand is not regulated, known about or exposed to our consumers.
> *Mr. Kennedy*: I am grateful to my right hon. Friend for that. I read those reports this morning. Given that this party supports the Government when they are positively engaged in Europe, we should use that positive engagement to insist that such ludicrous states of affairs are not allowed to be maintained. I could not agree with my right hon. Friend more. [Official Report, 20 October 1999; Vol. 336, c. 449]

The main focus of criticism is the EU, whose job of protecting consumers and European businesses has not been fulfilled satisfactorily according to Kennedy and his party colleague. Kennedy uses the word "ludicrous" to describe the current state of affairs, which is another strong word that deepens the negative view of EU policy implementation – which is now portrayed as not only crazy and insufficient, but also absurd. All in all, Kennedy's contribution to the debate does not seem to qualify as Europhile but as decidedly Eurosceptic, although of the soft kind. Again, this criticism of the EU for not doing enough is at odds with a general call for less protectionist measures especially in the realm of agriculture. Instead, it seems the Lib Dem leader makes a case for more and better controls of EU regulations protecting the EU market against competitors from other countries here. The EU is portrayed as a referee failing to ensure everyone in the game adheres to the rules and plays fair – the values of equality, fairness, and the rule of law can be identified as underlying basis for the assessment made by Kennedy.

Kennedy also makes the argument that the Lib Dems are always in favour of being "positively engaged in Europe", but reiterates that this is a pragmatic strategy based on the belief that this will earn the UK government more room for manoeuvre and a stronger place in negotiations when it comes to pushing through measures in British interests. The EU is more of a further level of governance that should be used and played in order to further British interests and ensure others, be they in other EU member states or outside the EU, play by the rules. The clear focus on "us", encompassing the government, political parties like the Lib Dems, as well as British farmers and consumers as sitting in the same boat and being unfairly treated by foreign ('other') actors, is striking.

The last paragraphs of Kennedy's speech focus on the single currency and link this topic with agriculture in the UK:

> The second much broader issue is that of the single currency. I am glad that Britain in Europe campaign was launched last week and that it has a healthy degree of cross-party support, which is important. The Government must recognise, however, that there has been a significant change in grass-roots farming opinion on this matter. My view is based on discussions that I have had in the past couple of years. Because of the strength of the pound over the past period, the increasing perception among the agricultural community in this country is that a commitment on the part of this country to a single currency would be in the long-term interest of UK agriculture.
>
> [...]
>
> I appreciate that the Minister is constrained by the policy of the Chancellor, the Foreign Secretary and the Prime Minister, who from time to time seem to have the same policy on this issue. None the less, I hope that he will acknowledge that there will be real long-term benefits to British agriculture if we are coherently and sensibly part of a single trading currency zone within Europe.
>
> [...]
>
> No one who has considered the issue sensibly would argue that the single currency is the panacea for all ills in the agricultural sector or elsewhere. Of course it is not. It is a technical as well as a political and a constitutional judgment. On balance, it brings merits and benefits and that is why I am in favour of it for agriculture, as for other things.
> [Official Report, 20 October 1999; Vol. 336, c. 449–450]

Kennedy draws attentions to a shift among "grass-roots farming opinion" towards a pro-euro attitude. An interesting rhetorical trick is that he claims to be in direct contact with the people on the ground, having discussed their opinions over a long period of time. He can, therefore, counter any criticism aimed at the EU or the euro for being elite projects that are out of touch with real people. He also demonstrates that he really cares and listens to farmers and their concerns. The argument is that the strong pound makes exports into the Eurozone more expensive, which poses a problem for farmers reliant on such exports. Kennedy claims that those farmers see it this way and have, therefore, changed their opinion to support the introduction of the euro. Appearing only to relay the thoughts and conclusions of another imagined community, the "agricultural community in this country", Kennedy argues that joining the euro "would be in the long-term interest of UK agriculture". Therefore, he links the current problems to the currency and emphasises that any decision on the euro should respect possible future scenarios – especially those in which British food products are exported to the rest of the European Union. Economic prudence and foresight are the values underlying Kennedy's recommendation to join the euro for the British primary sector's sake.

Kennedy parries the Minister's answer to that by playing at apparent disagreement among cabinet members over European policy and the euro in particular, but wants to make sure his views are registered: he repeats that he sees "real long-term benefits to British agriculture" in British membership in the Eurozone. The words he uses to describe this policy alternative to the government's wait-and-see tactics are "coherently and sensibly", implying that the Lib Dems have a more logical approach and the rest is just a patchwork of irrational decisions which will ultimately hurt British interests in the domain of agriculture. The key point here is the timescale: the Lib Dem leader proposes to look at the bigger picture and future developments, and might be interpreted as arguing that potential short-term quibbles will be worth it in the long run. This is a soft criticism of short-term, survey and poll results-oriented government policy with frequent changes and U-turns when public opinion sways. Answering a further intervention, Kennedy allows that the euro is "no panacea for all the ills in the agricultural sector" but insists that all things considered "it brings merits and benefits and that is why I am in favour of it for agriculture". The Lib Dem leader uses agriculture as a peg for addressing another topic, basically moving the focus of his debate contribution to the euro but always comes back to it by singling it out as an important branch of the economy which would be influenced by the development.

"Amendment of the Law" (21.03.2000)

The next intervention comes some five months later, and Kennedy vents his frustration at the Government's claim that there are no major problems in rural Britain:

> The other area that was not touched on, which has suffered so significantly as a result of that combination of circumstances, is agriculture. I am beginning to think that the

Chancellor must have believed the Prime Minister when he went to the south-west a few weeks ago and told an incredulous local population that life in rural Britain was really going rather well. That is not the case. The farming industry is in deep recession, and it is an absolute disgrace that the Chancellor, with vast sums at his disposal, is unable to announce today that he will access the agri-compensatory funds available from Europe; and Liberal Democrat Members will continue to campaign on that issue. [Official Report, 21 March 2000; Vol. 346, c. 881–883]

This rather scathing criticism of the Chancellor Gordon Brown with regard to his handling agricultural policy has a domestic focus. One element of the CAP, the agri-compensatory funds, is only mentioned at the end of his intervention on behalf of farmers across the UK who suffer from a recession in their sector. Kennedy's concern is obviously for "life in rural Britain", and he presents the farming industry as central to it. Surprisingly, a moral judgement is cast: Kennedy calls it an "absolute disgrace" that those farmers in need do not receive financial compensation although funds on EU level would be available for exactly such as purpose. In this speech, the argumentation concerning the CAP is reversed: instead of calling for reforms and less protectionist policies, Kennedy condemns the Chancellor for not using EU money to shore up one particular industry branch.

"European Council (Seville)" (24.06.2002)

On the European Council in Seville on 24 June 2002, Kennedy ties up enlargement with the CAP by arguing:

On the issue of enlargement, which we strongly support, and the intended progress, which is also very much to be welcomed, can the Prime Minister explain how that can be squared when no meaningful decisions have yet been arrived at and, apparently, no substantial discussions have taken place on reform of the common agricultural policy. Surely one must predate the other. [Official Report, 24 June 2002; Vol. 387, c. 616]

As already shown in the chapter on enlargement, these two policies are closely interlinked in the Lib Dem line of argumentation. Reform of the CAP "must predate" enlargement. The Lib Dem leader thereby clarifies the opposition to the CAP and their resistance to pay even more when economically weaker countries (with agriculture representing a high share of their economy) join. This might, on the one hand, be termed 'kicking away the ladder'; i.e. not giving the same subsidies that one enjoyed to boost one's own economy or certain sectors of it to weaker countries but insisting that they battle market forces and conditions without such payments. To be fair, however, it has to be said that the position is consistent, since the Lib Dems have been calling for CAP reform ever since – and the Lib Dems were not in government to abolish the protectionist measures sooner (and indeed, neither at this point in time).

The word "reform" suggests making the present form better, improving it in some way, and thereby shows the Lib Dem opinion that the common agricultural policy is not in line with their values and worldview and has to be amended – if not scrapped altogether.

"European Council" (28.10.2002)

Only months later, Kennedy heavily criticises the lack of progress where reforms of the CAP are concerned:

> On the specific issue of common agricultural policy reform, which has to be the big disappointment of the weekend, too little progress—if, indeed, much progress at all—was achieved. Will the Prime Minister acknowledge that the agreement reached simply to cap subsidies is not a long-term solution? Does he agree that Commissioner Chris Patten was correct yesterday when he said that far-reaching reform remains inevitable? In that context, we have to get away from the wastage of EU resources and the unfair discrimination against emerging economies elsewhere, in the third world in particular. We also have to recognise the unfair penalties that the existing CAP imposes on our hard-pressed agricultural community in Britain.
>
> How does the Prime Minister reconcile the outcome of the summit with the commitment to the phased withdrawal of EU subsidies in favour of the wider Doha commitments, to which we are already a signatory? Does he see any potential in coming times for assembling a coalition of interests within existing EU member states towards that end? [...] Will the Prime Minister acknowledge that our country would have greater leverage, not least on agricultural reform, if we were seen to be more of an active participant at the top table in Europe, especially as we are the fourth largest economy in the world? Are we not in danger of missing the boat at the formative stage of the single currency in the same way as we did at the outset of the establishment of the CAP? [Official Report, 28 October 2002; Vol. 391, c. 547–548]

The short interval lets us guess that the issue is considered important by Kennedy. The word choice hints at strong feelings (and, therefore, a high distance towards Lib Dem goals and values): the description of CAP reform as "the big disappointment of the weekend" is a clear negative judgement of the developments and shows that they did not go in the desired direction. Kennedy assesses that "too little progress, if, indeed, much progress at all" points to the alternative goal the Lib Dem leader would like to see realised, which is probably the abolition of the CAP or at least a severe cutback. In a similar vein, all decisions reached at the European level are criticised as not enough – highlighted by the adverb "simply" which suggests that the measures taken are half-hearted and not suited to deal with such a big issue. The other aspect of the criticism aims at the timeline – the Lib Dems obviously push for long-term, i.e. fundamental, change of the policy (with supposedly no possible way back). Using the word "solution" in this context suggests that the CAP as such should be perceived as a problem – and doing nothing, therefore, is no option for a responsible politician. Problem-solving is a main virtue and an important criterion to measure political effectiveness and success. The government is, therefore, portrayed as weak if they cannot push through the measures needed to 'solve' the problem CAP. This is the Lib Dem leader in proper opposition mode. He seeks support for his position by quoting the British member of the European Commission, Chris Patten, as an ally – which seems highly telling, since the latter was actually a member of the CON at the time. It seems that when it comes to economic policy, the Lib Dems are prepared to side with the CON MPs in order to further their own agenda, their proposed alternative goal amounting to abolish CAP and establish a free market for agricultural products from within the EU. Competition and free trade are clearly prioritised over the social and cultural aspect of farming. The basis for the CAP, namely the desire to become and remain independent from other countries in case of food shortages (a lesson from the after-war period), as well as the aim to preserve cultural landscapes and traditions, is left out of the argumentation, showing that international economic liberalism is more important to the Lib Dems than those other aspects. The details of the "far-reaching reforms" being "inevitable" in Patten's and Kennedy's opinion are not specified either, but the word "inevitable" seeks to frame their proposed goal of completely overhauling the policy as being without a reasonable alternative and only a matter of time. The people responsible for the delay thus appear as not quite up to date and not effective enough to bring this result about sooner than later.

The words "wastage" and "unfair discrimination" serve to paint the CAP in a negative light, for both indicate phenomena that nobody could publicly condone and which violate not only universal but arguably also essentially British values such as prudence, thriftiness, and fairness, which the Lib Dems stand for and which should find broad support among listeners and voters. Very interestingly, the Lib Dem leader proceeds to underlie his claim by connecting the CAP to "unfair discrimination against emerging economies elsewhere" – the new member states with weak economies are obviously not included, for he mentions "third world" countries "in particular". Thus, the argumentation goes like this: let agricultural products be produced where it is cheapest to do so, and let's import them without protecting the single market farmers from that competition. It is a classical liberal economic reasoning topped with an international cooperation and solidarity 'cherry'. The Lib Dems thus manage to come across as caring, concerned with fairness and world-wide justice, while the goal remains the same the CON pursues: the complete abolition of the CAP.

Added almost as an afterthought, Kennedy also brings up British farmers as stakeholders in the debate. Again, the CAP is described as "unfair" and the word "penalties" implies that the EU is a punishment apparatus that subjects the British to unfair rules and makes them suffer on purpose, whereas the "hard-pressed agricultural community in Britain" is presented as victim. Thus, an opposition is created between a poor but hard-working "community" living in Britain which stands no chance against the CAP rules and the EU which upholds them on the other hand. Everyone opposing changes to this policy must, therefore, appear as an enemy to British farmers, and everyone (especially government members) who does not do their utmost to bring about that change can, therefore, not care much about the British farmers. The fair treatment of other EU farmers is not mentioned as a policy goal by the Lib Dem leader, who clearly foreground national interests here.

Kennedy then seamlessly links the CAP to international trade and the Doha round. Equating CAP with "EU subsidies" and insisting these must be phased out to honour commitments already made and to allow for free trade to flourish. He suggests that finding allies to achieve this end in negotiations with the other EU member states (so-called like-minded states) and argues that with a different strategy, the UK might influence policies on a grander scale and to a greater degree in its own interest, as would have been desirable with respect to the CAP. Kennedy claims that joining in European integration developments would mean greater leverage to actually give those policies a spin into the right direction, but as an outsider, the UK cannot exercise a lot of influence.

"First Day" (13.11.2002)

> We welcome the fact that the Government again rightly pay tribute to European enlarge-
> ment remaining the big goal, a view that we share. However, as we did in exchanges a
> couple of weeks ago after the last summit, we have to enter the reservation—I think the
> Prime Minister, the Foreign Secretary and the Chancellor would agree—that despite the
> agreement, which goes up to 2006, Europe will have to revisit the common agricultural
> policy if it is serious about making a success of enlargement. We hear nothing positive
> from the Conservatives on that because they have nothing to contribute. I say in passing
> that when agricultural matters are considered, it is important that the Prime Minister,
> with an eye to the many fragile communities around our coastline and country, puts
> maximum political support behind the plight of the fishing communities, which face an
> uncertain future. [Official Report, 13 November 2002; Vol. 394, c. 38]

Although the main focus of the debate and his remarks is on enlargement, Kennedy nevertheless formulates a "reservation" – it is CAP reform. Kennedy reminds the listeners that he has made this priority clear in previous debates, and he is obviously not willing to let it go. He claims that CAP reform has to happen and that the developments on the EU level, namely the agreement to enlarge in the time to come, stretching 4 years ahead, is not a reason to abandon those reforms but indeed a prerequisite. Kennedy warns that it is necessary to reform CAP – and the actor responsible is identified as "Europe". This rather vague reference to the European Council and Parliament, the EU organs where those decisions have to be taken does not serve to attribute responsibility where it belongs and thus criticism directed at decisions. It is not clear where British politicians come in, but it is possible that the listeners do not understand "British ministers and the PM as well as MEPs" but imagine a monolithic other when hearing that "Europe" has to act "if it is serious about making a success of enlargement and thereby implies that any politician not dedicated to CAP reform is guilty of the same charge.

With the formulation "I say in passing", Kennedy suggests to listeners that what follows is less important. In the typically British way of using understatement to mask emotions attached to an issue, it could also be a rhetorical trick to avoid the impression that the Lib Dems call for protectionism or subsidies because they care about people, which would run counter to the image of sober, pragmatic liberalism, and economic responsibility. Tellingly, it is the reference to the "many fragile communities around our coastline and country" which is introduced in this way. The description of the fishermen as a "community" and as a "fragile" one at that, a community plagued by "plight" and an "uncertain future" suggests an urgent need to help them, and implies that it is the Government's task to do just that (he addresses the PM personally). It is worth noticing that in this respect, Kennedy appeals to patriotic feelings of solidarity when he speaks of "our coastline and country". The coast as a quintessential space for an island (not forgetting Northern Ireland, part of another island) and (once) proud seafaring country is named first and is followed by country. The use of the pronoun "our" suggests that all people living in such environments are part of a larger (and indeed imagined) community of British people who all have to stand together in the face of adversity. *Ex negativo*, this implies that EU policies put British people at risk and make them suffer, and that this is due to that and the weakness of the government which has not done enough to amend the situation. It could be that the regulation of using the sea, a quintessential part of British economic activity and history, touches a deeply rooted tradition of regarding the sea as a guarantee or opportunity to make a livelihood, to trade with others and protect the country from outside attack. With the EU's system of fishing quotas and policy of granting every country the same right to fish wherever they like, including British waters along the thousands of miles of coast, an uneasiness with the situation may be linked both to economic concerns as well as deeper, cultural and historical reasons. Britannia does not rule even its very own waves any longer where fishing is concerned – it may well be a large trawler from Spain instead.

When it comes to agricultural and fishery policy, the Lib Dems gear up to be a very critical opposition party indeed, and nothing positive is heard on this EU policy – despite Kennedy's claim that this strategy is followed only by the CON, a further jab at the largest opposition party and their remarks on European policy developments.

"European Council (Copenhagen)" (16.12.2002)

> Given that some of the continuing entrenched aspects of the common agricultural policy have become even more entrenched as a result of some of the decisions that were reached at the summit, what prospect does the Prime Minister see, with enlargement ahead of us, of achieving the genuine, long-term reform of the CAP that is inevitable, desirable and will come about only if our country plays its full part at the top table of Europe? It will not be achieved on the country club membership basis advocated by certain people. [Official Report, 16 December 2002; Vol. 396, c. 542–543]

In the next instance, Kennedy repeatedly uses the word "entrenched", which is part of warfare vocabulary. The metaphor is a sign of deeply felt antagonism between the UK and other EU member states in this policy area, reminding the listener of the long and terrible conflict between European powers, with the trenches a symbol for World War I and a stalemate situation upheld regardless of the victims it claims. Kennedy accuses the PM of being part of such a political trial of strength and not having managed to come closer to winning but only to have allowed the issue to fester and the trenches to be dug deeper because no party wants to budge. Kennedy repeats his call for "genuine, long-term reform of the CAP", implying that everything else if disingenuous cosmetics. He proceeds to present this political goal once again as "inevitable", implying that all other ways are a dead end and there is no alternative than to follow his advice, and further makes it clear that this would be in the Lib Dem's interest – he assesses CAP reform as "desirable". He then repeats his suggestion that the previous and current governments·have adopted the wrong approach to achieve this goal by not engaging fully with every step of European integration.

While Kennedy is, therefore, arguing to stay on board with every measure towards an ever-closer union, it is not that he approves of all of them but rather sees this as the better negotiation strategy. By going along with the rest, he hopes to be more influential when it comes to how the policy developments look like in detail and shape future policies before they are decided upon. This may be considered a rational, practical pro-Europeanism and not a whole-hearted support for the EU as such. According to the definition by Szczerbiak and Taggart (2008: 240–241), this approach would fall into the category of soft Euroscepticism qualified opposition to a specific EU policy and argumentation using or in favour of the national interest, i.e. British farmers as epitomes of the whole people. Kennedy concludes that the only way to gain more clout in negotiations and thus more success in pushing for CAP reform is to engage more and throw the weight behind EU integration. The use of the word "only" suggests that there is no alternative to this proposal and that the Lib Dems have the magic recipe to prevail on the European level, suggesting that when it comes to Europe, the Lib Dems are the one party with the competence and knowledge to deal with this effectively and in the national interest. Using the expression "top of the table", Kennedy suggests that the UK's right and rightful place is as leader in the European Union, not as just another member.

Hand in hand with this goes the assumption that the EU member state "at the top" will then have the power to impose its will on the others, rather than accept "defeat" or being content with slow-paced and gradual reform negotiated with a view to consensus. This might be considered a wide gap between political cultures – the logic that the stronger and fully engaged country will also decide the direction works in a majority-based voting system but not in an organisation where all views are sought to be reconciled and minority opinions are taken seriously. It is the opposite of quick efficient decision-making at the expense of the minority promulgated by the British system, and thus the PM's role in European negotiations is judged as weak according to British standards. The Lib Dem leader might be right, however, that the UK's negotiating position is not strengthened by staying outside important developments. The "country club membership" he refers to is probably meant to suggest a "light" version of a real (gentlemen's) club where the important people meet as opposed to one in a rural area. "Certain people" is a further jab at the CON, not at the Government, and can be seen as a further evidence of the Lib Dems opposing the Opposition instead of Government.

"G8 Summit" (04.06.2003)

Commenting on the UK's policy goals to be pursued at the G8 Summit in 2003, Kennedy expresses the Lib Dem policy goal to bring about further cuts of subsidies in the agricultural sector by tying together the CAP and protectionism: "Does the Prime Minister see scope for the cutting of farm subsidies and export credits?" [Official Report, 4 June 2003; Vol. 406, c. 164] This shows that the whole idea of an EU-wide support for one sector goes against the Lib Dems' liberal market agenda and that Kennedy is prepared to exert pressure on the Labour government to cut back on this, even if this puts the UK in direct conflict with other member states and their interests. Where the CAP is concerned, the Lib Dems' own ideology is clearly rated more important than consensus within the EU.

"European Council" (21.06.2004)

Does the Prime Minister agree that the new threats facing Europe, particularly global terrorism and climate change, as well as long-standing problems such as reform of the common agricultural policy, will be given better effect in a collective way as a result of the procedures outlined in the treaty? Will he indicate specifically the prospects under the provisions in the treaty for tackling the CAP—such a long-running source of frustration for successive Governments and this country as a whole? [Official Report, 21 June 2004; Vol. 422, c. 1086–1087]

In the context of the debate on a European Constitution, the CAP is cited in a list of problems and is ranked only third after global terrorism and climate change. This enumeration suggests a similar salience shared between these three issues. Compared to the former two, reform of the CAP seems ridiculously overstated and inflated beyond its real importance – global terrorism and climate change arguably are a threat to life and survival whereas CAP is mainly a question of money. This list shows how Kennedy prioritises CAP as a political issue and pushes it up to the top of the agenda. He describes it as a "long-standing problem[...]". In this respect, the general preference for international cooperation is emphasised in the hope that the constitution will help to move in the direction the Lib Dems want (probably a reference to proposed majority voting on issues such as CAP reform where formerly every country had to approve and, therefore, wielded a de facto veto). The combination of the words "collective" and "better" is clear evidence for this. In a dramatic expression, Kennedy then proceeds to title CAP as "such a long-running source of frustration", and not only "for successive Governments" [sic] but, in an interesting generalisation, also "for this country as a whole". The CAP is, therefore, painted as a nuisance directed against the UK as a country, and thus against the imagined community living in this country. Frustration is a negative emotion and the formulation suggests that the Lib Dems along with all other British politicians feel that way. An opposition between the EU and the UK is established, with the added characteristic that this has been going on for a long time ("long-running"). Even though this assessment only applies to the CAP, there is an inherent danger that this image transfers to the EU itself – an ever-ongoing nuisance for everyone British.

"European Council, Brussels Summit" (24.03.2005)

The next instance of the CAP being discussed in Parliament is in 2005, when Kennedy brings it up in a remark on the UK rebate:

> On the UK rebate, will the Prime Minister acknowledge that that will always come back to the argument that France would have to accept fundamental reform of the CAP before it could make progress by being critical and carping about the UK rebate? Given the domestic referendum concerns of the President of France, which we all recognise, does the Prime Minister hold out much prospect of being able to be a little more persuasive with him than was obviously the case in the past two or three days? [Official Report, 24 March 2005; Vol. 432, c. 1019]

Not for the first time, it is France which is directly named as the opponent by Kennedy, after the issue of BSE had (literally) died down. The country is named, not a certain minister as part of the EU Council or the president, which serves to imagine an "other" as opposing actor. This invokes the impression that the whole country is geared towards stripping the UK of benefits and is "critical" about the UK guarding its interests in the budget debate. This rhetoric choice might even bring to mind a rhetoric of war, where it is one country against another. At least no specific people or institutions are mentioned, which makes it hard to arrive at a nuanced judgement of the different positions. France is not only identified as an opponent attacking the UK rebate (and, therefore, endangering financial advantages for the UK) but also as the principal hurdle preventing "fundamental" CAP reform. The Lib Dem leader seeks the PM's approval on the negotiation strategy to trade concessions on CAP reform against concessions on the issue of the UK rebate. Obviously, Kennedy believes France to be the main beneficiary of CAP and, therefore, sees it as unjustified that they criticise the UK's benefitting from another arrangement with the EU. The criticism voiced by a French politician that the UK rebate was not fair is, therefore, refuted as unfounded and played back at France, who has "started" the negotiation deadlock by insisting on the CAP remaining as it is. The portrayal of France as "carping" is a person-ification, attributing a negative and particularly annoying type of communica-tion and behaviour. Working together with a person wont to carp, thus working with countries like France on an EU level, is, therefore, irritating and no one could be blamed for trying to avoid it. In the case of CAP, the Lib Dem discourse on Europe and cooperation with European member states can thus be classified as verging on Euroscepticism – a general complaint about having to deal with irritating others. Although it is limited to this specific policy area and is, there-fore, no to be seen as hard Euroscepticism, the negative discourse may well be strengthened by Conservative and also government rhetoric in this area – and may not be contained to CAP, but influence the whole attitude towards collaboration on EU level altogether.

"EC Budget" (20.06.2005)

> The Prime Minister was undoubtedly correct over the past few days not to agree to a fudged deal over the budget. There is still time to agree a new package before 2007. But the Prime Minister did not begin to make the public case for reform, especially of the common agricultural policy itself, until it became clear that the United Kingdom rebate was under threat. In retrospect, surely that was a mistake. Why did he wait so long to make that coherent case for reform? [Official Report, 20 June 2005; Vol. 435, c. 528]

Taking up the same interlinked issues of the UK rebate and CAP reform some three months later, Kennedy lends his support to the government's decision not to agree on an EU budget deal, which he qualifies as "fudged". This description implies a lack of straightforwardness; it suggests that the other EU partners have offered the UK unfavourable terms. Fudging can be defined as "a method of dealing with a problem that does not solve it completely but hides its difficulties" ("Fudge"). Such evasive behaviour that ignores British interests or does not reflect them sufficiently is being ascribed to the EU as a whole, using an apostrophe. This can be seen as problematic since the whole organisation is caught up in this negative assessment.

The Lib Dem leader reassures the listeners that there is still time to reach a new deal over the EU budget but then tells off the PM for not having insisted strongly enough on reform earlier so he is now in a difficult position, seen as obstructing the reaching of a deal and making up conditions he did not prioritise before. Consistent with earlier suggestions on negotiation strategy, this could mean that Kennedy is worried about the constructive image that he claims would allow the UK to play a more influential role. He emphasises the importance he accords to "making the public case for reform", thus pointing out how crucial open and public discourse is when it comes to European policies. This can be read as a criticism of Blair's strategy not to mention European policy, thus keeping this controversial topic out of public debate and minimising the risk of it causing a breach within his own party or among voters. Daddow comments that Blair did indeed show "a tendency to dampen rather than stoke the European debate" since 2001 (2011a: 6). Kennedy takes up the role of opposition party leader when he openly assesses this as a "mistake" on Blair's side, and claiming that Blair failed to make a "coherent case for reform" until then.

This is a further intervention that is far from being uncritically and wholeheartedly pro-European but reveals a more deeply-running aversity. Getting what you want from the EU (partners) is, it seems, a game of weighing your

option during tough negotiations and timing your claims in order to succeed –
which can be taken to mean getting what you want and not what might be best
for the EU as a community as a whole or a compromise. The strong objection
to a "fudged" deal is surprising since a pragmatic 'muddling through' and slow
evolvement by small reform steps instead of revolutionary clean slates has often
been said to be in line with British preferences. This might be one of the factors
explaining why the Lib Dems were not seen by voters as convincing when they
argued for staying in the EU.

"EC Budget" (19.12.2005)

> Given the ideals that the Prime Minister properly set out at the beginning of the UK
> presidency, there is a great deal of disappointment with its conclusion, not least where
> common agricultural policy reform is concerned. First, is not the truth of the matter
> that the stitch-up between France and Germany over CAP reform, to which the Prime
> Minister had to put his name, that took place two years ago is what has made the British
> position so difficult today?
> Secondly, the French managed to call his bluff on the issue at the summit. The Prime
> Minister has said: "and then to open up the prospect of a radically reformed Budget
> midway through the next Budget period." The French Foreign Minister has said that
> there will be no reform of CAP before 2013. Those two statements do not marry up.
> Will the Prime Minister confirm that when the much-vaunted review takes place, it will
> consist of a review by the Commission, which will result in a document being submitted
> to a subsequent Council of Ministers, which will decide the matter? The review carries
> no more force or persuasiveness than that. [Official Report, 19 December 2005; Vol. 440,
> c. 1568–1569]

Commenting on the concluding second British EU Council presidency, Kennedy
sums up the results as a "disappointment"; the CAP is once more the only policy
area that is explicitly named in this regard. Kennedy thus accords a high salience
and importance to CAP and uses it as a yardstick for the success of the British
presidency.

Interestingly, it is now two member states that are explicitly mentioned
relating to CAP reform: France and Germany, who work together. Kennedy does
not describe this in a neutral way but uses the word "stitch-up" to characterise
their relationship, which indicates that they have teamed up to work against
the interests of the UK. A stitch-up is understood to be "a dishonest or unfair
arrangement or result" ("Stitch-up"). In this meaning, values like fairness and
honesty are reclaimed for the British side, which suffers from the dishonest and
unfair deal between the two other countries. The big word "truth" suggests that
Blair does not want to point a finger at his "partners" or that he is too naïve to
notice their wrongdoing. The formulation that the PM "had to put his name"

to France and Germany's unfair arrangement suggests that Blair was forced or was too weak to insist on a better deal. Kennedy refers to this deal of two years earlier to explain why the PM supposedly did not succeed this time. Kennedy characterises the "British position [as] so difficult today", making out the present state of affairs between the UK and the EU (partners) as problematic (even though the PM has presented them as ok), and attributing the seeming difficulties to dishonest behaviour by France and Germany in the past.

In a further take on CAP, "the French" are again the main opponent and Kennedy judges their answer to the British as having "managed to call his [the PM's] bluff" – which marks them as a tough negotiation partner and the PM as a fool or someone inexperienced enough to let himself be caught in such a situation. Calling someone's bluff is a metaphor taken from the realm of gambling – thus the French are shrewd (poker) players in a game called EU negotiations. In such a game, the aim is winning which can only be achieved by making the opponent lose their whole stake or give up because the prospect of winning fades or they do not want to take any more risks. The stake is money, of course – along with saving one's face and demonstrating superior skills or just pure chance – but this metaphor does not suggest that EU politics are something serious and substantial but a game for people who have money and time to lose or are desperate or even addicts. Paying money to the EU thus appears as honouring debts equated with paying the price for bad luck or unwise gambling, not investing in something worth having and not paying for a service or products or helping poorer countries prosper, as is the (at least official) case with development aid, for example. The timescale of reforming CAP becomes a stake in a game of cards and the PM a foolish player, not a responsible politician negotiating to keep partners on board while pushing for policy changes in the (arguably) national interest. Kennedy further accuses the PM of misrepresenting the results of the negotiations, pointing out that the French have contradicted him on the timescale for CAP reform. While the PM proposes he will be able to achieve "a radically reformed Budget" (the EU budget period is a one-year interval which is negotiated and agreed upon in advance). It is likely, however, that the PM refers to the EU's long-term budget plan, the so-called 'Multiannual Financial Framework' providing the grand lines of spending for a seven-year period in advance – meaning he refers to the current budget period from 2006 to 2013 (which would be followed by the one from 2014 to 2021). This means that the French have practically excluded CAP reform from negotiations over the next multiannual financial framework period and thus put it out of reach from the present government. This assessment shows that the Lib Dem leader doubts the PM's negotiation strength against the French and is not happy with the outcome. Again, it is the UK pitted against France in CAP affairs; and France seems to win.

The next verbal attack in the speech is aimed at the review process – Kennedy mockingly calls it "much-vaunted" and thereby makes it clear that he does not put much store by it. He names every single step the review process entails and concludes: "The review carries no more force or persuasiveness than that", meaning it is a paper tiger and there will be plenty of opportunity for any member state (like France) to veto it again in the Council of Ministers. Implicitly, both the EU institutions and their processes are portrayed as weak and designed in a way that allows France to sabotage UK interests. Furthermore, the PM cannot make sure that UK interests are protected, either. This rather damning statement is in line with the other references both to the CAP and to France and the EU whenever CAP is concerned.

7.4.3 Menzies Campbell

Sir Menzies Campbell discussed the CAP twice during his time as leader. The first occurrence was during a session of PMQs:

"Questions" (10.05.2006)

"Does the right hon. Gentleman understand the extent of anxiety and hardship that has been caused in rural areas by the Government's mishandling of the single farm payment scheme?" [Official Report, 10 May 2006; Vol. 446, c. 308] In this mention of the CAP instrument of single farm payments, the Lib Dem leader's criticism is this time not directed at the policy itself, but at the PM himself following an incident where the government did not pay out the money to the farmers when it was due. This intervention can thus be categorised as "real" opposition. Implicitly, the single farm payment is recognised as crucial for British farmers – without the payment, "anxiety and hardship" are the consequences. This question may be counted as a grudging admittance that the CAP has positive sides to it, and it can be guessed that this was with farmers as an important voter group in mind.

"European Council" (25.06.2007)

The second instance was during the debate on 25 June 2007 concerning the European Council meeting. After cautioning against protectionism generally in a clear bid for more free trade in a globalised world, Campbell singles out agriculture and asks: "What flexibility does the EU Trade Commissioner now have in relation to agriculture for the purpose of achieving a successful outcome to the Doha round?" [Official Report, 25 June 2007; Vol. 462, c. 27] The CAP is portrayed as a vehicle of protectionism and thus clearly belongs to the kind of policies that need to be axed in order to achieve a desirable state of affairs. The main values underlying this (rhetorical) question are flexibility, which is expressly stated, and international cooperation to achieve economic success. The political goals are free trade, and more precisely successful trade relations based on international cooperation that is beneficial for the UK as a member of the EU. The way to reach this goal can be deduced from the apparent worry about the negotiation position – the Lib Dems obviously feel this can be got by a clear commitment to free trade and thus a strong negotiation position when dealing with trade partners all over the world. The self-image of a strong UK can be classified as within the EU; when it comes to international trade, the Lib Dems accept that the EU brings more to the negotiation table than the UK alone. However, the CAP is seen as one policy that stands against the political goals the Lib Dems advocate and which thus limits the bargaining power of the EU in terms of trade. The underlying value can be seen as economic rationality (when free trade is accepted as a mantra); thus, international trade is rated higher than protecting the interests of EU farmers.

7.4.4 Vince Cable

Cable refers only once to the CAP:

"Intergovernmental Conference (Lisbon)" (22.10.2007)

In this debate, Cable dedicates one remark to the CAP: "Will he at last give us a timeline for fundamental reforms of the wasteful, economically illiterate common agricultural policy?" [Official Report, 22 October 2007; Vol. 465, c. 27] He expresses a very clear negative judgement by describing it as a "wasteful, economically illiterate" policy, and urgently calls for "fundamental reforms". This choice of words to describe the policy clearly conveys the Lib Dem position on CAP – they cannot accept it in the current form because it stands against their values of economic rationality, i.e. policy choices made on the basis of (neo-) liberal economic theory, and of prudence and thriftiness. With a Labour government in power, the idea that this party is not the most competent when it comes to the economy is aligned with their apparent support or unwillingness (or incapability) to bring about "fundamental reforms" of the CAP – thus, support for the EU in this regard is somehow framed as financially irresponsible and hurting UK interests in the area of trade. With this position, the Lib Dems come close to their proclaimed opponent in all matters European, namely the CON.

7.4.5 Summary

The CAP was on the Lib Dem agenda right from the start and was mentioned in 17 debates overall, making it the fourth most discussed topic. Its salience peaked in 2002 and 2005, which coincided with disagreement over CAP on the EU level, mainly between France and Germany on the one hand and the UK government on the other hand. Yet after Vince Cable's remark in October 2007 the topic was abandoned, and the Lib Dems focused on other EU policies. Nick Clegg did not mention CAP at all during his time as party leader of the Lib Dems in opposition.

Judging from the word choice and metaphors used in the Lib Dem speeches on CAP, the assessment of this particular EU policy was overwhelmingly negative – except for one, where progress with reforms was welcomed. All "reforms" the Lib Dem leaders called for aimed at reducing protectionist measures and cutting the overall costs of the policy. Criticism of the CAP can be traced back to liberal values of fairness, free and open markets, competition, (cost) efficiency, and prudent spending of public money. All these were perceived as violated by an essentially protectionist mechanism to shield the EU's agricultural sector from global competition. The criticism of CAP as one, if not the, most important and most costly EU policy from its inception in 1962 (with a peak of 72 % of the budget in 1984) cannot be classified as being happily pro-European. On the other hand, criticism was always aimed at specific elements of the policy, not the EU as such, and progress in this context was duly noted and welcomed. The position of the Lib Dems towards this eminent EU policy can, therefore, be described as rationally critical and objective. According to the definition by Szczerbiak and Taggart, this approach falls into the category of "Soft Euroscepticism". The Lib Dems opposed the policy and consistently argued that it must be reformed in order not to hold other developments back and not to harm the British national interest. With regard to British farmers and their interests, however, the Lib Dems were not consistent in their liberal argument but called for support and financial aid in times of crisis, seeking to incorporate the social democratic strand into the policy approach while also foregrounding national priorities. It can be concluded that with regard to the CAP, the Lib Dems applied a double standard: one for the imagined community of British nationals, who deserve help, and all other European workers in this sector, who, in their line of argumentation, do not.

7.5 Bigger Is Better: EU Enlargement

"Accession to the EU is achieved by way of a treaty between all member states and the applicant country" (Blockmans 2015: 129). The EU institution in charge of the entire enlargement process is the European Council. Since they must decide unanimously, all member states can thus veto the accession of a new country at any stage. National parliaments also have a factual veto because each needs to ratify any agreed accession treaty (Blockmans 2015: 129).

Crucially during the researched period, the so-called Eastern Enlargement of the EU was implemented in 2004 after many years of debate and negotiations. In 2007, Bulgaria and Romania followed. Accession negotiations with Turkey were formally opened in 2005 and continued throughout the research period. Blockmans concludes: "As a subject of the first enlargement of the original European Communities, the UK continues to be a supporter of enlargement" (2015: 128). Indeed, Wall describes the UK's role on the matter of enlargement as "the principal champion" (Wall 2008: 179) and recounts that Blair swallowed the toad of generous CAP spending to safeguard France's and Germany's approval of the policy in 2002. However, Wall argues that at the same time "the enlargement of the Union has made it harder politically to argue that Britain should join the common frontier arrangements" (Wall 2008: 168). The UK thus opted out of the common agreements on asylum and visa.

> The UK was among the few member states willing to remove all restrictions on free movement from the moment of the 'big bang' accession of new member states in 2004, whereas many other member states insisted on transitional regimes. As a result, the UK experienced a particularly large spike in immigration, which has now pushed it into a more restrictive camp. (Blockmans 2015: 131)

The reaction to the high numbers of immigrants from the new EU member states Blockmans refers to also featured prominently both in the general election campaign in 2015 and in the EU referendum campaign. It is thus very interesting to investigate whether the freedom of movement was addressed in speeches concerning the Eastern enlargement.

Tab. 8: Lib Dem Leaders' Speeches Mentioning EU Enlargement

Leader	Date	Name of Debate
Paddy Ashdown	18.06.1997	European Council Amsterdam
Paddy Ashdown	15.12.1997	Engagements (PMQs)
Charles Kennedy	13.12.1999	Helsinki European Council
Charles Kennedy	11.12.2000	Nice European Council
Charles Kennedy	17.12.2001	European Council (Laeken)
Charles Kennedy	24.06.2002	European Council (Seville)
Charles Kennedy	28.10.2002	European Council
Charles Kennedy	13.11.2002	First Day
Charles Kennedy	25.11.2002	NATO Summit (Prague)

(*continued on next page*)

Tab. 8: Continued

Leader	Date	Name of Debate
Charles Kennedy	16.12.2002	European Council (Copenhagen)
Charles Kennedy	23.06.2003	European Council
Charles Kennedy	15.12.2003	European Council
Charles Kennedy	21.06.2004	European Council
Charles Kennedy	20.12.2004	European Council
Charles Kennedy	20.06.2005	EC Budget
Charles Kennedy	19.12.2005	European Council (Brussels)
Menzies Campbell	19.06.2006	Brussels Summit (EC)

Total: 17 Debates

Tab. 8 lists the 17 speeches dealing with EU enlargement. Concerning the chronological distribution, it emerged that Lib Dem party leaders debated the issue of enlargement of the European Union from 1997 until 2006, after which it dropped off the agenda. This means that only three out of five party leaders in the researched time span engaged with the topic: Ashdown, Kennedy, and Campbell. Compared to other topics such as the euro, enlargement did not receive much attention. This indicates a broad level of consensus across parties on the issue, where as an opposition party, addressing it does not promise much gain.

7.5.1 Paddy Ashdown

Paddy Ashdown addresses enlargement only twice: once in the debate on the European Council meeting in Amsterdam on 18 June 1997 and once on the European Council on 15 December 1997.

"European Council Amsterdam" (18.06.1997)

> That having been said, does the Prime Minister agree that the summit is marked not by the work it did, but by the work left to be done? Is it not true that there is a great deal of work to be done, perhaps at some future intergovernmental conference—surely there must be one— to prepare the way for enlargement and to complete the process of institutional change? Surely the right hon. Gentleman cannot be satisfied with the progress in, for example, the democratisation and accountability of the European institutions and in other areas that need to be dealt with before Europe can move forward. That is important, and I hope that the Prime Minister will agree. [Official Report, 18 June 1997; Vol. 296, c. 320–321]

While the main focus of his intervention is on other European policy areas, Ashdown comments on enlargement as well in this passage. What is especially striking is the fact that Ashdown uses the coordination conjunction "and" to express what in his way needs still to be done: he calls for an intergovernmental conference to deal with enlargement and additionally with institutional change. This makes all the difference because enlargement is not presented as an opposing movement to a further deepening of European integration but as one side of the same coin. However, the status quo is described in negative terms – according to Ashdown, the EU is not ready for enlargement and the Amsterdam treaty has left a lot of work to do in the area of institutional change. By using repeated rhetorical questions which he introduces with "surely", he presents this assessment as common-sensical and the only acceptable conclusion to be drawn from recent events.

Ashdown emphasises the values of democracy and accountability by criticising their absence from the current institutional make-up of the EU. He argues that in order to successfully enlarge the organisation, the notorious 'democratic deficit' in the EU has to be addressed, also to improve the legitimacy of the whole project. The lack of all the above endangers the progress of European integration according to Ashdown, and thus stands in the way of his party's policy goals. Consequently, he argues that a conference with other European leaders must be held to be able to "mov[e] forward". He explicitly calls for an "intergovernmental" conference, though, which highlights the importance he places on the national level and that the strategic competence to shape the future direction and form of the EU should lie with the member state leaders, not with supranational EU institutions.

"Engagements" (15.12.1997)

In the next instance, enlargement is the number one item that Ashdown addresses:

> First, I join the Leader of the Opposition in welcoming the move towards what the Prime Minister described as the "historic launching"—not continuation—of the move towards enlargement. That is very welcome, especially since it will be done on an inclusive basis. [Official Report, 15 December 1997; Vol. 303, c. 24–25]

Again, Ashdown uses the opportunity of the PM's statement on the next European Council meeting to make his party's position on enlargement known, highlighting the importance he as party leader accords to this issue. Again, he uses the verb "to welcome" twice when assessing the status quo – anything on the way to achieving enlargement is framed as positive and is obviously in line with the party's political goals.

Ashdown brings up the value of inclusiveness, which he equally welcomes and obviously supports. In what could be termed a modest proposal of an alternative way of presenting enlargement to the public, Ashdown points out that the word "continuation" would be more appropriate when describing enlargement of the

EU – and indeed, it had already evolved from a club of six to 15 in 1997. This might be an attempt to discursively align the Eastern enlargement with the rest of the EU's historical evolution, making enlargement sound like a natural process and thereby lessening the impression that this is a seemingly extraordinary development, which the PM's word choice of a "historic launching" implies. Thus, organic growth of an organisation uniting what belongs together is touted as the way to go.

7.5.2 Charles Kennedy

The next party leader who debated the enlargement of the EU is Charles Kennedy. In overall 14 different debates, from 1999 through to 2005, he addressed the issue. The first instance is the European Council in Helsinki in 1999.

"Helsinki European Council" (13.12.1999)

> On the all-important issue of enlargement—especially in respect of Turkey—does the Prime Minister agree that a seminal decision was reached in principle in Helsinki? However, Europe must be emphatic that, while wanting to welcome Turkey into the European community of nations in due course, Turkey must respond by a significant improvement in its domestic human rights agenda. We should not lose sight of that simply because of the bigger and welcome aim of enlarging the union in that geographic direction. [Official Report, 13 December 1999; Vol. 341, c. 641–642]

In the debate on the PM's statement concerning the outcomes of said European Council, Kennedy describes enlargement as the "all-important issue" and highlights Turkey as a candidate country eliciting special interest. The status quo is portrayed as positive – the summit has brought a decision Kennedy welcomes and sees as "seminal". Cooperation of member states on the EU level is thus portrayed as effective because important decisions are taken. A slight concession is made by qualifying the decision as regarding a matter of principle (where the devil may still be in the detail). The goals are very clear-cut: The Lib Dem leader wants the enlargement of the EU to go ahead and include Turkey as well, as long as the latter country brings its human rights record up to scratch.

A further political and strategic goal can be deduced from the last sentence: The Lib Dems are in favour of increasing the EU's sphere of influence towards south-east Europe. From the insistence on Turkey, a strategic interest in this NATO member becoming more closely allied with the EU can be inferred. With its huge market, an economic motive for supporting Turkish membership can be suspected as well.

In terms of values, respecting human rights is what the Lib Dem leader foregrounds and marks as a prerequisite for joining the EU. The EU is thus represented as a value community, although enlargement as such is termed the "bigger and welcome aim", specifically with regard to the geographical dimensions of the EU. A further value could be attributed to the assessment of enlargement as overall welcome: inclusiveness, as well as openness for international cooperation. However, the Lib Dem leader excludes any considerations pertaining to cultural closeness, religious identities, and the free movement of people within the EU from his argument – such values and cultural aspects seem not to weigh a lot compared to geography and human rights as a uniting factor.

Kennedy does not identify alternative ways of reaching the political goals that differ markedly from government policy – he demands that human rights play a major role in EU negotiations and urges the EU to stand united on that front and to be "emphatic", i.e. to defend their values and not give in to secure an economic or strategic gain.

"Nice European Council" (11.12.2000)

One year later, commenting on the outcome of the European Council and the ensuing Treaty of Nice, Kennedy has changed his positive assessment slightly:

> If the hon. Gentleman will allow me to continue, the accessor countries will gain admission to the European Union 14 years after the collapse of the Berlin wall. That is an intolerable time to take to enable the developed, integrated countries of Europe to open their doors to the supplicant accessor countries. Does the Prime Minister agree that more needs to be done to speed up the process of European decision making? [Official Report, 11 December 2000; Vol. 359, c. 356–357]

Interestingly, the candidate countries are called "accessor countries" – the word "accessor" is not listed in the *Oxford Dictionary of English*. Two other words are similar, namely "access", which relates to the technical and formal aspect whereby the candidate countries gain access to membership, and "accessory", which bears the connotation of something small that adds to the attractivity or functionality of a bigger entity but is not as important and indeed, in many cases, optional. The latter seems more likely to be intended, because the word "admission" is used in the same sentence and thus makes "access" redundant. The candidate countries are, therefore, not perceived as on a par with the existing EU member states and have to wait a long time to be allowed in, like people being humiliated by being told to wait in line and being scrutinised before being admitted to an exclusive establishment. The candidate countries are portrayed as suffering from the high standards set as an entry bar and dependent on the goodwill of the existing members. This interpretation is supported by the following word choice, describing the waiting time of "14 years after the collapse of the Berlin wall" as "intolerable". Here, a clear historic reference is made and the envisaged enlargement which includes eight former Soviet bloc countries is framed in the context of regime clash during the Cold War – apparently, with the end of that systemic conflict, the reason not to accept these countries as EU members has been eliminated in the view of the Lib Dem leader. Neither the Maastricht criteria which contain the legal requirements for joining the EU nor the complex transformation process on the political, legal, and economic levels are mentioned and thus excluded from the argumentation. EU enlargement is thus seen as a strategic option and less like a complex and detailed process requiring time and effort from both sides.

The description of the member states as "developed" and "integrated" which have taken their time to "open their doors" to the ten candidate countries which are termed "supplicant accessor countries" strengthens the impression of a clear power and relevance hierarchy, where the EU member states are definitely in a better position. The idea of a superior power graciously granting a share of a better way of life to "supplicants" rings tones of an empire mentality. The Lib Dems can, therefore, be said to tap into imperial feelings of being in possession of superior knowledge on how to run an economy and of an organisation of public life that others desperately seek to emulate or become a part of, as in the Commonwealth of Nation for instance. Granting certain freedoms to citizens may be considered part of the package.

In terms of institutional structure of the EU, the Lib Dem leader uses the opportunity to criticise the lack of efficiency when it comes to decision-making on the EU level, where a further underlying value of effective and efficient governance (as it is practiced in the UK with its majority system) is clearly discernible. Interestingly, this might be seen as a call for more powers for EU institutions to take decisions by majority instead of seeking a consensus every time. This can be seen as favouring more European integration and a supra-national approach for the sake of efficiency. The Lib Dems are thus prepared to give up veto rights and arguably a little sovereignty for the sake of reaching bigger political goals and also values. The criticism of EU decision-making processes can thus be termed rational and in favour of more competences concentrated at this level in order to improve and speed up results, not as anti-EU.

"European Council (Laeken)" (17.12.2001)

The next time Kennedy takes up enlargement again is in the following year, in the debate on the European Council in Laeken:

> The need for such a development is underpinned by what the Prime Minister said about the process of enlargement. Those of us who were Members of Parliament a decade or

so ago and remember that Monday afternoon after the weekend the Berlin wall came down—and the huge sense of political liberation that accompanied it—will remember that all the talk was of enlargement, but a decade later, the over-ossified structures have not yet enabled so many of the aspirant states to join. Something that will assist progress in that matter is to be welcomed.

As the Prime Minister acknowledged, that progress must also be accompanied by changes in our internal procedures here. Last week, the Leader of the House published modernisation proposals for the House to discuss. I commend to the Prime Minister an idea that does not appear in those proposals but on which we as a Parliament should reflect, and that is the need for more effective scrutiny on the Floor of the House of the monumental amount of legislation from Europe, which many of us have felt has never been adequately scrutinised. Is that something that the Prime Minister wishes to consider? [Official Report, 17 December 2001; Vol. 377, c. 27–28]

Kennedy once again connects the issue of enlargement with a call for structural reform of EU institutions. In a further reference to the past, Kennedy describes enlargement as the first thing on every parliamentarian's mind after "the Berlin wall came down", thereby according a huge importance and high salience to it. The fact that the process of actually achieving enlargement took more than ten years is presented as a yardstick for the efficiency of the EU as a whole, i.e. the period of time it takes to implement a political goal, to achieve tangible results is the measure of good governance. In that regard, the Lib Dem leader sees room for improvement and makes this very clear by criticising "the over-ossified structures". Something that is ossified is like a fossil, an anachronism unable to function properly in the present (let alone the future). It paints the EU as a dinosaur, as an organisation moving so slowly its central organs have begun to petrify. It is the opposite of an evolving, agile, flesh-and-blood learning organism needed to meet the challenges of the twenty-first century. Kennedy underlines that anything leading to more "progress" is desirable. The EU is thus not portrayed as a time-honoured and venerable institution but an organisation in danger of becoming obsolete because it cannot keep up. This assessment shows that the underlying value of efficiency is strongly felt by the Lib Dems but might also make the listener wonder since the British have always been very proud and appreciative of ancient traditions and institutions, such as the UK parliament which is addressed in the next paragraph. (But then again, with the majority electoral system, efficient decision-making is ensured. The Lib Dems consistently argue that any reform in the direction of the British system is to be welcomed.)

The Lib Dem leader calls for reforms in the House of Commons, too, to allow for "effective scrutiny". The value accorded to national scrutiny of European policies shows the respect for parliamentary sovereignty and is perhaps not

surprising in a party that since 1923 has held a role in opposition, with parliament as the only place they can exercise power. The jab at the amount of EU
legislation to be considered in the HoC which Kennedy characterises as "monumental" can, on the one hand, be said to reflect badly on the EU because it creates
a huge amount of work with which parliament cannot cope any longer – a claim
echoing a common criticism that the EU produces too many laws, unnecessarily
meddling in all kinds of aspects of daily life, and on the other hand to refute the
claim just made that the EU is too slow and ineffective to pass important legislation. The overall effect could be that the EU is perceived as bureaucratic and
unnecessary, inefficient when it comes to important decisions while producing
countless laws pertaining to unimportant things – the exact opposite of a (neo-)
liberal ideal of a "lean" state.

The candidate countries are titled "aspirant countries" again, which discursively deepen their image as underdeveloped countries (as opposed to the
"developed" member states mentioned in the year before) striving for (indeed
aspiring to) higher ideals, i.e. eager to join an organisation governed by a single
market, civil freedoms, and democracy – all values that the Lib Dems hold dear
and which, therefore, comes across as an attractive organisation.

"European Council (Seville)" (24.06.2002)

> On the issue of enlargement, which we strongly support, and the intended progress,
> which is also very much to be welcomed, can the Prime Minister explain how that can
> be squared when no meaningful decisions have yet been arrived at and, apparently, no
> substantial discussions have taken place on reform of the common agricultural policy.
> Surely one must predate the other. [Official Report, 24 June 2002; Vol. 387, c. 616]

Half a year later, Kennedy takes the next European Council (in Seville) as an
opportunity to reiterate the Lib Dem position that they "strongly support"
enlargement and are happy about progress in that policy area. However, Kennedy
clearly formulates a condition: "reform of the common agricultural policy" is, in
his view, an essential prerequisite for enlargement: "one must predate the other".
In an apparent paragraph about enlargement, the argument thus turns into a
vehement call for CAP reform, together with his criticism that "no substantial
discussions" were held on that subject. The two policy areas are discursively
bound together, with a time element inserted – so whoever wants enlargement
must also endorse CAP reform – and so progress in the latter area becomes a
yardstick of successful progress on the former issue. Underlying values seem to
point in an economic direction, with market rules a paramount Lib Dem concern. Although it is not spelled out, the fact that many candidate countries had

and have a large agricultural sector and are thus likely to profit from EU subsidies in this regard may well play an important role in this argument, too: the EU budget must not be stretched to this level because as a net contributor to it, the UK would have to pay more. This is neither a popular move nor does it tie in with the ideal of a lean state and free markets since the CAP is viewed as essentially protectionist.

"European Council" (28.10.2002)

> In the context of this weekend's summit, we welcome the further progress made on enlargement, although perhaps the Prime Minister, like me, reflected just a few minutes ago on the fact that, if enlargement is to be made a reality, those who pay lip service to the practicality of enlarging the European Union also have to go through the motions and the Division Lobby of the House to give effect to treaties such as the Nice treaty, rather than opposing them at every juncture. Some of the comments that we heard a few minutes ago need to be viewed in that context.
>
> Will the Prime Minister also acknowledge that aspirant states wish to come into the Europe Union? Although it is marvellous that they are at last being liberated from old-style central command-and-control economies, they are none the less finding that existing member states and the Commission are still putting too much red tape and bureaucracy in their paths. Further emphasis needs to be given on ensuring that the enlarged Europe that evolves is more liberal and more free-trading than it is at the moment. [Official Report, 28 October 2002; Vol. 391, c. 547–548]

In the parliamentary debate on the European Council in autumn of 2002, Kennedy refers to enlargement positively again. The word combination "further progress" elicits an impression of a positive dynamic which reflects on the institutions responsible for it – the scathing judgement of the EU of a slowly-moving dinosaur has been replaced. The criticism is, this time, directed at MPs in Westminster: linking enlargement to EU treaties like Nice, Kennedy decries opposition to the latter as effectively obstructing the former, and with the judgement that they only "pay lip service" to their proclaimed goals of enlargement thus accuses (mainly CON) MPs of hypocrisy or double dealing when they do not vote accordingly in House of Commons decisions.

The candidate countries are called "aspirant" once more, which implies that their past was not good and they now aspire to something higher, introducing a hierarchical element where the EU comes out on top and appears like an attractive option when viewed from an outside perspective. This might also be a call for some UK listeners to remember the EU's merits.

Assuming that the jab at "too much red tape and bureaucracy" is meant to pertain to the economic aspect of the EU, it seems that Kennedy then reminds

listeners of the Lib Dem criticism in that respect and reveals their apparent preference for a lean state or at least less and flexible regulations. The hierarchy is very
clear: the UK economic model is good, more should be done to make the EU
resemble it even more, and the "old-style central command-and-control economies" which are clearly placed in the past as out-dated and overcome are at the
bottom of the race. This implicit feeling of superiority illustrates that enlargement
has a strong link to the regime conflict of the Cold War and that the Lib Dems see
their economic policies on the winning side. This assumption is further illustrated
by the word choice "liberated" – implying the value of freedom, another central Liberal value which is positively connotated, and suggesting that the former
Soviet bloc countries were enslaved or sieged and that the EU with its economic
system embodies the freedom they now deserve. By choosing to solely highlight
the economy, Kennedy draws attention to this aspect and downplays all others.

A very clear reference to political goals is made in the last phrase: the Lib
Dems want the EU to become "more liberal and more free-trading" in the future,
i.e. to transform the organisation according to their own values. The alternative
policy that is suggested between the lines of this statement is that the government should use the opportunity of enlargement negotiations to put more pressure on its EU partners to attain these goals.

"First Day" (13.11.2002)

> We welcome the fact that the Government again rightly pay tribute to European enlarge-
> ment remaining the big goal, a view that we share. However, as we did in exchanges a
> couple of weeks ago after the last summit, we have to enter the reservation—I think the
> Prime Minister, the Foreign Secretary and the Chancellor would agree—that despite
> the agreement, which goes up to 2006, Europe will have to revisit the common agri-
> cultural policy if it is serious about making a success of enlargement. [Official Report,
> 13 November 2002; Vol. 394, c. 30–38]

A few weeks later, on the 'First Day' debate of the new parliamentary session,
Kennedy repeats that the Lib Dems share the government "big goal" of enlarging
the European Union. The alternative views are then followed by the conces-
sionary adverb "however": the CAP is again presented as an obstacle to the "success of enlargement" and that anyone "serious" about achieving the latter must
agree with their view that CAP reform is necessary. Thus, there is a two-fold
structure – the Lib Dem leader always begins by welcoming an overall development or aspect which is then followed by a criticism of another aspect or detail.
According to the rules of good feedback, this can be classified as constructive
criticism, and ties in with the Lib Dem's self-proclaimed aim of being a "constructive opposition".

"NATO Summit (Prague)" (25.11.2002)

Does the Prime Minister share my curiosity? We just heard the argument that greater coherence and integration of NATO—a wider NATO—and, at the same time, greater coherence and integration of the defence realm in Europe are bad ideas, but if that is the case it is puzzling that countries are queuing up to join both organisations. Instead, they see the success and future stability that such membership and cooperation can bring. [Official Report, 25 November 2002; Vol. 395, c. 308]

Only two days later, on the occasion of the NATO summit in Prague, Kennedy points out a shared factor of the enlargement of NATO and that of the EU: "countries are queuing up to join both organisations". The Lib Dem leader attributes this fact to the "success and future stability that such membership and cooperation can bring" and, thereby, refers to the value of cooperation instead of insisting on national sovereignty. Obviously, stability (which we can take to mean peace in the realm of defence alliances) and success warrant integration and make it worth it. The outside perspective is mentioned as well: if other countries deem both organisations so attractive they want to join rather sooner than later, it must mean something. Kennedy here exposes the dilemma: if the candidate countries are accepted as on a par and experienced enough in the domain of foreign policy to be taken as witnesses or role models for a course of action, the image of the UK as a superior power with its ancient tradition of diplomacy and worldwide military engagements automatically loses its nimbus and becomes one country of many instead of a still sovereign nation in this domain that is central to a country's outside image and relevance in the eyes of realist politicians.

Of course, defence as a part of foreign policy is classified as "high politics" and a central competence of a state, and Kennedy refers to the CON leader's (who spoke just before him in the debate) criticism of closer cooperation and integration as tantamount to losing power in such an important policy area. Kennedy attacks this attitude by using the words "curiosity" (as to how this view can be justified) and "puzzling" (to indicate that there are obviously facts that speak against the conclusions drawn). Thus, the alternative is to reject the CON's proposal to oppose further integration of the organisations the UK is a member of on the grounds of a differing world view and instead to embrace cooperation with other countries to achieve stability and peace. This is part of a pattern where the Lib Dems agree with the Labour government and attack the CON's position instead, which may seem rather unusual for an opposition party. The political aims may converge but the world views and, therefore, the proposed course of action differ wildly.

"European Council (Copenhagen)" (16.12.2002)

I thank the Prime Minister for his statement and join him in congratulating the successful Danish presidency.

> Judging from the House's reaction to the remarks of the leader of the Conservative party [sic], it widely shares the view that we felt no sense of history when the right hon. Gentleman described a time of such historic groundbreaking achievement for Europe and for the spread of democracy, stability, peace and security across the continent as 13 wasted years. I thought that that referred to a different period in history relating to the Conservative party [sic].
>
> None the less, the 18 years of unbroken Conservative Government in this country certainly helped to build the single European market. It helped to extend qualified majority voting—thanks to Mrs. Thatcher and the Conservative party [sic] - and it even helped to pave the way for the enlargement process on which Conservative Members seem to be trying to pour cold water today. They have no sense of history and even less sense of the future—that is the Conservative party [sic].
>
> Given that some of the continuing entrenched aspects of the common agricultural policy have become even more entrenched as a result of some of the decisions that were reached at the summit, what prospect does the Prime Minister see, with enlargement ahead of us, of achieving the genuine, long-term reform of the CAP that is inevitable, desirable and will come about only if our country plays its full part at the top table of Europe? It will not be achieved on the country club membership basis advocated by certain people.
>
> Would not Britain's hand in Europe be strengthened more generally if we showed greater political resolve on the single European currency? Increasingly, we risk marginalising ourselves, as well as suffering domestic economic disadvantage, due to continuing uncertainty about a referendum and about the Government's long-term political commitment on the issue.
>
> I welcome the decision reached about Turkey. It is important that over the next two years there is full and active engagement with the Turkish authorities—not least as regards human rights—to ensure that as and when accession negotiations with Turkey are held, they are based on stability and dependable understanding as regards not only the commitment of the Turkish democratic authorities to Europe itself, but the need to maintain the fundamental values of human rights that Europe enshrines and to which we are signatories. [Official Report, 16 December 2002; Vol. 396, c. 542–543]

Kennedy makes a speech on the occasion of the European Council in Copenhagen. Beginning with a positive note – congratulating other country leaders for their achievements on the European level – sets the tone and lets the listener assume that the agenda of the Danish was in line with their own political aims. The word "successful" brings across an image of a positive and well-working EU where political actors can reap success and bring the whole organisation forward in the Lib Dem's sense. Kennedy chooses to then launch a heavy and lengthy criticism of the previous speaker, the CON leader. In this way, the Lib Dems position themselves once more as supporters of government and opposition to the biggest opposition party itself. This could also be a rhetorical technique to establish some political opponent (otherwise he would just have to agree and sit back down – so no alternative to government policy would be presented which is not a good strategy to win elections).

The last paragraph is dedicated to Turkey, whose candidacy is further supported by the Lib Dems. The development in this regard, namely the official opening of accession talks and the conferral of candidate status to Turkey, is welcomed. This time, however, the emphasis placed on human rights is more pronounced and is presented as a non-negotiable condition to join the EU. The latter is not mentioned explicitly but the term "Europe" is used, which points to the conclusion that Kennedy here refers to the Convention of Human Rights which hinges on the Council of Europe, not the EU, and which has a wider membership base. Kennedy thus commits his party both to further enlargement but also to human rights and British membership in the Council of Europe and the European Convention of Human Rights which has nowadays become a major controversy because it entails being subject to decisions by the European Court of Human Rights.

"European Council" (23.06.2003)

> My right hon. and hon. Friends and I certainly welcome the acceptance of the Convention's proposals in principle, and it is worth reminding ourselves that, not that many years ago, it would have been unthinkable that 15 existing member states and 10 accession countries could reach even this degree of consensus for sensible cooperation over the development of the EU. [Official Report, 23 June 2003; Vol. 407, c. 712–713]

Addressing EU enlargement indirectly in the speech on the next EU Council, Kennedy refers to the "accession countries" and praises the degree of "sensible cooperation" demonstrated by making decision by finding a consensus among 25 countries. This is a clear hint that the developments on the EU level are in accordance with the values Kennedy as the Lib Dem Party leader advocates and which are also shared by the other members of the parliamentary party, his "right honourable and honourable friends", the address used in the House of Commons for MPs from the same party.

"European Council" (15.12.2003)

In the last intervention addressing enlargement before the actual Eastern enlargement came into effect on 1 January 2004 (debate on 'European Council'),

Kennedy links the issue with the EU constitution: in this speech, Kennedy for the first time discursively connects the issue of enlargement with the endeavour to codify an EU constitution. He is very clear, more so than any other party leader, that in his and his party's view, a constitution for Europe is a good thing and enlargement a highly salient reason for taking this stance:

> May I stress to the Prime Minister that the Liberal Democrats remain firmly of the view that there remains the need for a constitution – a codification of European operating procedures – not least because of the welcome enlargement that is now in front of us and that those who seek some comfort from the difficulties of the weekend overlook the much bigger picture? Those of us who were Members of Parliament at the time remember the Monday after the weekend when the Berlin wall came down and all those countries of central and eastern Europe that had been under the tyranny of the communist regime in the Soviet Union suddenly began to experience liberation. That was the big picture and the big prize for Europe, and we must not lose sight of the fact that, despite the political difficulties that were encountered at the weekend, the constitution will give effect to an enlarged Europe. That is a pivotal point, which those of us who are of a pro-European slant are correct to emphasise.
>
> [...]
>
> Finally, will he confirm that it remains the Government's intention to secure a decent and deliberative outcome to the Convention process, arriving at a workable constitution for an enlarged EU? That is in British interests, and it is profoundly in European interests as well. [Official Report, 15 December 2003; Vol. 415, c. 1326]

With using the word "remain" concerning the political convictions of his party, Kennedy paints a picture of a reliable and consistent party which does not change according to opinion surveys and is not afraid to stand up for their beliefs. This is further strengthened by the adverb "firmly", suggesting uprightness and strength (of character). Kennedy argues that a written constitution would be beneficial and make cooperation within a group of 25 countries easier. Again, he refers back to the fall of the Berlin wall and the ensuing end of the Cold War a historic background against which the development must be viewed and is directly related to, making it "welcome" to those already on the "winning" side of liberal and democratic convictions. The soon-to-be members are once more framed as victims of the "tyranny of the communist regime" who can now taste freedom after liberation. It is telling that the prospect of the accession of the "central and eastern European countries" are described as a "big prize" – something to win, something that rewards for efforts made in the past and something valuable. This attribution of merely passive and almost monetary qualities highlights the dimension of economic gain expected from an enlarged EU. The constitution is thus also presented as a necessary step to take full advantage of this prize, not as an inherently welcome development. Kennedy stresses that the argument for the constitution must hinge on enlargement to convince others of its merits and that this argumentation is common to all pro-European forces in parliament, making it look like a purely technical issue that is strategically positive but not otherwise good. This pragmatic reasoning smacks of self-interest and political strategy that is not well suited to inspire real passion for the project. The CON MPs will address this argumentation by disclaiming the assumption that the constitution is necessary for enlargement, which they also support.

Interestingly, we can perceive a self-description of the Lib Dems as pro-European here and a sense of a community with others of the same opinion: "those of us who are of a pro-European slant are correct to emphasise" that the constitution enables enlargement goes his reasoning. Once again, he backs the PM in this position and decries the criticism of a constitution voiced by the CON leader who spoke just before him. At the end of the speech, he calls for a constructive British contribution to the constitution negotiations and claims that this "is in British interests" (which obviously come first and legitimises the goal) as well as "profoundly in European interests as well". This addition brings the Lib Dem view across that by playing a constructive role in key EU policy projects concerning the future and make-up of the organisation itself is in the national interest and that it is a win-win situation because British and European interests coincide in this instance. He wants to see a "decent and deliberative outcome" from the negotiations, implying values of fairness and constructive cooperation.

Further on, Kennedy refers to the "bigger picture" and to a sense of history when he calls for a positive stance on the EU as a whole and to set aside memories of difficult negotiations and conflicts with the other EU members over political goals – in this line of thinking, details become less important and are, therefore, no cause for blocking important developments (like the CON MPs) because it is more about the bigger picture of a clash of systems that can now be resolved peacefully (and with the added bonus of enjoying the feeling of superiority that in the UK, the freedoms were already in position whereas others had to go without).

"European Council" (21.06.2004)

It is surprising that nothing is noted on the actual enlargement coming into force before June 2004, when Kennedy returns to the subject in the debate on another "European Council" half a year later:

> May I, on behalf of my right hon. and hon. Friends, give a general welcome to the fact that this compromised treaty was agreed and unanimously endorsed by 25 member states and Governments over the course of the weekend? Will the Prime Minister

acknowledge that, given the welcome and historic enlargement of Europe and the triumph of democracy, and of socially fair market democracy at that, the model that operated for a Europe of six was simply not applicable to a Europe continuing to develop with a membership of 25? [Official Report, 21 June 2004; Vol. 422, c. 1086–1087]

Kennedy again stresses that the developments on EU level are in accordance with his party's political goals by using the word "welcome" and underlining the unanimity of the now 25 members. This points towards the conclusion that consensus and cooperation find Lib Dem approval, values that may not always be honoured in the British political system. This is made even more likely by the appearance of the word "compromised" as qualifying the treaty, together with "agreed", which conjures up an atmosphere of peaceful cooperation between partners on the EU level. The recently completed enlargement is mentioned and described as "welcome and historic" as well as a "triumph of democracy", framing enlargement to the east as a step towards *The End of History* as proclaimed by Francis Fukuyama (2006), where he forecasts that after the fall of the Iron Curtain, ideological struggles will end with the victory of western (neo) liberal (market) democracies. Kennedy seeks to implant the value of fairness into this model, adding the care for individuals that cannot compete successfully in a purely liberal, market-oriented system and thereby introducing social policy as an important element of Lib Dem political goals, although the mention of this in an inserted apposition suggests that this is only a minor aspect and that the most important point is democracy, not social fairness.

Enlargement is further portrayed as a development calling for institutional change and reform of the EU as a whole because the structures have to keep up with the size of the organisation. All in all, the EU is presented as a well-working organisation incorporating contemporary values on the winning side of history which is also capable of internal development and reform through decisions reached by consensus.

"European Council" (20.12.2004)

Kennedy keeps up the pattern of commenting on Enlargement every time a debate regarding a European Council meeting takes place (but not in between):

I thank the Prime Minister for his statement on the significant summit of a few days ago. Does he agree, when we hear some of the sceptical sounds that are made about Europe, that after a summit that has welcomed the finalising of accession treaties with Romania and Bulgaria and set dates for their accession, thereby opening important accession discussions with Turkey and Croatia, it is a bit odd that all the welcome new countries—democracies emerging from the shadow of the cold war—are queueing up to join the institution, while others would have us believe it is a manifest disgrace and disability to us all? People should reflect on that when they hear some of the nonsense that is talked about the welcome progress on the European front.

Does the Prime Minister agree that opening discussions with Turkey sends a positive signal about the European Union to the rest of the world? The European Union is open, secular and united by democracy and human rights. Given that, will the Prime Minister go a little further than he went in his statement about how he—or the Foreign Secretary—views the squaring of the circle regarding Cyprus and the legitimate, continuing interests of our country in that context? I appreciate that that is a difficult question. [Official Report, 20 December 2004; Vol. 428, c. 1924]

Kennedy starts with a description of the summit as "significant", thereby according it significance and prominence among other such European summits. In a distinct effort to counter the (Euro-) sceptic narrative presented by the CON, Kennedy argues that the fact that even after the large-scale enlargement, there are still countries wanting to join the EU, which he presents as a consequence of its attractiveness. With this description of the status quo, he seeks to invalidate the "skeptic [sic] sounds" from the CON leader illustrating his stance that "Europe" is a "manifest disgrace and disability to us all" in the Lib Dem leader's words. Again, Kennedy includes himself (and probably his party) in this "us" – an attempt to appear as part of a community embracing all UK citizens.

The new member states are characterised as "democracies" and again, the historical reference to the Cold War is directly attached to them as a further quality.

The wording "European front" is a metaphor from the domain of war to denote European policies and cooperation, in general. This seems wildly inappropriate for a political party which sees itself as pro-European and seeks to oppose the Eurosceptic discourse of the CON and wishes to frame enlargement as "welcome progress" on the European level.

"EC Budget" (20.06.2005)

On Thursday, when the Prime Minister addresses the European Parliament, he will be required to set out his vision of how Europe will develop. Can he give us some more detail this afternoon about what that vision will be? In that regard, does he agree that, especially in the Balkans, the prospect of EU membership is a great driver for positive change as well as for regional stability? Will he ensure that under his presidency Britain maintains the momentum for that enlargement? [Official Report, 20 June 2005; Vol. 435, c. 528]

The difficult question of a "vision of how Europe will develop" is addressed by the Lib Dem leader during the debate on the EC budget. He tries to get the PM to spell out such a vision and seeks his agreement on the issue of further enlargement. He singles out the Balkans as the region in whose direction the next expansion should be going because of the need for stability. In an interesting description of the political ends enlargement could further, he points out that the "prospect of EU membership" can be a "great driver for positive change". It can be guessed that this positive change encompasses the values held dear by the Lib Dems, including democracy, the rule of law, and peaceful cooperation with neighbouring countries. As a former war zone, the argument made here is that the Balkan countries should get all the help associated with being EU membership candidates (financial support, help with establishing structures, and institutions) that is possible in order to achieve a state where those values are implemented in words and reality. It becomes clear that the Lib Dem leader sees enlargement as an instrument of foreign policy that is in accordance with their worldview that international cooperation is beneficial for all sides and the way to go to avoid conflict.

"European Council (Brussels)" (19.12.2005)

In the debate on the EC budget on 19.12.2005, Kennedy confirms the Lib Dem position on enlargement:

> As the Prime Minister knows, the Liberal Democrat party has consistently supported the enlargement of the EU and welcomes that development, which, following the collapse of the Berlin wall, is good for us in Europe and for the world generally. I acknowledge that that development must come with a financial price tag in order to meet moral, political and economic objectives. Having achieved a degree of expansion, we also welcome the opening of accession talks with Turkey and Croatia and the approval of candidate status for Macedonia in this presidency. [Official Report, 19 December 2005; Vol. 440, c. 1568–1569]

The keyword "consistently" is used to demonstrate a quality which is rare in political life: consistency. It is probably used to show that the Lib Dems are dependable and true to their proclaimed aims (which might serve to distinguish them from parties in government, where compromise and strategic choices according to public opinion may dominate the agenda). It also shows that the Lib Dems have a pro-European self-image and are proud to have always been in favour of enlargement. The fact that enlargement has taken place is described as "good for us in Europe and for the world generally". Interestingly, a clear self-image of the Lib Dems as representative of the whole UK as a community which in turn is as well a part of Europe – or the Lib Dems as part of a pan-European community which is not specified in more detail – is inherent in the formulation. The assessment that cooperation with others is good for both one's own country as a part of Europe as well as "for the world generally" points to the conclusion that the Lib Dems have a world view where international cooperation brings benefits for all, be they directly involved or only concerned by association. The attempt to frame enlargement as a development in the tradition of the "collapse of the Berlin wall" means the Lib Dem leader uses an historical argument – in this logic, everyone who sees the fall of the Berlin wall (as a *pars pro toto* for the end of the Cold War) as something positive must also embrace enlargement of the EU. In this vein, enlargement becomes a victory of one's own system of government and economy – which is all too often accompanied by a feeling of superiority. It is not learning from one another and seek a new relationship respecting diverging historical experiences but to hurry the Eastern European candidate countries to become like oneself, i.e. better, so they can fit it and function as part of the single market.

Kennedy accepts that enlargement costs money – and as a net contributor to the EU, this includes UK tax money – using the word "acknowledge", which can be interpreted as support for the government decisions or tolerance (without really being in favour). This may be seen as an altruistic move, almost like spending money on development and aid. What is more interesting, however, is that Kennedy proceeds to justify this position by citing "moral, political and economic objectives", in this order. Moral objectives in enlargement policy have a subtext of superiority, or at least of having had more luck than others which creates a moral obligation to help and support, to extend a helping hand to the poor underdeveloped candidate countries of the former Soviet zone. Political objectives seem more tangible and justify rational, pragmatic self-interested goals. Economic objectives seem very clear and weigh heavily despite their being moved to the end of the list (thus keeping up appearances and disguise self-interest with grand words and gestures pertaining to morality).

The Lib Dems stay consistent in their support for enlargement and verbalise that it is a good thing that Turkey, Croatia, and Macedonia may be next to join, while not elaborating on any specific reasons on this occasion.

7.5.3 Menzies Campbell

Campbell is the last party leader in the research period who commented on enlargement.

"Brussels Summit (EC)" (19.06.2006)

> I welcome the renewed commitment to enlargement and, although there is no doubt that there are particular difficulties that attach to Turkey, it has been the view on both sides of the House that Turkey's accession to the European Union is essential for the future of the European Union. [...]

The Prime Minister is right to accept that a union of 25—soon to be 27—cannot operate within a framework designed for six. In the meantime, what practical steps can be taken for reform and does he remain committed to a referendum if there are any proposals for constitutional change that would significantly alter the relationship between Westminster and Brussels? [Official Report, 19 June 2006; Vol. 447, c. 1070–1071]

A political discourse analysis of this speech must draw on the previous results. Commenting on the PM's statement on the outcomes of the summit in Brussels, Campbell evaluates the status quo as positive by using the verb "to welcome", thereby lending opposition support to the government position to advocate further enlargement of the EU. However, he also portrays the status quo concerning the institutional make-up of the EU as inadequate for the enlarged EU by agreeing with the PM's assessment that the original framework was designed for a much smaller number of member states and, therefore, has to be changed in order to work for the present. This becomes clear in Campbell's calls for "practical steps for reform".

Interestingly, the insistence on the PM's promise to legitimise any further competence transfer to the EU by holding a referendum in the UK is not what one would have expected from a self-proclaimed "Europhile" party and indicates that public opinion must have changed in such a pronounced way that the Lib Dems have integrated it into their political aims. With hindsight, it is interesting to follow up the actual policy proposal to pass legislation which would subject any further competence transfer to the EU to an obligatory referendum in the UK.

Campbell then proceeds to present his party's policy goal in this policy area: he explicitly adds the application of Turkey to become a member of the EU to the list although he concedes that there are "particular difficulties" in this case. However, judging from this word choice, Campbell believes that any existing factors which might prejudice Turkey's accession are mere "difficulties" and can thus be overcome, and he cites cross-party support in the HoC for this position. Indeed, he concludes that "Turkey's accession to the European Union is essential for the future of the European Union". The word "essential" underlines the importance the Lib Dems obviously accord to further enlargement. Possible hurdles are acknowledged – taking into account earlier speeches by Campbell's predecessors, he probably refers to issues such as a doubtful record on human rights, but not basically insurmountable 'cultural' arguments like the fact that Turkey is a Muslim country. Thus, by quoting only technical or legal obstacles which can be remedied, the goal of including new members is rated more highly than possible objections or supposedly incompatible cultures. In terms of values, this points to a strictly rational, market-oriented position. The idea that the EU can only be successful in future if it includes new members with big new markets rests on ideas that growth is essential and ignores uneasiness on a cultural, religious, or, otherwise, identity-related score. The EU is thus imagined as an economic and legal community, not a cultural union where all members share similar values and religious backgrounds.

In conclusion, it can be said that the government position to further enlargement is unwaveringly supported by the Lib Dems. When it comes to EU enlargement, any criticism expressed by Lib Dem leaders does not aim at the policy goal itself, but at the handling and implementation of it both by the EU and the Labour government, e.g. the perceived delays in decision-making on the matter on the European level and the PM's failure to speed up the process and overcome resistance by other EU members.

7.5.4 Summary

Overall, the analysis of the speeches by Lib Dem leaders which addressed the issue of EU enlargement led to the following results: it emerged that they debated the issue from 1997 until 2006, after which it seemingly dropped off the agenda. This means that only three out of five party leaders in the researched time span engaged with the topic.

Concerning their arguments, EU enlargement was presented as welcome and as a goal which merited working hard towards to; however, only if certain conditions such as the promotion and joint acting on the basis of shared values like free (Liberal) but also social market economy were met. Democracy and human rights were equally mentioned. They formulated certain "reservations" including institutional reform (which they argued was necessary if enlargement should be successful) and a reform of the Common Agricultural Policy (CAP). All in all, they perceived the road to enlargement as a positive direction which was indicated by their talking about "moving forward", i.e. progressing, which has a positive connotation.

The analysed quotations in the speeches from 1997 to 2006 showed a distinctly political argument being made by the Lib Dem party leaders, by virtue of references to history and to the expansion of the political system of democracy. This was clearly addressing the change in the former Eastern bloc countries and their transition after the collapse of the Soviet Union. Before entering the European Union, the candidate countries had to incorporate the *acquis communautaire* into national law and thus came closer to the political system of the other member countries. The discourse also contained a geo-strategic dimension. Not least, however, economic considerations were mentioned: hoping for market democracy in the new member countries implied expectations of new markets and trade partners.

The candidate countries were referred to as the "the aspirant states", which suggests that the EU was seen as something positive and desirable, some sort of "higher" form of organisation that other countries aspire to. This implied that their situation at the moment of speaking was not ideal and that they obviously wished to ameliorate their position by joining the EU. A second expression, namely "the supplicant accessor countries" put the candidate countries again in a (discursively expressed) inferior position; the EU member states were called upon to grant their plea for accession, it seemed. This presented the motives of the UK as one of the members as purely philanthropic and generous, as benefactors to less lucky nations, and negated the expected benefits which surely played a role, too. In conclusion, the UK was presented as a benign power which champions and helps less fortunate countries on their way to enjoy privileges like human rights and a "fair market democracy".

Where Europe was mentioned, the Lib Dems referred to "the fundamental values of human rights that Europe enshrines and to which we are signatories", presenting their role in Europe as upholders of human rights and the EU by implication as an association held together by shared values. This might also have been a reference (or rather a jibe) towards the CON's plan to withdraw from the European Convention of Human Rights (signed by Tony Blair in 1997). Furthermore, the Lib Dem leaders presented their interpretation of historic events leading to the creation of European integration: "the whole European ideal was built out of the ashes of the second world war [...] and [...] the goal of growing stability, security and maintenance of peace and prosperity is something of which we should never lose sight". These grand words claimed the existence of a "European ideal", i.e. a standard the member countries try to achieve. Additionally, they stated their goal of "ensuring that the enlarged Europe that evolves is more liberal and more free-trading than it is at the moment". Here, the clear call for reform became apparent and also the focus on economic aspects of the European Union. As a Liberal Democrat, the speaker calls for a more liberal Europe and explicitly mentions free trade as an underlying aim of supporting enlargement. It can be concluded that the speakers wanted the audience to accept their beliefs that enlargement would be a step towards a reformed (i.e. changed for the better) EU, that enlarging means to "move forward". It is to be noted that the EU was never mentioned explicitly; instead, it is "Europe" that was talked about. The word 'Europe' was obviously deemed more suitable to designate lofty and perhaps also vague values than the institutionalised (and un-loved) European Union which they saw as in need of reform to match the high standards expected of a liberal Europe, a beacon of human rights.

When it came to the self-image the Liberal Democrat leaders entertain of the UK, it can be concluded from the analysis above that "Britain" was presented as a model of democracy and a socio-liberal market economy which is part of a European value community. This is thus the identity the Lib Dems seemed to accord to the UK in Europe. The UK was portrayed as an important player and a champion for other countries wanting to profit from the same favourable circumstances. It follows that the Lib Dems drew a positive and constructive image of the UK in Europe and as part of the EU with the aim that the audience accepts this image and the conclusion they draw from it, namely that supporting enlargement is a noble deed and that the EU is something positive to which other countries aspire. The audience addressed was, on the one hand, other parties in parliament, but on the other hand also the larger public.

8. Conclusions

This study set out to uncover how the party's position on European policy was expressed and justified, ultimately seeking to achieve a more detailed and differentiated understanding of the underlying identity concepts and inner logic of the contributions by Lib Dem party leaders when debating European policy in the British Parliament. The following questions were addressed:

- How important was the topic "Europe" in the New Labour years? How often was it addressed?
- How were Britain and Europe portrayed in Lib Dem party leader's speeches during the Blair and Brown governments?
- Which discursive strategies were employed and how did the party leaders use certain words and metaphors to characterise both Europe and Britain? What did their "discourse reality" concerning the British-European relations look like?
- How did they seek to rebut Eurosceptic positions and political offers in the UK?
- When it comes to specific European policies, which course of action did the Lib Dem party leaders, as members of the opposition, propose and which arguments and rhetorical devices do they use to justify their recommendations?

To answer the first question, a corpus containing all 546 separate parliamentary debates with oral contributions by Lib Dems party leaders was created. These speeches were, in a first step, analysed in terms of the topics they addressed. The debates where a European dimension became apparent were collected in a further, smaller corpus containing 115 debates altogether. With a share of approximately 20 %, the relevance of the Lib Dem discourse on European policy issues could be confirmed. A subsequent second content analysis of corpus two resulted in the following clusters categorising the content of the speeches: the euro and EMU, foreign and security policy, EU treaties, the EU's Common Agricultural Policy, and the EU enlargements. These five topics were brought up most frequently by Lib Dem party leaders.

The lines of argumentation, employed metaphors, and the images of Britain and Europe differed among these topic clusters. The questions regarding these facets of the discourse will thus be answered chapter-wise summaries in the following:

The euro was the topic most often addressed in the Lib Dem discourse on Europe. The salience of this topic was high from 1997 to 2003, with a further peak in 2008. All Lib Dem leaders argued consistently in favour of joining the single currency, but they nevertheless reasoned that this decision must be based on economic soundness and pragmatic reasons prioritising the national interest, not on any ideological preference or antipathy vis-à-vis the EU as such. The arguments presented to justify their support for the policy goal of the UK joining the single currency were, therefore, that joining the euro equalled increased bargaining power on the EU level, and that the UK needed to join the single currency to protect the national economy and industry branches from disadvantages stemming from the euro-pound exchange rate and better currency stability within the eurozone. The metaphors and word choice to describe the decision to join the euro included 'grasping a nettle' and 'crossing the Rubicon' as well as avoiding the unwelcome development that other EU member states could 'surge ahead' as in a race. These rhetorical choices suggest that it was a necessary if not entirely desirable decision – yet on balance, the benefits for the UK would weigh out any unpleasantness.

The image of the UK in relation to Europe was that of a country deserving a top position among European Union member states. In terms of Anderson's concept of imagined communities, a self-understanding of the British nation as a special, naturally strong, and economically successful one was adopted. 'Europe', on the other hand, was cast as a place where the fiercest competition to this imagined community loomed. The EU itself was portrayed as an organisation pursuing an agenda which could compromise the British national interests, e.g., during the financial crisis, but also as a haven of stability and economy-friendly conditions. Therefore, joining the euro or having access to the decision-making process at least was framed as the only way to safeguard British interests. The Lib Dem leaders lent vocal support and tried to encourage Labour to make this hard decision, whereas they fiercely attacked the CON as ideologically misguided and pandering to popular fears. A sharp contrast to this marked the Lib Dem discourse towards the end of the research period, when the euro crisis had set in: Europe was described as a source of contagious economic trouble instead. Interestingly, the call for a referendum to legitimise a possible decision to join the euro came up quite early in the debate and was repeated with increasing urgency. Apparently, the Lib Dems doubted that the British public would accept the decision made even by a freshly elected government with a large majority. However, the Lib Dem leaders consistently claimed the government could win a referendum easily if they only defended the decision to join publicly instead of avoiding the issue, which according to them ceded the power to determine the 'regime of truth' in the discourse on the euro to the Eurosceptic Official Opposition.

The Lib Dem discourse focusing on foreign and security policy, the second-most debated topic, can be differentiated into two distinct lines of argumentation: the Lib Dem leaders advocated cooperation, even sharing sovereignty with the other European member states where policy aims in the areas of cost efficiency and peace-keeping coincided, framing 'Europe' as a community of trustworthy allies sharing the same priorities and values. They accepted the UK as one country among many which could profit from the combined strength of an alliance. Europe was thus imagined as a community of friendly nations that could use economies of scale and cooperate to bring peace. However, the Lib Dem leaders insisted that national sovereignty should be safeguarded when it came to the deployment of British soldiers. This confirms Anderson's claim that the sacrifice of lives for the sake of the nation goes right to the heart of the nature of this particular kind of imagined community. Even though the Lib Dems had actually opposed the wars in Iraq and Afghanistan, they were prepared to prioritise British soldiers' needs over any solidarity on the EU level and were not willing to support a military solidarity requirement in the EU, while also opposing the unquestioned support for NATO member USA's military missions. Here, they made it clear that their primary concern was security in Europe, thus distinguishing a common European interest from the US-American one. They justified their policy approach once again with the claim that it was the "sensible" and "intelligent" way to manage things, whereas any appeals to emotions, be they fear or pride in the past, were discredited as irrational.

The Lib Dem position on treaty change, the next big topic cluster, was supportive in that they advocated the signing of all the proposed EU treaties in the research period, namely the Treaty of Amsterdam, the Treaty of Nice, the EU Constitutional Treaty, and the Treaty of Lisbon. The overall goal of seeing the UK at the "top table" in Brussels was translated into advocacy of treaty acceptance, arguing that opt-outs would mean a loss of influence. Moreover, the institutional changes effected through further treaties were discursively constructed as prerequisites for the EU enlargement. This general support was carefully framed as purely rational and being in the British national interest, not as a general, fixed position of the party. Any emotional elements in the discourse, be it fears by Eurosceptics or alleged enthusiasm on the part of the Lib Dems, were firmly rejected, and no references to a European identity or unquestionable solidarity with other EU members states were made. On the other hand, other MPs who opposed treaty change were classed as irrational fearmongers who did not have the British national interest at heart. Yet a certain wariness of alleged centralising tendencies within the EU also became apparent in the Lib Dem discourse: the UK was evoked as a model for openness and transparency compared to the European way of reaching consensus, and while the EU Constitution was thus advocated, it was framed as a safeguard for national powers from being grabbed by EU institutions, with veto rights in certain policy areas such as taxation, therefore, declared essential.

After the EU Constitution had fallen through in two referendums outside of the UK, the Lib Dems insisted that a referendum in the UK was still needed to address the virulent domestic Euroscepticism. By 2006, it became clear that they considered a referendum to legitimise any further treaties inevitable. In October 2007, after the Treaty of Lisbon had been agreed and Gordon Brown had not held a referendum on it, even the holding of an in/out referendum became a Lib Dem policy goal, highlighting as how fundamental the issue of legitimacy for any further EU treaty was judged by the Lib Dems then. Obviously, they could not imagine that a majority of voters would choose to ignore all of their rational arguments. Although the Lib Dem MPs had overall been fairly united in their voting behaviour when it came to divisions on matters of European policy, one case of 'rebellion' occurred when Nick Clegg "ordered his MPs to abstain on a Conservative amendment on a Lisbon referendum" (Lynch 2011: 220). This shows how difficult it was for the Lib Dem leader to keep up the appearance of a marked difference to the CON's position when, in essence, both parties had argued that a referendum on EU policy was necessary and desirable, albeit with opposing hopes for the outcome.

The salience of the CAP, the fourth most discussed topic, was closely linked to negotiations about its reform on the EU level in 2002 and 2005, after which the Lib Dems dropped the topic. Judging from the word choice and metaphors used in the Lib Dem speeches on CAP, the assessment of this particular EU policy was overwhelmingly negative since it was seen as opposing liberal values such as fairness, free and open markets, competition, (cost) efficiency, and prudent spending of public money. However, the criticism was always aimed at specific elements of the policy, not the EU as such, resulting in the verdict that the Lib Dem discourse on Europe contained only "Soft Euroscepticism" in this regard. The Lib Dems applied a double standard, though: one for the imagined community of British nationals, exemplified in this case by farmers who deserve help, and one for all other European workers who are clearly seen as outside the community.

The last specific discursive formation was concerned with EU enlargement, which stayed important from 1997 until 2006, with the accession of Romania and Bulgaria in 2007 not mentioned once. Concerning the Lib Dem arguments,

EU enlargement was presented as an important goal; however, only if certain conditions such as the promotion and joint acting on the basis of shared values like free (Liberal) but also social market economy were met. Democracy and human rights were equally mentioned, thus creating an imagined value community including all other EU member states as well as the candidate countries. Yet there was a discernible hierarchy expressed by terms like "the aspirant states", which suggested that the EU was something positive and desirable, some sort of "higher" form of organisation that other countries aspire to. This presented the motives of the UK supporting the enlargement as purely philanthropic and generous, as benefactors to less lucky nations, and remained silent on the expected benefits for the UK. In conclusion, the UK was presented as a benign power championing less fortunate countries on their way to enjoy privileges like human rights and a "fair market democracy", like in the Empire and later the Commonwealth of Nations. 'Britain' was presented as a model of democracy and a socio-liberal market economy which is part of a European value community. It follows that the Lib Dems painted a positive and constructive image of the UK in Europe and as part of the EU in the context of enlargement.

All in all, in a context where "the British were kept in a permanent state of discursive war with the continent, in which a hegemonic Eurosceptical [*sic*] discourse acted as both frame and limit on the way the British people called Europe to mind" (Daddow 2011b: *New Labour* 65), the Lib Dem leaders relied on 'traditional' approaches of legitimising their policy goals with claims that these were in the national interest in four out of five topic clusters, with EU enlargement as the only exception. With hindsight, it can be concluded that criticism of the EU and some of its policies (even if it was not of a general nature) as well as the support for vetoes and 'red lines' were not suitable means to establish a powerful pro-European counter discourse. Additionally, the Lib Dems completely rejected any appeal to emotions or pathos as valid rhetorical devices to convince voters; instead, they relied on hard-headed rational arguments weighing costs and benefits of EU policies and even membership. This discursive strategy was upheld until the fateful (and from the perspective of pro-European forces, unsuccessful) Brexit referendum in June 2016. An added problem was to voice criticism or propose reform of the EU without using the same words as the Eurosceptic 'opponents' upholding the dominant regime of truth. Metaphors employed to describe the UK-EU relationships were mainly drawn from the domain of war and conflict as well as sports competition imagery.

A further finding is that throughout the parliamentary speeches by Lib Dem leaders, the term "Europe" was often used as a synonym to refer to the European Union, its member states, or institutions instead of citing the correct

name for a European institution. It could also include candidate countries for
EU membership, or a more vaguely defined value community. This imprecise
use of the term arguably makes it difficult to differentiate between criticism of
specific EU policies or decisions which would fall under the definition of "soft
Euroscepticism" and the more general negative assessment of the whole project of EU integration made, e.g., by the CON during the same period. It can
be argued that even well-founded and justified criticism voiced by leaders of
the Lib Dems with the aim to prove they were not blindly advocating European
integration at all costs could thus only be attributed negatively to the EU as
a whole and failed to establish a credible and recognisable pro-European
counter-discourse.

The Lib Dems sought to rebut Eurosceptic positions and political offers in the
UK by attacking the proponents of such positions by trying to make out they
were ideologically opposed to EU membership. Furthermore, the quality of the
proposals themselves was attacked and decried as insane and unrealistic. The Lib
Dems tried to appear as the only reasonable voice proposing a way forward that
put the national interest first, unlike the two bigger parties which they accused
of being preoccupied with short-term party-political gain. It seems that today,
these preoccupations continue to riddle the Brexit process, but the Lib Dems still
struggle to make their voice heard loudly enough.

8.1 Evaluation

So, did the Lib Dems live up to their image as a pro-European party in the end,
or did they leave the Eurosceptic discourse unchallenged, unable to transcend
the "frame and limit" of the dominant Eurosceptic discourse? The results of this
study have shown that there is no overarching answer, but different EU policy
areas have to be looked at individually. Overall, the argumentative and rhetorical
strategy employed by the Lib Dems has obviously not been sufficient to accomplish the feat of countering the hegemonic Eurosceptic discourse in the UK.
They could not challenge the Eurosceptic discourse to a degree sufficient to make
it unstable and allow it to be significantly altered. In the terms introduced by
Foucault, they failed to establish an alternative 'regime of truth' that was accepted
by the audience. This became evident most clearly in the 2016 Brexit referendum
result as well as in the general election outcome in June 2017, where the Lib
Dems were the only nation-wide party to campaign on a pro-European ticket
but did not succeed to convince voters with this strategy, illustrated by a further small loss in vote share compared to the disastrous election results of 2015
("Election 2017").

Regarding the question of support for referendums on European policy or indeed even membership of the European Union, it has to be noted that referendums as such have no traditional place in the British political system; indeed, the first nationwide referendum in the UK ever was held on the continued membership in the EEC or "common market" in 1975, after Wilson had negotiated a 'better deal' for Britain. A reason for this is the doctrine of parliamentary sovereignty, which is factually undermined by popular votes which, although not legally binding, create significant pressure on MPs and government members to support whichever outcome lest they should appear as unresponsive to people's concerns. Concerning the question of referendums on European policy, it was thus especially interesting to analyse the reasoning behind Lib Dem calls for a referendum both on entry into the single currency as well as on the proposed EU Constitution, which was consistent with the Eurosceptic policies by parts of the CON as well as UKIP.

In Lib Dem discourse, the issue of accountability and legitimacy within the British political system became entangled with European policy. Ultimately, the supposedly Europhile party ended up calling for the in/out referendum alongside professed Eurosceptics in the CON and UKIP, which has contributed to the process of Brexit currently underway. The reasoning behind this policy choice, however, was very different from Eurosceptic campaigners who saw the opportunity to exit the hated EU; quite the contrary, the Lib Dems acknowledged that they had not succeeded in changing the dominant discourse through parliamentary debate contributions, and so a public campaign to stay in the EU was seen as the only way to 'clear the air' and settle this controversial issue once and for all. It seems that they, similarly to their former coalition partner, simply underestimated the rhetorical force of the case for leaving. Looking at the results of this study, it can be concluded that despite their best intentions, the Lib Dems actually contributed to a continuous discourse casting various EU policies and EU member states as unsympathetic towards the British national interest. Thus, on the whole, they confirmed the image of 'Europe' as a club of continental countries pursuing their agenda regardless of common-sense, rational, and legitimate British interests.

It seems, therefore, that not only PMs seek to protect and are influenced by "an inherited view of the British national interest" (Wall 2008: 185, see also Black 2006: 3); the Lib Dems did neither succeed in overcoming this narrow view of good politics centred on the national aspect, nor in establishing a British identity that embraces and includes a European dimension, thus extending the limits of the imagined community beyond the shores of the British Isles.

It is likely that there are more factors not covered by this study which could help to explain the results and put them into a wider context and into perspective. Oakland suggests that

> in recent years [...] opinion polls indicate increasing dissatisfaction with politicians and authority figures; scepticism at the performance of institutions and their bureaucracies; disengagement from formal political engagement reflected in low election turnout and reduced membership of political parties; but a trend towards political action represented by public protests, demonstrations, petitions, media campaigns and membership of single issue or special-interest groups. These attitudes partly reflect an individualistic, independent and dissenting British tradition that has been historically cynical, irreverent and critical about state structures and powerful individuals. Institutions such as the monarchy, Parliament, law and the Church have had to earn the approval and support of the British people, which could also be taken back. (2011: 17–18)

This points to scepticism towards power structures as something inherently and traditionally British and may serve to at least partly explain why the issue of accountability is so important to many Britons. Euroscepticism could thus be seen as a natural by-product of such an "irreverent and critical" British attitude. Wall, with his insider knowledge as a long-time civil servant, claims that "one feature that is common to most Whitehall departments, and which goes wider and deeper than their individual ethos, is an instinctive dislike of EU legislation" (Wall 2008: 200). It seems that the dominant 'regime of truth' that casts Europe as something negative and un-British is incredibly pervasive and permeates all levels of government – and public servants continue to work in this domain for a long time, unaffected by party positions.

Moreover, the "lack of deep-seated public support in Britain for the European project" (Wall 2008: 172) in the UK generally and a "deep suspicion of French policy and motives" (Wall 2008: 172) among British politicians and civil servants, especially in the area of defence, meant that even had the Lib Dems argued more convincingly in favour of EU policy proposals, their implementation and legitimacy would probably have remained questionable and controversial nevertheless. In addition to that, the British media (especially the Murdoch press) are also frequently cited as another important factor perpetuating a Eurosceptic discourse in the UK (see e.g. Daddow 2012; Wall 2008: 180).

On the European level, the years following the global financial and economic crisis (from 2008 onwards) and the euro crisis have seen evidence of many challenges and problematic issues facing the European Union: a lack of confidence in its ability to manage the crises, a lack of trust in its institutions, and in its central promise to deliver prosperity and peace to its member states, combined with dissatisfaction in its structural make-up, especially the perceived democratic deficit and its image as an elite project. In many member states, Euroscepticism, populism, and right-wing nationalism combine into increasing support for parties promising the exit from the EU. A lack of solidarity or sense of community is another symptom. These factors are thus not unique to the British context but may well have played their part in the complex issues debated within the British political discourse on Europe.

Furthermore, the rise of populism constitutes a further challenge: Johnson argues that, similarly to developments in other European countries, "confidence in traditional political methods and in the dominant class of political entrepreneurs through whom Britain is governed has diminished and is unlikely to be restored by mere palliatives" (N. Johnson 2005: 20). Indeed, in many EU-countries, parties defined as right-wing and/or populist have been winning worryingly high numbers of votes for some time now and in many countries, they are represented in parliaments or even at government level, thus being relevant political actors (Grabow and Hartleb 2013: 13). This means that to win enough votes to govern, the established parties might feel the need to address similar issues in similar rhetoric. This means that even though UKIP was not represented at parliamentary level during the researched period, they still might have represented an influence on the Lib Dem leaders' rhetoric and choice of topic in debates; to confirm this hypothesis, however, more in-depth research and a comparison would of course be needed. However, as Grabow and Hartleb point out, this phenomenon is not unique to the UK, but true for many EU countries (2013: 13). Brok confirms this when he observes that "[n]ational self-interest and prejudices against European neighbours and fellow European citizens are increasing" (2013: 3), so it can be argued that this phenomenon appears Europe-wide. The foregrounding of such national motives in the discourse of the "most Europhile of all British parties", however, is quite frankly disappointing and leads to the conclusion that the British political discourse definitely contains examples of "Soft Euroscepticism" even from the parts of professed pro-European parties.

8.2 Lib Dem Discourse on Europe after New Labour

On 6 May 2010, the General Election produced the following result: The CON won 306 seats (36.1 %), whereas Labour only won 258. The Lib Dems were still the third biggest parliamentary party with 57 gained seats – this meant a hung parliament. After frenzied negotiations, a CON-Lib Dem coalition government with David Cameron as Prime Minister and Nick Clegg as Deputy Prime Minister was formed (J. Schmidt 2011: 459). One of the most divisive issues was, again, the European policy to be pursued by the coalition. The 2016 Brexit referendum result as well as the poor election results in both the general election in 2015 and 2017, respectively, however, illustrate that not much can have changed during Clegg's new position as Deputy Prime Minister. This means that despite the increase in power, which according to Foucault is the prerequisite for "produc[ing] reality" (1979: 194), the Lib Dems could not transcend the dominant discourse in favour of a more pro-European stance.

In the end, then, it is a look into the past which might generate some hope for the future: The UK has made tremendous contributions to a European cultural heritage – be it the rights enshrined in Magna Carta, be it Shakespeare's works, be it technical and cultural inventions like the steam engine or football, or indeed newspapers (Sicking and Müller 1999: 7). It can be concluded that in a post-Brexit world, it will be incumbent on cultural links and relationships, and cooperation in the area of science as well as on interpersonal contacts, to uphold the connection between Britain and Europe. Possibly, the looming British exit from the European Union with its incalculable effects on the economy, on mobility and diversity in the UK may contribute to such a change in perception that the Lib Dem (and New Labour's) discursive strategy could not bring about. Ultimately, the dominant 'regime of truth' in British political discourse might thus be successfully challenged and changed into a more European-friendly one in the future. It seems that the Lib Dems have not given up yet and may still play a part in this – however, they should review their discursive strategies in the light of the results of this study.

Appendix

The entirety of oral contributions made by Liberal Democrat party leaders during the Labour governments, 1997–2010, are available online on the Hansard web pages. All links provided here have been verified and last accessed on 21 August 2017.

Paddy Ashdown:

1997/98	http://hansard.millbanksystems.com/people/mr-paddy-ashdown/1997
1998/99	http://hansard.millbanksystems.com/people/mr-paddy-ashdown/1998
99/2000	http://hansard.millbanksystems.com/people/mr-paddy-ashdown/1999

Charles Kennedy:

99/2000	http://hansard.millbanksystems.com/people/mr-charles-kennedy/1999
2000/01	http://hansard.millbanksystems.com/people/mr-charles-kennedy/2000
2001/02	http://hansard.millbanksystems.com/people/mr-charles-kennedy/2001
2002/03	http://hansard.millbanksystems.com/people/mr-charles-kennedy/2002
2003/04	http://hansard.millbanksystems.com/people/mr-charles-kennedy/2003
2004/05	http://hansard.millbanksystems.com/people/mr-charles-kennedy/2004
	https://publications.parliament.uk/pa/cm/cmvol424.htm
	https://publications.parliament.uk/pa/cm/cmvol425.htm
	https://publications.parliament.uk/pa/cm/cmvol426.htm
2005/06	https://publications.parliament.uk/pa/cm/cmvol428.htm
	https://publications.parliament.uk/pa/cm/cmvol429.htm
	https://publications.parliament.uk/pa/cm/cmvol430.htm
	https://publications.parliament.uk/pa/cm/cmvol431.htm
	https://publications.parliament.uk/pa/cm/cmvol432.htm

https://publications.parliament.uk/pa/cm/cmvol434.htm
https://publications.parliament.uk/pa/cm/cmvol435.htm
https://publications.parliament.uk/pa/cm/cmvol436.htm
https://publications.parliament.uk/pa/cm/cmvol437.htm
https://publications.parliament.uk/pa/cm/cmvol438.htm
https://publications.parliament.uk/pa/cm/cmvol439.htm
https://publications.parliament.uk/pa/cm/cmvol440.htm

Menzies Campbell:

2005/06	https://publications.parliament.uk/pa/cm/cmvol441.htm
	https://publications.parliament.uk/pa/cm/cmvol442.htm
	https://publications.parliament.uk/pa/cm/cmvol443.htm
	https://publications.parliament.uk/pa/cm/cmvol444.htm
	https://publications.parliament.uk/pa/cm/cmvol445.htm
	https://publications.parliament.uk/pa/cm/cmvol446.htm
	https://publications.parliament.uk/pa/cm/cmvol447.htm
	https://publications.parliament.uk/pa/cm/cmvol448.htm
	https://publications.parliament.uk/pa/cm/cmvol449.htm
	https://publications.parliament.uk/pa/cm/cmvol450.htm
2006/07	https://publications.parliament.uk/pa/cm/cmvol451.htm
	https://publications.parliament.uk/pa/cm200607/cmhansrd/cmallfiles/mps/commons_hansard_2450_od.html

Vince Cable:

2006/07	https://publications.parliament.uk/pa/cm200607/cmhansrd/cmallfiles/mps/commons_hansard_2413_od.html
2007/08	https://publications.parliament.uk/pa/cm200708/cmhansrd/cmallfiles/mps/commons_hansard_2413_od.html

Nick Clegg:

2007/08	https://publications.parliament.uk/pa/cm200708/cmhansrd/cmallfiles/mps/commons_hansard_2631_od.html
2008/09	https://publications.parliament.uk/pa/cm200809/cmhansrd/cmallfiles/mps/commons_hansard_2631_od.html
2009/10	https://publications.parliament.uk/pa/cm200910/cmhansrd/cmallfiles/mps/commons_hansard_2631_od.html

List of Figures

List of Tables

Works Cited

Primary Sources

List of debates with interventions concerning Europe by Paddy Ashdown:

1997

Official Report, 14 May 1997; Vol. 294, c. 70–75.

Official Report, 04 June 1997; Vol. 295, c. 386.

Official Report, 18 June 1997; Vol. 296, c. 320–321.

Official Report, 09 July 1997; Vol. 297, c. 940–941.

Official Report, 29 October 1997; Vol. 299, c. 894.

Official Report, 03 December 1997; Vol. 302, c. 347.

Official Report, 15 December 1997; Vol. 303, c. 24–25.

1998

Official Report, 21 January 1998; Vol. 304, c. 1007–1008.

Official Report, 28 January 1998; Vol. 305, c. 343.

Official Report, 24 February 1998; Vol. 307, c. 177–178.

Official Report, 17 March 1998; Vol. 308, c. 1120–1128.

Official Report, 29 April 1998; Vol. 311, c. 322–323.

Official Report, 05 May 1998; Vol. 311, c. 569.

Official Report, 20 May 1998; Vol. 312, c. 962–963.

Official Report, 17 June 1998; Vol. 314, c. 374–375.

Official Report, 08 July 1998; Vol. 315, c. 1068–1069.

Official Report, 21 October 1998; Vol. 317, c. 1273–1274.

Official Report, 04 November 1998; Vol. 318, c. 864.

Official Report, 24 November 1998; Vol. 321, c. 38–46.

1999

Official Report, 10 February 1999; Vol. 325, c. 314–315.

Official Report, 23 February 1999; Vol. 326, c. 187–188.

Official Report, 09 March 1999; Vol. 327, c. 200–205.

Official Report, 17 March 1999; Vol. 327, c. 1117–1118.

Official Report, 29 March 1999; Vol. 328, c. 735–736.

Official Report, 08 June 1999; Vol. 332, c. 469–470.
Official Report, 09 June 1999; Vol. 332, c. 641–642.

Interventions by Charles Kennedy:

1999
Official Report, 19 October 1999; Vol. 336, c. 257–258.
Official Report, 20 October 1999; Vol. 336, c. 444–450.
Official Report, 27 October 1999; Vol. 336, c. 1012.
Official Report, 17 November 1999; Vol. 339, c. 32–38.
Official Report, 13 December 1999; Vol. 341, c. 27–29.
2000
Official Report, 16 February 2000; Vol. 344, c. 942.
Official Report, 21 March 2000; Vol. 346, c. 881–883.
Official Report, 27 March 2000; Vol. 347, c. 27.
Official Report, 17 May 2000; Vol. 350, c. 326–327.
Official Report, 21 June 2000; Vol. 352, c. 343–344.
Official Report, 05 July 2000; Vol. 353, c. 326.
Official Report, 12 July 2000; Vol. 353, c. 863.
Official Report, 24 July 2000; Vol. 354, c. 767–768.
Official Report, 22 November 2000; Vol. 357, c. 304–305.
Official Report, 11 December 2000; Vol. 359, c. 356–357.
2001
Official Report, 20 June 2001; Vol. 370, c. 55–62.
Official Report, 14 September 2001; Vol. 372, c. 609–610.
Official Report, 14 November 2001; Vol. 374, c. 853.
Official Report, 28 November 2001; Vol. 375, c. 963–964.
Official Report, 17 December 2001; Vol. 377, c. 27–28.
2002
Official Report, 06 March 2002; Vol. 381, c. 295–296.
Official Report, 18 March 2002; Vol. 382, c. 26–27.
Official Report, 17 April 2002; Vol. 383, c. 599–602.
Official Report, 22 May 2002; Vol. 386, c. 286–287.
Official Report, 19 June 2002; Vol. 387, c. 270.
Official Report, 24 June 2002; Vol. 387, c. 616.

Official Report, 03 July 2002; Vol. 388, c. 218–219.

Official Report, 28 October 2002; Vol. 391, c. 547–548.

Official Report, 13 November 2002; Vol. 394, c. 30–38.

Official Report, 25 November; Vol. 395, c. 39.

Official Report, 27 November 2002; Vol. 395, c. 308.

Official Report, 16 December 2002; Vol. 396, c. 542–543.

2003

Official Report, 24 March 2003; Vol. 402, c. 25–26.

Official Report, 09 April 2003; Vol. 403, c. 293–294.

Official Report, 21 May 2003; Vol. 405, c. 1006.

Official Report, 04 June 2003; Vol. 406, c. 163–164.

Official Report, 23 June 2003; Vol. 407, c. 712–713.

Official Report, 05 November 2003; Vol. 412, c. 791–792.

Official Report, 26 November 2003; Vol. 415, c. 32–37.

Official Report, 15 December 2003; Vol. 415, c. 1325–1326.

2004

Official Report, 20 April 2004; Vol. 420, c. 161–163.

Official Report, 14 June 2004; Vol. 422, c. 525.

Official Report, 16 June 2004; Vol. 422, c. 768–769.

Official Report, 21 June 2004; Vol. 422, c. 1086–1087.

Official Report, 30 June 2004; Vol. 423, c. 290–292.

Official Report, 03 November 2004; Vol. 426, c. 302.

Official Report, 08 November 2004; Vol. 426, c. 574–575.

Official Report, 23 November 2004; Vol. 428, c. 27–36.

Official Report, 20 December 2004; Vol. 428, c. 1923–1924.

2005

Official Report, 16 March 2005; Vol. 432, c. 274–277.

Official Report, 24 March 2005; Vol. 432, c. 1019–1020.

Official Report, 17 May 2005; Vol. 434, c. 49–54.

Official Report, 15 June 2005; Vol. 435, c. 255–256.

Official Report, 20 June 2005; Vol. 435, c. 528.

Official Report, 22 June 2005; Vol. 435, c. 793.

Official Report, 11 July 2005 a; Vol. 436, c. 570–571.

Official Report, 11 July 2005 b; Vol. 436, c. 585–587.

Official Report, 13 July 2005; Vol. 436, c. 828–829.
Official Report, 18 July 2005; Vol. 436, c. 1078–1079.
Official Report, 19 December 2005; Vol. 440, c. 1568–1569.

Interventions by Menzies Campbell:

2006

Official Report, 15 February 2006; Vol. 442, c. 1415–1416.
Official Report, 22 March 2006; Vol. 444, c. 305–308.
Official Report, 10 May 2006; Vol. 446, c. 308.
Official Report, 07 June 2006; Vol. 447, c. 244–245.
Official Report, 19 June 2006; Vol. 447, c. 1070–1071.
Official Report, 04 December 2006; Vol. 454, c. 26–27.

2007

Official Report, 12 March 2007; Vol. 458, c. 27–28.
Official Report, 21 March 2007; Vol. 458, c. 833–835.
Official Report, 25 June 2007; Vol. 462, c. 26–27.
Official Report, 03 July 2007; Vol. 462, c. 823–824.

Interventions by Vince Cable:

2007

Official Report, 22 October 2007; Vol. 465, c. 26–27.
Official Report, 6 November 2007; Vol. 467, c. 34–37.
Official Report, 14 November 2007; Vol.467, c. 677–678.
Official Report, 17 December 2007; Vol. 469, c. 602–604.

Interventions by Nick Clegg:

2008

Official Report, 26 February 2008; Vol. 472, c. 922.
Official Report, 27 February 2008; Vol. 472, c. 1085–1086.
Official Report, 05 March 2008; Vol. 472, c. 1739.
Official Report, 17 March 2008; Vol. 473, c. 622–623.
Official Report, 19 March 2008; Vol. 473, c. 933–934.
Official Report, 21 May 2008; Vol. 476, c. 314–315.

Official Report, 11 June 2008; Vol. 477, c. 304.

Official Report, 23 June 2008; Vol. 478, c. 30–31.

Official Report, 10 July 2008; Vol. 478, c. 1554–1555.

Official Report, 08 October 2008; Vol. 480, c. 271–272.

Official Report, 20 October 2008; Vol. 481, c. 28–29.

Official Report, 17 November 2008; Vol. 483, c. 28–29.

Official Report, 15 December 2008; Vol. 485, c. 821–822.

2009

Official Report, 11 March 2009; Vol. 489, c. 290–291.

Official Report, 23 March 2009; Vol. 490, c. 27.

Official Report, 23 June 2009; Vol. 494, c. 666–667.

Official Report, 24 June 2009; Vol. 494, c. 790.

Official Report, 28 October 2009; Vol. 498, c. 280–281.

Official Report, 02 November 2009; Vol. 498, c. 590–591.

Official Report, 14 December 2009; Vol. 502, c. 650–651.

2010

Official Report, 20 January 2010; Vol. 504, c. 308–309.

Official Report, 29 March 2010; Vol. 508, c. 514–515.

Secondary Sources

Anderson, Benedict. *Imagined Communities: Reflections on the Origin and Spread of Nationalism*. Revised and extended edition, Verso, 1991.

Austin, John Longshaw. *How to Do Things with Words*. Oxford University Press, 1975.

Baedermann, Tim. *Der Einfluss des Wahlrechts auf das Parteiensystem*. Nomos, 2007.

Barker, Chris. *Cultural Studies: Theory and Practice*. 4th edition, SAGE, 2012.

BBC. *Election 2017: Results*. 2017, http://www.bbc.com/news/election/2017. [Last access 27 April 2019]

Bevan, Shaun, and Peter John. "Policy Representation by Party Leaders and Followers: What Drives UK Prime Minister's Questions?" *Government and Opposition*, vol. 51, no. 1, 2016, pp. 59–83.

Birch, Anthony H. *The British System of Government*. 10th edition, Routledge, 1998.

Black, Jeremy. *The European Question and the National Interest*. Social Affairs Unit, 2006.

Blockmans, Steven. "Enlargement". *Britain's Future in Europe: Reform, Renegotiation, Repatriation or Secession?* Centre for European Policy Studies (CEPS); Rowman & Littlefield International, 2015, pp. 127–131.

Brok, Elmar. "Foreword". *Exposing the Demagogues. Right-Wing and National Populist Parties in Europe*, edited by Karsten Grabow and Florian Hartleb, 2013, pp. 3–5.

Budge, Ian, editor. *The New British Politics*. 4th edition, Pearson Longman, 2007.

Cabrera, Miguel A. *Postsocial History: An Introduction*. Lexington Books, 2004.

"Camp." Macmillan Dictionary, https://www.macmillandictionary.com/dictionary/british/camp_1. [Last access 27 April 2019]

Casey, Terrence, editor. *The Blair Legacy: Politics, Policy, Governance, and Foreign Affairs*. Palgrave Macmillan, 2009.

Chaim, Perelman. *The New Rhetoric and the Humanities. Essays on Rhetoric and Its Applications*. Reidel, 1979.

Charmley, John. "Splendid Isolation to Finest Hour: Britain as a Global Power, 1900-1950". *The Foreign Office and British Diplomacy in the Twentieth Century*, edited by Gaynor Johnson, Routledge, 2005, pp. 130–146.

Chilton, Paul A. *Analysing Political Discourse: Theory and Practice*. Routledge, 2004.

Churchill, Winston. *The United States of Europe*. University of Zurich, 19 September 1946, http://www.winstonchurchill.org/resources/speeches/1946-1963-elder-statesman/united-states-of-europe. [Last access 27 April 2019]

Clarke, Harold D., Matthew Goodwin and Paul Whiteley. *Brexit. Why Britain Voted to Leave the European Union*. Cambridge UP, 2017.

Coakley, John. "Mobilizing the Past: Nationalist Images of History". *Nationalism and Ethnic Politics*, vol. 10, 2004, pp. 531–560.

Cole, Matthew, and Helen Deighan. *Political Parties in Britain*. Edinburgh University Press, 2012.

Colley, Linda. *Britons. Forging the Nation 1707–1837*. Yale UP, 2005.

Cowles, Maria Green, et al., editors. *Transforming Europe: Europeanization and Domestic Change*. Cornell University Press, 2001.

Daddow, Oliver. *Britain and Europe since 1945: Historiographical Perspectives on Integration*. Manchester University Press, 2011a.

Daddow, Oliver. *New Labour and the European Union: Blair and Brown's Logic of History*. Manchester University Press, 2011b.

Daddow, Oliver. "The UK Media and 'Europe': From Permissive Consensus to Destructive Dissent." *International Affairs*, vol. 88, no. 6, 2012, pp. 1219–1236.

Däwes, Birgit. "Local or Global? Negotiations of Identity in Drew Hayden Taylor's Plays." *Global Challenges and Regional Responses in Contemporary Drama in English*, WVT, 2003, pp. 217–231.

Diez, Thomas. *Die EU lesen: Diskursive Knotenpunkte in der britischen Eurodebatte*. Leske + Budrich, 1999.

Díez Medrano, Juan. *Framing Europe: Attitudes to European Integration in Germany, Spain, and the United Kingdom*. Princeton University Press, 2003.

Dunleavy, Patrick. *Developments in British Politics 8*. Palgrave Macmillan, 2006.

"EU Constitution Summit 'May fail.'" *BBC*, 7 December 2003, http://news.bbc.co.uk/2/hi/europe/3298441.stm. [Last access 27 April 2019]

European Commission. *EU Treaties*. https://europa.eu/european-union/law/treaties_en. [Last access 27 April 2019]

European Commission. *The History of the European Union 1970-1979*. http://europa.eu/about-eu/eu-history/1970-1979/index_en.htm. [Last access 27 April 2019]

European Commission. *The History of the European Union 1945-1959*. http://europa.eu/about-eu/eu-history/1945-1959/index_en.htm. [Last access 27 April 2019]

Fairclough, Norman. *New Labour, New Language?* Routledge, 2000.

Fairclough, Norman, and Isabela Fairclough. *Political Discourse Analysis*. Routledge, 2012.

Forster, Anthony. *Euroscepticism in Contemporary British Politics: Opposition to Europe in the Conservative and Labour Parties Since 1945*. Routledge, 2002.

Foucault, Michel. *Discipline and Punish. The Birth of the Prison*. Vintage Books, 1979.

Foucault, Michel. "Method." *Cultural Theory and Popular Culture: A Reader*. 4th edition, edited by John Storey, Pearson Education, 2009, pp. 313–319.

Foucault, Michel. "Truth and Power." *Power. The Essential Works of Michel Foucault 1954-1984*, edited by James D. Faubion, Penguin, 2002a, pp. 111–133.

Foucault, Michel. "Question of Method." *Power. The Essential Works of Michel Foucault 1954-1984*, edited by James D. Faubion, Penguin, 2002b, pp. 223–238.

Frenken, Wiltrud, et al. *Political Speeches: Historical &Topical Issues*. Schöningh, 2008.

"Fudge." Macmillan Dictionary, https://www.macmillandictionary.com/dictionary/british/fudge_1. [Last access 27 April 2019]

Fukuyama, Francis. *The End of History and the Last Man.* Free Press, 2006.

Geddes, Andrew. *The European Union and British Politics.* Palgrave Macmillan, 2004.

Gellner, Ernest. *Thought and Change.* Weidenfeld and Nicolson, 1964.

George, Stephen. *An Awkward Partner: Britain in the European Community.* Oxford University Press, 1998.

Giddings, Philip J. "Purpose and Prospects." *The Future of Parliament: Issues for a New Century.* Palgrave Macmillan, 2005a, pp. 257–269.

Giddings, Philip J. "Westminster in Europe." *The Future of Parliament: Issues for a New Century.* Palgrave Macmillan, 2005b, pp. 215–227.

Giddings, Philip J., and Helen Irwin. "Objects and Questions." *The Future of Parliament: Issues for a New Century,* edited by Philip J. Giddings and Study of Parliament Group, Palgrave Macmillan, 2005, pp. 67–77.

Glencross, Andrew. *Why the UK Voted for Brexit: David Cameron's Great Miscalculation.* Palgrave Pivot, 2016.

Grabow, Karsten, and Florian Hartleb. "Mapping Present-Day Right-Wing Populists." *Exposing the Demagogues. Right-Wing and National Populist Parties in Europe,* edited by Karsten Grabow and Florian Hartleb, 2013, pp. 13–44.

Grob-Fitzgibbon, Benjamin. *Continental Drift. Britain and Europe from the End of Empire to the Rise of Euroscepticism.* Cambridge UP, 2016.

Grond, Petra. *When Maggie Speaks: Die Reden der britischen Premierministerin Margaret Thatcher - Eine Studie in Politischer Rhetorik.* Karl Stutz, 2004.

Guisan, Catherine. *A Political Theory of Identity in European Integration: Memory and Policies.* Routledge, 2012.

Heindrichs, Sebastian. *Die Europapolitik Grossbritanniens unter besonderer Berücksichtigung der britischen Position zur Osterweiterung der Europäischen Union und der Regierung Blair.* Logos, 2005.

Hennink, Monique, et al. *Qualitative Research Methods.* SAGE, 2011.

Hennessy, Peter. *Muddling through: Power, Politics, and the Quality of Government in Postwar Britain.* Gollancz, 1996.

Hunt, Lynn. "Introduction: History, Culture, Text." *The New Cultural History,* edited by Lynn Hunt, University of California Press, 1989, pp. 1–22.

Ichijo, Atsuko, and Willfried Spohn, editors. *Entangled Identities: Nations and Europe.* Ashgate, 2005.

Ipsos MORI. *Issues Index: 1997-2006.* 2006, https://www.ipsos.com/ipsos-mori/en-uk/issues-index-1997-2006. [Last access 27 April 2019]

James, Scott, and Kai Opperman. "Blair and the European Union." *The Blair Legacy. Politics, Policy, Governance, and Foreign Affairs*, edited by Terrence Casey, Palgrave Macmillan, 2009, pp. 285–298.

Jansen, Hans-Heinrich, et al. *Grossbritannien, das Empire und die Welt: Britische Aussenpolitik zwischen 'Grösse' und 'Selbstbehauptung', 1850-1990*. Brockmeyer, 1995.

Jennings, Will, and Shaun Bevan. *UK Policy Agendas Project*. http://www.policyagendas.org.uk/. [Last access 27 April 2019]

Jessop, Bob. *The Future of the Capitalist State*. Polity, 2002.

Johnson, Gaynor. "Introduction: The Foreign Office and British Diplomacy in the Twentieth Century." *The Foreign Office and British Diplomacy in the Twentieth Century*, Routledge, 2005, pp. 1–12.

Johnson, Nevil. "What of Parliament's Future?" *The Future of Parliament: Issues for a New Century*. Palgrave Macmillan, 2005, pp. 12–21.

Jones, Alistair. *Britain and the European Union*. 2nd edition, Edinburgh University Press, 2016.

Jones, Bill, and Philip Norton, editors. *Politics UK [includes the 2010 General Election]*. 7th edition, Pearson Education, 2010.

Kamm, Jürgen, and Bernd Lenz. *Großbritannien verstehen*. Wiss. Buchges, 2004.

Kastendiek, Hans, and Richard Stinshoff. "Zur Entwicklung Großbritanniens seit 1945." *Länderbericht Grossbritannien. Geschichte, Politik, Wirtschaft, Gesellschaft*, edited by Hans Kastendiek and Roland Sturm, 3rd revised edition, Bundeszentrale für politische Bildung, 2006, pp. 95–116.

Kavanagh, Dennis et al., eds. *British Politics*. 5th edition, Oxford University Press, 2006.

Keller, Reiner. *Doing Discourse Research: An Introduction for Social Scientists*. SAGE, 2013.

Kingdom, John E. *Government and Politics in Britain: An Introduction*. 3rd edition, Polity Press, 2003.

Kingdom, John E., and Paul Fairclough. *Government and Politics in Britain*. 4th edition, Polity Press, 2014.

Kuckartz, Udo. *Qualitative Inhaltsanalyse: Methoden, Praxis, Computerunterstützung*. Beltz-Juventa, 2012.

Leith, Murray Stewart, and Daniel P. Soule. *Political Discourse and National Identity in Scotland*. Edinburgh University Press, 2012.

Ludwig, Andreas N. *Auf dem Weg zu einer "Achse Berlin-London"? - Die Deutsch-Britischen Beziehungen im Rahmen der Europäischen Union unter Gerhard Schröder und Tony Blair (1998-2002)*. Diplomica, 2011.

Luhmann, Niklas. "Sinn als Grundbegriff der Soziologie." *Theorie der Gesellschaft oder Sozialtechnologie*, edited by Jürgen Habermas and Niklas Luhman, Suhrkamp, 1971.

Lynch, Philip. "The Con-Lib Agenda for Europe." *The Cameron-Clegg Government: Coalition Politics in an Age of Austerity*, edited by Simon Lee and Matt Beech, Palgrave Macmillan, 2011, pp. 218–233.

MacDonald, Robert H. *The Language of Empire: Myths and Metaphors of Popular Imperialism, 1880-1918*. Manchester University Press, 1994.

Mautner, Gerlinde. *Der Britische Europa-Diskurs: Methodenreflexion Und Fallstudien Zur Berichterstattung in Der Tagespresse*. Passagen, 2000.

Mayring, Philipp. *Qualitative Inhaltsanalyse: Grundlagen und Techniken*. 11th edition, Beltz, 2010.

Meier-Walser, Reinhard C. *Die Tories Und der 'Dritte Weg': Oppositionsstrategien Der Britischen Konservativen gegen Tony Blair und New Labour*. vol. 23, Hanns-Seidel-Stiftung, 2001.

Morisse-Schilbach, Mélanie. *Diplomatie und Europäische Aussenpolitik: Europäisierungseffekte im Kontext von Intergouvernementalismus am Beispiel von Frankreich und Grossbritannien*. Nomos, 2006.

Musolff, Andreas. *Mirror Images of Europe: Metaphors in the Public Debate about Europe in Britain and Germany*. Iudicium, 2000.

Negrine, Ralph, and Colin Seymour-Ure. "The Challenge of Adaptation." *The Future of Parliament: Issues for a New Century*. Palgrave Macmillan, 2005, pp. 257–269.

Nünning, Ansgar, and Vera Nünning. "Fictions of Empire and the Making of Imperialist Mentalities: Colonial Criticism as a Paradigm for Intercultural Studies." *Intercultural Studies. Fictions of Empire*, edited by Vera Nünning and Ansgar Nünning, vol. 58, C. Winter, 1996, pp. 7–31.

Oakland, John. *British Civilization: An Introduction*. 7th edition, Routledge, 2011.

Open Europe. *EU Survey*. 2007, http://archive.openeurope.org.uk/Content/ documents/Pdfs/constitutionpoll.pdf. [Last access 27 April 2019]

Pine, Melissa. *Harold Wilson and Europe: Pursuing Britain's Membership of the European Community*. vol. 21. Tauris Academic Studies, 2007. International Library of Political Studies.

Risse, Thomas. "A European Identity? Europeanization and the Evolution of Nation-State Identities." *Transforming Europe: Europeanization and Domestic Change*, Cornell University Press, 2001, pp. 198–216.

Robbins, Keith. *Britain and Europe, 1789-2005*. Hodder Arnold, 2005.

Roederer-Rynning, Christilla. "The Common Agricultural Policy: The Fortress Challenged." *Policy-Making in the European Union*, 7th edition, edited by Helen Wallace et al. Oxford University Press, 2015, pp. 197–219.

Rose, Andreas. *Zwischen Empire und Kontinent: Britische Außenpolitik vor dem Ersten Weltkrieg.* Oldenburg, 2011.

"Rubicon." *Macmillan Dictionary*, http://www.macmillandictionary.com/dictionary/british/rubicon. [Last access 27 April 2019]

Russell, Andrew, and David Cutts. "The Liberal Democrats after Blair." *The Blair Legacy. Politics, Policy, Governance, and Foreign Affairs*, edited by Terrence Casey. Palgrave Macmillan, 2009, pp. 65–79.

Ryle, Michael. "Forty Years on and a Future Agenda." *The Future of Parliament: Issues for a New Century*. Palgrave Macmillan, 2005, pp. 3–11.

Said, Edward W. *Orientalism*. Routledge and Kegan Paul, 1978.

Said, Edward W. *Culture and Imperialism*. Knopf, 1993.

Schmidt, Gustav. "Einleitung: 'Britain and Europe - Britain in Europe': Das Spannungsverhältnis zwischen wirtschaftlicher Eigenentwicklung, europäischer Verteidigungsgemeinschaft und atlantischer Sicherheitspartnerschaft nach dem Zweiten Weltkrieg." *Grossbritannien und Europa - Grossbritannien in Europa. Sicherheitsbelange und Wirtschaftsfragen in der Britischen Europapolitik nach dem Zweiten Weltkrieg*, edited by Gustav Schmidt, N. Brockmeyer, 1989.

Schmidt, Johann N. *Großbritannien 1945 - 2010: Kultur, Politik, Gesellschaft.* Kröner, 2011.

Seldon, Anthony. *The Blair Effect*. Little and Brown, 2001.

Sicking, Manfred, and Olaf Müller, editors. *Vom Empire nach Europa: Grossbritannien im Umbruch: Tony Blair, Internationaler Karlspreis Aachen 1999*. Einhard, 1999.

Silverman, David. *Interpreting Qualitative Data*. 5th edition, SAGE, 2014.

Smith, Anthony D. *Chosen Peoples*. Oxford University Press, 2003.

Smith, Anthony D. "The Poverty of Anti-Nationalist Modernism." *Nations and Nationalism*, vol. 9, 2003, pp. 357–370.

Spiering, Menno. *A Cultural History of British Euroscepticism*. Palgrave Pivot, 2015.

Stiegler, Bernd. *Theorien der Literatur- und Kulturwissenschaften: Eine Einführung.* Wilhelm Fink, 2015.

Stiersdorfer, Klaus. "Linguistic Turn." *Grundbegriffe der Kulturtheorie und Kulturwissenschaften*, edited by Ansgar Nünning, J.B. Metzler, 2005, pp. 132–133.

"Stitch-Up." *Macmillan Dictionary*, http://www.macmillandictionary.com/dictionary/british/stitch-up_2. [Last access 27 April 2019]

Storey, John. *Cultural Theory and Popular Culture. An Introduction.* 7th edition, Routledge, 2015.

Stuart, Mark. "The Role of Parliament under Blair." *The Blair Legacy. Politics, Policy, Governance, and Foreign Affairs.* Ed. Terrence Casey. Palgrave Macmillan, 2009, pp. 178–189.

Summo-O'Connell, Renata. "Imagined Australia: A Provocation in Four Stages." *Imagined Australia: Reflections around the Reciprocal Construction of Identity between Australia and Europe*, Peter Lang, 2009, pp. 3–11.

Szczerbiak, Aleks, and Paul Taggart. "Theorizing Party-Based Euroscepticism: Problems of Definition, Measurement, and Causality." *Opposing Europe? The Comparative Party Politics of Euroscepticism*, vol. 2, OUP, 2008, pp. 238–262.

Teubert, Wolfgang. "A Province of a Federal Superstate, Ruled by an Unelected Bureaucracy - Keywords of the Euro-Sceptic Discourse in Britain." *Attitudes towards Europe. Language in the Unification Process*, edited by Andreas Musolff. Ashgate, 2001, pp. 45–86.

Thackeray, Frank W. *Events That Changed Great Britain since 1689.* Greenwood Press, 2002.

The Conservative Party, and Liberal Democrats. *Programme for Government.* 2010, https://assets.publishing.service.gov.uk/government/uploads/system/uploads/attachment_data/file/78977/coalition_programme_for_government.pdf. [Last access 27 April 2019]

Tönnies, Merle, and Claus-Ulrich Viol, editors. *British Political Speeches: From Churchill to Blair.* Reclam, 2001.

Ungari, Elena. "Perceiving Europe and Australia and Constructing an Imagined Australian Identity in 'The Aunt's Story' by Patrick White." *Imagined Australia: Reflections around the Reciprocal Construction of Identity between Australia and Europe*, Peter Lang, 2009, pp. 353–366.

UK Government. *John Major.* https://www.gov.uk/government/history/past-prime-ministers/john-major. [Last access 15 Sept. 2017]

UK Parliament. *List of Previous Commons Recess Dates.* https://www.parliament.uk/about/faqs/house-of-commons-faqs/business-faq-page/recess-dates/recess/. [Last access 27 April 2019]

UK Parliament. *Parliament's Role.* http://www.parliament.uk/about/how/role/. [Last access 27 April 2019]

Viebrock, Helmut. "Einleitung." *Rhetorik und Weltpolitik. Eine Interdisziplinäre Untersuchung politischer Reden von W.E. Gladstone, J. Chamberlain, und B. v.*

Bülow, edited by Helmut Viebrock and Hans Jochen Schild, F. Steiner, 1974, pp. 9–11.

Viebrock, Helmut. "Vorwort." *Rhetorik und Weltpolitik. Eine Interdisziplinäre Untersuchung politischer Reden von W.E. Gladstone, J. Chamberlain, und B. v. Bülow*, edited by Helmut Viebrock and Hans Jochen Schild, F. Steiner, 1974, pp. 7–8.

Wall, Stephen. *A Stranger in Europe: Britain and the EU from Thatcher to Blair.* Oxford University Press, 2008.

Wanninger, Susanne. *New Labour und die EU: Die Europapolitik der Regierung Blair.* Nomos, 2007.

Watt, Nicolas. "No Special Treatment for UK over Europe, Says Angela Merkel." *The Guardian*, 27 Feb. 2014, http://www.theguardian.com/politics/2014/feb/27/angela-merkel-uk-strong-voice-eu-membership-parliament. [Last access 27 April 2019]

Watts, Duncan. *Britain and the European Union: An Uneasy Partnership.* Sheffield Hallam University Press, 2000. Politics 2000.

Western European Union. *Home.* http://weu.int. [Last access 27 April 2019]

Wintour, Patrick, et al. "Mandelson Enters the Euro Debate." *The Guardian*, 21 May 2003, https://www.theguardian.com/politics/2003/may/21/uk.eu. [Last access 27 April 2019]

Wodak, Ruth, and Michael Meyer. *Methods of Critical Discourse Analysis.* 2nd edition, SAGE, 2012. Introducing Qualitative Methods.

Worcester, Robert. "Foreword." *Explaining Cameron's Coalition: How It Came About. An Analysis of the 2010 British General Election.* Biteback, 2011.

Young, Hugo. *This Blessed Plot: Britain and Europe from Churchill to Blair.* Macmillan, 1999.

Young, John W. *Britain and the World in the Twentieth Century.* Arnold, 1997.